10,000
WAYS TO
CHANGE
YOUR LIFE

10,000
WAYS TO
CHANGE
YOUR LIFE

Pamela J. Ball

ARCTURUS

Published by Arcturus Publishing Limited
For Bookmart Limited
Registered Number 2372865
Trading as Bookmart Limited
Desford Road
Enderby
Leicester
LE9 5AD

This edition published 1997

Printed and bound in Great Britain

© Arcturus Publishing Limited/Pamela J. Ball
443 Oxford Street
London W1R 1DA

ISBN 1 900032 61 9

CONTENTS

PREFACE

Some years ago a friend painted a picture for me which consisted merely of triangles of various colours. When asked why, he replied that, for some reason, I always made him think of threes of all sorts. I found out later that my birth number is three, and most of the studying and learning I have done has usually had three aspects to it – the physical, the mental and the spiritual. In addition, there has always been a strong emotional or passionate commitment to everything I have explored. This book is no exception.

The book falls naturally into three sections. The first deals with a number of difficulties and problems we all come up against. If these difficulties or problems are sufficiently testing we will come to a point where we are left with little option but to seek an explanation and/or to try something different. Often it needs only a very small change or attitude to bring about major change in our lives. Once we understand why things happen we are able to make those very subtle changes that make life more bearable. Sometimes there may be an enforced major external change – such as bereavement or loss of employment – which forces us to reassess our lives and our dreams. When we are able to deal with these positively, we can once again allow ourselves to enjoy the life we have.

Quite deliberately, the first section of the book contains only suggestions for change. At no time is it right for anyone to say 'You should/must do such and such'. Free will is an integral part of decision-making and it is entirely up to the reader to decide what he or she is or is not capable of doing. What is offered is encouragement to experiment and follow a line of thought or enquiry.

Section Two consists of tips, techniques and alternative ways of looking at things in order to make changes. It is a glossary of information to help your understanding as you delve deeper into your own psyche. It contains terms and words (from aura through magic to yoga), information on alternative therapies and healing, on world religions, deep thinkers, philosophers and mystics who may or may not influence your thinking, and basic knowledge of esoteric practices such as crystal therapy, divination and meditation.

The entries in Sections One and Two are listed alphabetically. There is extensive cross-referencing, with suggestions in bold type to make the search easier. Where an entry to which you are referred is found in a section other than the one you are consulting, the appropriate number is shown after the cross-reference – for example, **aura (2)** would indicate that the entry is to be found in Section Two.

As you delve deeper into understanding your own inner workings and thought processes, it is possible that you will find a more structured approach necessary. This is provided in Section Three. When something has stood the test of time, and also turns up in many different forms, it has to have some validity. The belief that within each of us there are certain subtle energy centres, or chakras, which can be activated by various disciplines and techniques belongs to Eastern philosophy. In Western psychology it is recognized that a child develops into a competent adult through much the same process of growth. An adult who wishes to develop and understand 'the meaning of life' must widen his or her understanding by venturing firstly into more magical and later into more philosophical realms. Along the way there may be many detours and blind alleys, all of which add up to a development of the spiritual self and a profound understanding of our relationship with our fellows, our environment, our soul and our universe. Section Three charts a course through a maze of information, from the practical through to the spiritual.

No one can make all the changes that may be desirable, or even necessary, all at once. The suggestion is that you experiment with what works for you. It is possible to move around within the sections in various ways – the choice is yours. The only thing we ask is that you enjoy your journey.

PAMELA J. BALL, NEWBURY,
MAY 1997

PROBLEMS
OF A
LIFETIME

A

ABUSE

The term 'abuse' is difficult to define, because what one person may regard as abuse, another may not. Of all the many types of abuse, child abuse is perhaps the one that springs most readily to mind. This type often arises out of a lack of understanding of the growth processes that a child goes through. The fact that a child cannot hit back makes it a ready target for adult frustrations, particularly in families where violence is the norm.

For those who have suffered abuse as children, and who want to begin to change their lives and their perceptions, it is often therapeutic to learn to understand and control anger, and to use ways of getting in touch with the inner self, initially through physical **therapies (2)** such as the **Alexander technique**, **rolfing** and **massage**. Later some form of spiritual healing can often be of help.

Another form of abuse that is becoming increasingly common is **drug abuse**. In modern society technological progress provides room for **boredom** and **alienation**. As people look for new means of artificial stimulation, the opportunities are there to abuse the substance that gives a 'high'. But it is possible to bring about peak experiences without resorting to artificial stimulation – for example, by changing one's lifestyle and moving towards personal or spiritual development.

A third form of abuse is sexual abuse. This tends to run in families, although in many cases abusers are family friends rather than family members. This kind of abuse is difficult to prove, because the victim is often not believed or is afraid to betray his or her attacker. Help is needed in later years to release the abused individual's suppressed feelings, for example by psychotherapy, Freudian or Jungian analysis, or relationship counselling.

One relatively unpublicized form of abuse is that of the elderly (see **Ageing**). Pressures on funding, resulting in fewer trained staff, and the move towards care in the community have shifted the burden of caring for elderly relatives to families. This can put an intolerable strain on loved ones and lead to both intentional and unintentional mismanagement. Such abuse can also take place within situations where staff are available. These problems can be handled through support for carers and more efficient training in the care of the elderly.

Finally, there is what is known as **psychic abuse** (2). If one believes in a connection in the electro-magnetic fields surrounding each of us, it follows that a transfer of energy between individual fields can take place. Psychic abuse occurs when someone with a stronger field misuses or abuses the connection with another. This can take the form of leaching energy (see **Incubus** and **succubus** in Section Two) or in attempting to influence someone else's actions in a negative way (see **Psychic attack** in Section Two).

ACNE

Acne is a skin condition that is thought to be the result of hormonal changes in puberty. There is no known prevention or cure, though treatment can be given in a number of ways. The male hormone testosterone stimulates the sebaceous glands in the skin to produce an oily substance known as sebum. If these sebaceous glands are blocked, they can be invaded by bacteria and cause inflammation of the surrounding tissues. When scar tissue forms this becomes known as cystic acne.

The management of acne consists of careful cleansing of the skin, a change of diet to exclude oily and fatty foods and to include plenty of fruit and vegetables, and an increased intake of vitamins; vitamins C and A are particularly helpful. Gentle skin defoliation using a mildly abrasive sponge can relieve the symptoms, again provided that all implements are kept scrupulously clean. Long hair can sometimes exacerbate the problem. Because the self-image of young people can be so poor at this time, psychological support and reassurance can often allow them to come through this period without too much damage. Acne occurs more often in boys than in girls, although increased awareness in hygiene should see a levelling out among the sexes.

ADDICTION

An addiction can be either physical, psychological or both. Broadly, it can be defined as something without which one cannot get through a day. Often that 'something' is a substance, typically alcohol, drugs (recreational or medicinal), tobacco or food.

Therapists and helping agencies have identified an addictive personality type, often a very intense individual who may, while appearing to be extrovert, be fairly introspective. Many addicts start off by needing the lift or 'buzz' (for example, of tranquillizers in the case of depression or of recreational drugs) that the substance gives them. The physical addiction kicks in later, and the individual has to get used to handling the ups and downs of his own particular habit. As the body becomes acclimatized to the use of a substance, a craving is set up which must be fed. In cases of addiction to medication, such as sleeping pills, this craving is fed 'legitimately' by the continued use of the substance. Efforts to break the cycle are often not made until the individual concerned realizes and accepts he has a problem.

Alcohol addiction can come about in a similar way. The chemical changes that occur through the continued use of alcohol result in a dependency that can become crippling, both for the individual and his family. While alcoholism is taken to be a daily dependency, there is also what is called the 'bouter', a person who goes on binges for a period and then abstains for long periods. This pattern is similar to that seen in eating disorders. There may be an addiction to the pattern of behaviour as much as the situation.

A further and not so easily recognized addiction is that of obsessive behaviour towards other people, giving rise to the stalking phenomenon (see **Obsession**) and also the problem of co-dependency (see **Dependency**). The latter is most easily recognized in the battered wife syndrome, where the woman continually returns to a difficult situation.

ADOLESCENCE

Adolescence can be an extremely difficult time both for young people and their parents. Huge confusions can be thrown up by the bodily, emotional and spiritual changes that occur. Self-doubt becomes the norm, and as the youngster experiments with both new-found freedoms and restrictions, the dividing line between child and adult becomes blurred and often indecipherable. The young person becomes conscious of bodily changes, of difficulty in understanding his sexuality, and of new feelings which arise because of this. The recognition of **loneliness**, being 'different from other people', and fear of the future, can come to the fore. The teenager becomes more aware of family problems and of parental discipline. This can be particularly painful as the child reaches for **independence** and becomes aware that it is not in his power to rebel. New dilemmas such as whether to go with the crowd and to experiment with **drugs** and **alcohol** have to be tackled.

For parents, issues around their expectations for, and of, their children will need to be faced. They may become jealous (see **Jealousy**) of the opportunities offered to the young person and try to project their own wishes and career choices on him. It will, for instance, be hard for someone who is intellectually able to realize that their child may never reach the same standard. **Sexuality** may also become an issue within the family environment as the young person grows into a desirable adult.

A question that often arises is that of **control**. Just as the young person must learn to take charge of his life, so also the parent must learn to eventually relinquish control. Achieving a balance during this transition process can be a time of arguments and pain. One way out of the possible impasse is to learn to communicate fully and honestly. Equally, both parties must learn to respect one another's parameters and to allow room for growth. There are many suggestions given in this book which will help in the handling of adolescence.

ADOPTION

It is natural for an adoptee to want to know what characteristics he might have inherited. Such knowledge can be important from a health point of view – for example, whether there is a tendency to heart disease or some genetically inherited problem. The need to understand one's background can become a concern, particularly in the teen years, or times of 'rites of passage'. Understanding where we came from is an important part of discovering who we are and of coping with our sense of being different from other people. The need to understand another's motivation can also be strong. What, for instance, made the natural mother give up the child? What made the adoptive parents choose that particular child? What was their motivation for adoption?

However loving the care given by the adoptive parents, there may be an inexplicable sense of loss. Although institutionalization is less likely nowadays, there can still be a sense of not belonging or, in later years, of having to conform in ways only half understood. Each child will experience the consequences of their own adoption in unique ways.

AGEING

The process of ageing can be frightening. Not only are there physical changes that many consider inevitable, but there are also mental ones. Physical changes can range from grey hair through sagging muscles – perhaps with pain and stiffness – to sickness and disease, such as **asthma**, **diabetes** and gynaecological or prostate problems. Mental changes can range from occasional memory lapses through isolation from one's contemporaries to **depression** and nihilism (the sense that there is no meaning to anything, that one might just as well not exist).

Fitness and exercise can be a help in managing some of the degenerative changes associated with ageing. Gentle exercise such as swimming, **yoga (2)** and **t'ai chi (2)** all help to maintain both physical and mental flexibility. Changes in **diet** and sleeping patterns can also add a new zest to life. Learning organizations, such as the University of the Third Age and Positive Ageing, form a basis from which to utilize hitherto untapped talents.

Middle age particularly can give a new perspective to life. It is possible that issues such as a parent's helplessness and death have to be faced and because of this the question of one's own mortality becomes an issue. It is often at this time that spiritual matters become of interest and the search for a greater meaning results in investigation into such concepts as survival beyond death, the **higher self** (2) and **religion** (2). By this time children will be growing up and there may well be more time, and possibly more money, with which to pursue new activities. Often, as the family needs less attention, the focus can move outside the home into help and service within the community.

In many cultures the elderly are treated with reverence and respect. In the West, however, advances in technology and the fact that many families no longer remain in one geographical area, mean that the experiences of older people are made less use of. This can lead to two different types of isolation. Older people can feel alienated from the rest of society, and society can become impatient with them, particularly for their relative lack of ability to keep pace with the intricacies of modern life. With this alienation, a rich area of wisdom and life experience can be lost. As scientific advances and modern medicine enable people to live longer, the necessity of maintaining the quality of life increases.

ALLERGY

An allergy can be defined by a simple sentence. If you can prove that a particular substance is making you unwell, you have an allergy. Perhaps a better word to use is a sensitivity to that substance. This could be a food substance, a natural environmental element such as pollen, mould or animal substance, or a chemical pollutant such as a material derived from petrol. This last group appears to be causing more problems the more consumer-conscious we become. Often, people who suffer from allergies are sensitive to more than one group of irritants. For instance, an individual who is sensitive to pollens may also be sensitive to cheap perfumes.

There are several stages of allergic reaction. The first is exposure to the offending substance when nothing overtly happens. During this stage the body produces antibodies and becomes sensitized to the offending material, which causes a reaction the next time the individual is exposed to the substance. Adaptation occurs after frequent exposure when the body becomes accustomed to the problem and the majority of symptoms subside. This does not mean that the problem has gone away, since there is almost always a further stage, called maladaption, when resistance runs out and symptoms return. This stage may also involve **addiction**, when symptoms are relieved by an intake of the offending substance.

Food allergies

Management of food allergies is possible once the offending foods have been identified. The main requirement for this is patience and determination. As with any natural healing method it is likely that you will feel worse before you feel better, which may be confusing. This is because your body has got to get rid of the various toxins which have been taken in over the years and whose effects it will have got used to carrying. Generally it takes two weeks to eliminate the effect of the foodstuffs on your body, and four weeks before the improved diet has any effect. During this period of abstinence, be kind to yourself – which does not mean rewarding yourself with the food you are sensitive to, although it is perfectly natural to want to do just that.

There are three ways to detect food sensitivity. All consist of eliminating foodstuffs from the diet for longer or shorter periods and then testing, by monitoring the reaction as foods are re-introduced, thus enabling a safe repertoire of foods to be built up. During the period of testing at least one food per day can be introduced, more if there is no reaction. Some people are sensitive to foods in combination (e.g., eggs and cheese). Others may find that some foods are initially safe, but that allowing a build-up by eating them too often gives problems.

The 'easy elimination' diet can be carried out between fourteen to 21 days. During the period of the diet it is important not to smoke and to look at your drug intake, whether recreational or medicinal. The Eight Foods diet – i.e., two foods from each food group (proteins, vegetables, fruit and complex carbohydrates) – can be tolerated for seven to fourteen days. It is more rigorous than the elimination diet, but can quite quickly bring about an improved state of health. A fast of between four to seven days can achieve spectacular results, but is not recommended because it reveals all food sensitivities at once – a carefully monitored return to normal eating is a better method. A fast to detect food sensitivity should be undertaken only if other methods have failed. Dealing with a food allergy while in certain conditions – for instance, pregnancy or diabetes – requires careful, expert management and should not be undertaken unless it is properly supervised.

Natural environmental problems

Many people who suffer from hay fever and other allergic reactions to inhaled substances find that their symptoms are improved by the total or partial removal of the irritant. For instance, at its very simplest level, it is unwise to keep a cat if a member of the family is hypersensitive. However, if the sufferer is sensitive only to cats, some other pet may be suitable. This may sound like stating the obvious, but it highlights the importance of management in this particular sensitivity. Good nutrition and vitamin and mineral supplements can often be helpful, too. They do not of themselves cure the problem, but make it more manageable. Having identified the irritant and the group of irritants it belongs to, the sufferer can avoid similar products. Someone sensitive to grass pollen may, for instance, find it worthwhile to eliminate from their diet all members of the grass family – such as wheat, rye and corn – during a time of extreme sensitivity. Experimentation of this kind can be extremely beneficial to the sufferer.

Chemical pollutants

Our increasing use of high technology, and simultaneously our alter- ation and depletion of natural resources, have led to an increased use of chemicals and artificial substances. Many of these are petroleum derivatives, once thought harmless but now discovered to be a source of problems for many people. As with other forms of allergy, this type requires patience to identify the substance or combination of materials causing the problem. A sufferer may find that she is not sensitive to a favourite perfume, but to the propellant in the perfume bottle! Careful management – without becoming paranoid – also pays dividends here.

Exposure to a new work environment can be hazardous for some individuals. Responsible employers will enforce proper safety measures in the workplace, and ensure that such agents as photo-copier fluid and adhesives are properly stored and handled. Problems arising out of electro-magnetic sensitivity are increasingly being given credence. Some people are sufficiently aware of changes in these very subtle energies to be upset by them. The electro-magnetic field surrounding each of us (see **Aura** in Section Two) is measurable and changes in it are registered in different ways. If an individual finds himself feeling ill and uncomfortable in an environment containing many electrical machines, it may be worthwhile suspecting such sensitivity.

Sufferers from allergies and sensitivities often feel burdened psychologically. If you are a sufferer, or someone who is caring for a sufferer, it may be worth listening to the language used to describe symptoms. Statements such as 'It feels like a band round my chest' might indicate not only the physical condition, but also some constriction experienced by the patient in their lives. Simple **creative visualization** (2) exercises – perhaps seeing the band being broken, thus allowing a deep breath– may help. 'My skin feels raw' might suggest the need for better defences against difficulty. Conversely, this statement can also suggest a sense of contamination on some level other than the physical. (The section on **Body awareness** in Section Two highlights possibilities.) Treatments such as **acupuncture**, **homeopathy**, **osteopathy** and **psychotherapy** (see entries under **Therapies** in Section Two) may help in managing allergies, as can changes in lifestyle such as a new job, a change of pace or a change in relationship.

Because allergies are often symptoms of sensitivity it is worthwhile looking 'behind' the problem to discover whether a different perspective might help. Referring to the **chakra** chart in the introduction to Section Three may give an insight into a different sort of self-management. For instance, problems with breathing may behelped by **colour therapy**, spiritual **healing** or by simply learning to express oneself better (2). Problems with food may be helped by coming to an understanding of our emotional make-up.

ANGER

Anger is an attempt to deal with a perceived wrong. This may be in the present moment, or may be as a result of something that happened some time ago. Anger starts off as a reaction, but if allowed to continue it becomes part of a habitual response to the perception that one is not being treated properly, or that 'It's not right', whatever 'it' may be. The expectation then arises that one is not going to be treated fairly, and a vicious circle is built up. People who are often angry are frequently looking for trouble, and while they attribute aggressive behaviour to others may see hostile conduct where there is none. It is their way of interpreting external circumstances that is faulty.

Anger is a common emotion, and has enormous group and individual consequences. It can lead to violence of all sorts. This may be violence against self, others, the home environment, or the world in general. It shows itself in verbal abuse, mental cruelty, road rage, and riotous crowd behaviour. If anger is suppressed it results in resentment, poor communication, apathetic behaviour and may even contribute to eating disorders (also see **Anorexia** and **Bulimia**).

Angry people often find it very difficult to accept that they have a problem. Some therapists believe that the original anger stems from the difficulties that the individual experienced during the process of birth. Much benefit has been gained by the release of the emotions apparently retained or created during birth (see **Primal therapy** under **Therapies** in Section Two). Others believe that anger materializes out of the socialization that we all experience as we learn to live in groups. This may arise out of the will to survive, and the aggression that would be needed in primitive society. Anger, channelled properly, becomes passion and a useable commodity in the right circumstances.

Managing anger

Learning to handle anger can be hard. First you must find out what makes you angry at any given moment. The technique for dealing with the emotion when it arises centres on slowing down and getting a perspective on your feelings. It will probably involve the use of deep breathing (2) techniques and possibly some kind of **mantra** or positive **affirmation** (2).

Unfortunately the sufferer often finds himself committed to a course of action before he has a chance to use these techniques. However, with practice, one can develop a sort of automatic response mechanism that helps towards self control. One theory being worked on is that we are born either angry or placid.

Whatever the root causes of anger, we as individuals have to take responsibility for it if it is a feature of our behaviour. It is worthwhile, therefore, finding out the pattern of our anger and keeping a diary. Do you, for instance, flare up very quickly? Is your anger over quickly? Are you 'slow to burn' or do you simmer with resentment? Are there certain situations that inevitably make you angry? As the pattern of your anger takes shape, try reaching back into your memory to past occurrences that have made you angry. The more you find out about the pattern of your anger the better position you will be in to decide what to do about it.

Handling anger is a six-fold process:
1) Finding out what the common factors are.
2) Trying to remember the first time you felt this way, and what the circumstances were.
3) Deciding how old you were, and whether your behaviour would have been appropriate at that time.
4) Recognizing that your behaviour is child-like (not childish) and that a different response to events could be developed.
5) Resolving to develop more appropriate behaviour.
6) Confirming this appropriate behaviour by first practising it and then fine-tuning it.

It should be remembered that in order to handle anger properly one needs to understand the emotion and not suppress it. Often the process reveals that the underlying emotion is not anger at all but some other, such as jealousy or hurt. Much can be accomplished by dealing with that feeling in an appropriate way, such as forgiving the person concerned, letting go of the trauma or using **creative visualization** (2).

Once it is understood, anger can be used constructively, for example in campaigns where forceful action is needed or as a tool in motivating oneself towards positive action. Finally, controlled passion can be developed in order to achieve a change in attitude to long-held beliefs and principles.

ANOREXIA
Also see **Eating Disorders**

Anorexia nervosa is a serious disorder of perception. The word anorexia means loss of appetite, but when the disorder gets to the point where there is extreme emaciation (thinness or starvation), it can cause a great deal of distress. In a few cases it is a symptom of psychiatric disorder such as depression or schizophrenia, but in many cases it occurs because of an identification of slimness with sexual attractiveness. Medically, the effects of anorexia nervosa, often hidden in the earlier stages by the sufferer, are obvious. In anorexia there is extreme thinness, with a loss of a third or more of the body weight, coupled with tiredness and weakness. In females, menstruation often ceases altogether; some explanations of the disorder involve the notion that the sufferer is afraid to grow up. Death from starvation, or suicide, is common, affecting approximately 10 per cent of cases.

Personality problems and the persistence of the disorder can make treatment difficult. Management of the disease consists of ensuring that the sufferer receives an adequate diet and assistance in understanding the problem. This may have to be done in hospital, because the individual will fight against being fed. Therapy can consist of working with the frightened inner child, and using body care methods such as **massage** and **shiatsu**. It is important to enhance the patient's self-image, and his or her 'right to belong'. Frequently there is a particularly intimate relationship with one parent, who, despite the problem, the sufferer can be anxious to please. Even after normal weight has been regained, sufferers may need to remain under psychiatric care for months or years.

ANXIETY

Anxiety affects both the mind and the body, causing tension, trembling, nausea and churning stomach. There may also be diarrhoea, backache and sometimes palpitations. In some cases these physical symptoms can be attributed to other causes connected to major illnesses such as cancer, heart attack, diabetes and so on. This increases fear, thus locking the individual into a spiral of anxiety.

Anxiety is vital in order to cope with dangerous situations or difficulties and arises from the so-called 3F response. This consists of a very basic reaction to danger, and is present in all animals. First there is Fright, which then triggers a physiological response that releases various hormones into the system. Then there is Fight, which means that the danger is confronted. When this is not possible, there is Flight, which means that we remove ourselves from the situation. In today's highly technological society it is often impossible to get away from stressful situations, and this sends our responses into overdrive. The sufferer from anxiety used to be given little sympathy, particularly when no physical cause was found for the various symptoms, but attitudes have changed. Problems with excess anxiety are now extremely common and probably one person in ten will consult a doctor about them at some time or other.

A particular type of personality seems to be prone to anxiety attacks. Many medical practitioners have experience of patients who have become dependent on them, either because they are kind or because a physical examination is comforting and reassuring for the patient. Much more is now understood about anxiety, and victims can find various ways of helping themselves. Prescription drugs – such as beta-blockers and tranquillizers – can help for a while but they gradually become less effective the longer they are taken. There can also be a psychological, if not a physical, dependency on them. They may also give rise to some very odd side effects when the treatment is stopped (see **Drug Dependency**).

Anxiety can interfere with everyday life. In the absence of real fear, or when fear is still present long after the danger has past, it is possible to suffer from various **negative thoughts** and **phobias**. These can lead to various behaviour patterns that inhibit the enjoyment of life. For instance, in trying to avoid things or places that cause anxiety, the sufferer may compound the problem by making them harder to face the next time. There is also the realization that relief is only temporary, causing anxiety over what might happen rather than what is happening. Avoidance becomes a way of life rather than a defence mechanism.

Re-building confidence can be difficult unless the process is taken very gently. Firstly do easy things; by becoming competent in these you will be able to move on and tackle slightly more difficult tasks, and by developing competence in these you can later attempt even more difficult assignments until these, too, no longer make you anxious. Always remember that it takes some time (normally at least six weeks) to build any change in behaviour. Above all, do not become anxious over the new behaviour.

Anxiety itself does not cause heart attack or stroke, nor does it cause nervous breakdown. It does, however, make you feel tired by using energy needlessly. Anxiety may be a symptom of disorders of the thyroid gland, the menopause and depression, but in any of these other recognizable symptoms would also be present.

Managing anxiety

In an effort to handle the symptoms of anxiety it is worthwhile listing some of the ways in which they can be alleviated. Different types of anxiety can be handled in different ways, and identifying the methods appropriate to the management of each will allow you to make choices and enable you to gain more control over your life.

Many alternative therapies such as **aromatherapy**, **massage**, **cranial osteopathy** and **homeopathy** can help in the control of anxiety (2). When in a state of anxiety the sufferer is often tense and hunched up. Techniques such as the **Alexander technique** and disciplines such as **qi gong** and **t'ai chi**, which are martial arts, or **yoga** can give relief (2). Relaxation can help to relieve muscular tension, tiredness and worry, and also to reduce the speeding up and mental 'chatter' that occur in anxiety.

There are also several techniques that you can apply to handle anxiety symptoms when they present themselves or in order to reduce the likelihood of them appearing at all.

● Rapid anxious breathing, which is a normal bodily response when faced with danger, can make you feel dizzy, shake, give you a rapid heartbeat and cause tingling in your hands and feet. These symptoms can usually be controlled by breathing at the rate of 8–12 breaths a minute.

● Try to turn your attention away from tense, worrying thoughts – thoughts that tend to produce a vicious circle – and concentrate instead on something pleasant. A calm sea or a warm summer's day in the country are ideal images. Use the image of a time when you were particularly happy.

● You can try to concentrate on what is going on near you. This shifts your focus away from yourself, outwards, and allows you to develop your powers of observation and objectivity. Simple activities such as counting the red doors in your street, observing the cracks in the pavement, or counting how many breaths it takes to get to the end of the road can be very helpful.

● Physical activity such as walking, gardening, swimming or weightlifting can help, because such activity links in with the Fight stage of the 3F response.

● Mental activity such as working out a complex problem, or compiling a list of long words and their meanings, can break the cycle, provided you do not transfer the anxiety to the problem or list itself.

● Comfort and a calming effect can be gained by using a particular space or place such as a park or church as a sanctuary.

● Rushing can create anxiety, as can being overly conscious of time. Plan what you have to do in advance in order to avoid rushing. Divide your tasks into:

1) What you must do.
2) What you ought to do.
3) What you would like to do.

Tackle them in that order and you will probably find that you get just as much done.

By studying your patterns of thinking you will be able to find out exactly what thoughts upset you (see **Negative Thoughts**). Practising identifying such thoughts can be considerable therapy by itself, because it keeps the mind occupied and gives you the opportunity to turn such thoughts into positive **affirmations** or presuppositions – e.g., 'I can't do that!' becomes 'I could do that if.......'. Often talking this change through with someone else will clarify your own thoughts.

Meditation techniques can be helpful in handling anxiety, as can many other spiritual disciplines such as **prayer**, **chanting** and **colour therapy** (2).

ARTHRITIS

Arthritis means inflammation of a joint, and is a term used to describe many types of joint disease. Often there is no actual inflammation present. In the most common type of arthritis, osteo-arthritis, there is a wearing away of the protective cartilage with which the bone is surrounded. This results in the bones becoming thickened and rubbing against one another, causing pain and stiffness. More women than men seem to be affected by arthritis, which tends to run in families. Symptoms vary from the very mild, which can often be handled by a change in lifestyle, to the very disabling, when many alternative therapies, such as **acupuncture**, **osteopathy**, **shiatsu** and **massage**, can help (2).

With rheumatoid arthritis, to which women again seem to be more prone than men, initially there may be flu-like symptoms with raised temperature, hot swollen joints and stiffness. The bone ends of the joints may become eroded, and the over-production of synovial fluid that lubricates the joints can cause swelling. It is as though the body is attempting to defend itself, possibly against a virus, and continues to do so long after the original attack. Flare ups and remissions are characteristic of this type of arthritis. About twenty per cent of sufferers recover completely.

Arthritis tends to require individual treatment, and no single regime will suit all sufferers. If one particular type of pain-killer does not work, it is worthwhile experimenting until an effective one is found. Exercise is an important part of management, so that mobility is maintained for as long as possible. Some holistic practitioners have always advocated exercise as a way of minimizing the possibility of such diseases developing. Swimming, walking and cycling are all good for strengthening muscles, and helping to support the joints. **Yoga**, **t'ai chi** and **qi gong** are also of use in self-management, assisting in reducing stress and changing the sufferer's attitude (2). Because they are so gentle and not forced, they can bring about a lasting improvement.

Finally, food supplements such as fish oils, evening primrose oil, selenium and extract of green-lipped mussel can, together with changes in diet, such as eliminating red meat, make this disease manageable.

ASTHMA
Also see **Allergies**

Asthma is a respiratory disorder characterized by breathlessness and wheezing caused by inflammation of the bronchial airways, bronchiole (small air passages) contraction and excessive mucus secretion. When not allergy related, attacks can be set off by stress, infection, strenuous exercise and sometimes even cold air. A bad attack causes sweating, rapid heart-beat and extreme gasping for breath. Asthma often occurs in more than one member of a family.

Any treatment that influences respiration or acts directly on the lungs can be of help. Some people need drugs that react on the sympathetic nervous system, but these can sometimes over-stimulate the heart and should not be used for long periods. Corticosteroids have been used to control asthma, but can cause **drug dependency**.

In stress-related asthma the management of attacks can help the sufferer to feel differently about himself. 'Trigger situations' – in which agents of distress occur, such as cigarette smoke or extreme cold – can be avoided. The learning of techniques to avoid or handle these situations can give the sufferer confidence. **Relaxation** and **breathing** exercises can also relieve the symptoms (2).

In some cases vitamin B6 can help, as can a vegetarian diet. Breathing difficulties can be eased by the use of eucalyptus and peppermint. **Aromatherapy**, **homeopathy**, **Chinese medicine**, **reflexology** and **acupuncture** may also help in management (2).

The following yoga exercise may help at the beginning of an attack, to give you the feeling of being in control:

Sitting on your heels, move your head backwards as you inhale and forwards as you exhale. Repeat the movement up to six times.

B

BACK PAIN

A number of different groups of disorders of the spine can lead to back pain. These include mechanical and structural problems (the so-called slipped disc), inflammation as a result of infection; disorders of the structure of the bones of the spine; and tumours of various sorts. The types of back pain dealt with here are those that will respond to manipulation or are **psychosomatic** (2) in origin.

Back pain is one of the commonest causes of absence from work, and often manifests in times of stress. Tension in the muscles and ligaments can cause tremendous problems, and often is made better by what is jokingly called the 'talking cure'. When a different perspective is put on a problem, the individual can relax and deal with the difficulty. Back pain often arises from a feeling of not being supported (see **Body Awareness** in Section Two). Heat is one of the most effective ways of relieving the symptoms of back pain (the simplest method is to apply a hot water bottle to the affected part) while not altering the actual problem.

Massage can be helpful for those whose discomfort is caused by knotted or strained muscles rather than a chronic structural problem. It can be used as a precursor to other forms of treatment, such as **osteopathy** or **chiropractic** manipulation (2). When dealing with psychosomatic problems, massage can make early trauma more accessible.

BED-WETTING

Bed-wetting is a problem that arises both in childhood and old age. In either case it can be caused by an inability to control the muscles of the bladder, and particularly during sleep can indicate that the individual is deeply relaxed.

Bed-wetting may indicate a problem with the prostate in men and a gynaecological disorder in women. Often the **guilt** or shame associated with bed-wetting will make it worse, so support and understanding are necessary. In some cases bed-wetting may be symptomatic of a problem with self-image (how the person sees himself). Exploration by skilled **counselling** can often uncover hidden worries. Changes in **diet** may help, as may **shiatsu** or **reflexology** treatment (2).

BEHAVIOUR

A perceptive individual will often be able to recognize certain types of behaviour as indicating particular states of mind. Each of us has what might be called idiosyncratic behaviour; that is, certain mannerisms and habits that are ours alone. If those mannerisms are 'trade marks', a departure from them may well indicate a difficulty. For instance, someone who is normally a bright and breezy character may become very withdrawn and morose when experiencing difficulty. Neurotic behaviour and moodiness can often be identified as child-like, and may give some indication of the nature of the problem. In such cases it is worthwhile trying to decide at what age such behaviour would be appropriate, and then consulting the **chakra** chart in Section Three to explore the difficulty further.

BEREAVEMENT

In any situation where there is loss, there is bereavement. When someone moves away, for instance, those left behind will experience a kind of bereavement, not necessarily as final as that caused by death but nevertheless a bereavement. When a relationship ends there is also bereavement, and perhaps one that is doubly difficult, since there is not only the loss of the partner and of the relationship, but also of personal constructs like self-esteem, a hold on the future, and, if the break-up has been acrimonious, those physical and material things that have become familiar to us.

Psychologically the whole panoply of negative emotions is experienced in bereavement. There is an urge to search for the lost person. When there has been a death, this can take the form of attempting to contact the deceased in some way. This may range from continually visiting familiar places to exploring **spiritualism**, and making contact through a **medium** or channel (2). This same behaviour is seen in the break-up of relationships, and may lead to the problem now known as stalking. There is also the need to try to find out 'what went wrong', often accompanied by massive feelings of **guilt** or **anger**. These feelings may then fade into feelings of regret. With efficient **counselling** (2) the bereaved person is helped to realize that these feelings are perfectly normal and natural and are part of the process of letting go of the loved one. Frequently, the bereaved person will 'see' the other individual, or will mistake someone in the street for the person they have lost. Many people will experience the presence of the loved one after death, particularly in the first few weeks. These are known as apparitions, and it will depend on the bereaved person's beliefs as to how these are dealt with. Some may believe they are simply products of a fevered imagination, while others will accept them as reassurance from the deceased that they still exist, albeit in a different form.

Spiritually, bereavement touches our deepest and most private areas. However sophisticated and technologically expert we become, there is within each of us the hope that we do not cease to be after death. We may feel that we live on in our deeds, or in our families. We may also believe that our spirit does not die or that our energy continues in a different form. Whatever our beliefs, it is a test of faith when someone we care about leaves us to cope alone.

There are many simple things that can be done during the process of bereavement, both by the person who has been left behind and by friends and family. It is probably wise to allow the former to set the pace in any help that needs to be given. Initially there may be a need to protect oneself and others from the 'intrusion' of the outside world, or there may be the need for the help of friends. Some sufferers may need help with the everyday tasks that are necessary to continue with life. Others will prefer to do them themselves. The process of bureaucracy can help to accommodate one to the loss, and this is so not just in loss through death, but also in the break-up of relationships. Thus, the preparation of some ritual which marks the change can be cathartic, whether this is a private or a public ceremony. This can be as simple as the destruction of love letters, the changing around of furniture in what had been a shared space, or a funeral or memorial service.

At some point in the bereavement process, it will be important to deal with 'unfinished business'. There will be things that have not been said, actions that have not been taken, difficulties that are unresolved. If possible these should be externalized; writing a letter to the one you have lost can be effective. In the case of a broken relationship, this need not be sent; it is often enough to carry out the activity, to create the space where positive thoughts and actions can be substituted for negative ones. Often we realize that the mourning period is over when we are able to talk to others about our experience in order to help them.

BLOOD DISORDERS

There are many blood disorders that can be alleviated by means of a self-help regime. This, as always, does not mean self-diagnosis. If you think you have a problem you should seek help from your doctor or your health practitioner. The information given below is suggested as a back-up to any other advice.

Anaemia

The most common cause of anaemia is lack of adequate dietary iron. Symptoms and signs include fatigue, breathlessness, dizziness and poor concentration. Megaloblastic anaemia – caused by deficiency in B12 or folic acid – gives the same symptoms plus a sore mouth and tongue. In both cases the condition can be improved through dietary means, the former through using animal products, dark green leafy vegetables and dried fruits. The latter improves through an increased intake of B12, often by injection, or by folic acid (see **Diet**). The most common cause of anaemia in women is heavy blood loss through menstruation.

Blood Pressure, high/low

There are no obvious symptoms of high blood pressure, though the condition can lead to stroke, heart attack, kidney failure and eye damage. **Aromatherapy** (2) treatment consists of relaxing massage, using any of the essential oils, but principally lavender. Low blood pressure can occur for various reasons – injury, shock and psychological trauma, for example – but it is often seen when there is low blood sugar. One way of dealing with it is to eat little and often. **Acupressure** (2) and **stress** relief can ameliorate the condition, as can **homeopathy**. **Yoga** (2) and dietary change (for example, a switch to vegetarianism) may also be beneficial, as may calcium, magnesium and potassium.

Bruising

This can sometimes appear without the individual realizing he has knocked or injured himself. **Herbal** remedies such as witch hazel can help to lessen the discoloration. Vitamin C, bioflavinoids and zinc can lessen the ability to bruise. **Hydrotherapy** and **homeopathy** practitioners can also be consulted for suitable remedies (2).

Chilblains

These painful, itchy swellings appear as a result of poor circulation. **Aromatherapy** (2) treatment is as for Raynaud's disease (see below). **Massage** (2) and **Chinese medicine** (2) may bring relief.

Cholesterol, high

An excess of cholesterol is thought to contribute to the risk of heart disease. Changes in **diet** in order to reduce cholesterol levels include avoiding red meat, foods with saturated fats and full-fat dairy produce. Fish oil has been shown to reduce cholesterol, as have oat and rice bran and whole grain cereals. The management of **stress** is an important factor and both **relaxation** (2) techniques and aerobic **exercise** can reduce high levels of cholesterol.

Gangrene

This results from insufficient circulation of the blood to an area of flesh. The conditions of diabetes, arteriosclerosis and thrombosis can give rise to gangrene. Conventional treatment can be supported by **massage** (2), a high intake of vitamin E and stopping smoking. Poor circulation can often lead to bacterial infection.

Gout

This is caused by a build-up of uric acid crystals in the joints. Often confined to the big toe, gout may result from kidney malfunction or over-indulgence. Some drugs can make the condition worse. Alternative management of gout would involve a change of **diet** – avoiding alcohol, reducing the intake of some foods, such as fatty fish and shellfish (which stimulates the production of uric acid) and using charcoal tablets to reduce acidity in the system. **Homeopathy** (2) can also help. **Reflexology** (2), often massaging a related zone area, will bring relief.

Raynaud's disease

In this circulatory disorder large blood vessels become hyper-sensitive, preventing adequate blood-flow to the extremities. Increasing the intake of iron can help the circulation, as can **herbs** (2) such as cayenne pepper and ginger. An **aromatherapy** (2) massage using oil of black pepper and rosemary may be beneficial, as may a prescription of cinnamon twigs and angelica. Aerobic **exercise** such as walking, running, swimming and skipping increases the blood flow.

Thrombosis

This is an injury caused by a blood clot from either accumulated fats in the blood or a sluggish blood-flow. **Diet** changes should consist of more fatty fish (such as herring, mackerel and kipper), eating fresh garlic and onions, and taking vitamin E daily (200–300 mg).

Varicose veins and haemorrhoids

When the valves in veins become weakened the blood can no longer flow properly and the veins themselves become knotted and twisted.

Haemorrhoids are varicose veins which occur specifically around the anus. Varicose veins and haemorrhoids can be made worse by constipation, pregnancy, the menopause and obesity. **Hydrotherapy** (alternating hot and cold water) can bring relief, as can **yoga**, including deep breathing and stretching exercises (3). Dietary help consists of using vitamin C and E and increasing the intake of foods such as cherries, rosehips and buckwheat, which contain rutin. Varicose ulcers occur when a sore associated with varicosity fails to heal. Essential oils (2) as appropriate can help the healing process.

BOREDOM

Boredom is thought of as a sign that mental stimulation is lacking, but is in fact much more than that. It can often signify that the inner self (the spiritual self) is aware of the need for change. It is as though there is a blockage between the personality and inner motivation. Right from the time a child is born and becomes aware of its surroundings, it is receiving stimulation and gradually widening its areas of perception. When the need to change perception ceases, or there is no motive to be curious, then boredom sets in. The nature of the boredom will depend on individual character. For instance, an extrovert will lack external stimulation, whereas an introvert will find difficulty in remaining connected to his inner motivation. The way to deal with this is to deliberately instigate change, however small. Simply taking a different route to work or school can begin a process of stimulation. Changing the order in which one carries out the daily routine can alter one's perception. Taking up a hobby that requires mental effort can help, as can exploring a new concept.

Boredom can sometimes be an early sign of depression and senility. As the individual becomes less mobile or less able to take in information, repetition of the same routine can become boring. In many instances of crime, particularly juvenile, boredom is a prime factor. While many youth and community projects are initiated to handle such boredom, there is also the problem that they are begun by authority figures who do not necessarily allow young people to take responsibility for themselves. One of the ways of dealing with boredom may be to ensure some kind of interaction between age groups within the community.

BULIMIA
Also see **Eating Disorders**

Bulimia is an eating disorder characterized by eating large quantities of food in a short period of time. It mainly affects intelligent young women who after bingeing secretly make themselves vomit in an effort to cancel out the effects of their over-eating. In many cases bulimia is not recognized by friends or family until the pattern of binge/vomiting has become well established. Many young women binge only occasionally: others have a regular daily pattern. Usually social or mental **stress** lies at the root of this disorder. Management consists of identifying the stressful factors and dealing with them at source. Only when the individual pattern is known can dietary measures be introduced. Physical problems usually arise because of the changes in blood acidity through the vomiting or the use of laxatives or diuretics. Muscular weakness can occur; there can be heartburn and sore throat.

Psychological difficulties are similar to those of **anorexia nervosa**, and are often associated with problems of self-image and competence. Bulimia is often considered less serious than anorexia. This is not necessarily true, though it does respond to treatment more readily.

Spiritually it could be said that in the bulimic there is an instinctive recognition that a void needs to be filled. There is also a recognition that the '(w)hole' is not being filled in the correct way and that there is a need to keep the void clear and uncontaminated. This does mean recognizing one's limitations, as well as accepting one's potential in whatever is closest to one's heart. Often achieving a balance between limitation and potential is sufficient to enable the individual to stop the destructive cycle.

Affirmations (2) can help in creating the right atmosphere for success. Patience with oneself, and a willingness to accept outside help, in order to break out of the secrecy trap, are huge steps forward in self-management. Finding a purpose or focus in life, often one that has an impact on other people or on the outside world, may also help to make positive use of an energy that can be destructive. Often ego problems, ranging from extreme self-criticism to a belief that one is responsible for the world's ills (a juvenile type of megalomania), need to be dealt with.

Healing (2) can take place when the sufferer is able to achieve some kind of integration of self. Some progress may be made when there is a recognition that the impulse to binge and then vomit is a form of self-punishment, or that the impulses that arise may be a way of trying to experience a different reality, one that no one else can control.

C

CANCER

This book is not the correct place to go into depth insofar as all the various cancers are concerned, except to note that each and every system of the human body can produce abnormal cell growth. There have been healings of various cancers that are nothing short of miraculous, although the medical profession will not admit to such cures, preferring to believe that the cancer is in 'remission' – that is, at this point in time the cancer is no longer active. What is agreed both by alternative therapists and doctors alike is that it is the individual's attitude to the illness that will play a large part in his or her management and possible recovery from the disease. The more positive the attitude, the more the possibility that the self-healing available to each individual will be awakened and made use of.

With cancer more than any other illness there has to be an acceptance that such an illness is a 'soul choice', although not a conscious one. This means that the individual has a life lesson to learn while going through the experience. Sometimes that lesson may be to treat themselves with more dignity, care and attention. Sometimes it may be to try to live life to a maximum potential, perhaps to learn to accept assistance from other people. Each individual's experience will be entirely unique, as will be the experience of the people caring for the sufferer.

Practically, changes in **diet** commensurate with the needs, wishes and desires of the person concerned can help. Often, a vegetarian diet can make a difference. This may be because the system does not become overloaded with the toxins accumulated by an ordinary diet. Many of the alternative **therapies** (2), such as **reflexology**, **shiatsu**, **acupuncture**, **acupressure**, which work with the body's energy flow, can aid the healing process. **Creative visualization** (e.g., seeing the growth shrinking until it disappears, or visualizing an 'army' of healthy cells overcoming the invaders) will also activate the healing process. A variation is to envisage the chemotherapy 'army' being assisted by the body's defensive troops, and then the debris being cleared away. It should be stressed that each person must develop his own techniques and visualizations. A competent therapist can only assist in the process of developing a routine.

With the onset of cancer various fears need to be addressed. The most obvious one is the fear of dying. This can be broken down into several different aspects. One is the actual process of dying itself, and whether this can be accomplished with dignity. Another is the fear of not having done what one intended to do with one's life. A third is the fear of there being no continuation of life after **death**. A fourth is the difficulty of leaving others behind. While all of these fears can be met, they can only be tackled at the appropriate time. The things that need to be tackled first are such issues as personal care and support in order to do away with unnecessary stress. On this front, it is often appropriate for the sufferer to do what is possible to 'wipe the slate clean' of old difficulties and hurts. While some would feel that this is a preparation for death, it can also be seen as husbanding the energy that is necessary for survival.

Some form of belief, either in a **religion** (2) or some other philosophical system, may be an important source of support for the sufferer. **Prayer**, **chanting** and **spiritual healing** may all be used to back up one's system of belief (2).

It must not be forgotten that carers of people with cancer also need help, and in this **counselling**, **stress** management, perhaps **massage** (2) or other forms of bodywork can bring great relief and ease the pressure.

CELEBRATIONS

There are many who will be surprised to find celebrations in a list of problems. There are, however, several ways in which such occasions can be difficult. Often such times can give difficulty because of the high expectations that surround them. They are often family occasions when old animosities and old hurts resurface. The participants may well be over-tired or under stress. Everything is done to excess and this can lead to bad behaviour.

Often the rituals associated with these occasions, such as Christmas and birthdays, may be used for comfort or as a means of escape. The perennial ceremony of filling the stockings may reassure some and bore others. By practising tolerance, it is suggested, a great deal can be learnt. But often family rituals have developed simply as a way of bypassing problems.

Perhaps the greatest tolerance or honesty that one needs is with oneself. If you find such occasions difficult, can you be honest enough to accept that you yourself may be the problem? If so, what can be done? Perhaps you need to relax a little (see **Relaxation Techniques** in Section Two). Honesty with others may be called for, but this does not mean telling it like it is, but rather avoiding conflict until a more appropriate time or even creating an opportunity to agree a code of behaviour before trouble begins.

Sometimes, celebrations can have the shadow of the past hanging over them. Uncle Jack (with apologies to any Uncle Jacks who may be reading this) may sing along to a favourite song at a certain point. If he would be hurt not to do so, then let him. If you are uncomfortable, leave. With consideration for the greater good, these occasions can be enjoyed.

Pagan and tribal societies may have something to teach us, for their celebrations are used quite deliberately to release tensions. When the festivities are over, work resumes as normal.

CELIBACY
See **Sexuality**

CHASTITY
See **Sexuality**

CHOICES

Most of us dislike making choices because we do not know what the outcome of our choice will be. The ability to make choices does not develop in a child until the age of two. The necessity to differentiate between two courses of action in terms of right and wrong is learnt later, and the ability to choose the best option for oneself personally even later still. Subsequently one learns to consider what effect the choices one makes may have on other people. Making choices is actually a process of going through these various stages.

Let us suppose that you decide to make a change in your career. The process begins by deciding between staying where you are and moving on. By concentrating on one option (e.g., staying where you are), a decision must be made as to whether you will ask for a pay rise or not. You must decide which action is feasible. The process of choice is a type of pendulum swing between 'If this......then that'. If, for instance, you know that a pay rise is unlikely the right decision will be to leave.

Having decided to leave, you may find that the people you work with will have difficulty with a particular contract as a consequence of your departure. Your decision then has to be taken in the light of what will be best for everyone. Conversely, your decision may be to leave without asking for a pay rise. You are then in a position to take responsibility for the choices you make, without needing to put the blame on anyone else. It is for you to decide at which point you take responsibility for your own decisions. The mature individual will consider all the options available before making a choice.

CHOLESTEROL
See **Blood Disorders**

COMMUNICATION

Communication has had many thousands of words written about it, many theories put forward and many attempts made to define it. Despite this, to communicate is something that many people find extremely difficult to do.

It is perhaps worthwhile defining for yourself what you consider communication to be. Is it stating clearly what you mean? Is it listening to what others have to say? Is it expressing what you feel or what you think? Is it using words, gestures or body language?

It would probably be safe to say that in communication there are three basic actions. These are listening, interpreting and giving feedback. Listening is of prime importance. When we remember that a child learns to speak and understand by listening to what is going around him, we have some concept of the importance of the art of listening. At first, listening is taking in sounds, then making sense of them, and then attaching meaning to them. To follow a process through, let us use an example. A mother uses the word 'sausages' and indicates what a sausage is. The child learns that certain sounds mean 'sausage'. To communicate his need for a sausage the child then tries to reproduce the sound, which may come out as 'le-le-les'. The mother then has two options: she can correct the child's speech or can accept his version of the word, understanding his meaning. If she uses his version of the word, a loop has been completed where both understand one another although the child has not learnt correctly. If we then go one stage further and sausages become known as 'le-le-les' in the family, a localized system of communication has been set-up. (This has a parallel in the computer industry where three-letter acronyms (TLAs) are understood within the industry but not elsewhere without explanation.)

Explanation, or rather clarification, is an equally important aspect of communication. When meaning is clarified, one is often able to hear what is behind the communication. The meaning or the intention is clarified and interaction is enhanced. There are many suggestions made as to how to enhance our ability to communicate, but perhaps the most important one is the ability to give feedback. This can be done both verbally and non-verbally. A smile and a touch can both be equally valid, and sometimes more effective than words. So also can some of the mirroring techniques used in **Neuro-linguistic programming** (2). Many management training techniques highlight the need for good communication and the importance of explanation, the reason being that if a person knows why something has to be done, he will do it more willingly.

COMPLAINING

When someone gets into the habit of complaining, it can often be because their perception of themselves – or of others – is distorted. Complaints arise because the individual feels that he has had something done *to* him. This suggests that he is powerless within the given situation. Complaining indicates a discontent with the way that we are being treated, or with what is being given to us. Legitimate complaints indicate our ability to be assertive and to put right something that has gone wrong. But complaining as a habit indicates an attitude to life that is essentially negative (see **Negative thoughts**).

Changing such an attitude can be difficult. It requires looking positively at what is taking place. We may have learnt as children that complaining brought us attention, or that there is some other pay-off we can have. We may, for instance, feel that complaining indicates our ability to be in control of our own lives. This is a mistaken assumption because this type of control is of a negative kind. When trying to change this kind of behaviour, it is important to realize that a habitual pattern first needs to be stopped and then a new response initiated. Techniques such as handling change, positive **affirmation**, **meditation** and **chanting** can all be useful in breaking old patterns (2).

CONFIDENCE

Confidence is knowing that you have the ability to do something. In the process of learning, you discover how to do something, then learn further to do it better. For instance, a child learns to stand up, then to walk, then to walk properly and finally learns how to run. In physical terms, this suggests first finding a means of being able to maintain a balance. Confidence is the ability to keep up an internal balance, whatever the external circumstances may be. Self-confidence, therefore, is the ability to make correct choices that will preserve the equilibrium you have learnt. Self-confidence is also being able to maintain a balanced viewpoint about oneself, no matter what the circumstances. It is knowing what one can do and what one can't. Confidence-building can come from **yoga**, which teaches correct balance on a physical, emotional, mental and spiritual level, and learning how to practise some of the ancient techniques, such as **t'ai chi** and **qi gong (2)**. **Meditation**, **chanting** and **creative visualization** all help to establish and hold balance (2). An effective meditation is to visualize an old-fashioned pair of scales swinging gently and eventually coming to rest in perfect balance. Hold this image for as long as possible.

CONTROL

There are three aspects of control that need to be considered when trying to instigate change in our lives. The first is control of the circumstances around us. Quite literally, circumstance means that which surrounds us. The popular belief is that we are not in charge of our circumstances – they just happen. This is not strictly true. A more accurate way of looking at it would be to say that we draw towards us the experiences that we need for growth. If this is so, then ultimately we are always in control, although sometimes it may not feel that way. Once a change in attitude occurs, we are more able to be objective and less likely to make mistakes. We are able to have confidence that we have made a correct judgement, and are therefore more able to maintain control of the situation, of people and of self.

CRUELTY

There are many types of cruelty, most of which could be safely said to arise from one person's need to have power over another. There can be physical cruelty where there is violence against the person. This can often be against children who are not able to fight back, or against the elderly who may be too frightened or too weak to do so. There may also be cruelty to animals, again because they are not able to retaliate. Often such cruelty arises from **anger** or frustration, and the bully will need to learn how to handle these emotions in order to ensure that damage is not done. It is not for the victim to handle the emotions, although this is often what happens because the victim will try to make the situation better by placating the cruel person.

If this sort of situation is allowed to continue, then bullying takes place, which is cruelty in a prolonged form. Once the weak spot in one's armour has been found, then the truly cruel person will work on that weakness constantly. This then becomes mental or emotional cruelty. An example of this might be the kind of bullyiny that goes on in schools when a child is picked on by his peers for being smaller and perhaps less able. Similarly a younger member of the family may find himself blamed for everything that goes wrong within the family, and ultimately comes to believe that he is blameworthy. Perhaps the most effective way of teaching a child to deal with this is to have him see himself surrounded by a protective shield that no-one can get through unless he allows it. (Children are much better than adults at this type of visualization, because they do not need to rationalize their actions.)

Cruelty, bullying and harassment within the workplace can be very difficult to deal with, particularly if the one doing the bullying has authority on his side. Often a code of conduct needs to be agreed between management and personnel, for dealing both with bad behaviour and with grievances. These procedures should not give either side an advantage, and need to be strictly adhered to if conflict situations are to be avoided. One technique that can be employed to help the victim deal with the problem is to perceive the persecutor as a child of about two years old. This often reveals weaknesses that have not been seen before, and by removing the fear element allows the victim to take control of the situation in an appropriate manner.

Lastly, from a spiritual point of view, it is worthwhile looking at how the **victim** is co-creating a situation in which he can be bullied. It may be, for instance, that this feeds the 'Poor me' side of their personality. It could also suggest that in continually finding themselves in such situations, they need to learn how to take back their own power and not to be intimidated. It is helpful to remember that cruelty to others arises out of a feeling of inadequacy.

D

DEATH

It has been said that we are only truly alone when we die. Certainly each experience of death is totally individual. There will always be fear associated with dying, as mentioned in **ageing**, but a great deal can be done to 'lighten the load'. One of the fears is of what happens to us afterwards. This can range from what happens to the body, to what happens to the essential us.

Even before we have a terminal illness or have reached our four score years and ten, it is a good idea to have clarified our wishes and to have made them known to our nearest and dearest. When making a will it is wise to include instructions as to what you want done with your remains. Do make sure, though, that if your instructions are at all unusual, they can be carried out. If, for instance, you wish to donate your organs (such as your kidneys) on your death, then be sure to have filled out a donor card. It is unfair to expect others to make decisions such as these when they are mourning your loss. If you wish your body to be disposed of other than in the conventional ways of burial or cremation, ensure that this is possible. There is a growing fashion for disposing of the body in an ecologically acceptable way, such as by using biodegradable coffins. If this is your wish, then do make sure it is feasible.

The way you wish to be remembered or for your life to be celebrated is also something that needs to be considered. Those who are left behind are going to both want and need, as part of their own grieving process, to carry out your wishes. Try to have a thought as to what may be appropriate. You may wish that no dark clothes are worn, you may wish that there are no flowers, or lots of flowers, you may wish that your funeral arrangements are according to your own belief system, and so on. Many people do not wish to consider such details when they are fit and healthy, but in the event of your death being sudden consider the consolation your relatives would derive from knowing what your wishes were. It would be something for them to hold on to in times of shock.

Many people are afraid of the actual act of dying. No-one likes to be helpless or to feel that they are not in control of something that is happening to them, and death combines both these fears. Older people may wish to die at home, whereas others may prefer a hospital or hospice environment. For others, the place is immaterial or has to be where care is available. If you or your relatives have the opportunity to do so, try to make the surroundings as comfortable as possible. If you have religious beliefs, then have them followed.

The Living Will is a way of having your wishes about your treatment made known. While not legally binding, and final decisions are probably best left to your medical practitioner, it does set out whether treatment is to be carried out in certain circumstances, whether attempts should be made to revive you and so on. Think very carefully about these issues while you are able to, and because you appoint a proxy – who is usually a near relative or close friend – be very clear that you do not cause problems for him or her.

Another fear that can arise is that of what is going to happen to those left behind. On a practical level it is wise to make as much provision for them as you can long before the thought of death arises. In practice this is often not done. For many the thought of taking out insurance or making a will simply brings death closer or makes it more frightening. It is worthwhile remembering, however, that life is going to be difficult enough without your presence, without any additional practical worries. It seems to be easier to think of what will happen after death as we get older; it is as though something in us accepts that life can and will go on without us.

Perhaps the worst fear of all is that of taking a long time to die. In this day and age pain management is much better understood and more readily available. In addition to **drugs** such as morphine there are ways of controlling pain using the body's own endomorphic system; small electrical impulses can be used to activate the body's ability to kill pain. It is at this time that alternative or complementary therapies come into their own, bringing physical relief and spiritual ease. **Spiritual healing** (2) and the laying on of hands may bring much comfort – as can **counselling** (2) – in order to deal with any unfinished business, such as broken relationships and past hurts. Many **religions** (2) can help to alleviate distress by focusing on issues such as living life in a way that leaves no loose ends. Also, by giving some hope of an existence after death (and possibly the principle of reincarnation), there is a greater sense of permanence.

The possibility of not having done enough is another fear that can arise when faced by death, particularly an untimely one. What can be accomplished should perhaps be given priority, and the ability can be cultivated to let go of those things that do not really matter. Spiritual practices such as **meditation**, **chanting** and **prayer** can help (2).

DEPRESSION

Depression is a mood of sustained sadness or unhappiness and is believed to be far more common in women than in men. Clinical depression involves a degree of hopeless despondency, dejection, fear and irritability out of all proportion to any external cause. Chronic depression is the return at frequent intervals of feelings of intense misery, negative thoughts, self-doubt, tearfulness, guilt, sleeping difficulties, severe headaches and loss of appetite and sex drive. There is an important difference between normal unhappiness and genuine depressive illness, in that it is often impossible to recover from the latter without some kind of external help.

There are several causes of depression. Frequently there is a tendency to view oneself as being undesirable or worthless. The sufferer often views the world as a hostile place in which deprivation and suffering are inevitable and failure and punishment are to be expected. It is as though the individual has no longer the ability to adapt to circumstances. Depression often manifests as, or is precipitated by, a seriously afflicting major life event, such as **bereavement**, **retirement** or loss of status. Post-natal depression is slightly different in that it generally arises from physiological hormonal causes, coupled with the life-changing event of having a child. This type of depression responds well to support, both for the change of lifestyle and the management of the psychological difficulties which may arise.

Suicide is a risk in people who are clinically depressed, and is especially common in elderly people. This is a form of nihilism where nothing matters, not even survival. First attacks tend to come between the ages of 50 and 60 in women. It is thought that post-menopausal depression attributable to hormonal changes may be the cause, though there is no positive proof of this. It is more likely that a combination of factors comes into operation. Children may be leaving home, the woman is aware of the ageing process, she feels less attractive and less needed than before, and there is more time in which to brood. Depression may also hit men who are high achievers, or who have gone through divorce or the loss of access to their children.

It is very important to recognize the signs of true depression so that urgent treatment can be given, as the condition can be relieved at this early stage. Anti-depressant drugs can be of help, but often do not 'kick-in' until about two weeks after first taking them. Many forms of self-help techniques can be put into practice immediately. **Aromatherapy** (see under **Essential Oils** in Section Two) using clary sage oil can help, **Bach Flower remedies** (2), particularly Rescue Remedy, sweet chestnut and mustard, are of use; however, if the cause of the depression is known, other of these remedies may be more suitable. **Exercise**, because it relieves stress and releases certain hormones into the bloodstream, can lift depression, as can dietary changes which exclude junk food and include vitamins, particularly the B group. Natural tryptophan and D,L-Phenylalanine (DPLA) may also help, although the latter should not be taken by people with kidney problems or high blood pressure.

Counselling (2) or psychotherapy may be suggested, and some life-management techniques may also help. For instance, laughter has been found to lift the mood, and rediscovering a sense of humour or new activities can shift the black cloud. **Creative visualization**, particularly using colour (see **Colour Therapy**) (2), will also work, as will a technique called 'Time Control'. This latter is akin to retraining. The individual undertakes not to allow himself to be depressed, initially for a short period, sometimes as short as half an hour. This initial period is then extended progressively until eventually a whole day of non-depression is achieved. It is often better if there is a small reward given for each personal milestone passed. The sufferer must be patient and not become disheartened, because, as always, it takes at least six weeks to achieve a change in behaviour.

In addition to these methods, an understanding of **anxiety** and **negative thoughts** can be of great assistance.

DIABETES

There are two types of diabetes: insulin-dependent and non-insulin-dependent. The first is treated by insulin injections and **diet**. Around one in four people with diabetes have this type. It is the most severe form and usually develops under the age of thirty.

Non-insulin-dependent diabetes affects the remaining three out of four diabetics. It is also known as maturity-onset diabetes and is more common among elderly people, especially if they have been overweight for twenty years or more. The complications for these sufferers are due both to obesity and to the diabetes – which can affect the tissues of the eye, the kidneys, the heart and blood vessels and the nervous system. This type most readily responds to **diet** management.

Exercise is of particular use in keeping diabetes under control, as are **yoga** and **creative visualization**. A suitable visualization might be to picture the blood becoming 'clean' and free of impurities.

DIET AND NUTRITION

Although certain suggestions are made throughout this book as to the possibilities of experimenting with various types of diet, it cannot be stressed too strongly that no particular diet is right or wrong. Everyone has the right to try different patterns of food intake, and to change that pattern if so desired. Much is made in today's society of the necessity and determination that is needed to stick to a particular diet when it is sometimes wiser to listen to what your own body and metabolism needs. What is needed is a basic appreciation of what healthy eating is about. It would be more exact to call it healthy nutrition rather than healthy eating. This entails knowing what each food type is and knowing how to get the best benefit from your food. The four food groups are:

● Fats, including saturated fats (mainly from animal sources), and unsaturated fats (from vegetable oils and oily fish).

● Carbohydrates – these include simple ones (such as sugar), and complex ones (such as wholegrain products).

● Protein – foods such as meat, fish and soya protein.

● Fruit and vegetables. Fibre is contained in fruit and vegetables, and also in complex carbohydrates which are wholegrain products.

Attitudes often determine people's eating habits – the beliefs and values that a person has will affect how he thinks about food. As an example, the breakfast habits that people had 75 years ago, when fat-filled foods were the norm, are very different from those of today, when fibre-rich foods are recognized as improving health.

Health considerations may take second place to habit, cheapness, and a liking for certain foods. People will not simply buy a food because they have been told it is good for them – they also have to like it.

Food preparation may also be a consideration in eating habits. When cake mixes were first introduced they were disliked because there was very little to do in their preparation. In many instances, the preparation of food is an act of love and a ritual that satisfies a deeper need. In certain religious belief systems specific foods may or may not be eaten. These restrictions are observed to a lesser or greater degree by believers. Some of the better known religious restrictions are:

Hindu – Tend to be strictly vegetarian – no meat or fish; beef and pork are especially forbidden. Some people may eat eggs. Alcohol is forbidden, and there are also some periods of fasting.

Jewish – Pork is forbidden, and also considered unclean. Meat must be Kosher, and milk and dairy products must not be eaten with a meal of meat, or, indeed, cooked with the same utensils.

Muslim – Again, pork is forbidden. Meat must be Halal, which means that it is slaughtered in a prescribed fashion. However, fish with fins and scales are permitted. Alcohol is forbidden. Fasting (including no water) is observed during the daylight hours of Ramadan.

Rastafarian – The food here must be I-tal. Eggs and meat may be forbidden, as may salted and canned foods.

Sikh – The orthodox are strict vegetarian. Eggs are not permitted, neither is alcohol. Beef and pork are forbidden. There is a great deal of variation in dietary observances in Sikh communities.

In Section Three dietary suggestions are given which will enhance the healthy maintenance of the body and spiritual development. Also see the entry for **Diet** in Section Two.

DISABILITY

It takes a great deal of courage to deal with disability of any sort, both for the people who are disabled and their carers. From a physical point of view there is often **pain** to be dealt with. The qualities of patience and fortitude have to be developed on both sides. This is not easy.

Starting with disablement at birth, there always arises in the mind of the parents the question as to whether such a birth defect could have been their fault. While this is a time when mutual support is of prime importance within a relationship, it will depend on the character and personality of the parents as to whether that support is forthcoming within their relationship. Fears have to be faced and difficulties considered, and, arising from that, the whole dynamic of relationships within the family has to be examined. There is a belief that from a spiritual point of view the birth of a disabled child represents some kind of karmic lesson (see **Karma (2)**) to be learnt. Certainly, other members of the family will be profoundly affected by it. Older children must learn to adjust to the presence of a disabled child, and it will depend on what age they are when the new baby arrives as to how they cope with the ensuing difficulties. In later years, for instance, they may need help in working through their own attitude to disability. Children born after the child who is disabled will often develop an unusually mature attitude towards their sibling.

Disability arising through injury or disease can be even more difficult to cope with. Initially there is shock and trauma, both for the person concerned and his family and friends, and there is often a whole new search for meaning. Psychological **counselling** is of prime importance during this time. **Stress** management will often help and at this stage some people will explore alternative **therapies** (2).

Spiritually, people may turn towards **healing** (2) in the hope of changing their lives and even in the hope of a 'miracle'. At this point it is vital that the healer adopts a responsible attitude. Much can be done to make things easier for the sufferer, to help him understand the wider implications of the problem. Any improvement is through the establishment of a relationship between the individual and his own belief system, and it is in this sense and to this process that the healer lends his energy and his ability to channel healing energy. If and when a 'miracle' does occur the healer accepts this with humility as being part of the plan for that particular person.

The disabilities associated with old age need careful management. Again, alternative therapies such as **massage**, **reflexology** (see under **Therapies** in Section Two) and other forms of bodywork can assist in mobility, together with specific sensitive **counselling** and **healing** (2) where appropriate. Some conditions, such as arteriosclerosis and **Alzheimer's disease**, lead to a loss of reality for the sufferer. In these cases the healer can often help the families of sufferers by giving them a safe space in which to express their distress.

DISCIPLINE

Discipline does not usually make a great deal of sense until one is older. It is a learnt skill that allows you to create a suitable structure within which to run your life successfully. Parents will impose 'discipline' on young children without explaining the reasons why. The easiest example of this is perhaps that of sensible bedtimes. The child is told to go to bed at a time when he is not tired, and to get up when he is (see **Ritual** in Section Two). Discipline for a child is exceptionally difficult, because there may be one set of rules and regulations for home and another for the world outside. The fact that those rules may be created for the easy running of society will mean very little to a child who has not yet learnt to conform.

Learning to conform is perhaps the best way to think of discipline, particularly self-discipline. When you discover what works as a structure for you, it is sensible to develop a set of behaviours that will allow you to maximize the energy you have available. It is, however, difficult to maintain those behaviours as a matter of course, and you may often have to bypass your own inertia. One way of overcoming this is to develop a 'time contract' with yourself. Here is an example:

Time Contract
I agree to make full use of my time by:

- Developing a list of priority items to do each day.
- Guarding against unnecessary interruptions (asking people to call back, etc.)
- Keeping appointments on time, apart from emergencies.
- Not allowing 'casual' visitors to use up too much time.
- Making time for people who need me.
- Doing important things rather than procrastinating.
- Developing my own interests and those of others.
- Keeping accurate records wherever possible.
- Setting realistic deadlines for assignments and projects.
- Planning 'quiet times' regularly for self-reflection and realistic day-dreaming.
- Allocating the proper time for appointments and visits etc.; keeping to them.
- Stopping to assess my time management performance.
- Helping others to improve their self-discipline.
- REWARDING MYSELF FOR GOOD DISCIPLINE BY –

(Please fill in your own reward; e.g., relaxing, a massage, working out.)

Signed..

Fear must be dealt with in learning discipline. Often this can be a fear of change. You need to ask yourself what you are most afraid of. Might it be success *or* failure? Or maybe the fear of being beyond discipline? Whatever it is, face the fear honestly. Be gentle on yourself and give yourself time. As always, remember that it takes at least six weeks to change a behaviour pattern.

DRUG ABUSE

A drug is any substance, not including most foods, that affects the body in any way. Tobacco, alcohol, coffee and tea are all drugs, so most people are drug takers, and are addicted, though these habits are not regarded as 'abuse'. There are others who do not consider that the occasional use of marijuana or cocaine is 'abuse'. Drugs such as betel nut, pan or opium are used conventionally in various parts of the world, and the users do not consider themselves as 'abusers'. Often drugs are prescribed for various medical conditions, and patients can, through overdosage and misuse, abuse drugs such as valium or librium.

Drug abuse really means the use of any drug that is disapproved of by most members of society. The class of drugs used to alter the state of the mind for recreational purposes is often divided into 'soft' and 'hard' drugs – hard drugs are those liable to cause major emotional and physical dependency, such as heroin and morphine. This dependency can lead to crimes of stealing and mugging in order to fund the 'habit'.

Drug Types:
DEPRESSANTS

Alcohol The history of alcohol consumption goes back thousands of years, although the term 'alcohol' has only been linked with 'spirituous' liquids for some three hundred years or so.

Alcohol depresses the central nervous system and can cause a number of changes in behaviour. Even a low intake can impair judgement and co-ordination, though this may have more to do with an individual's own capacity. Alcohol can induce relaxation, suppress anxiety and may inspire confidence. However, as more is drunk and its toxic effect increases, euphoria often gives way to depression. Intoxication occurs because of the slow rate at which the liver is able to break down the alcohol – a maximum of one ounce per hour. Being drunk can last up to twelve hours. Once the body develops a dependency on drink, a sudden end to its consumption may lead to withdrawal symptoms, such as tremors, hallucinations and convulsions. Permanent damage can occur – to the brain and liver – if consumption is heavy and over a long period.

The type of alcohol drunk socially by many of us (as whisky or vodka, for example) is ethyl alcohol, an anxiolytic which is a product of fermentation. Similar to ethyl alcohol but not fit for human consumption is methyl alcohol, known colloquially as meths (methylated spirits). Even when taken in small doses, methyl alcohol can result in blindness and death.
Street Name Booze.

Barbiturates This is one of six categories of depressants, or 'downers', the others being benzodiazepines, methaqualone, ethchlorynol, chloral hydrate and meprobamate. Depressants have been used in the treatment of insomnia and anxiety since the early 1900s – and have always been a target for abuse. This situation is not helped by the fact that barbiturates have, until recently, been regularly prescribed by general practitioners without any monitoring of the results. Barbiturates are associated with several thousand accidental and intentional deaths per year.

Barbiturates depress the central nervous system and produce depressant effects similar to those of alcohol. There are thousands of derivative barbiturate acids, of which only 15 or so are used medically. They were originally used to replace drugs such as opiates, bromides and alcohol in order to provoke sleep. The body develops a tolerance to barbiturates with regular use that can become a need for more frequent, larger doses. The problem is that tolerance to the lethal level does not increase, and thus frequent use will bring the user closer and closer to the lethal limit. Barbiturate abuse can result in two kinds of addiction: psychological and physical dependence.

Effects may include a sense of excitement before sedation takes place. Symptoms also include slurred speech, lack of co-ordination, clammy skin and coma. When taken with alcohol the chances of death from overdose are increased.

PAINKILLERS/NARCOTICS

Many of today's painkillers or narcotics contain natural alkaloids found in opium poppies. Narcotics, also known as opiates, are painkillers that may also be used in the treatment of sleeping problems. The term opiates is used to distinguish drugs that are derivatives of opium, e.g., heroin, morphine and codeine. The term 'opioid' is used to refer to those natural or synthetic compounds that trigger morphine-like effects.

Opioids work by attaching themselves to specific opioid receptors in the nervous system. This then relieves pain and induces a feeling of euphoria. When pain receptors are activated, a nerve impulse is triggered that travels from the site of the injury along sensory fibres to the spinal cord, through to the brain – specifically to the thalamus. This area generates an awareness of pain, while the cortex gives a sharper perception of the pain. The pain receptors in the brain are temporarily blocked by the analgesic influence of the body's own endorphins. Because this effect is very brief, however, it is sometimes necessary to continue the analgesic (pain-killing) effect for the good of the patient. This is where opiates come in, commonly morphine. Chemically similar to the body's natural painkillers, morphine connects easily to the same pain receivers as those endorphins, and stops, for a longer period of time, the pain signals being sent to the brain. The problem is that morphine suppresses the body's production of its own natural painkillers and therefore makes the body dependent on the drug. Once this dependency is established – and then discontinued – the pain signals are allowed to flow without the natural effect of the endorphins. This painful transition back to normal is known as drug withdrawal.

Heroin/H Pure heroin is a white powder with a bitter taste. Cut heroin is different in colour and taste, due to the manufacturer's process of 'cutting' (adulterating) the heroin with food colouring, cocoa, sugar or bicarbonated soda. Another form of heroin is 'black tar' – a processed form that may be sticky like tar or hard like coal. It is dark brown or black.

Heroin produces a feeling of euphoria, most often followed by nausea, vomiting, and drowsiness, also itchy eyes, constricted pupils. Overdose symptoms include clammy skin, shallow breathing, coma, and possible death.

Street Names H, Black tar, KFC, Junk, White lady, Scag, Syrup.

Methadone German scientists synthesized methadone during World War 2 because of a shortage of morphine. Although different from morphine or heroin, the drug produces many of the same effects. It became widely used in the 1960s for the treatment of narcotic addicts. The effects of methadone differ from morphine-based drugs in that they last longer, allowing administration only once a day in heroin detoxification. However, tolerance and dependence may develop along with withdrawal symptoms, which are more prolonged.

Street Names Dolly, Dolophine, Meth.

Morphine Morphine (one of the most effective pain-relieving drugs, and also one of the most highly addictive) is the principal constituent of opium, ranging in concentration from 4 to 21 per cent. Its effects include euphoria, followed by nausea, vomiting, severe cramps and drowsiness. Other drawbacks are itching, watering eyes and constricted pupils.

Street Names Emma, Gunk, M, Morpho.

Opium At least 25 alkaloids can be extracted from opium. These fall into two general categories, each producing different effects. One is morphine and codeine, which are used medically as analgesics and cough suppressants. The second is papaverine (an intestinal relaxant) and noscapine (a cough suppressant). Misuse leads to addiction and other symptoms.

Street Names Black stuff, Hop, Poppy, O.P.

STIMULANTS

Two of the most widely used stimulants are nicotine – found in tobacco products – and caffeine. When used in moderation, these stimulants tend to relieve fatigue and increase alertness. There are, however, more potent stimulants which, because of their ability to create a dependency, are supplied only on prescription. Users will say they use stimulants to feel stronger, decisive and more self-absorbed. Chronic users often follow a pattern of taking 'uppers' in the morning and 'downers', such as alcohol, at night. The use of stimulants may result in a temporary sense of exhilaration, energy, hyper-behaviour, un-tiredness and loss of appetite. It may, however, also induce feelings of anxiety and apprehension and be followed by a period of depression, known as a 'come-down' – this is not a pleasurable experience. The pattern of abuse becomes very hard to break. Recognizable symptoms include insomnia, dilated pupils and trembling. The long-term effects of stimulant-use can include paranoia and violent behaviour.

Amphetamines and their derivatives – street names 'speed', 'splash', 'crank' and 'meth' – as well as cocaine, LSD, PCP and THC are all examples of drugs that act on the central nervous system and specifically the brain. The effect of amphetamine stimulation is a marked decrease of fatigue, diminished appetite, insomnia and increased alertness. 'Designer' drugs of this type have been illegally manufactured to create the effects of drugs that have been banned because of their inherent dangers and propensity for abuse. Misuse often occurs when the individual is looking for some change in consciousness, which apparently cannot be achieved without artificial stimulants.

Hallucinogenic or psychedelic drugs are stimulants that alter sensory perception and normal thought processes. The exact trigger that causes the psychic effects of LSD is unknown, but the role of the receptor sites for the neurotransmitter (a kind of chemical messenger) serotonin is key. Serotonin is thought to be involved in sensory perception, sleep inducement and mood control. The limbic system is the part of the brain that deals with emotion and behaviour. When some parts of this system have been stimulated, they produce feelings of intense punishment, while other areas produce feelings of intense pleasure. When nerve cells are activated by a nerve impulse (specific to this area) serotonin is released from their nerve endings. It is believed that LSD inhibits the initial receptors of the serotonin-producing neurones, causing a decrease in the ability of serotonin to inhibit the postsynaptic neurone. The effect of LSD is that it allows 'excitatory' neurotransmitters to influence the postsynaptic neurone (the nerve on the other side of the gap) and increase its propensity for uninhibited 'firing'. This influence may account for the changes in behaviour produced by the drug. Also, it is believed that it is the resultant effect of extreme sensory input reaching the brain that accounts for the associated visual hallucinations produced.

Cocaine/Crack Cocaine is extracted from the leaves of the coca plant, which has been grown in South America for many years. The leaves of the plant are chewed for refreshment and relief from tiredness. Elsewhere in the world pure cocaine was used in the late 19th century as an anaesthetic. The intensity of the psychological effects of cocaine depends on how quickly it enters the bloodstream. Intravenous injections and smoking produce an immediate, intense experience. Sniffing cocaine has the effect of sharpening perception for a short period of time.

The usual form in which cocaine is sold - cocaine hydrochloride - is insensitive to heat. The conversion of cocaine hydrochloride to cocaine base yields a substance that becomes volatile when heated. 'Crack' is usually vaporized in a pipe or smoked in a 'joint'. Inhalation of the fumes from 'coke' produces intense effects that are very quickly over, followed by a 'come down'. This leads to repeated doses and hence addiction.

Because of its pleasurable effects, cocaine has the potential for extraordinary psychic dependency, and in the male may appear to enhance sexual performance. Effects can include feelings of euphoria, heightened sensory awareness, paranoia, confusion, anxiety, irrational behaviour and hallucinations.
Street Names Coke, Cola, Charly, Ice, Snow.

Marijuana The term 'marijuana' is used to refer to the cannabis plant and to any part of it that produces somatic or psychic change. A tobacco-like substance produced by drying the leaves and flowering parts of the plant, marijuana varies significantly in its potency, depending on the source.

The initial effects of the drug include feelings of euphoria and well-being, relaxed inhibitions, a sense of humour about almost everything, and hunger pangs (munchies). Other effects may include a significant increase in heart rate, dry throat and mouth, bloodshot eyes, short-term memory loss, difficulty with comprehension and co-ordination. It may also produce feelings of paranoia as well as psychosis. In some cases it may cause panic attacks.

Street Names Dope, Weed, Puff, Hash, Herb, Bud, Ganja, Grass, Dubie, Spliff, Reefer.

MDMA, MDA and other 'designer' drugs such as MMDA (ecstasy) MDEA (eve), DOM and DOB are chemical variations or modifications of amphetamines and methamphetamines. These drugs can be very dangerous, because they may be many times stronger than the drugs they are meant to reflect. Initial effects include feelings of warmth, confidence and enhanced thinking, as well as an exhilarating rush; other effects may include chills, sweating, nausea, fainting and blurred vision. Psychologically, there is often paranoia, depression and anxiety.

Street Names X, E, Ecstasy, MDM, XTC.

Mescaline The main active ingredient of the peyote cactus is the hallucinogen mescaline, which has long been used by North Mexican Indians as part of traditional religious rites. Mescaline can also be produced synthetically. A dose of 350 to 500 mg of mescaline produces illusions and hallucinations lasting from 5 to 12 hours. Overdose may lead to psychosis and possible death.

Street Names Buttons, Mesc, Chief, Seni.

Nicotine Nicotine is the active ingredient in tobacco and acts as a stimulant. In its pure form nicotine is colourless and has a potent odour and strong acid taste, and is also highly poisonous – in fact, one drop of 50 mg can kill a person within minutes.

Cigarette smoke contains about 4,000 chemicals, many of which are cancer-causing. Smoke from a tobacco plant includes such toxins as tar, carbon monoxide and nicotine. Tar, which is made up of many other chemicals, has cancer-causing agents in itself, such as nitrogen oxide and hydrogen cyanide. But it is nicotine that is the most dangerous substance in tobacco. Nicotine is highly addictive and damages many organs in the body. In smoking more than 90 per cent of the nicotine in a cigarette is absorbed in the lungs and will quickly enter the cardiovascular system. Nicotine is a very fat-soluble substance that easily enters the cell membranes where it first stimulates, then depresses, the vital respiratory centres of the brain.

Low doses of nicotine may increase mental awareness, induce a feeling of euphoria and relaxation. High doses may induce low blood pressure and also a cessation of activity in both the intestines and bladder. Tobacco smoke has an adverse effect on the bronchial tubes and lungs – common lung cancer has its beginnings in the bronchial walls.

PCP Phencyclidine Hydrochloride was first developed in 1959 as an anaesthetic to be used during surgical procedures. However, because of adverse effects, including delirium and confusion, it is no longer given to humans.

In the 1960s PCP emerged as a street drug and soon became well known for its weird and volatile effects. Most drug users stayed away from it because of these effects. However, since the 1970s the drug's 'attractions' (e.g., the feelings of heightened stimulation, strength, invulnerability, mood elevation and euphoria) have led to a resurgence in its use. Adverse effects include agitation, paranoia, suicidal impulses, physical violence and aggression, and even death due to respiratory failure. The effects of PCP can begin at any time from 2 to 15 minutes after use and last up to 6 hours. A drug-induced psychosis may set in 3 or 4 days after taking the drug.
Street Names Angel dust, Crystal, Rocket fuel, Killer weed.

Psilocybin Like the peyote cactus, psilocybe mushrooms have been used for centuries in traditional Indian rites. When they are eaten, these 'sacred' or 'magic' mushrooms affect mood and perception in a similar way to mescaline or LSD. Their active ingredients, psilocybin and psilocyn, are chemically related to LSD. They can now be made synthetically, but much of what is sold under these names is made up of other chemicals.

The effects of psilocybin may include altered vision, changes in perception, illusions, hallucinations, dilated pupils, anxiety, and depression that may lead to suicidal feelings. There is a danger that it could also cause organic brain damage and produce periodic flashbacks months after taking it. Overdose may cause agitation, convulsions and death.

Street Names Fungi, Magic mushrooms, Shrooms, Silly putty, Spores.

DYSLEXIA

Dyslexia is a disorder of interpretation. It was first recognized – in the mid-19th century – as a difficulty in interpreting letters, but is sometimes seen as a difficulty in interpreting meaning. Dyslexia is not a disorder of vision or spatial orientation, but a subtle kind of disorder in the area of language – of how to express and recognize thought. It is recognized that dyslexics excel in the creative arts, architecture and engineering (all branches of endeavour that are to do with the creation of form). Injury to the brain, often while still in the uterus, sometimes results in thought and speech disorders, known as the aphasias, meaning 'not speaking'.

Anatomically the brain is divided into halves with dense collections of nerve cells closely packed together inside the skull. The two cerebral hemispheres are approximately – though not exactly – symmetrical. It has been discovered that about 90 per cent of right-handed people have speech controlled by the left hemisphere, as do approximately 70 per cent of left-handed people. 15 per cent of left-handed people have it controlled by the right, and 15 per cent by both. In much of the research the area of the brain chosen for study was the *planum temporale*; part of the surface of the temporal lobes on each side of the brain. It was discovered that the left hemisphere is involved in the production of language. The right hemisphere is generally said to be concerned with visuo-spatial tasks and processes information simultaneously and holistically (as a whole). It is also thought possible that many of the skills required for music are controlled from the right hemisphere.

Earlier research had shown that there was asymmetry between the two *plana* in 75 per cent of cases studied. When the brains of those with learning difficulties were examined, the *plana* were more often than not symmetrical. In addition, the brains examined showed structural abnormalities, including *ectopias* (intrusions of cells from one layer to another) and *dysplasias* (disorganized cells within a cell layer). It is therefore sensible to suppose that the balance between the two halves of the brain is different in dyslexics, and that because of the presence of ectopias and dysplasias, connections have been formed in odd ways. It then follows that the brain mechanisms available for interaction with the environment are likely to be different.

The science of speech sounds, insofar as they convey meaning, is known as phonology, while 'phonological processing' refers to operations by which stimuli are interpreted in terms of the speech sounds involved. Many dyslexics get over the problem of interpretation by bypassing the area of the problem, for instance by using a tape recorder rather than recognition of the written word, or a computer fitted with speech recognition in order to express thoughts or knowledge.

E

EATING DISORDERS

Problems with eating are now much better understood than they were previously. It has been recognized that there is a fairly intimate connection between eating and sexuality. If we think of sexuality in terms of masculine/feminine, active/passive, penetration/receptivity and not just in terms of gender, it is probable that there is some confusion over such issues in the minds of those who suffer from eating disorders.

In addition, it may be crucial to recognize the connection between feeding in the sense of nurturing, and the child-like need to be comfortable. Many eating disorders appear to include regressive behaviour (going back to a younger sort of behaviour) and are to do with self-image.

One of the main causes of **anorexia nervosa** is the sufferer's perception of his or her attractiveness, whereas sufferers from **bulimia** are known to have difficulty in feeling complete. It is accepted that comfort eaters may well be trying to either cover something up or to 'fill themselves up'. Most of these difficulties tend to arise during puberty, and are helped – or hindered – by the attitude of the people around the sufferer.

When looked at from a spiritual point of view, it is perhaps easier to see how disorders of perception can arise in the young person. From about the age of ten, the emphasis is on learning how to express oneself properly. Added to that, philosophical concepts such as the meaning of existence, both personal and otherwise, present themselves for consideration. In relation to the chakra chart in Section Three, the difficulties which can arise are feelings of futility, lack of direction and helplessness, or indeed impotence – of being out of control or in the grip of a force greater than oneself. Eating disorders will reflect the distortions that occur in the management of all these factors.

Fasting (see **Diet** under **Crown Chakra** in Section Three) has a long history, as a means of cleansing away both physical and spiritual toxins. In animals fasting occurs instinctively when they are sick. This impulse may be at the root of some eating disorders, while in others it may be the fear of not having enough.

While it is appreciated that many eating disorders do not respond well to treatment, it may be that a course in spiritual development – such as learning to understand the **chakras**, backed up by physical therapies such as **massage**, **aromatherapy** and other deep bodywork – will help (**2**). Spiritual **healing** and the **laying on of hands** may also make a difference (**2**).

EDUCATION

The term 'education' often brings to mind children and the process of being taught, of learning how to conform to the beliefs and norms of society, as well as understanding the manipulation and workings of letters and figures. However, education can be very much more than that, as educationalists such as **Rudolf Steiner** and **A. S. Neill** (see under **People** in Section Two) have shown.

When the inquiring mind is given an opportunity to explore without restriction, it will follow what at first seems to be a random course, but will then gradually become more and more focused as the interest is caught. This principle is understood in the handling of gifted children and also of those with learning difficulties. To become a fully rounded individual, however, social skills need to be developed. This can be done by using the child's main interest as a 'hook'. For example, with a child interested in aeroplanes, the teaching of numbers could be introduced through an understanding of speed, as could concepts of fast and slow. Understanding colour could be introduced through painting, or social skills through team work and so on.

Education is not just about having young people learn, however. It is also recognizing that we can all learn from one another. Often we learn more about ourselves by helping others to understand our own particular passion. A good teacher is one who loves his subject. Being prepared to be open to new learning means we keep our minds agile. Particularly when one is depressed, having the courage to accept something new can often lead us away from such a state.

Education was once the province of religious establishments, and for those capable of understanding, these establishments still remain a rich source of knowledge. For instance, a comparison of beliefs can lead one through to one's own truth. If one is also happy to rely on **intuition** and **inspiration** (**2**), one's own course of learning can be developed.

EMPLOYMENT

It may seem strange to include this topic in a section on problems and difficulties, but there are many ways in which it can be a problem. The most obvious is a lack of employment, which can lead to a lack of self-esteem and respect from others. There is also a problem with lack of skills and therefore direction in life. In today's fast-moving society, where technology moves forward by leaps and bounds, the individual may be unable to keep up with changes. Lack of employment can also lead to boredom and alienation from others. It may be that this can be alleviated by some voluntary work or re-training, but it can be extremely difficult to remain motivated under such circumstances. Some of the techniques in Section Two, such as coping with change or the 'time contract' (see **Discipline)** may help. Lack of employment can also lead to depression and family problems .

But for those in work, other problems may occur. Not enjoying a job can give rise to difficulties. **Stress** is now accepted as something that causes loss of a great deal of productive time. A classic example is the customer care manager who had to take time off work because of a problem with her ears (see **Body Awareness**). If a creative person is not allowed to use that creativity within the framework of his job, then some other outlet must be found – perhaps art, music or theatre may give a respite. Employment may also give a problem if career management is not part of everyday planning. For instance, a factory that uses people on a temporary basis may not perceive a need to train people extensively. This then puts the responsibility onto the individual. Aat this point career counselling may help to find out what talents might be developed and whether such skills might be of use in the company.

Finally, employment in the sense of remaining busy is important. In retirement, for example, keeping an interest in what one is doing can lead to a successful change in lifestyle, as can being prepared to use one's wisdom and experience in a wider community sense.

ENEMIES

Almost invariably, as we attempt to change our lives, many of those people who have been our friends fail to understand our motives and find our new selves difficult to handle. We may not be asking them to change, but they become confused by new thoughts, ideas and concepts. In our eagerness to share new information, it is very easy to create enemies. We may be too fanatical or dogmatic. We may become boring or didactic.

Enemies are usually made due to intolerance of one sort or another, and while it can be a problem in the search for wholeness, communication, understanding and patience can usually overcome the difficulty. In this context we need to understand our enemies' fear. Certainly there will be fear for us and also fear of what we can do.

This last fear can be broken down into two aspects: fear of what we can do to them and fear of what we can do to their lifestyle. If in our own minds we are clear that we do not wish to 'take any prisoners' then we do not need to get caught up in their fears and doubts. Equally, if we are aware that our own fears can create problems, we can look long and hard at how we can be affected by fear and can deal with that. We will not, therefore, get into situations where we make enemies. We may disagree with others – and they with us – but equally we will not find ourselves in situations where our harmony is disturbed.

ENVIRONMENT

Many elements need to be looked at when considering our environment. Our own personal space is important to us from a comfort point of view. It is believed that where there is overcrowding the sensitive **aura** (2) is compromised, thereby making it difficult to maintain internal balance. **Meditation**, **chanting** and disciplines such as **yoga**, **qi gong** and **t'ai chi** all help to maintain this balance (see entries under **Therapies** in Section Two).

The development of a personal 'spot' or place, which can be perceived as a source of energy, is an important aspect of looking after oneself. Arising from this, the immediate environment – such as a bedroom or workspace – then becomes important. Much has been done to understand the human being's needs. Personalizing such space may be a throwback to establishing territorial rights in the same way an animal does. Decorating such space can have the dual effect of personalizing it and of placating the gods, demons and ancestors. Making the energy right and ensuring that it flows correctly is seen in **feng shui** (2), the layout of churches and in sacred geometry.

In the wider sense, being aware of the environment in a global perspective carries this principle one stage further. In being conscious of the use of energy, we also become aware of the use of finite resources. We therefore need to understand the interaction between the various systems, both man-made and natural, that support life. This leads naturally to ecology and how to conserve and maximize the resources we have.

On a more subtle and spiritual level, this in turn leads to what might be called our cosmic responsibility. If this world of ours is to carry on, we must be aware of how our actions will affect us in the future. This again means being conscious of our responsibility to a greater whole, and creating an environment that will sustain and nurture us.

ENVY
See **Jealousy**

EPILEPSY

There is reason to believe that the 'electrical' disturbances that occur during an epileptic fit or attack are similar to the changes in brainwave patterns shown in **mediums** (2) and channellers when working in trance. In some families with experience of psychic experience there is a history of grand or petit mal. Many of the symptoms experienced by sufferers of epilepsy are also experienced during the development of the 'siddhis' or powers such as **clairvoyance** (2) and clairaudience. For some reason, the development of these faculties – as well as epilepsy – can occur after head injury. The Dutch clairvoyant Peter Harkos is a case in point.

Stress management techniques such as **massage, relaxation, aromatherapy** and **meditation** are useful in the management of epilepsy (2). Some success has also been achieved with both **colour** and **crystal therapy** (2).

ESTEEM

When we think of esteem, we usually think of self-esteem, in the sense of feeling good about ourselves. This includes both who we are and what we do. It has been recognized only relatively recently that a baby appears to be aware of what is going on around it even before birth. It is also thought that the baby is aware of the mother's thoughts and feelings while it is still in the womb. Thus on some level the body will be aware of whether it is wanted or not, and may therefore form an image of itself accordingly. This first image is the one on which all future perceptions are built. Positive **affirmations** (2) and such techniques as found under **Base Chakra** in Section Three can help.

EUTHANASIA

Euthanasia is such an emotive subject that it is perhaps wise to sort out one's own feelings and ideas about it. There are two conflicting and perhaps irreconcilable views on this subject. The first is that one cannot 'play God' and decide at what point someone else is going to die. The second is that one would not let an animal suffer in the way that people with terminal illnesses sometimes do.

Euthanasia touches on personal responsibility at both its lowest and highest levels. If the individual concerned has strong views on the subject, then provided that they do not involve anyone else in their decision about their own life, they cannot be faulted. Almost inevitably, however, someone else – whether a relative or medical attendant – has to become involved, if only to be informed of their decision. The Hippocratic oath states that life should be prolonged, and it is perhaps unfair to expect someone who has taken this oath to go against it.

The advance of medicine and medical technology has considerably affected the way people are able to survive, and also the way people regard their lives. Life expectancy has increased considerably during the last thirty years, because many illnesses that were previously fatal are no longer. As our understanding grows the issue becomes one of maintaining the quality of life.

Euthanasia touches on aspects of **religion**, ethics and indeed

karma (2). We have to be able to take personal responsibility for our own beliefs, and also to recognize the impact that our decisions have on other people.

EXERCISE AND FITNESS

Exercise and fitness, though natural and normal, are yet very difficult to maintain. The muscles, respiratory system and heart are interrelated and benefit from a good exercise regime. It is impossible to change one aspect of the body without changing another, and it is important that the activity is enjoyable. Exercise can take many forms – from half an hour's walk in the park to a heavy workout, from swimming and dancing to **yoga** and **t'ai chi** (2). For such activities to be beneficial they must be regular and undertaken at least three times a week.

The body functions only to the level of the demands placed upon it. As fitness increases, the rate at which the heart has to work falls and becomes more efficient, and the pulse rate also drops. The heart does less work, but at the same time the other systems function more easily. The degree of attainable tension in the muscles is increased, the ability of muscles to utilize glucose and fatty acids in the presence of lowered insulin level is enhanced, and the ability of the liver to maintain the supply of glucose to the blood, and hence to the muscles, during strenuous exercise is improved.

Exercise throughout life is one of the most important preventives of arterio-sclerosis, which occurs when the arteries get clogged up or closed by fatty deposits. This condition reduces the blood flow, causes heart attack, stroke and eventually gangrene of the limbs. Arterio-sclerosis increases among women who have passed the menopause, because they are no longer protected by their hormones.

Exercise on a regular basis can have a profound effect on **depression**. This is partly because of the release of natural endorphins (mood changers) but also because of the self-discipline required. Regular habits can develop a framework around which the life can be structured and give it purpose.

One note of warning. Some people find exercise addictive. This is thought to be because of the release of endorphins and adrenaline, so care should be taken to keep exercise to a moderate level.

Exercise for at least twenty minutes a day, three times a week, is beneficial for most people, and helps to control blood pressure, **diabetes**, low blood sugar as well as obesity.

F

FAME

Many people would not consider this to be a problem. However, it is probably one of the most life-changing events there can possibly be. Andy Warhol is reported to have said that "In the future, everyone will be famous for 15 minutes". In theory this is about as much as anyone needs. It depends to a certain extent on how one becomes famous (or infamous). If it is for something that can be admired, an act of bravery for instance, fame may not last very long – about as long as the event remains newsworthy. If it is for an action that goes against the norms of society, one may remain famous as long as the transgression remains an issue.

Sudden unintentional fame can bring with it quite a problem. It forces people who thought they knew you well into thinking about you in a different way. It can indeed make you think differently about yourself. You may become aware of new talents, abilities and achievements.

Fame that arises out of a particular talent (for example, acting or playing an instrument) carries with it a certain degree of responsibility to the public. If the individual is well adjusted and emotionally balanced, this may not be a problem and may be accepted as 'part of the job'. If, however, the individual has difficulty with an aspect of themselves – such as being painfully shy – they may find it difficult to adjust from introversion to the extroversion expected of them. In some cases such difficulties may lead to substance abuse. There is a very fine line between allowing space for public demands and the right to personal privacy.

Barriers have to be put firmly in place at the beginning. It is unreasonable to court publicity on the one hand, then complain about it on the other. Boundaries that may not have been necessary in the past have to be accepted as a way of life. For the famous, fear may become a constant companion and have to be lived with on a daily basis. The syndrome of 'stalkers' is a case in point. One theory is that such people are trying to share the limelight of their heroes and heroines.

While there is a sense of responsibility associated with being famous, there is also a danger of losing one's individuality. The expectations, desires and adulation projected onto famous people can be a hard burden to bear. Any minor transgression can be blown up out of proportion, causing anxiety and distress to the person concerned and also to family and friends. A person cannot lead a normal life if they are continually aware of the effect, or possible misreading, of every action undertaken. Developing some form of spiritual discipline, such as **meditation**, **chanting** or **t'ai chi**, could help the individual to cope with this pressure (see entries under **Therapies** in Section Two).

FAMILY

The aspect of family life that appears to give the most problem is that of relationships. When two people decide they love one another enough to live together or to get married, they bring to that relationship a fair amount of ' baggage'. They will have formed ideas about themselves and their function in the world, about what is right or wrong, about what they can and can't do. All of these ideas will need reassessment in the light of the relationship they have formed. They may discover that their assumptions are wrong or that they are capable of doing unimagined things. They may find that previously unacceptable qualities in themselves take on new meanings. Thus a new relationship is an ideal time to reassess oneself, and one's family and the way it functions. Is there, for instance, a common pattern of behaviour that everyone follows unthinkingly? For example, in some families the habit of saying 'Take Care' on parting is actually an admonition to be good, while in others it may be an expression of fear about what might happen, or indeed have a hundred and one other subtleties of meaning. (This phrase can, of course, also be totally meaningless.)

New relationships may also involve becoming more tolerant of other people. Mother-in-law jokes have always been a source of mirth, but it does have to be remembered that a son or daughter's new friend can cause a huge upheaval in relationships within the family. If there is active dislike, should this be stated? Is the family ethos one of honesty and integrity, so this can be stated without prejudicing the family structure? If brothers and sisters already have cause to be jealous, a newcomer may give focus for these negative feelings.

A similar huge shift in perception occurs when children come into a family. It has been said that parents do not know whether they have done a good job with their own children until they become grandparents. Certainly, when this happens an awareness of continuity is inescapable. Parents begin to realize that their children are fully adult, and children begin to realize that they must develop a sense of responsibility that includes the care of other people. There is a shift of focus away from the selfish to the more altruistic.

With the birth of a first child a woman's perception of herself undergoes a more profound shift than at any other time in her life. She must get used to feeling totally different about herself and her body. Emotionally, as well as practically, she requires a great deal of support. The old tribal way of women who have gone through the same experience supporting a new mother has mostly been replaced, and nowadays support may come largely from professionals with whom there is not such an easy relationship. The new mother is likely to question her own competence, beliefs and awareness at this time. Sensitively handled, and using techniques such as **aromatherapy** massage, peri-natal counselling, **relaxation**, and perhaps **yoga**, difficulties such as post-natal depression can be averted (2).

For many new mothers keeping a diary can be of tremendous help, both early on and later when other children arrive. Many women develop a highly charged awareness of their own **intuition** (2), and of spiritual questions that may not have troubled them before. This is a good time to look to the future, to try to get some perspective on what life is likely to hold. Such thoughts should not, however, be allowed to become a cause of anxiety or take you away from the here and now.

As the family grows (and grows up) many changes occur quite naturally. Having to move to accommodate a growing family or to take up different employment, for instance, is known to be highly stressful for everyone concerned. It is only now being realized that the ability of children to relate to other people can be affected by major moves in childhood, depending on the age at which this happens. Management of change and recognizing the stages that are gone through can help.

Family structures can also change as a consequence of illness or death. As older members of the family become incapacitated, the demands on others increase (see **Ageing**), putting relationships under strain, stirring up resentments and changes in perception of loved ones. Perhaps the most profound example of this is Alzheimer's disease. To see a once competent person reduced to a shadow of themselves calls on all the qualities of compassion, courage and love, to enable the correct decisions for all concerned to be made.

Finally, the structure of a family relationship can be a problem, as people are just beginning to realize. When a marriage breaks down, both parties may remarry. Any children of the previous relationship lose their former security and must now accommodate many other relationships, as will be seen in the diagram below. The realization that he or she may not be quite so important after all can cause great distress. This problem can be made worse if there is animosity.

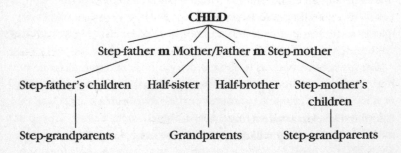

FATIGUE

There is a distinct difference between the fatigue caused by effort, whether sustained or otherwise, and fatigue caused by there being something clinically wrong. The condition of ME, for instance, results in an inability to sustain any effort whatsoever for more than very short periods, thus badly affecting the sufferer's quality of life. Chronic fatigue can have a profound effect on not just the sufferer but also family and friends. **Diet** and vitamins play a huge part in the management of fatigue. The B vitamins, which feed the nerves, are particularly of use but should not be taken late in the day because they may interfere with sleep. Sleep patterns should also be examined; for instance, if the individual is waking at a particular time during the night. **Acupuncture**, **acupressure**, **shiatsu** and/or **yoga** may be used to identify and deal with both the physiological and psychological dimensions of fatigue (see entries under **Therapies** in Section Two).

Fatigue can arise when we do not want to face a difficulty. This form of refusal and withdrawal can be self-defeating, because the problem will cause disturbed sleep and get us into a vicious circle of worry, fatigue and insomnia.

One way of dealing with a disturbing problem is to ask yourself the so-called journalistic questions of what, when, where, how and why. Here's an example:

- What is my problem? I am having difficulty studying.
- Where did it come from? I am not good at concentrating.
- When does it trouble me most? After about half an hour.
- How do I deal with it? Break down my study period into blocks of 20 minutes, change subjects if necessary, and then come back to it later.
- Why does this happen? I have not developed a discipline for myself.

Action: Develop a system that works for me.
Obviously the reader will develop his own answers further.

FEAR

Fear is first and foremost a physiological reaction. When one is threatened by danger the adrenal glands react to protect the individual. They initiate the reaction of fright, fight and then flight. Fear is a complex blend of all three of these reactions, and it will depend on the presenting danger which reaction becomes paramount. Alertness to danger gives options of action, of either remaining to confront the danger or of fleeing the scene.

If the danger is of an emotional nature, risk is often a factor, and again it will depend on the individual as to how the risk is assessed. (Some techniques for managing fear are shown under the **Throat Chakra** in Section Three.)

Much fear is based on not knowing. This can be not knowing what is going to happen, what the risks are or what our actions will bring to the surface. One way of handling fear is to ask four questions:

- What does this fear do *to* me?
- What does it do *for* me?
- What do I get out of not beating this fear?
- What do I get out of beating it?

FERTILITY/INFERTILITY

Fertility and infertility issues have a great deal to do with self-esteem and self-image. A woman's sense of self is rooted in her ability to bear children – or to choose not to. When a woman has a problem conceiving, almost inevitably she feels responsible. While intellectually she may know that there is good physical cause for her infertility, on an emotional level it precludes her from becoming a 'total woman'. In other words, she has no choice in the matter. Many conventional medical programmes have been instigated to allow women to bear children, but much can be done in the alternative field for both men and women.

In some quarters it is accepted that vitamin E can help both partners to achieve maximum fertility. As always, it is best to consult your health practitioner for individual advice. **Aromatherapy** (2) oils, by relaxing the partners, increasing sensuality and acting on the hormones, can help conception. These oils can be used in massage, while bathing and to enhance the atmosphere in the bedroom. The old idea of oysters being an aphrodisiac has some validity because it is now known that zinc – which is present in oysters – enriches the mobility of sperm (zinc levels drop significantly during periods of frequent sex).

Male infertility, while less widely talked about, is as problematical for men insofar as self-image is concerned as female infertility is for women, because so many men measure their masculinity by their sexual prowess. A man's realization that he is 'firing with blank rounds' can be devastating. The support and assistance that women tend to be able to call upon is not as available to men, who do not easily talk about such matters. Equally, many men do not appreciate that alternative **therapies** (2) can help them as much as their partners. Learning techniques such as tantric **yoga** (2 and 3) can also help to achieve potency.

Anxiety can compound the problems surrounding fertility and conception, so stress and anxiety management play an important part in treatment. Libido falls in times of stress, hence the necessity to prioritize one's needs and desires. Both men and women can find it extremely difficult to achieve a satisfactory sex life if they are under pressure at work. **Relaxation** (2) and small changes in **diet** (2) may go a long towards creating the right circumstances for conception. A positive holistic approach using **meditation** (2), **creative visualization** (2), **exercise** and healthy self-management will also have the effect of helping to keep both partners focused on their wish to have a baby.

The issues of fertility and infertility may not be based purely within the physical, but may have deeper significance and be connected with other abilities, fears and doubts; for example, the individual may doubt his adequacy as a parent. Spiritual **counselling**, **healing** (2) and awareness are integral to the process of becoming a parent.

FETISHES

A common misconception is to regard a fetish as being an action and to associate it with sexual behaviour. The fetish object is seen as some kind of trigger for action; for example, in the case of someone who cannot perform sexually without the presence of his or her particular fetish.

A fetish is, in fact, the concentration of energy into an object – as becomes apparent if one looks at the use of fetish objects in Native American culture. Tribal fetishes, such as feathers and beads woven in particular patterns, were worn by a warrior in the hope that the energy they represented would become part of his make up. Such an acknowledgement of the power of the gods would, it was believed, encourage them to look favourably upon him. By giving the individual a point of concentration or focus, energy is increased and becomes more available for use. The spread of Shamanic knowledge is leading to the incorporation of such fetishes in the ceremonies and **rituals** of other cultures. Nowadays, an altar which holds effigies of Buddha and a cross may well also include a Shamanic fetish.

FITNESS
See **Exercise and Fitness**

G

GAMBLING

It was not until fairly recently that gambling was seen to be an **addiction**. The rather fanciful idea of Lady Luck favouring her own can be traced back to pagan times when lucky gamblers were thought to be the beloved of the goddess of good fortune. She was seen as being capricious and prone, occasionally, to mockery. Risks were taken in order to gain her approval, and one of these risks was trying to guess what would happen – for example, which way a leaf would fall, which way a frog would jump. In fact, trying to calculate an element of chance.

While gambling is far more sophisticated nowadays , it still rests on calculating that element of chance. 'Form' is studied, particularly where horses or greyhounds are concerned, and chance weighed accordingly. The opportunity to win (or lose) a fortune is one that everyone appreciates. The traditional flutter on major sporting events suggests that everyone, even those who would not normally gamble, will relax their principles once in a while, just for the fun of it.

The National Lottery takes advantage of this need for fun. The chances of winning the jackpot on this are said to be approximately 14 million to one – nobody would dream of betting on a horse with those odds. When the imagination is captured, and the idea of having wealth presented, the individual is allowed to dream and plan what will be done with the winnings. One suspects that being able to dream of such an occurrence is perhaps as important as the winning. Those, who capitalize on these dreams, such as bookies and other commercial enterprises, are peddling false hopes and ideas. Often the people who can least afford it are the ones who spend the most and become addicted – not just to the lottery itself but to the idea of winning.

Gambling can have a profound effect on both the individual gambler and his family. As with any **addiction** or **obsession**, everything may become focused on feeding the habit. Food may be in short supply, anti-social behaviour may occur, family relationships broken, children may show **anger**, **anxiety**, **fear** and insecurity and often isolation. Their relationships with one another may be either exceptionally close or extremely distanced as a method of self-defence. This self-defence, sometimes leading to **aggression**, may also be shown towards the non-gambling members of the family, behaviour recognized as being dysfunctional without there being a solution to it.

When a gambler is unable to handle his failure to win, family and friends may be pulled into his depression. This can often lead later to deep-seated difficulties with others who are perceived to have the same personality traits. There is often a projection by those who have experienced the problems associated with gambling at second hand – for instance financial mismanagement – onto their own personal relationships.

One other aspect of gambling which must be considered is that of the corporate gambler. Someone who is an inveterate risk-taker may be seen as the blue-eyed boy until something goes awry, and then he may be perceived as a gambler. His behaviour is condoned when the risks he takes produce lucrative deals. However, when things go badly the risk-taker is alienated and made into a fall guy.

GOSSIP

If we consider gossip as an inappropriate way of speaking, the problems it can cause become obvious. The originator of the gossip may purport to be acting 'from the best of motives' and may feel that people need to know the titbit of information being offered. Those who listen to gossip, believe it and then pass it on are taking a vicarious pleasure in other people's lives. Salacious gossip – that is, the type that brings about an 'oo-er' reaction – makes us feel good, possibly because the subject of the gossip has been naughtier than we are and has been found out. Malicious gossip which is designed to hurt is an abuse of information, often twisted to suit an individual's purpose. The need to hurt or to harm someone else often arises out of a desire for some kind of justice.

Dealing with gossip can be done in one of several ways. If the gossip is about you, there is an old wisdom which states that while they are talking about you they cannot be talking about someone else. You can choose to ignore it on the grounds that it is beneath your dignity. Perhaps the most efficient way is to confront the person concerned, and ask them what you and they are going to do about it. This has the effect of taking the wind out of anyone's sails.

GREED

Greed has always been considered a sin, yet it is now only just being recognized that psychologically it may arise from a **fear** of **loss**, or a lack of fulfilment. If it is based on fear, it may be worthwhile trying to identify what the fear is. We may fear not having enough, not being sufficiently strong to get enough or even be fearful of being pushed out of the way. Such greed may concern food and also spread out into other basic needs such as warmth and shelter. It may arise from a strong need for survival.

When greed displays as a need for material possessions the underlying problem may be one of insecurity. The thought is 'If I have this, then I must be alright.' Greed of this sort may also reflect a quest for power, and, particularly when it is associated with deviousness and getting the better of other people, a dislike of society. Greed and hoarding – which can be a fear of letting go – often go together.

Being greedy for **love** or approval is another form of neediness. We do not necessarily need the person, but we do need the feedback and the 'feel-good' we get from the interaction. Greed can also manifest as a fear of the future. If we do not know what the future holds for us we may be very 'grabby' in the present in an effort to insure against possible future difficulty and disaster.

In terms of personal development, greed is often associated with the first three **chakras** (see Section Three). The type of greediness will often give a clue to what is actually out of balance, and form a basis for readjustment. If there is a lack of fulfilment in the individual's life (for instance if he perceives himself as unable to have successful relationships), he may become an attention seeker in the hope that this will fulfil the lack of a one-to-one relationship. Work could then begin on the second chakra, perhaps in the process taking him back to the time when he was two or thereabouts, to find out what he feels he has missed.

GRIEF

Grief is an emotion which arises out of any kind of **loss**. When a young child is left in hospital without knowing that his parents are coming back to collect him, he will show signs of inconsolable grief. While on the face of it this grief can be assuaged, such apparant desertion can have a profound effect on the child in later life.

Grief over the loss of a relationship is just as profound (see **Bereavement**). Grief over the loss of an object, particularly if it has sentimental value, is often used as a displacement activity for the loss of a loved one.

Life holds many disappointments. Grief at a lack of achievement is often not understood. One is expected to get up and go on as though nothing has happened, rather than allowing time to come to terms with and express that disappointment. Such grief can often be worked through in a physical manner through **exercise**, but may also require **counselling** (2), career management or other therapies.

H

HATRED

Poets and songwriters are well aware that the emotions of hate and **love** are very closely linked. Both are strong emotions and are not particularly open to being rationalized. If one is hurt badly enough, love can turn to hate. Conversely, what appears to be hatred often has elements of extreme sexual attraction.

Hatred arises out of **jealousy** and lack of understanding. Family feuds, for instance, which have escalated into hatred can be destructive in the extreme, sometimes with children adopting the feud without actually understanding the reason behind it. Often it is not until the grown adult decides to deal with the outstanding issues that have always existed in the background of his life - as a kind of 'chatterbox' refrain - that emotions of this sort can be understood and relinquished.

Feelings of hatred are destructive to the individual who holds them and need to be expelled if he is to develop. Racism and sexism also arise from fear. They are instances of a group hatred which can, with learning and experience, be recognized as inappropriate. In terms of personal development, work on the **heart chakra** (3) is required if feelings of hatred occur.

HELP

'Help, I need somebody' - the words of the Beatles' song express a basic need in everybody. Help is perhaps the most difficult thing in the world to ask for. We may be too proud, too insecure or just too stubborn to recognize that our need for help may satisfy someone else's need to give. There are various types of help that we may require - some may be material, some emotional and some spiritual.

Help with material things can be both easy and difficult to accept. Clothes, for instance, passed between families can be very acceptable, whereas financial assistance may be difficult for both parties to handle. The recipient may feel beholden, whereas the giver may feel obliged to help. This is obviously not always so, but such help can often create enormous difficulty. Emotional assistance and support can sometimes be much easier, although at the same time it can also be very draining. Spiritual help, provided it is not given in a dogmatic fashion, can be the easiest of all, because the help given arises out of a mutual respect for one another.

Help is a matter of give and take and of being there for one another. Provided it is not used as a weapon or taken for granted, it can be an act of **love** between the recipient and the giver. We should be able to listen to what is needed rather than give what we think is necessary.

HOME LIFE

In today's society, where two incomes are often necessary, the quality of what was once seen as home life may seem to have diminished. This is a subjective interpretation, however, because people's needs over the last two generations have changed significantly. As families have become more mobile, activities have become more diverse. Whereas formerly more was done together as a family group, there now tends to be more individual activity. This certainly allows each person within the unit to develop his own skills, attitudes and behaviours, but inevitably leads to less interaction between family members.

As working patterns change, there are more single-person households than ever before. **Marriage** patterns are also changing and more couples are living together without needing marriage, perhaps until children arrive. It is also accepted that people may be happier living together without formal recognition. Joint responsibilities, such as a mortgage or similar financial commitments, may tend to tie people together beyond the life of the relationship.

Supportive groupings such as house and flat shares generate a type of home life that is totally different from family life. This type of grouping is often necessary for the young adult after he leaves the family home but before he settles down into marriage and domesticity. As the extended family – the network of aunts, uncles, cousins and so on – is no longer apparent, support has to be sought from other sources. Perhaps an ideal grouping could be several non-related families who are able to give mutual support to one another. This may then fulfil the differing emotional needs of the disparate members of the group. This way, the experience of the older generation can be combined with the dynamism of the young.

Another aspect of home life which needs to be considered is the care of people with special needs, such as the elderly, the sick and those with learning difficulties or disabilities. Support can be given through many aspects of alternative and complementary medicine to enable people to look after their own, although the cost of this to the carer is not always adequately recognized.

For most people home is synonymous with security and stability. Individual needs may differ, but a roof over one's head is a primary necessity and one that enables the majority of us to handle almost any other difficulty.

HOSTILITY

Hostility can be one of the most difficult emotions to handle. Often the sufferer cannot understand why he feels hostile. In many cases the cause can be traced to childhood, specifically to the 'hostile' mother, whose own hostility may derive from not wanting the child, a difficult birth, feeding difficulties or sheer inexperience.

A different type of hostility is experienced in sibling rivalry. It has been said that there is no right time to have a second baby, and the various types of hostility encountered in the older child may vary according to the age of that child. Whether that child has learnt to handle his feelings will depend on what he has been able to understand, and how he has been treated. If hidden feelings of hostility persist into later life, these can be dealt with by **counselling** or working with the **chakras** (see Section Three).

Relationships in later life can often be soured by such basic childhood antagonism, particularly if the sibling is of the opposite sex. Sigmund Freud suggested that difficulty in male/female relationships was caused by penis envy, although this explanation may have been more appropriate to the times in which he lived. **Jealousy** and hostility over previous relationships, or imagined infidelity in present ones, can cause a great deal of distress and often arises from a basic insecurity.

An additional cause of hostility between men and women sometimes arises nowadays, particularly in the workplace. Men may feel, for instance, that a woman boss deals unfairly with them and has personal preferences. Women may feel that their personal talent or style is not appreciated. Clear communication of such feelings by either sex is helpful in lessening tension. Another area where there can be hostility is between generations.

During the **ageing** process, misunderstandings and difficulties can occur. These may arise from young to old and vice versa. The older people may resist changes in behaviour and attitude, while the younger may be impatient; also see **Ageing** and **Youth**. Again honest communication and tolerance may help.

HYPERACTIVITY

When hyperactivity occurs in a child it is often evident from birth and seemingly unconnected with any obvious cause. It may be that the behaviour is caused by an **allergy** to certain food colorants. Hyperactivity can be very debilitating for friends and family alike, because the child may become uncontrollable to a point verging on **violence**. The child becomes bored (see **Boredom**) very quickly and is prone to frustration. Mental stimulation can give some relief; physical restraint does not usually work.

From a psychic point of view, a competent clairvoyant may be able to ascertain whether the problem is **diet**-related or has some other physiological cause. Many of the alternative **therapies (2)**, such as **massage**, **reflexology** and **shiatsu**, may help to alleviate the condition. Working on the third and seventh **chakras** (see Section Three) can also help.

I

IMITATION

There is a saying that imitation is the sincerest form of flattery, and in many ways this can be true. If one's personal qualities are such that they are worth imitating, then it is flattering to be imitated. However, there needs to be a degree of humility in accepting that it is primarily the qualities that are being admired and not necessarily the person.

In making changes in personal development there is a technique which entails choosing someone you admire and using them as a role model. This may be someone in your own family, a person you work with or a public figure. It is not necessary to follow them slavishly, but to base certain aspects of your conduct on theirs. For instance, let us suppose you admire someone's management technique. It might be worthwhile approaching them to find out how they developed it, where they trained and so on. You could then incorporate any tips they give into your own personal style to create success. Through this type of imitation, we are often able to link into something within ourselves which has previously been hidden and access information which would not otherwise be available. This, in turn, allows us to maximize a potential that is totally our own.

IMMATURITY

If being mature means acting responsibly, then being immature means not acting in a way that is commensurate with a set measurement of growth. A child will often hear the word 'immature' and have that measurement imposed on him by adults. It is believed that by a certain age a child will have achieved certain milestones in learning, or will have passed certain landmarks in the moral sense. Equally, when one area of growth occurs too quickly, another area may prove to be immature. Many child prodigies or exceptionally gifted children have not developed the social skills to accompany their particular gift.

Immaturity in adults may arise from a fear of having to take responsibility for themselves. The 'Peter Pan' mentality arises from a need to be free and yet, at the same time, to be able to take risks with that freedom. Conversely, such immaturity can come from never having been allowed to take responsibility and work out who one is. This is perhaps where personal development can come into its own, in that it is possible to go back and regrow the parts of the personality that have been left behind. One technique which is suitable for undertaking this process is **psychosynthesis** (2).

IMPOTENCE
See **Fertility**

INFERIORITY

To feel less than someone or something – the definition of 'inferiority' – is natural in childhood when we are surrounded by the incomprehensible and things that other, 'bigger' people seem to take in their stride. A wise parent will reassure the child through explanation and ensure that he grows through each new experience. But if a child is made to feel inadequate in some way, this natural feeling can crystallize into a sense of not being good enough, clever enough, or able enough, and years later surface as a sense of inferiority. Often such a feeling can be handed down subliminally from parent to child, through many generations, without anyone realizing that this is happening. If, for instance, a family believes that it is a victim of circumstances, the expectation will develop that something awful is bound to happen. If, with practice, that expectation and attitude can be changed, the whole family can benefit. It is not until the individual realizes that such feelings are a real block to progress that they can be dealt with successfully, by means of **affirmations**, **neuro-linguistic programming**, **psychotherapy** and other therapies (2).

Often inferiority develops when an individual does not successfully move from being competent at something to being confident of their abilities. Lack of confidence can generate fear, whether fear of one's ability or fear of the outcome of one's actions. This can happen if in childhood there was not time or space to experiment with or practise the skills needed to be a successful person. It may be that the child's first creative efforts were belittled, or that there was not the time or energy to encourage self-expression. Such 'missing out' can often be dealt with in adult life by relearning a skill or subject within a different context. A lack of ability in mathematics, for instance, might be tackled through an interest in **astrology** (2). Also, by being able to stick at something and not give up, a feeling of inadequacy can be transformed into a sense of achievement.

Physical and mental handicap can also increase feelings of inferiority or inadequacy. For instance, until **dyslexia** (1) was accepted as a problem, many children were considered stupid and unteachable. Nowadays the problem is better understood, and different methods of instruction and high technology are harnessed to enable the child's true creativity to be realized.

Many **religions** (2) stress the idea of the individual being only a very small unit in a vast eternal plan. This can have the effect of making a person feel helpless in the face of superior and overwhelming forces, and confirm his sense of inferiority. It is better that each of us should be encouraged to feel that our co-operation is needed to enable the world to function properly, and to recognize that however insignificant we are, there is still a greater power that cares.

Positive **affirmations** (2) can help us to overcome feelings of inferiority – for example, a statement such as 'Each day I become more and more confident in my abilities'. **Meditation** (2), **active imagination** (2) and martial arts, such as **t'ai chi**, can also be of benefit.

J

JEALOUSY
Also see **Hostility**

Jealousy is possibly the most destructive emotion of all, and certainly the most basic. There is actually a line on the hand which indicates the likelihood of a possessive temperament. Jealousy often originates from possessiveness within relationships, and possessiveness arises from **fear**. Often that fear comes from not understanding the basics of relationships. A young child will not understand that mother or father must turn their attention towards something else occasionally, whether that is another child or a job. If the child forms the impression that something or someone is more important than he is, the natural reaction is jealousy. If that feeling is buried or the child is not taught how to deal with it by, for instance, plenty of reassurance, the emotion may surface at inappropriate times. This could happen at the beginning of a relationship or when a partner takes up an activity that does not include the possessive one. The feelings that arise need to be dealt with, if necessary through **counselling**. Once they are understood, a huge weight will be lifted from the sufferer.

Another kind of jealousy is that of ownership. This is the basis of many arguments that arise at times of **bereavement**, or when someone has won a great deal of money. The individual who has not benefited from the bequest or the competition is jealous of the one who has. The feeling towards the 'lucky' one is more akin to resentment, and can usually be let go once this is recognized. Resentment which escalates into jealousy can also manifest in the work situation, for instance when someone is promoted.

JINX

The word 'jinx' can be used in two ways. First, it may be applied to objects and places that bring bad luck. Its second use applies more directly to people. One of the most common 'jinxes' is experienced with electrical equipment. This may have to do with a particularly strong electromagnetic field (see **Aura** in Section Two), which some people have. It may also emanate from disturbed energy that a person attracts.

The strange coincidences that occur around certain people can sometimes lead them to feel that they are abnormal in some way, thus heightening their sense of being jinxed. This can often start during the teenage years, when the personal energy is unstable, and can be similar to **poltergeist (2)** activity.

JUDGEMENT

The idea of judgement first occurred in both ancient Egypt and India. The principle is that the soul is weighed and if found imperfect goes to hell, and if not goes to heaven. It is said that a period must elapse during which the soul atones for certain past misdeeds and is then judged. There are three possible outcomes to this process: liberation, rebirth or damnation. Paradise, heaven, hell or purgatory are therefore of our own making.

It is widely accepted nowadays that we each create our own judgement day and that a life properly lived while on earth is judged to be sufficient to allow spiritual progress (see **Karma** in Section Two).

K

KLEPTOMANIA

Kleptomania is a condition which occurs when someone makes the assumption that they have a right to other people's possessions. As with other **phobias** and psychological difficulties, its origins are difficult to trace. It may stem from the acquisitiveness of the child before he has learnt to differentiate between what is his and what is someone else's. In terms of personal development, work within the concept of the subtle bodies (see **Clairvoyance**) may be of help in redefining what is necessary for the individual and what is not, and in readjusting his notion of personal boundaries. Kleptomania can also be seen as a distortion of an altruistic impulse, the desire to share everything.

L

LETHARGY

Lethargy consists of a basic feeling of tiredness, often combined with a sense of futility. It is difficult to decide which comes first because, almost inevitably, these two feelings 'feed' one another until they become indistinguishable.

The feelings of negativity connected with tiredness can arise from overwork, bad diet, bad sex, or almost anything that forces us beyond our own boundaries.

A feeling of futility arises when it seems that there is no way forward. Often the question 'Why me?' or 'What have I done to deserve this?' arises. This is often connected with a sense of alienation from the rest of the world. In terms of personal development, the problem of lethargy can arise from **boredom** with current circumstances and the need for change. It can also arise from the overuse of recreational **drugs** or **medicine**. When working with the **chakras** or spiritual centres, such feelings are associated with the fifth or throat chakra (see Section Three).

Dealing with lethargy entails firstly making small changes in one's life or lifestyle which will shift the focus from lethargy – an internal feeling – to something outside oneself which may be of interest. When lethargy appears as part of the mourning process in **bereavement** or loss, there is no harm in going along with these feelings so long as one does not get in a situation of wallowing in self-pity.

Medically, lethargy can be a warning of something more serious, such as diabetes, M.E., multiple sclerosis and other nerve-wasting diseases.

LIFE

The life we live on this earth could be said to be simply part of a greater journey. This concept allows for the idea of our existing before we became physical beings, and also of our continuing to exist on some plane after our physical death. There are countless possibilities as to the meaning of this life and which ones we choose to explore and how we tackle them will depend on our belief system. If the belief is that we are here to experience rather than to suffer, life can become a positive happening. If we believe that what happens to us is preordained and we have no control, then we may suffer. Viewed in this way, life could become very negative. Reconciliation of these two beliefs would give us the concept of free-will and a middle way. Certain events may be preordained, but more important is how we handle life changes and life events. Esoteric sciences such as natal astrology – an assessment of the influences on your life at the moment of birth – and **palmistry** (2) can make us aware of our potential and can enhance our understanding of what life has to offer. Spiritual development, using a system such as the understanding of the **chakras** suggested in Section Three, can widen our comprehension of why certain things happen to us. There is a saying that 'life is what gets in the way of plans', but with enough information we can train ourselves to maximize our potential. The quality of life then becomes something to be appreciated and the problems (many of which are tackled in this book) are offset by the beauty which life contains.

LONELINESS

All of us experience loneliness at some time, and not always when we are physically alone. We can feel lonely in the most unlikely situations – for example, at a football match, in a pub, at home, or with family.

There are many people who will remain in a relationship that does nothing for them simply because they dislike spending time alone. Others seen as loners by their friends and family may show no inclination to join in with group activities, and, indeed, may feel pressured by the presence of too many people. Social conditioning usually dictates that we learn to relate successfully with others at a fairly early age. People who work with children have noted what might be called 'sandpit' behaviour. Below the age of two, a couple of children will play quite happily in a sandpit, but at opposite ends. At about the age of three they will play together and learn to be more sociable. Previously they will have guarded their own territory or personal space with some **jealousy.** Loneliness in adults often occurs because they are unwilling to let others into their own personal space; also see **Auras.**

We can learn much from being alone, not least the qualities of self-reliance and self-sufficiency. Periods of aloneness can be instrumental in helping us understand others. Finally, it is perhaps worthwhile remembering the three stages of growth that occur through spiritual development. Firstly there is loneliness, secondly there is aloneness – when one learns to value and understand one's individuality – and thirdly there is all-oneness, when one realizes that one is part of the greater whole.

If loneliness is a problem, then help may be gained through **counselling** (2) or group activities. The initial step towards group activities may seem to be more than you can cope with, but when entering a new group it is worthwhile remembering that among its members there is likely to be someone who is feeling even more lonely than you. By making contact with that person, you can take the first steps to dealing with your own loneliness.

LOVE

Love is the most sought after, inexplicable, wonderful and painful puzzle known to humankind. It is the theme of countless songs, films, books and poems, as well as the catalyst for numerous crimes of passion. To put 'love' into words – that is, the type of love that exists wholly between two people – would be a tough task indeed. In fact, in the face of 'true love' words can become meaningless and dull, poetic or otherwise. Love is neither logical nor scientific, in the sense that objective reasoning in order to prove a subjective form is to slightly miss the point. In essence, you couldn't bake a cake without knowing what the exact ingredients were.

Parental love is crucial. As a child we are dependent on our parents for everything we need, the most important need being for love. At that stage of life, we are unable to comprehend rejection as rationally as we do when we get older (and even then it is not taken lightly). However, for children, their whole world revolves around the parental love and guidance they receive and any misappropriation of it will be heartfelt. To receive too little will have after-effects somewhere along the line, yet to receive too much in the wrong way may cause a differ-ent type of reaction later. Here we come back to the question of not just what love is, but how one gives and shows love. This applies to all aspects of love, whether it is between siblings or friends. There must be understanding and communication – if there isn't, togetherness becomes much harder.

Learning how to communicate through touch can be a huge breakthrough, because it means that we have learnt to handle both our own personal space and that of others. Many who have not learnt how to be demonstrative within the family situation are amazed at the freedom they feel when they have given themselves permission to hug others. Love is an exchange of energy and power, and nowhere is this more clearly felt than in the spontaneity of young love. The stomach churning uprush of mutual attraction holds within it so much energy which can be used in so many ways, ranging from the sexual to the spiritual. Each type of love is different, and it is this which gives it its beauty.

M

MANIC DEPRESSION

To be a manic depressive is to experience extremes of two conflicting emotions. It has been said that one cannot see the mountain properly unless one sees it from the valley – a description that fits manic depression well. People with this condition experience the full intensity of both states, sometimes swinging wildly between them. When the sufferer is in the manic phase there is nothing but the idea which has taken over. This can be a highly creative period, but often does not ultimately lead to anything concrete. In the depressive stage the individual becomes withdrawn and unable to cope. Often the sufferer is only marginally aware of the slide into **depression** or the compulsive behaviour which rises to mania.

There is no single cause of manic depression. It is controllable by **medication**, and alternative **therapies** (2) tailored to the need of each individual can be of assistance. Some relief can be gained through an understanding of the psychic implications behind the condition. An understanding of the **chakras** (see Section Three) can bring some relief in cases where it is possible to identify at what level of awareness there may have been trauma.

It is said that many comedians are manic depressives, and one wonders whether the ability to laugh at the ridiculous is perhaps a way of covering up a deep sadness and hurt. In order to get through life, a façade that becomes a public persona is created – an effective way of hiding the depression which is constantly present.

MARRIAGE

In palmistry, the lines which used to be known as marriage lines are nowadays usually called relationship lines. This shows the change in thought in the space of one generation. Perhaps the first change to contribute to this was the advent of the birth control pill. This gave women control over their own bodies, but also meant that they could develop a degree of independence and decide for themselves the direction in which a relationship might go. The pill allowed women to make their own choices and gave them the means to say 'No' to pregnancy. This in turn brought about a change in the laws to do with the termination of pregnancy.

At around the same time consumerism became an issue. Young couples wanted more material goods, and they wanted them immediately. This necessitated a double income, which itself highlighted the ability of each person to be financially independent when necessary. At the same time women were being encouraged to beome more educated (often to a high standard), which again freed them from the home and brought the realization that they need not be drudges. Marriage had been an institution to which one was committed, before God and one's friends, and within which some people were trapped. The emphasis shifted to making a commitment to the relationship, with the recognition that the relationship could fail. Thus, to live together was – and is – more of a risk emotionally, while also generally being more sensible financially. Expenses could be shared without, in theory, creating financial problems if the relationship broke down.

Thus the two main reasons for marriage – procreative and

economic – have become less valid than formerly, although interestingly the comparatively recent fashion for prenuptial agreements and legal agreements has probably taken the place of the marriage vow 'With all my worldly goods I thee endow'. This seems to be more of a 'Thou shalt have – with conditions'. Although sensible, such an attitude starts the relationship off on a negative foot. The emphasis is more on preserving what is rightly yours than creating a mutually shared base.

Many relationships work perfectly well without marriage, and others which have worked well while the couple were living together break down when marriage, or even the idea of marriage, is introduced. It is often worthwhile considering very seriously how the relationship may be changed by making a promise which one may not be able to keep. Particularly for young people today, it can be more important to be with someone because you want to rather than because you feel you have to. The arrival of children can alter the picture considerably, changing people's security needs.

Our attitudes to marriage are often formed by our experience of other people's marriages. A difficult relationship between parents can affect the individual's attitude to partnership of any sort, while an easy relationship can set up expectations which may not be possible to realize within one's own relationship.

There are clear divisions in people's attitudes to marriage. Approaching it from a religious point of view, the ceremonial making of promises can be important; approaching it from a more secular point of view, there can be financial advantages in the long term as well as the short term. From an emotional point of view, the knowledge that one is supported by the partnership can give a great deal of satisfaction.

Something that must be realized is that a committed relationship such as marriage needs to be constantly open to change. As people mature, their needs alter and therefore the relationship must take account of this. It may be, for instance, that shyness in one partner – which seemed charming initially – becomes a problem to the opposite partner as his or her career opportunities expand. Relationship counselling, and other aspects of personal development, can help to accommodate change.

MASOCHISM

Masochism is often a form of self-hatred in which the individual takes pleasure in hurting himself. Many people regard it as a form of sexual deviance, but masochism finds expression in all sorts of other ways. The need to be controlled, for instance, can lead to the 'martyr' syndrome where the individual feels put upon no matter what happens. Putting himself in the position of **victim** and therefore being persecuted is another form of masochism, as is hypochondria. The phrase 'having enjoyed bad health' is very apt here, because many hypochondriacs take pleasure in exploring the symptoms they have, and perhaps deciding what they have not got but may well suffer from in the future.

The 'buzz' that the individual receives from masochism will depend on the personality, and what he considers pain to be, since this can be physical, emotional or spiritual. A prime example of masochism is the practice of self-flagellation once widespread in monastic orders.

It is very easy to be judgemental about masochism, particularly when it is associated with sex. However, no-one has the right to judge other people, not even an individual who is fully conversant with the motives behind an action.

MEDIA

Are the media too intrusive? Is media coverage of controversial subjects too one-sided? It is possible that the man in the street is being told only what those in authority decide he needs to know, and that misinformation is being used as a form of control. It has often been said that one man's truth is another man's lies. Each individual has to decide for himself and use his **intuition** (2) to determine what he should believe.

The media can be used to good effect for humanitarian projects, such as Live Aid. Without the wide attention that such projects attract, the plight of people less fortunate than ourselves would not be recognized. When traditions such as Children in Need appeals are established through the media, a fine line has to be drawn between the desire to give and charity fatigue.

It would be naive to suppose that those artists who participate are not motivated by a desire to enhance their profile, and equally naive to believe that the organizers are not aware of the collective guilt tapped into by such programmes. By concentrating on the giving and introducing an element of competition into a small timeframe, people are more motivated to give. The repetitive format of such occasions can be either intensely irritating or humorous, depending on your point of view.

If we look at giving from the point of view of self-development, there are two types of generosity. Projects such as Comic Relief and Live Aid appeal to our emotional side, while the lone collector on the corner appeals to our altruistic and perhaps wiser side. Giving is part of the development of both the third (solar plexus) and fifth (throat) **chakras** (see Section Three) – an emotional response followed by self-expression.

MEDICINE/MEDICATION

Within the field of medicine there have been many breakthroughs in the last fifty years – some bad and some good. The discovery of penicillin led to the development of many of today's antibiotics, without which countless numbers of people would have died. At the same time, sensitivity to those same antibiotics causes problems for others.

Conventional medicine tends to isolate the various components of substances and use them in isolation. This can cause an imbalance, leading to resistant 'superbugs' and new viruses. 'Folk' medicine, on the other hand, tends to involve the balancing of various substances, and tends to treat the cause rather than the symptom.

Many plants used in **herbalism** (2) produce no side effects, because they are processed in such a way as not to unbalance the complex chemicals contained in them. By isolating these complex chemicals the balance is upset (as in the case of the conventionally prepared drug digitalis, which comes from the foxglove), thus expos-ing patients to the possibility of side effects.

The breakthroughs occurring in cancer management are as much to do with drug administration as with the potency of the drugs used. For example, it has been discovered that patients often do better when chemotherapy is administered before an operation than after it. Alternative **therapies** (2) (such as aromatherapy, reflexol-ogy, massage and stress management) can be used successfully to back up this regime, rather than in an attempt to repair the damage already done.

There can often be a difficulty with prescription drugs in that, because they are administered by a professional, the patient trusts what he is told and prescribed. Occasionally, as initially with the administration of **tranquillizers**, the long-term effects are not fully known or understood. Many people are still suffering from the effects of spontaneous **addiction** to such substances.

It should also be noted that it is not only conventional medicine that can produce problems. Each of us needs to be aware of our own idiosyncrasies. There may be sensitivities and **allergies** to some **herbal** and **homeopathic** substances, and overuse of these can be just as risky. It is the mark of a good practitioner to ascertain such sensitivities.

MOTIVATION

Each of us is motivated by different things. Some people may be motivated by financial gain, others by fame or status and others still by the emotional satisfaction they gain from having achieved their aims. Yet another group may be able to perform more success-fully if their work environment or relationships with othersis to their liking. Lack of motivation can lead to problems such as **boredom**, failure and **lethargy**.

It is useful occasionally to apply management techniques to one's life and to decide which factors are most important. These can broadly be described as Basic Needs, Safety Needs, 'Belonging' Needs, Ego Status and Self-Fulfilling Needs.

1) Basic Needs: Survival and the satisfaction of physical needs such as warmth, food and sufficient material gain to satisfy those needs. Within the work situation these can be met by incentives, bonuses, pay, good working conditions. Relationships which are struggling often become bogged down in arguments about basic needs.

2) Safety Needs: A secure environment and support for you as an individual with minimum criticism. There needs to be freedom from fear, a degree of reassurance and a satisfactory level of activity.

3) 'Belonging' Needs: The ability to be a successful part of a social group by making friends and being able to spend time socially with others. These factors demand the creation of a friendly environment and the ability to involve other people in joint concerns.

4) Ego Status Needs: The desire for respect and recognition for who you are, to receive praise for what you do and to get individuals to think of what you do as important.

5) Self-Fulfilling Needs: Also known as Actualization, this suggests that individuals need to be involved in decision making and given the freedom to plan and live their lives in their own way. Individuals are stretched by challenging activities which have interest for them. The highest form of self-fulfilment is being yourself in any situation.

If you have answers that are, for example, high in safety needs and low in ego-status needs you will respond negatively to attempts to motivate you by stressing possibilities for change, if you feel there are risks involved. The 'reward' has to be appropriate to your own profile. Someone who is altruistic may not feel rewarded or motivated by money.

Decide how important each of these factors is in affecting your attitude to your life. Indicate this by marking the chart with a cross on a scale of 0 (not important) to 10 (extremely important). Then circle (again on the scale of 0 to 10) to show to what extent this is being met in your life.

FACTORS	0	1	2	3	4	5	6	7	8	9	10
Security (2)											
Status (4)											
Physical work conditions (1)											
Achievement (5)											
Advancement (4)											
Job interest (5)											
Recognition of achievement (4)											
Personal relationships with authority figures (3)											
Personal relationship with partner (3)											
Personal relationships with family (3)											
Personal life (1-5)											
Financial gain (1,2,3 or 4)											
Individual growth in activities (5)											
Responsibility (5)											

Which of the factors are the most important to you?
Which areas are least fulfilled? What can you do about them?

NEEDS   **ACTIONS**

....

....

....

....

....

Ascertaining Motivational Skills

Most people underestimate their skills and abilities. There are three types of skills:

Functional, transferable skills These are skills which can be used in a wide variety of settings and which we often forget we have: for example, communication skills.

Personal skills These relate to you as a person, and come from your natural inclinations: for example, the ability to work alone or to handle yourself well in stressful situations.

Learnt skills These are what we traditionally think of as skills. They depend very much on what we have assimilated: for example, the skills and knowledge of a snooker player.

By looking at the skills you have, especially the functional skills, you can begin to look realistically at opportunities to change your life. To see which you prefer, sort out the skills you feel you have into five columns:
1, Totally delight in doing; 2, Enjoy doing very much; 3, Like doing; 4, Prefer not to do; 5, Strongly dislike doing.
Then within each column sort the skills into those activities at which you are – 1, Highly proficient; 2, Competent or 3, Poorly skilled.

Some examples of activities or skills are shown below. Highlight the skills you feel you use at present:
Gardening, Decision making, Liaison, Maintaining records, Selling, Planning, Organizing, Using physical abilities, Observing, Budgeting, Being a host or hostess, Dealing with feelings, Teaching, Making changes, Motivating, Entertaining, Performing, Portraying images, Skilled craftwork, Food preparation, Carpentry, Intuitive perception, Evaluating, Writing, Tending animals, Negotiating, Nurturing and Nursing, Meditating, Counselling, Visualizing, Classifying, Composing music, Generating ideas, Implementing, Designing, Supervising.

N

NAMES

There is a belief that parents instinctively give their child a name that contains within its meaning that child's greatest lesson in life. This would suggest that great care should be taken in choosing a name to avoid the possibility of foisting some great difficulty on your offspring! Equally, to choose an extremely fashionable or perhaps outlandish name may dog the child in later life. A nickname that is given in childhood may, for instance, suit you when young but be highly embarrassing when older. You may choose to be known by friends as one derivative of your name, by workmates as another and by your full name by your family.

One way of checking the appropriateness of your name may be to calculate its numerological value (see **Numerology**, under **Divination** in Section Two).

NEGATIVE THOUGHTS

Negative thoughts have been likened to a 'chatterbox' in the mind, always there waiting to pop up. It is as if there is a distortion in the mechanism that internalizes information from the external world and does not allow the process of rationalization to take place. Often the individual is conscious of the hidden agendas and suppressions which seem to have allowed these thoughts to develop an existence of their own, but does not know how to deal with them. While some would feel that nothing can be done, others are aware that it is possible with discipline to reprogramme the 'chatterbox' using autosuggestion or affirmations (2).

The individual may find himself worrying about all sorts of things. These may range from the bodily reactions that occur in stressful situations, such as breathing difficulties and sweating, through feelings and thoughts of inadequacy to worry over the consequences of one's actions. If there is nothing else to worry about, the person may worry about the future. Learning to focus on the immediate will help to make negative thoughts manageable. The martial arts, for example – such as **qi gong, t'ai chi** and aikido – teach this. They help to eliminate tension and leave one free to respond immediately to the situation.

Meditation (2), listening to music, playing golf, all are ways of 'switching off'. Meditation can also make us aware of our thought patterns and enable us to choose better habits. It can help eliminate the inner dialogue and worries about performance and poor self-image. It is also important to have a sense of purpose, a belief in a meaningful world such as comes from spirituality.

There are some peculiarities specific to negative thoughts:

● They happen very rapidly, and are automatic
● They are often difficult to ignore
● They usually involve considerable twisting of facts, and wrong assumptions, and often arise from long-held beliefs and values, sometimes originating in childhood.
● The person with negative thoughts accepts them as being perfectly believable and makes no attempt to question the logic of his thinking.
● Speculation, reasoning or contemplation alone do not give rise to negative thought.
● There is no sequential order in these thoughts: they are just there, and often block problem-solving.
● Though they may seem over the top to anyone else, they are usually seen as perfectly reasonable by the person concerned.
● The individual is often unaware of, or disregards, the influence these thoughts can have on his life, until such thoughts create a crisis situation.
● There is often a pattern of negative thinking in the family group.

O

OBSESSIONS

Obsession may be defined as 'domination of the mind by one idea'. This means that one can be obsessed by almost anything. Most people think of obsession as being to do with a love object, whether that be a person or a thing. However, the thing we are obsessed by may also be something we hate. For instance, family feuds can be obsessive, with the real reason for them becoming lost in the mists of time.

Often obsession goes hand in hand with what might be called an addictive personality. This is someone who can just as easily be addicted to a substance as to an action or a person, and it is often this syndrome that is the principal obstacle when trying to wean people off drugs or alcohol. The reformed addict may become just as obsessive and fanatical about not using stimulants as he once was about using them.

Fear can also give rise to obsession. This is often caused by an insecure personality who is afraid of losing something or someone, possibly because they feel they do not deserve to have whatever it is in the first place. This can be seen in obsessions over money, people or objects. Obsessive behaviour (repeating the same type of behaviour over and over again although that behaviour is unnecessary) usually stems from the need to control one's surroundings. A further type of obsession can be the phenomenon known as stalking. This arises out of a sense of possessiveness; for the victim it verges on being possessed.

The more positive aspects of obsession are the determination and **motivation** that are needed to carry out such devotion to a single cause. Had, for instance, Florence Nightingale not been obsessed by her need to look after the soldiers in the Crimea the whole nursing profession would probably not have been revolutionized. One problem with this so-called creative neurosis is that once the task has been fulfilled, life has little else to offer.

P

PAIN

Pain is a sign of distress – that there is something wrong. There are several systems in the body which can go wrong, and any difficulty will usually be translated into a warning signal. For this reason no pain, however minor, should be ignored. Advice should always be sought from your health practitioner or doctor in the first instance. There are, however, several self-help techniques which may help in the management of pain.

The musculature is the system of the body that reacts most quickly to any strain placed upon it. Our immediate reaction to pain is to rub the affected part, thus increasing the flow of blood to the area. Over-stretched or under-used muscles will often be eased by massage. Other methods can be used to manage muscular pain. The use of topical applications such as creams or lotions, particularly if they contain herbs or other agents with pain-relieving properties (see **Herbs** in Section Two), is effective. A form of **hydrotherapy** (see **Therapies**), consisting of the application of hot and cold water alternately to the affected part, may also bring relief. This is most effective when done with a shower attachment, because the force of the water will also help the circulation. It is equally effective, however, with total immersion, say in two basins, or with hot and cold flannels. In the latter case, ice added to the cold water may help. **Relaxation** techniques (2) may also be of help, as sometimes can visualization exercises. A very simple method that can be used with the hot and cold water treatment is to visualize the water washing away the pain.

Skeletal and joint problems can often be helped by changes in **diet** (1 and 2). Osteoporosis, for instance, is known to be associated with a lack of calcium, following hormonal changes at the menopause. Vitamin and mineral supplementation can help. The use of tissue salts (homeopathic preparations of the various salts found in the body) can replace those substances leached by modern life.

The various organs of the body may show their distress through pain. A pain in the stomach, for instance, can have many causes, ranging from the simple to the complex. Natural therapies will often give relief and can also be used to enhance, but not to be a substitute for, other methods of treatment. By treating the problem holistically it may be possible to prevent the pain re-occurring. In Chinese medicine each organ corresponds with, or rules over, emotions and feelings, so it is possible to cure the cause of the difficulty rather than simply relieve symptoms. Thus the pain of a misfunctioning kidney can be translated into a difficulty in eliminating unwanted thoughts. Learning these correspondences in the body (see **Body awareness** in Section Two) means that we have a self-help tool and that we may be able to put the problem right by using essential oils which have diuretic properties.

While most pain is physical in origin, some may be **psychosomatic**. Once we recognize the various traumas that we have endured, we may learn to understand ourselves better through our management of pain.

PANIC

During a panic attack you are likely to breathe very fast and/or deeply. This will have the effect of reducing the amount of carbon dioxide you have in your lungs and creating unpleasant body sensations which are likely to make you afraid. A vicious circle of fear, leading to overbreathing, which leads to unpleasant body sensations (faintness, dizziness, tingling, headaches, racing heart, flushes, nausea, chest pain, shakiness, etc.), which cause more fear, which leads again to overbreathing and so on, becomes established.

To stop this very nasty process, you have to raise the amount of carbon dioxide in your lungs. You can do this in two ways:

● Hold a paper bag over your nose and mouth so that no air can get to your lungs from outside, and breathe the air inside the bag for several minutes until you calm down.

● If you are in a situation where it would be embarrassing to use a paper bag (say in a supermarket), alter your breathing so that you breathe in less air. You can do this most easily by slowing down your breathing in small steps. Attempt to breathe in smoothly and slowly and to let your breath out just as slowly. As you slow your breathing the depth of each breath is bound to increase. However, try to avoid a very big increase in depth because this would undo the good you have done by slowing down. The ideal you are aiming for is smooth, slow, regular and fairly shallow breathing.

If you have managed to slow your breathing for a few seconds but feel out of breath and have a strong urge to take a quick gulp, don't. Resist by swallowing a couple of times – that should get rid of the urge; if it doesn't, then go ahead and take a gulp **BUT** once you have let the air in **HOLD IT** for about five seconds and then let it out **SLOWLY**. By holding a gulp for a few seconds you are preventing a lowering of your carbon dioxide levels.

To sum up, breathe in and out as slowly and evenly as you can and avoid any big increase in depth as you do so. To help yourself you could:

1) Count to yourself while breathing. To start with say 'one thousand' to yourself while breathing in and 'two thousand' while you breathe out, so your breathing would be:

| *in* | *out* | *in* | *out* |
| one thousand | two thousand | one thousand | two thousand |

and so on.

2) You might be able to say more to yourself while breathing in and out, and so take longer doing it. For example:

| *in* | *out* |
| one thousand, | two thousand one thousand, two thousand |

| *in* | *out* |
| one thousand, | two thousand one thousand, two thousand |

The feeling of being out of breath that people sometimes get when anxious is paradoxically often caused by breathing too much. Taking in less air for a little while will often make the sensation disappear. We don't know why some people become breathless after over-breathing, but it is a well established fact that they do.

PHOBIA

A phobia is an unreasonable dislike of something. Usually such a fear arises deep in the unconscious and can often be traced back to child-hood. Often arising from a **fear** which has got out of hand, such a condition requires of both sufferer and carers infinite patience and understanding.

There are numerous examples of the syndrome. Obsessive Compulsive Disorder, for instance, occurs when the sufferer has to go through a particular sequence of actions in a certain manner until a certain point is reached. Often the sufferer will have to go back to the beginning of the sequence and start all over again, if, according to the individual concerned, something has been missed out or has not been done properly.

Phobias may not manifest until there is some kind of trauma, which acts as a trigger. Agoraphobia and claustrophobia (respectively, a fear of open spaces and a fear of enclosed spaces) may be present in a mild form which is manageable, only to be triggered by a shock such as **bereavement**. Algophobia is a morbid fear of bodily pain, and prevents any kind of enjoyment for fear of injury.

One of the most common phobias is the fear of spiders. In this type, there may be a connection with the archetypal image of a **mandala** (2), which is a device for opening up the unconscious, hidden area of ourselves. The mandala can often be seen to pulsate in the same way as a moving spider. In various cultures the spider is depicted as having strange powers. This belief is so widespread, there has to be some kind of latent awareness which is triggered in arachnophobia. Often **counselling** (2) and desensitization techniques can help.

When conventional methods of help fail in the management of phobias, some form of regression therapy to uncover the cause of the phobia can be worthwhile. Regression is going back into past experiences in this life, and for some individuals experiences in past lives. Past life experience appears – if the regression is deep enough – to offer some clues as to the cause of phobias. In the hands of a competent therapist, this latter technique enables the sufferer to experience the origin of the particular difficulty in the previous existence. Detractors of the method claim that there is no evidence to confirm or deny the existence of such a past life, but what is indisputable is that many phobias have disappeared (or lost their intensity) as a result of this type of treatment.

PSYCHOSOMATIC ILLNESS

Our mental state can have a profound effect on our body. The most obvious example of this is **stress**, a common physical manifestation of which is stiffness in the neck and/or shoulders. We often say 'Oh, it's a pain in the neck', without actually appreciating that we may be opening ourselves to the possibility of difficulty in that area.

Psychosomatic illness suggests that part of our awareness has become shut down, and is not functioning properly. In other words, the flow of life energy is inefficient and is not connecting the most important facets of our lives – the spiritual, mental, emotional and physical. Wherever there is a difficulty, **pain** acts as a warning. It indicates that a level higher than that on which we experience the pain is uncomfortable. Thus physical pain may have an emotional origin, emotional difficulty may arise from a mental distortion, and mental distress may have a spiritual cause. The difficulties which we experience spiritually – real distress at our inability to improve our lives – often need an understanding of concepts such as **karma** (2) (the laws of cause and effect). Formerly – in the wake of popular understanding of the early psychoanalysts – psychosomatic problems tended to be dismissed as of no account. This attitude is rapidly changing as more and more evidence arises to show that such problems act as an early warning system of difficulties which can be healed from a different viewpoint.

The significance of **pain**, and its possible psychosomatic underlying causes, is dealt with more fully in the entries under **Body Awareness** (2), but it must be remembered that no pain should ever be ignored. The help and knowledge of a qualified medical practitioner should be sought to enable appropriate therapies to be utilized. Many orthodox doctors now acknowledge the help they receive from alternative therapists, such help ranging from **spiritual healing** and the **laying on of hands** to techniques such as **massage** and manipulation (2).

Psychosomatic problems may also be used as a form of diagnosis in order to understand one's own perception of the life one leads. Without a doubt, a problem such as **arthritis** or paralysis has a profound effect on both the sufferer and his carers, and not just from the aspect of loss of physical mobility. If the sufferer can become open to the deeper implications and significance of the stiffness and rigidity from which he is suffering, some relief may be obtained both physically and spiritually from the letting go of long-held beliefs and attitudes which may inhibit spiritual progress.

There is a body of belief that certain tendencies to illness in families are not just genetically inherited. They are also inherited through attitudes to the world in which we exist. If a mother expects a disaster to befall her children, her daughter is likely to be equally fearful for her own children. If it is considered 'normal' to suffer from certain illnesses, then an acceptance is engendered whereby the feeling is 'Nothing can be done'. Such thinking could equally be considered psychosomatic. Generally a change in attitude can have a profound effect on such difficulties.

Q

QUESTIONS/WHY?

Some people may say that life is full of questions, but it may be more appropriate to say that each individual is a question looking for an answer. We are born with an innate curiosity and a need to find out and know. Right from childhood and that very annoying period we all go

through when we continually ask 'Why?', it is as though we are perpetually looking for a rational understanding of why things are as they are.
As adults we dislike any evidence of our not totally understanding the
world we live in, and yet those childlike questions often reveal huge
gaps in our knowledge. It is as though at some point we stopped being
curious and became more accepting of the reality being presented to
us. This may have entailed accepting the reality of others as our own
and preventing ourselves from maturing in an appropriate way.

The question 'Why?' arises when the developing child questions not
what is but our beliefs. There is a story of the child who questions her
mother's way of cooking a joint of meat, by cutting off a corner. The
woman then in turn asks her mother the same question only to find
that it was because her pan was too small. The action had become a
ritual and had the child continued without questioning it this practice
would have become a belief. Once we begin to question belief we are
pitting ourselves against society, but equally we are opening out to the
possibility of change. If enough people question the validity of
something and agree on a course of action, it is possible to change the
culture of a community. This is seen in what has become known as the
Hundredth Monkey syndrome. Here, one small monkey recognized
that washing her potato in salt water made it taste better. Shortly afterwards this practice spread to other monkeys who could have had no
contact with the original monkey. In this instance the rightness of the
action was accepted without question once the initial change was made.

This can happen on a more general level when we hear of war,
murder, disaster, rape, etc. We may ask 'Why?' but feel we can do
nothing about it. On a more personal level, we may ask 'Why me?' and
then run the risk of falling into **victim** mode. If we are to change this,
we may need to ask ourselves five questions:

● What is the situation now?
● What do I want to achieve?
● What would 'good' look like?
● What shall I do next?
● How shall I measure success?

R

READJUSTMENT

There are many ways in which we must be prepared to make readjustments in our lives. Readjustment in the sense we are looking at it here is a readjustment back to a former state. The case of the lottery or pools winner who wins, spends, then returns to his former state is one of a double readjustment. It will depend a great deal on the personality of the individual concerned whether he is able to make the necessary mental change to enable him to handle such ups and downs. A phlegmatic personality will be able to accept such changes and adjust his behaviour accordingly. The more volatile personality will have more difficulty. Material adjustment is probably easier to cope with, whether that is to become poor or rich. Having been rich (see **Wealth**), the individual is more likely to appreciate any subsequent material gain; adjustment to poverty is sometimes easier in that out of necessity one develops certain techniques and tricks to deal with that state.

Emotional readjustment after, for instance, the break-up of a relationship or a realization within the way we handle relationships, can be more difficult. Here, patience is paramount, bcause the individual may not even understand his own reactions. It is impossible to return to one's former emotional state. We may attempt to do so and grow a defensive shell. More often than not, this defence mechanism will include the comfort of former habits and behaviour. We must also learn to accommodate the 'space' which has been left by the changes. This may mean making radical adjustments to other aspects of our life, such as how we use our spare time or what we do with other people, perhaps those who have formerly been our friends. Changes in the family (such as parenthood) also need to be treated carefully, and while the 'learning curve' may well be steep, readjustments can be made slowly. The need to be positive in any readjustment – and to appreciate that 'what is, is' – can be a major factor in our acceptance of our own personal change.

REGRET

Regret is a pointless emotion unless one is prepared to deal with it. It usually arises from a realization that we should have acted differently, or that someone else has not treated us properly. Acting against one's inner principles can bring regret, as can creating situations where others must do the same. Regret is an emotion which is backward looking, and is as much connected with forgiving oneself as it is with forgiving others. If you look at your actions, you may well find that you could not have acted in any other way in those given circumstances. If, for instance, you have lost your temper in an argument and said things that you have cause to regret, you may subsequently need to look at your motive for saying such things. You may have deliberately been using the other person's weak point to hurt them, you may secretly feel justified in what you said, or you may even be expressing a secret fear. Once you have uncovered your motive, or hidden agenda, then you can look to the past to uncover where this arises from, and deal with it. When you are able to let go of the bad feeling, you will be able to adjust your behaviour accordingly.

The 'Daily Balance Sheet' exercise is a good one for dealing with regret, because it enables you to deal with problems on an ongoing basis. At the end of the day, probably shortly before you go to sleep, you look back over your actions, speech, feelings and emotions and examine whether you have anything to regret. If you have done or said something that you feel is unworthy of you, visualize the situation, forgive yourself, then resolve to do better in the future. If someone else is involved you could send them positive thoughts so they are not affected by what you have done. This is using regret to move you forward, and helps to deal with feelings of guilt and of powerlessness.

REHABILITATION

The idea behind rehabilitation is to train an individual to re-belong to a society which is run according to certain rules and regulations. This pre-supposes that the individual wishes to belong and to conform. Since deviance from the given rules was probably part of the original aim, it is only if the individual recognizes that change is desirable (if not necessary) from the point of view of self-preservation that rehabilitation will work. Drug offenders, people with eating disorders, and people with drink problems, for instance, will only benefit from rehabilitation if they themselves have decided that their present way of behaving is inappropriate – that they are capable of modifying their actions with help from other people. At this point, work on self-image using alternative therapies such as **counselling**, **neuro-linguistic programming** (2) and personal development can provide motivation for change.

Professional counsellors may use the 'ownership' technique to achieve success.

- Help the individual to identify the problem.
- Agree the problem requires a solution.
- Agree a possible solution.
- Identify the benefits and attractions of this particular solution.
- Decide that the individual is the right person to achieve that solution.
- Achieve the individual's 'buy in' to the solving of the problem.
- Check the individual's competence and identify the additional resources needed.
- Allow the individual to own and be committed to the solution.

By achieving this owning both of the problem and the solution by the individual, rehabilitation – in the sense of re-joining society – can be achieved. It will not, however, deal with the problem of 'being different' from everyone else. This sense of alienation is often at the root of the problem, and therefore a further course of action may be needed to help the individual explore that alienation.

ROAD RAGE

This relatively new type of violent behaviour is perhaps a symptom of the stressful lives people lead. If, as popular belief would have it, the car is an extension of the personality, road rage is an expression of the aggression many people will normally hide or control. On finding that their own personal space has been violated, the normally reasonable individual will allow frustrations to spill over, and will react unfavourably to threats. Today, the 'gentle, New Age sensitive man' has found that there are fewer and fewer ways of dealing effectively with frustration. It is no longer right to 'kick the cat', so to speak, and therefore frustration is expressed in an inappropriate rather than a disciplined way. Interestingly, experiments with rats have shown that aggression escalates the more over-crowded their environment gets.

ROOTS

There is, in each of us, the need to understand our background and to appreciate 'whence we came'. This can range from a simple curiosity about our ancestors and how they lived - our roots - to a need to know who we are. Many adoptees are aware of a lack of continuity in their lives, and the birth of a baby or some change in their own circumstances can awaken a need to find out. Health checks may, for instance, spark a need for investigation.

There is always the possibility that in researching our roots we may discover something that does not tally with our idea of ourselves. This discovery can be difficult to accommodate both for ourselves and for others. It is always wise to remember that we are a product of both our genetic inheritance and our environment. Although certain genes may predispose us to certain tendencies and conditions, careful management of lifestyle, **diet**, attitude and **behaviour** can release hidden potential.

RULES/REGULATIONS
Also see Ageing

While some rules may seem pointless, many have been devised with a view to making society a better place. The reasoning on which they are based may no longer be as valid as it once was, but until better alternatives are found, the original rules are better than none. At some point in their lives most young people will question this argument and rebel against what they regard as regulations which seem inappropriate and outmoded. Such argument and continual questioning of long-established rules is what keeps a society vibrant and purposeful.

Following rules just because they are there can be seen by the young as boring and safe – and a prerequisite of maturity and age. It is true that as we grow older, we are generally less prepared to take risks and break rules and regulations. However, old age need not always mean having to conform.

S

SCHIZOPHRENIA

Symptoms of schizophrenia include hallucinations and delusions. Hallucinations can occur in any of the senses. The most common are auditory hallucinations which involve hearing voices talking to each other about the person who is suffering from schizophrenia. These voices may also speak directly to the sufferer. Others with this condition may simply hear unidentifiable noises.

A delusion is a fixed and bizarre belief in something in the face of evidence that would convince a mentally stable person that it is false. The sufferer will often feel persecuted, believing that there is a conspiracy to harm him. Often everyday events hold some special negative significance and may be further evidence to the sufferer of his persecution. In the acute stages of the disease, many sufferers believe that their thoughts are being interfered with. This may stem from the belief that their thoughts can be overheard by others; that other people's thoughts are being inserted into their mind; or that thoughts are being taken out of their mind against their will.

Paranoid schizophrenia is so called because the sufferer's hallucinations and delusions focus largely on one theme. This is often related to a belief that they will be harmed, attacked or killed. It is possible that this delusion arises because of a build-up of mental energy. A diagnosis of acute schizophrenia indicates that the person has only had the illness for a short time (2–3 months); if it extends beyond this period then it becomes chronic.

There are various traditional treatments for schizophrenia; antipsychotic medication (depixol, dozic, stelazine) acts to reduce the severity and frequency of hallucinations and delusions and helps people concentrate. These drugs can have a calming effect. Their main purpose, however, is to reduce the symptoms of schizophrenia. People with schizophrenia will often report feeling confused – these drugs help the brain to function in a more normal manner.

One of the most interesting discoveries to emerge from research is that the way a family communicates can have a profound effect on the development of schizophrenic illness. Insofar as the influence of the family has always been recognized, this is not new. However, new research stresses the importance of expressed emotion – that is, communication within a family.

Schizophrenic sufferers often complain about feeling tense or anxious (see **Anxiety** and **Negative Thoughts**), which in turn leads to a worsening of the schizophrenia. Therefore, **relaxation (2)** is a useful method of treatment – that is, using very specific procedures that will lead to a relaxed state.

SEX/SEXUALITY

There are so many hiccups and difficulties associated with sex that it is probably sensible to divide them into groups. There are, first of all, the problems which arise with one's own sexuality. Children recognize very early on the essential differences between male and female – differences which are often heavily reinforced by parents and other adults. The 'sensitive' boy and the 'assertive' girl are still seen as figures of fun by many, despite a general increase in awareness. This can often lead to doubts about appropriate behaviour, which then spills over into teenage difficulties.

Teenagers have to cope with many issues to do with sex. The first is the purely physical one of the growing body. As body shape changes there are inevitable comparisons to be made. These are on two fronts. Firstly, there is comparison with what is considered to be beautiful and/or sexually attractive – the Pamela Anderson ideal for men and the James Eden ideal for women. Secondly, comparisons are made as to what is thought to be normal so far as size and shape are concerned.

SEX/SEXUALITY

'Are my boobs big enough (or small enough)?' 'Is my penis the same as the boy's next to me?' The half joking language which is used to describe the sexual organs and the sexual act is in itself evidence of the embarrassment felt.

The teenager must also contend with the changing feelings and emotions about the opposite sex. Swinging wildly between extremes of love and hate, wanting and not wanting to be sexually mature, being attracted to someone physically and wondering why, all lead to confusion. All this may be exacerbated by the attitudes to sex and sexuality of the adults around. There is also a great deal of peer pressure to put up with. For boys it is mostly to do with 'performance'. 'Have you done it - or not?' 'Were you good at it?'. For girls the emphasis may be more on feelings. 'What did it feel like?' 'How did it make you feel?' At a time when it is important to 'belong', there is also the problem for young people of uneven development on a personal level. Some are more developed than others and therefore feel different.

There is also the question of principle. If young people have been taught that certain things are right and wrong, how do they decide what is right for them? Do they, for instance, have sex before marriage, or do they have sex with a member of the same sex? What is right, and what is legal? The only way to deal with any of these dilemmas is through experimentation, and wise counselling.

Perhaps the most important things to be learnt at this time are how to make decisions for oneself, and how to deal with the consequences of one's actions. There need not be embarrassment, for instance, if you have deliberately made a decision to remain a virgin, provided that you understand your own motivations.

A different type of 'performance' doubt is that which occurs in older people. Often because of, say, business worries, family difficulties, or some other external factor, the libido in both men and women can drop, almost to the point of non-existence. A fairly typical scenario is the young woman who has had a baby and whose sexual needs have changed because of this. At the same time a husband or partner is working extremely hard, and as a result is over-tired. There is a great deal of emotion surrounding the whole issue, and both end up

117

feeling frightened and rejected, and, perhaps worse, end up in the middle of real sexual difficulties. It is perhaps worth looking at the problem initially from a practical viewpoint. **Diet** may help to put some of the problems right. Vitamins – such as the B complex group to help calm the nerves, and vitamin E, which has an effect on the reproduction system, are worth trying. Foods and herbs which may help are to be found in the information on the **base chakra** in Section Three. Working on a more subtle level, the **Bach flower remedies** (2) may be of assistance, as may **massage**, **aromatherapy** and various forms of **counselling** (see entries under **Therapies** in Section Two). Problems with libido indicate that we need to look very carefully at our lifestyle, and where feasible make changes. A spirit of bravado and simply hoping that matters will improve without some action will not help.

This same attitude is unfortunately still seen at times in cases of sexual impotence. It is well known that the reproductive system reacts very quickly to problems in other areas, and probably none more so than psychological feelings and emotions connected with powerlessness. Much research has gone into the question of male impotence particularly, and drugs are available to help with the difficulty. A similar problem in women is the fear of frigidity. This is one that can arise from early sexual experience, and possibly abuse.

Deviant sexual behaviour can be a huge problem, not only to the individual, but also to friends and family. Behaviour which is unacceptable according to the rules and regulations of the society in which we live is usually considered to be deviant, but it is also probably more correct to consider behaviour which is not acceptable to the people concerned. A recent case in Britain has served to highlight this. Homosexual practices between consenting adults over eighteen is no longer a crime, but deviant sadomasochistic practices are deemed not permissible. There is a very fine line between what is deviant and what is dangerous. The exploration of sexuality and sexual practices can be both a moral and a legal minefield for everyone.

It is this fine line which is in question in other deviant behaviour, such as incest and paedophilia. In both cases the main issue is the imposing of another's will and actions on a person with no knowledge or defence. Perhaps the most difficult aspect for most of us to come to terms with is the destruction of innocence. An act which should be motivated by love becomes simply one of self-gratification. Much can be done in later years to put right the difficulties which may be left behind for the victim, but equally the perpetrator will need assistance and the motives behind the action will need to be explored. The individual himself may have been abused in a similar manner, for instance.

Having dealt with, or come through, the minefield that is sex, we are left with the sexual act as an expression of love and affection between two people. The supposed exhortation to young women in times gone by to 'lie back and think of England' has – in the main – long gone. It is much wiser and more satisfying to regard sex as a mutual pleasure between partners and to enhance the enjoyment it brings through the use of such body-based techniques as **massage** and **aromatherapy** (2).

BISEXUALITY

Bisexuality is defined as the inclination to have sex with both men and women. Often it can be more of a problem for other people than for the individual concerned. Official surveys show that at least 20 per cent of women and 30 per cent of men have engaged in, or are capable of, bisexual activity. Because bisexuality is often thought of as being the same as homosexuality, it receives the same stigma. The conflicts arising within the individual as a result of his or her bisexuality concern the balancing of differing needs, and only once these needs are understood and met can peace of mind be gained. These needs may be emotional as well as purely sexual in origin, such as the need for closeness and support.

The dissatisfactions with bisexuality can arise out of the knowledge that it is unlikely that there will be a primary relationship with one other person. These can be dealt with through sensitive **counselling** (2) and relationship management which is not designed to change the individual's sexual orientation but simply to give a greater understanding of self and personal issues. For instance, **jealousy** and frustration can be facets that only become apparent in an individual when he or she is in a bisexual relationship. These must be dealt with and understood if any relationship is to succeed. It is perhaps easier to think of such relationships as resembling a honeycomb, where only certain aspects of people's lives interact, sometimes out of necessity and sometimes out of choice.

Spiritually, bisexuality could be considered as an attempt to seek, if not create, a balance of energy within the individual. On becoming aware of an imbalance, a counter-balance is sought externally in a partner of either sex. In other words, the problem has more to do with partnering than with sex.

CELIBACY
Celibacy is a deliberate choice not to marry or to perform the sexual act. In this day and age, it suggests a decision to forego sex unless one is in a meaningful relationship. There can be periods of celibacy, for instance, when the workload is too heavy and the libido drops, when the health is compromised in some way, when the female partner is heavily pregnant or even at a time when there is confusion over various sexual issues. Celibacy may be chosen as a deliberate option prior to marriage when it might be seen as part of the commitment to the partner. Celibacy is also appropriate for many simply as part of being single.

CHASTITY
Defined as keeping oneself pure and unsullied, chastity is perceived as a much more feminine attribute than celibacy. With this, however, the implication is that the sexual act is denied, often because there is a dedication to a higher principle. While that dedication may be to preserve one's virginity, either until the right person comes along or because there is a sense of having consecrated oneself to the service of God or mankind, such an attitude is considered to be slightly old-fashioned in today's more permissive society. Many men and women experience a particular thrill in breaking the **taboo** of chastity.

HOMOSEXUALITY

There is still a great deal of misunderstanding over homosexuality – in Oscar Wilde's words the 'love which dare not speak its name'. Often taken to mean the performing of the sexual act between two men, it should be described as sexuality between like or like-minded people. The **media** tend to speak of homosexuals and lesbians, further confusing the issue.

There are many aspects of homosexuality which are of relevance to the wider community. Although not entirely a homosexual issue, the AIDS crisis has made many people aware of what it has cost our culture in terms of the premature loss of countless talented, creative people. The compassion and care shown within the gay community for its AIDS sufferers has, without doubt, radically altered the care of the terminally ill. A great deal may also be learnt about responsibility, sense of community, and ultimately the honest management of relationships. While gay relationships are often seen as shortlived and promiscuous, this is not necessarily so. Promiscuity may arise from the satisfaction of an immediate sexual need, whereas commitment to a relationship is – for most homosexual people – much deeper.

There is no single factor in determining homosexuality. Many theories have been put forward, and in former times as many 'cures'. Probably the theory which holds most credence, is – having recognized at a relatively young age a greater sensitivity, the young person perceives himself or herself as being different. This difference becomes more pronounced as the young person approaches puberty; needs incompatible with those thought normal by society require some satisfaction, and such requirements for closeness and support are most easily satisfied through the sexual act with another person of the same sex.

SEXUALLY TRANSMITTED DISEASES

These are infections, or sometimes infestations, which are transmitted through sexual contact.

AIDS (Acquired Immune Deficiency Syndrome) is a deficiency of the immune system. While there is no cure for the syndrome itself as yet, many complementary therapies can be used to help boost the immune system. **Diet** (2) is one area where huge differences can be made, by increasing the intake of beta-carotene – found in leafy vegetables and orange-yellow fruit, vitamin C and bioflavinoids, and zinc – while maintaining a highly nutritious intake free of junk foods. Herbal and **homeopathic** remedies are also of assistance, as are stress management techniques, **yoga** and **meditation** (2). **Chanting** and a belief in some kind of **religious** practice.

Chlamydia when left untreated can lead to miscarriage and infertility. In men there is burning and discharge, in women it causes burning and soreness accompanied by a vaginal discharge. Treatment is usually by antibiotics, backed up by strengthening the immunity through **diet**, **aromatherapy** and **Chinese medicine** (2).

Genital herpes is a sexually transmitted viral infection which, once caught, will recur, often during times of stress, and sometimes during menstruation and exposure to bright sunlight. Treatment consists of preventative care and **stress** management, **homeopathy** and **hydrotherapy** (2).

Genital warts require immediate treatment, since they are easily transmitted and there is some evidence to link them to cervical cancer. The usual treatment is by surgical removal.

Gonorrhoea is a sexually transmitted bacterial disease which can be passed from the mother to a new-born baby. Untreated the condition can lead to untimely death. Conventional treatment is with antibiotics. Complementary medicine advocates treatment via the immune system.

Infestations Crabs or lice cause itching in the pubic area. Lavender oil can be used to help this condition.

Non-specific urethritis causes burning and itching and can be

SKIN

helped either by tea tree oil or by boosting the immune system.

Scabies causes itching with raised lumps in the skin. Lavender oil, again, can help with the irritation. Additionally, the sufferer and those with whom he or she lives can treat the condition homeopathically with sulphur.

Thrush causes a white, creamy discharge which looks a little like cottage cheese. Treatment consists of avoiding yeast in any form, including foods such as bread, Marmite and mushrooms. Garlic is beneficial, but tea and coffee should be avoided and replaced by mineral water and herbal infusions.

Trichomoniasis is a parasitic infection which can be treated conventionally by antibiotics backed up by attention to the immune system through dietary changes such as the introduction of cranberry juice, live yoghurt, vitamins A, C, E and the mineral zinc.

SKIN

The skin is probably the most important organ of the body. It is one which deals with the secretion of sweat and thus has a part to play in health. It regulates the temperature of the body, and through the secretion of salts and minerals keeps this very delicate balance under control. The condition of the skin is a particular problem among teenagers and can be a cause of much embarrassment. If the appearance of spots is stress-related, this can be easily dealt with.

The skin is also important when a woman is pregnant. In pregracy hormonal changes can upset the balance in the skin. Adjustment to the growing baby and changes in texture and elasticity can be helped through **diet**, **massage** and the use of specific **essential oils**.

Looked at more broadly, the colour of one's skin can be a problem. There is a possibility of problems associated with self-image in children growing up within a racially mixed marriage or relationship. This needs to be handled sensitively, by instilling a strong sense of identity and self-awareness as early as possible.

SLEEP

When Shakespeare wrote 'Sleep that knits up the ravelled sleeve of care', he aptly described the function of sleep. In **shiatsu** (2) practice and other branches of Chinese medicine it is accepted that the meridians (lines of energy) connected with the various organs within the body can recuperate during the hours of darkness. Folklore also stresses the necessity of sleep, holding that an hour before midnight is worth more than two hours after. These two principles would at times appear to conflict with one another – until the lifestyles that these statements support are compared.

Most people are said to need about eight hours sleep per night, with that requirement reducing as one gets older. Young people need sleep in order to grow, because the growth hormone operates during that time. It may be that there is a connection between lack of this restorative sleep, hyperactivity and the rise in child violence. A balance between activity and rest is both important and necessary. This same balance is also necessary in adults, particularly if the individual leads a stressful lifestyle.

Exercise used in combination with a healthy **diet** (2) can give a more restorative sleep, which in turn allows one to deal with further **stress.** Care does need to be taken, however, to understand one's own sleep patterns. The problem of differing sleep patterns can lead to numerous problems within relationships. For instance, if one partner is a 'night owl' and the other is falling asleep by ten o'clock, some compromise needs to be reached. Other people may fall asleep early, only to wake half way through the night with some highly creative ideas or the solution to a problem, which can cause difficulties. Incidentally, it is interesting that the term 'sleeping with' someone is used as a euphemism for having sex. It pre-supposes that you are comfortable enough with your partner to allow your sleep to be disturbed!

When the pattern of your sleep changes dramatically it can be a warning that there is something wrong. In **depression**, for instance, sleep may be used as an escape mechanism in order not to have to deal with everyday reality. Waking in the night in order to pass urine, if it happens more than occasionally, may be a warning – for men – that the **prostate gland**, **kidneys**, or **bladder** are in trouble (see **Body Awareness** in Section Two). Such signs are always worth investigating.

The other sleep breaker is worry. Most people are familiar with the situation of waking in the middle of the night and becoming increasingly agitated over something about which very little can be done (at that hour anyway). When this occurs it is worthwhile examining past, present and future. Is there anything that you could or should have done, or done differently about the situation? Without giving yourself a hard time, note the possibilities and move on. Do not get 'stuck' in the past – tackle the present. Is there anything you need to do now to help the situation? You may need to write down your options of action in order to get a clear view of what you need to do. Does, for instance, what you feel you should have done tie in with one of those options? If not, let it go. If it does, consider it carefully and then plan what to do. Once you have done this, don't allow yourself to continue to worry – practise a breathing technique or a full relaxation and go back to sleep. Because you have done something positive and decided on a course of action, you should find this relatively easy; also see **Anxiety** and **Negative thoughts**.

True insomnia – an inability to sleep, which is more of a habit – can be very debilitating. It is worth remembering that studies have shown that ten minutes' **meditation** (2) is equivalent to four hours' sleep. Learning to meditate can take up some of the time you are not sleeping, and then allow you to use the rest of the time creatively and constructively. If sleep still eludes you, you may need to resort to **herbal remedies** (2), such as valerian or skullcap. These do not leave you heavy headed and disoriented when you wake up.

Other aspects of sleep which need to be considered are dreaming and **astral travel** (2). Dreaming is believed by many to be a kind of sorting activity which allows the brain to sift and categorize impressions and ideas picked up during the day. With practice it is possible to adjust dreams to create a positive outcome to a situation, through **lucid dreaming** (2). This initially entails waking oneself from sleep, deciding what you want the outcome to be, and changing the ending.

STRESS

We are always being told that stress is bad for us. However, it is not just stress but how we cope with that stress which is important. Different people feel stressful over different things. What is stressful for one person may not be so for another, and it is usually when we have not consciously 'taken control' that we come up against difficulty and possible burn-out.

Generally, stress can be divided into five types: altruistic (when our inner beliefs and principles are challenged), emotional, material, mental and physical. The first step is to identify and then manage your own particular type of stress. When one becomes aware of which particular type finds us most vulnerable, it then becomes possible to use 'diversification' techniques to cope with the problems which arise. Thus, emotional stress can be coped with by deliberately placing more stress on the physical level (e.g., a hard work-out at the gym), or can be used positively at the next level by choosing to give the mental level a 'kick-start' with an unexpected stimulus – e.g., the study of a new subject. This in itself is stressful, but could be called positive stress.

Stress responses questionnaire

Below are listed some statements that may apply to you when you are anxious. Tick either Yes or No. The answers you give will indicate the types of stress you react most strongly to.

	Yes	No
1) I dislike people more		
2) My heart beats faster		
3) I imagine terrifying scenes		
4) I feel I am losing out because I can't make decisions quickly enough		
5) I perspire		
6) I can't keep anxious thoughts out of my head		
7) I shake		
8) I get diarrhoea		
9) I can't keep anxious pictures out of my mind		
10) I pace up and down		
11) I feel depressed		
12) I want to shout		
13) I find it difficult to concentrate		
14) I am unable to move		
15) I worry over things that don't usually bother me		
16) My stomach knots up		
17) I feel like crying		
18) I get angry and irritable		
19) Trivial matters bother me		
20) I lose my temper for no reason over trivial things		
21) My eyes fill with tears easily		

Results: Check your answers with the list below. If you answer Yes to more questions in Row A, you react more strongly to Mental stress; if Row B, Physical stress; and if Row C, Emotional stress.

A.	3,	4,	6,	9,	13,	15,	19
B.	2,	5,	7,	8,	10,	14,	16
C.	1,	11,	12,	17,	18,	20,	21

STRESS EXPERIENCES

List both pleasurably stressful experiences and difficult stressful experiences and their sources and effects and then compare each group for similarities. Then decide on a strategy for action (overleaf).

Pleasurably Stressful Experiences –

_____

_____

Sources and Effects

_____

_____

Difficult Stressful Experiences –

_____

_____

Sources and Effects

_____

_____

Similarities –

_____

_____

Personal Coping Response

When under stress my main coping response is –

_____

_____

My back-up coping style is –

_____

_____

I need to develop the following coping styles –

_____

_____

Stress Management Summary
Write down the key points you have clarified about your stress reactions:

Key Sources of Stress

_____

Internal

_____

External

_____

SOURCES OF STRESS	ACTION

SUCCESS

Before one can deal with the problems associated with success, it is important to identify what success is. For some people it means financial stability, for others good relationships, and for others overcoming difficulties in everyday life. Often one's feelings about success are set in childhood by parents and society, whether this is to do with academic prowess, or one's ability to 'beat the system' or be socially competent. This expectation sets a standard which careful consideration may reveal has nothing to do with your own feelings.

Again, success within a career may not bring happiness, nor does it necessarily make the individual concerned feel successful. If a particular part of one's life comes fairly easily, the disappointments in another part may bring difficulty. It is sensible to aim for contentment rather than drive for success. While the feelings associated with success - the euphoria, the fulfilment and the sense of having succeeded against all odds - tend to be transient, contentment is lasting.

T

TABOO

Taboos are rules and regulations which are imposed within a culture, mostly by the elders of that culture, and supported by tradition. These rules are often developed in order to preserve the health or power of the group. Among such taboos are those developed to prevent, or, in some cases, to preserve inter-marriage in family groups. The idea is to preserve or guard against the weakening of certain characteristics. The most quoted example of this is the Amish group in America, which has experienced both of these aspects.

Many **rituals (2)** in the various **religions (2)** highlight the taboos associated with certain beliefs. At one time, it was forbidden for the groom to see his wife-to-be on the night before marriage - one presumes to preserve her status as a maiden, and his as a gentleman. In our age of freer relationships it is looked on as a pleasant superstition.

A taboo is based on a negative command – 'it is wrong to...' – and is restrictive in its nature. Many religious taboos were developed to prevent the acquiring of arcane or hidden knowledge, or to ensure that nothing could interfere with the power of the priests.

TELEVISION

Nowadays television plays a much bigger part in people's lives than it used to. Children, it has been suggested, watch far too much 'throw-away' television, resulting in a lack of **motivation** and, to a degree, a lack of basic literary skills. Too much poor-quality television viewing affects not only children on a motivational level. It is very easy for any of us to come in after a hard day's work and settle down in front of the television, without even thinking about it. Of course, television is not a wholly negative creation – it can be educational and informative as well as thought-provoking and moving. It can also help to widen our horizons beyond immediate concerns and be used positively to assist changes in lifestyle rather than as a means to blank out reality.

The biggest argument that television currently provokes is that over violence. One side states there is more violence in society now as a result of too much violence being shown on television, and the other that violence has always occurred but that we are now more informed about it. Neither side of the argument has been conclusively proved. However, if, for example, a situation occurs where television violence proves to be a deciding factor in the outcome of a court case, the floodgates may be opened for people to use television as an excuse for violent behaviour.

The use of language and behaviour which may be offensive to some people is another charge levelled against television. Short of turning the set off, such exposure is inescapable, especially by those who are most susceptible to its effects. One way round this is for parents to operate their control more judiciously and not rely on the general 'nine o'clock deadline'.

Another point worth considering is media coverage of events. Just as a business will tend to reflect the bias and beliefs of the managing director, so media coverage will often show a particular leaning towards a certain line of enquiry. A story by one newspaper or television programme will report in a 'tabloid' fashion which, it is claimed, is what their public want, while another paper or programme will adopt a more objective approach. But, as with the individual, so reporting is only a perception and it is ultimately up to each of us to form our own opinion. One self-management technique, for instance, suggests quite deliberately not reading or listening to information with a negative bias.

TRANQUILLIZERS

As has been mentioned under the entry dealing with **medicine** and **medication**, involuntary **addiction** to tranquillizers and sleeping pills is known to occur. When tranquillizers were first introduced not enough was known about them and their long-term effects. Believing them to be safe, many patients got into a pattern of overuse.

Much more is now known about such addiction and many self-help groups exist. If you are not within reach of such a group and wish to cut down or cut out the use of such drugs, it may be worthwhile to think about setting up your own self-help group using some of the alternative techniques dealt with in this book. It should be noted that for this method to succeed, there must be a genuine desire to cut down on dependency.

It is important to create the idea of a safe space. This involves a certain amount of trust – that the group is held in a place where individuals can be themselves, say and feel whatever they like (or not, as the case may be) and can share their fears and doubts without the worry of recrimination. Each person needs to feel that they are not being forced to come off their support system of drugs, but will do it because they want to. Regular meetings are therefore important, probably once every one or two weeks to give a sense of continuity.

Below is a suggested format for such a self-help group.

● Brief stretching out and breathing exercises (5 minutes)
● Short introduction of self or 'what's happened since we met' (10–15 minutes)

- Relaxation exercises followed by creative visualization (10–15 minutes)
- Dealing with self-image etc. (20 minutes). (See **Section Three**)
- Dealing with side effects using alternative substances and methods, for example, oils, vitamins, reflexology, self-caring.

This structure is used for the following reasons:
a) It becomes a familiar pattern yet allows flexibility.
b) It deals firstly with the physical symptoms, then the emotional/mental, and ultimately helps the individual to understand his own needs and motives.
c) The introduction of self in the first session allows for an assessment of where the individual members are coming from. The follow-ups can show the individual how to look for the positive side, and give help by not concentrating on the negative.
d) The **relaxation** techniques will assist those on sleeping tablets to learn more about their tensions and to use the technique as aids to sleep. **Creative visualization** (2) can help with relaxation and ultimately with achieving goals.

Working out a withdrawal plan

Tailoring a withdrawal plan to suit your own particular circumstances can be difficult and will depend on whether you are on a high dose of diazepam (Valium) or other type of tranquillizer, and also on whether you can expect the co-operation of your medical practitioner. You should be able to find out whether your capsules or tablets can be given to you in smaller quantities rather than the larger doses. For instance, you may be able to ask for tablets of 2 mg or less, instead of 5 mg ones. Equally with capsules you may be able to get smaller doses. If you have to go through a long-winded process of dividing tablets and capsules into halves and quarters this can be counter-productive and de-motivating.

The principle in reducing the dose is to keep to the time schedule that your body has become accustomed to. In the early stages of withdrawal you will need to keep to this because your body will be accommodating to the smaller dosages of drug. The speed with which you reduce or come off your drug intake will depend on several factors. Firstly, how long you have been using the drug. Secondly, how much you have been using, and thirdly, fears and doubts associated with having to do without the drug. The reason for needing sleeping pills and tranquillizers in the first place is obviously important and can range from insomnia and/or a bad sleeping pattern from an early age, to tranquillizers begun after operations such as hysterectomy or hip operations, or pain control such as arthritis or cancer. **Anxiety**, **anger** and negativity can also be reasons for needing tranquillizers.

Tapering off a normal anxiety dose can be different from reducing a severe anxiety dose. If the drugs are used only as an aid to sleep, for instance, reducing the dose can be relatively easy over a short time period. Larger doses will need a longer period of time – at least six weeks – and may possibly lead to different side effects. Again, it will depend on your personality whether you decide on the quicker, more drastic approach, or the slower approach recommended by many doctors and self-help groups. One suggestion is to reduce the dose every two to four weeks by approximately one eighth of the current dose.

It is almost impossible to avoid withdrawal effects no matter how slowly one reduces the intake. Some people will find it more painful to do it slowly, while others believe that increasing the withdrawal period simply lengthens the agony. It is for you to decide how capable you are, and when you want to start. The only 'good time' to start is now, so commit yourself to making the effort, rather than actually succeeding, and begin.

Some of the withdrawal symptoms which may occur and possible ways of helping with the problem are listed below:

Abdominal symptoms (cramp, pain, diarrhoea) – relaxation techniques, adjustment in diet.

Hyperventilation – breathing techniques, abdominal breathing.

Influenza – Vitamin C and zinc.

Muscular pain – gentle exercise.

Obsessions – checking things repetitively, e.g., irons, washing –

Vitamin B, Evening Primrose Oil.

Shifting ground and numbness – deep breathing.

Skin problems – start with gentle brushing of the skin if this is not too sensitive, relaxing bath oils, e.g. lavender and ylang ylang.

TRAPPED

In a situation such as a relationship or a job one may feel very trapped. How does one become trapped? Often it is for fear of hurting someone else, or for fear of making changes. It is possible to feel trapped by financial commitments, such as a mortgage or bank loan. Emotional commitments, such as duty to one's parents, and spiritual commitments, such as adherence to a particular type of belief, can also engender the same feeling.

Physical entrapment in a small space can be both a nightmare and an elevating experience. The sailor Tony Bullimore, who was saved after four days spent alone in his upturned boat in the middle of the ocean, described his experience later and said how he 'talked to God', although he confessed to being not particularly religious. In this instance, being trapped seems to have brought about a spiritual change.

One yoga exercise which is worth experimenting with is to close your eyes and visualize what it feels like to be very small in a large space, and then very large in an even larger space. Alternate these visualizations. You should get from them a totally different concept of the management of boundaries.

TRAUMA

The effect of trauma, whether it be physical, emotional or spiritual, can be profound. The element of unexpectedness involved in almost any kind of trauma seems to penetrate the being and hurt or harm on many levels.

Tragedies which attract media attention can provoke sympathy and horror in people far removed from the event. For those directly affected, either as victims, survivors or relatives and friends, trauma can manifest long after the initial cause, without a trigger. It is as if the individual only allows the emotions to surface after the practicalities associated with the incident have been dealt with. This syndrome is called post-traumatic stress disorder. Veterans of wars suffer similar anguish and difficulties long after the horrors that caused them have ended.

Trauma counselling, a relatively new branch of counselling, can have considerable effect in such cases. Other techniques which can help are those used in the treatment of **anxiety**, **phobia** and **stress**.

TRUTH

The search for truth, whatever that may mean, is a concept that many may find high-flown and esoteric. Truth can differ from moment to moment according to the knowledge and information that we have. What may have been true yesterday will not necessarily be true tomorrow. The **media**, for instance, present the truth as it is perceived by them, and truth will always have a personal slant fashioned by personal attitudes, beliefs and understanding. This is why **gossip** presented as fact can be damaging. We never truly know the truth, only what is believed to be true.

Children are often instructed to tell the truth, only to find that adults have been withholding the real truth 'for their own good'. Young children, for instance, are encouraged to believe in the existence of Santa Claus, only to discover later that he is a figment of someone's imagination. Yet at the same time Peter Pan's question 'Do you believe in fairies?' and the resounding positive response from the children in a pantomime crowd is an extremely poignant moment in its simplicity and truth.

Spiritual truth works according to the level of development one has reached. Awareness and objectivity reached through research and study give a totally different perspective to that of an emotional response. True spiritual truth is possibly when the former is confirmed by the latter.

In close relationships and also in situations where we may be harmed, there is a tendency to pervert the truth. Only the individual can decide whether the little white lie is appropriate in a particular circumstance and whether he or she will have to 'pay penance' for this. This is between himself and his conscience.

U

UNDERWORLD

The underworld, that is, the criminal side of life, or the 'underbelly of society', is not necessarily an aspect of life that involves the vast majority of people. However, we are all affected by non-legal activity to some extent, whether it be through taxation to compensate for financial loss or the emotional effect it may have on individuals.

It is probably true to say that the criminal underworld is slightly different in organization from the man or woman who goes out and commits a lone crime, but the knock-on effects of fear, insecurity and horror are much the same.

The 'underworld' has such negative connotations that it is perhaps difficult to recognize positive aspects. We do not perhaps have to be tolerant of people's actions but tolerant of their reasons for acting in the way they do. What is the difference, for instance, between someone who steals food because he is hungry, and someone who steals food to sell it on? They have both profited by another's loss.

The underworld in the sense of the negative influence underlying our thoughts, actions, and belief was in earlier times thought to be inhabited by phantoms and thought forms which had to be vanquished and understood. Each of us has to come to terms with the dark side of ourselves as successfully as we can.

V

VICTIM

Some people are perpetually victims. This tendency occurs in those who have a faulty attitude to their circumstances, and produces what might be called the 'Why me?' syndrome. The type of **questions** and statements which arise are 'What have I done to deserve this?', 'It wasn't my fault', 'But I didn't do anything', 'Why did this happen to me?'.

Feelings of futility and powerlessness indicate some kind of block in childhood which means that the child has not been able to take responsibility for happenings. This may well occur at some time between the ages of six and ten; some help may be gained by studying the third to fifth **chakra** information in Section Three.

Many people who have become victims – or like to play the martyr – have this type of behaviour for one or both of two reasons. The first is a straightforward need for reassurance of their own validity; the second is the need to have conflict within their life, and the actual enjoyment of being the victim. The conflict indicates that life is a struggle, and the satisfaction is a kind of 'negative reinforcement' of the victim's bad feelings about himself. To move away from this syndrome requires a gargantuan effort, and possibly changes in attitude and behaviour. This is especially the case when the behaviour is common to the family as a whole, and there is no help available to reinforce change. Perhaps one way, though, is to make very small manageable changes in just one area of life, and expand from that point.

Another area where victim mentality prevails is in the co-dependency triangle. This is broadly seen as two people being in a relationship where three roles are played out. One is victim, the second is persecutor, and the third is helper. Each individual moves from one role to the next, and like a hamster on a wheel keeps the cycle going. In some situations one of the individuals, by his behaviour, can actually help the other act as persecutor.

There are three roles that each person plays in any co-dependent relationship – Victim, Persecutor and Helper. Complete autonomy (represented by the asterisk in the diagram) is only reached when we refuse to play any of these roles and assume self-control. Prior to that, not only are our relationships with other people important, but equally significant is the way that we can persecute, help or victimize ourselves. This can turn us into martyrs – the type of statements made are shown in brackets in the diagram overleaf.

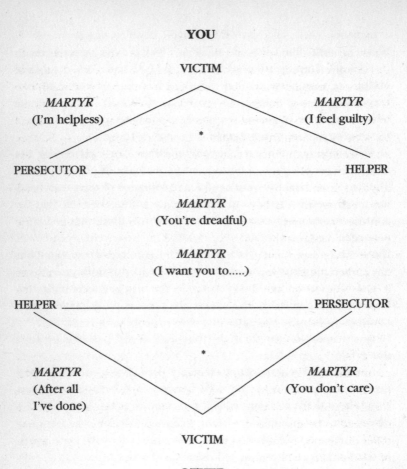

YOU

VICTIM

MARTYR
(I'm helpless)

MARTYR
(I feel guilty)

PERSECUTOR ———————————————————— HELPER

MARTYR
(You're dreadful)

MARTYR
(I want you to.....)

HELPER ———————————————————— PERSECUTOR

MARTYR
(After all
I've done)

MARTYR
(You don't care)

VICTIM

OTHER

This type of behaviour can be controlled by the individual gradually moving into his own power, and refusing to be either victim, persecutor or helper. This 'victim' type of behaviour is often seen where there is alcohol or substance abuse, but may also be apparent in sport-mad families or those involved in other highly focused activities.

VIOLENCE

It may be difficult to see how a book such as this can help to deal with this emotive subject. However, if we consider that the chief cause of violence is probably frustration of one sort or another, it is possible to trace the origins of this frustration back to childhood, and specifically to the level of development reached at around the age of two. As will be seen in Section Three, at this stage the child is trying to balance inner feelings with outer feelings – in short, to gauge whether he has control over what goes on around him and the degree of control imposed upon him by other people. If, for instance, the child recognizes that when it lashes out, or screams blue murder, parents are confused and upset, that indicates a kind of power and gives the behaviour meaning.

Parents or carers can have difficulty coping with violence, but if it is not curbed the child recognizes the validity of the behaviour and uses it as a weapon or tool. This is tantamount to the family accepting violence as the norm, particularly if the parents are given to similar outbursts. This same violent behaviour then seeps into society.

Few people nowadays will go to the aid of someone who is being, or has been, attacked for fear of personal harm. But this serves only to compound the problem, for the behaviour of the attacker may then escalate into viciousness. The more vicious people become the less society is able to deal with their behaviour. These aggressive tendencies need to be channelled, possibly through the martial arts or some other disciplined training, in order for the individual to learn a degree of self-discipline which moves beyond pure selfishness.

Many elderly people can permit themselves to be violent and vicious purely and simply because of their seniority. Aggression is unattractive in anyone, and although it often arises from **fear** it needs to be used solely as a defence.

VIRTUAL REALITY

While this term was coined by exponents of computer-aided imagery, it perhaps aptly describes the whole question of reality. If our own reality is what we create from our idea of how we believe things to be, then virtual reality is an approximation of a perceived reality, a sort of mirror of what may not have been real in the first place.

There is much concern over the loss of social skills because children are too involved in television and computer games. The question then arises as to whether this virtual reality, which ultimately will entail all the stimulation of the senses found in the physical world, can replace that physical reality. It is frightening to think of experiencing everything at one remove, as it were.

On the other hand, virtual reality may well enhance experience in different ways. While it may be used in fantasy and computer games, it can - and will - also be used to learn about other places and cultures and thus can only enhance our lives.

From a spiritual point of view, because there are so many different levels of reality, each of us should be able to identify the level of understanding at which we need to be.

W

WEALTH

Material wealth is something we all crave. With the advent of competitions, quizzes and, particularly, the Lottery, our perception of riches has changed. At one time most ordinary people would have considered themselves very fortunate to win a few thousands. Now the dream is not just to be comfortably off, but rich. The desire to have is is such that in Lottery roll-over weeks more people gamble than in ordinary weeks. Coupled with the desire for wealth is the recognition that in order for ordinary people to be rich there needs to be an element of luck or risk or both.

There are various problems associated with being rich. Being rich through an accident of birth does not necessarily bring happiness or contentment. It brings certain responsibilities which may not be willingly undertaken. It also gives the opportunity for a lifestyle which may in fact put people in danger; for example, a wealthy person may start to use drugs because others in his 'set' are doing it. Money does not always buy happiness, or even contentment.

At one time, 'marrying money' was seen as a form of **success**, hence the Victorian concept of making a 'good' marriage. As there is nowadays a blurring of class divisions it is more likely that people need not make such decisions, but there can be potential for difficulties in a relationship if one partner earns a great deal more than the other. If, for instance, a couple's lifestyle is built on two salaries, it can be very difficult to make adjustments to accommodate the arrival of children. There is a worrying trend which shows that family life is being eroded by the search for material success.

Y

YOUTH

Youth is seen as a problem by many people, and yet it can be one of the most exciting and fulfilling times of life. There are so many new things to learn and experience that there can occasionally be problems with overload of input. It is at this time, for instance, that the teenager will retire to his room and perhaps sit staring at the wall almost in sheer self-defence. There are increased parental expectations to deal with. The young person is expected to be 'sensible' without necessarily being allowed to experiment with what is feasible and what is not.

All those problems to do with becoming self-aware, such as looks, **behaviour**, **sexuality**, acceptable sexual behaviour, seem to happen at the same time. Each of these must be handled without causing too much disruption. It is a wise parent who is able to offer reassurance when necessary. Those issues which seem to be of paramount importance soon fade into insignificance the more the young person learns to fit in with his peers and be open to new experiences.

There are two aspects of youth that become important as one ages. The first, which probably arises from a fear of growing old, is the striving to remain young, as seen in the need for cosmetic surgery, collagen implants and so on. The second is the lack of understanding between young and old. While within the family, grandparents and grandchildren may achieve a good relationship, there may be difficulty in each generation's coming to terms with the other's culture. Rudeness and loud music can drive the older generation to distraction, while the vagueness and idiosyncrasies of the old can cause young people much annoyance. Tolerance is required on both sides.

Z

ZENITH

The Zenith is the highest point that one can achieve in any experience. It is therefore what is also known as a 'peak experience'. Each of us has capabilities that may remain untapped, until something in us clicks into place and craves a degree of excellence in everything we do. This striving for perfection can be both a problem and a blessing. If we are to live life to the full, each experience – however small – needs to be meaningful in some way or another, but often it is difficult to see how we have gained from what seems to be a negative experience. On the other hand, in recognizing that life deals out what is important for our spiritual growth, we will understand that whatever is happening to us is the best that we *have* expected. It may not be the best that we *can* expect, and this perhaps is the paradox we need to deal with. The more we expect of ourselves, the more we can expect to reach the high point in our experiences, and this leads us on to expect change.

KNOWLEDGE
OF A
LIFETIME

INTRODUCING CHANGE

Problems such as the ones dealt with in Section One can hinder us in any progress we may wish to make. Once a problem is understood, the next stage is to instigate change. That decision, however, can be almost as frightening as the change itself.

Changes – or, as some like to call them, transitions – can be handled much better if you are aware of the roles (such as organizer, planner, mover, supporter etc.) you prefer to occupy. You also need to be aware of what gives you stability in your life as you make the transitions you have identified as necessary. It helps to know how you handle change. Some people prefer to make a number of changes all at once, while others prefer to make minor adjustments and work up to major change. Sometimes, however, your way of adjusting can trap you into a set of behaviour patterns and responses which may need to be altered.
Some questions you may like to ask yourself are:

● How do I instigate changes in my life?
● How do I 'psyche up'?
● Do I tend to make many minor changes?
● Do I prefer to make several major changes?
● Do I forge ahead quickly when making changes?
● Do I wait for others to adjust to my changes?
● Do I expect others to change at the same time?
● How do I react to changes in others?

It is now recognized that there is something called the 'transition curve' which most people go through in one way or another while making changes. It is important to understand the process and stages of change in order for you to recognize where on the curve you are at any given moment, and to identify any assistance you may need. (It is worth remembering that we may be going through many changes and types of change at the same time, and may be at different points on the curve with each of them.)

When making radical changes in life, there is often a period of inertia – almost of not being capable of making any kind of move whatsoever. At this point **depression** can set in, because one is not in

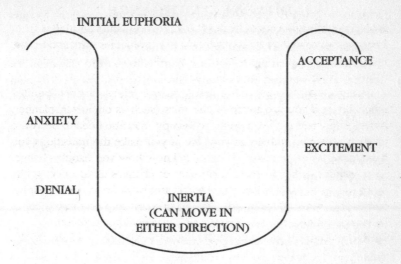

INITIAL EUPHORIA

ACCEPTANCE

ANXIETY

EXCITEMENT

DENIAL

INERTIA
(CAN MOVE IN
EITHER DIRECTION)

control of the situation and feels very small and defenceless. **Anxiety** of many types can become apparent. This may range from **fear** of not having completed something in the old situation to problems with performance in the new. There may also be anxiety because we do not know enough, or we do not have enough information – not necessarily one and the same thing. Perhaps we do not know what is an accepted code of behaviour.

It is helpful to find some sort of **ritual** or ceremony which will enable you to let go of the old situation. The 'leaving do' at the office is one such example in that it allows farewells to be said on both sides. This helps former colleagues to adapt, as well as allowing you the freedom to move forward.

The person who has gained some understanding of the process of change will be able to use self-knowledge to reduce pressure and to identify methods of stress management. These might include **yoga, t'ai chi** or simple **relaxation. Stress** (1) cannot be avoided in change, but it can be minimized by these methods. If one is not prepared to deal with the stresses of personal growth one may react by withdrawing from the situation. However, disassociation from the real difficulty will only serve to heighten feelings of anxiety, which in turn can lead to rigid thinking, inflexible behaviour, and eventually even to physical illness.

Below are some additional questions which may help you to think about how you as an individual best cope with making changes. The answers are yours and yours alone, and are simply designed to help you to handle the transitions, which hopefully this book will bring, in a calm and tranquil manner.

Identify major changes in your life in the past, both on a personal and a work level:
● How did you cope?
● How long did they take?
● How much stress was involved?
● Did they follow the general transition curve?
● Where are you now, either personally or in relation to work, on the curve?

In future transitions, what are your strategies for:
● Managing stress?
● Dealing with decisions?
● Are you aware of your own individual style of coping with change?
● What personal security needs do you have?
● What support systems do you have, or can you develop?
● What knowledge do you have and do you need for new situations?
● What skills do you have for coping with change?
● What personal changes do you expect to happen in the future? Can you plan and anticipate their effects?
● How will future changes meet your needs?

Often merely thinking about the process of change alerts us to the fact that we are capable of making changes in our lives. Losing the fear of change, and understanding how to manage both the fear and the change can be stimulating experiences in their own right.

We can help ourselves to make changes if we understand our reactions to change before we embark on the tips, techniques and alternative ways of thinking outlined in this section.

A

ABSENT HEALING

In the late 19th century there was great interest in healing at a distance and experiments were carried out to prove that one person's subjective mind could telepathically link with another's in order to bring about a physical cure. Among the people who experimented with this notion was Thomas Jay Hudson. His theory was that fundamentally the subjective mind was in harmony with the whole universe, and that illness was caused by a loss of harmony with nature. The essential balance might be restored with the aid of another subjective mind that reaches out to the contemplative mind of the client.

Hudson's experiments revealed that the best time to test this effect at a distance was while on the verge of sleep, when the healer's 'objective mind' was relaxed (see **Hypnagogic** and **Hypnopompic**). Hudson also found that the patient did not hamper the healer even when the former was aware of what was being attempted. In modern research this would be seen to contaminate results by allowing a 'placebo effect' to creep in. This has always given researchers into healing difficulty in quantifying results, because it is virtually impossible to reproduce exact conditions for experimentation and verification.

At present, there are many groups of people who meet regularly in order to give assistance to people who are suffering. Many individuals also recognize their own ability to heal at a distance. In the 20th century Lawrence LeShan attempted to gain first-hand evidence for Hudson's theory. In *Clairvoyant Reality* he tells of how, after one hour, his own group achieved success in several absent healing attempts. Other attempts, both in the laboratory and outside, by healers such as Matthew Manning, have also proved the value of such healing.

Remote viewing and remote diagnosis such as that used in **radionics** are also valid tools in absent healing. Here the healer uses either the clairvoyant faculty or the pendulum with a 'witness' - often the hair from a person's head – to ascertain what is the matter with the patient and then heal them. Sympathetic magic, which many associate only with witchcraft, as in the use of effigies and pins, may also be used by some healers. The type of healing used will depend largely on the belief system of the healer.

ACTIVE IMAGINATION

Jung used this term to describe a particular type of meditation that allowed him to create an inner world of beings who appeared to be completely independent of his own personality. The appearance of the Wise Old Man, whom he named Philemon, helped him to access ideas and concepts of which he was not consciously aware.

Philemon appears to be similar to the spirit **guides** and helpers who spiritualists claim are discarnate beings, though Jung was always careful to state in public that he felt Philemon was part of his larger psyche. In *Man and his Symbols*, which Jung co-wrote with four of his close associates, it is pointed out that active imagination is comparable to Eastern forms of **meditation**, such as Zen **Buddhism** or tantric **yoga**, and different from them in that there is no conscious goal or outcome.

Active imagination also corresponds in some ways to the sub-personalities that are uncovered in **psychosynthesis**, which is technique of **guided imagery** and similar to active imagination.) Active imagination allows one to access deeper levels of awareness than are normally available to the conscious mind. The technique can be used as an exercise by individuals or by groups.

ACUPRESSURE
See **Therapies**

ACUPUNCTURE
See **Therapies**

AFFIRMATION

An affirmation is a personal statement in which we believe. Positive affirmations are therefore positive statements in which we can have faith. Looked at as tools that we can use to change our lives, they are statements we make to ourselves which we come to trust.

Emile Coué, who developed the technique that he called **auto-suggestion**, was one of the first to put forward the theory that each of us has a conscious and an unconscious self and that either of these selves can influence the other. According to Coué, if we imagine that we cannot do something, we will be unable to do it. If, however, we believe that we can, we will succeed. He defined suggestion as 'the act of imposing an idea on the brain of another', and autosuggestion as 'the implanting of an idea in oneself by oneself'. One can suggest an idea to someone, but unless the recipient of the idea transforms it into autosuggestion, it will not work. Coué discovered that constant repetition resulted in the acceptance of an idea (see **Chanting**). Perhaps his most famous suggestion was 'Every day in every respect I am getting better and better'. This works as a method of healing both on a physical and on a mental level.

Coué identified a conflict between the conscious self and the unconscious self as a cause of negative thinking. This is true, in that the subconscious will accept a negative suggestion before it accepts a positive one. However, there is also a part of ourselves (see **Higher Self**) that is aware of what is right for us and is called into co-operation by positive statements. When we draw on this higher self, it is as though we are calling on someone with extra expertise who knows what needs to be done and will swing the decision the right way. When we have co-operation between the two parts of ourselves, we function much more effectively in the world.

When we make a positive affirmation, we must state our objective unambiguously. It is no use, for instance, making an affirmation for a new job and then finding that your new job pays less than your old one, if that was not what was wanted. Experience has shown that affirmations need to be as brief and succinct as possible to have the maximum effect. For this reason it is wise to spend time getting it right. Try to look at things as holistically as possible. What do you want, what do you need and what do you require? Needs are physical or material; wants are mental or psychological; and requirements are spiritual, satisfying a deeper feeling. Think about these areas as clearly as you can, then formulate the affirmation as concisely as possible. Check that it states your wishes and that it carries no negative implications for anyone else. Try also to ensure that it accurately reflects you and that its emphasis is right for you. A simple statement such as 'the universe is giving me what I deserve' is so general as to be meaningless. Your statement must carry your meaning.

Take some time every day to repeat the statement, out loud if possible, preferably repeating it at least nine times. Repeating the statement this number of times challenges your negativity on all levels – physically, mentally and spiritually. (In almost all systems of belief, there is recognition that the negative will not allow itself to be challenged more than three times. St Peter's denial of Christ is a good example.) Before too long, your affirmations will begin to have an effect on your life and things will begin to change. If you also use **creative visualization** and **chanting** with the same intent, the results should please you greatly.

Here are a few affirmations to help get you started:
- I see myself as a successful person.
- My relationships support and sustain me.
- My emotions truly reflect the way I feel.
- My work is creatively satisfying.
- I allow my innate wisdom to help me make choices.
- I am able to create for myself an acceptable here and now.
- I am able to create a future for myself which can be easily sustained.

Remember that these are only starting points and that your affirmations must be made personal.

AFTERLIFE

The concept of a life after death is an important aspect of many belief systems and has been with us for millennia. From the way primitive humans buried their dead we know that they believed in some form of afterlife. The ancient Egyptians believed that their dead were doomed to inhabit a shadowy world as thin fragile shades. The Mesopotamians named this place 'Kurnugia', which means the land of no return. The

Hebrews were consigned to darkness in their subterranean Sheol (the pit), which was described as the land of gloom and deep darkness. The spirits of the ancient Greeks experienced a rather aimless type of reality in Hades, or the land of illusions. This is similar to a modern day belief in limbo, and may also be where the idea of ghosts arose from.

A heavenly existence was at first regarded as a privilege for the chosen few, which is still reflected in some modern fundamentalist belief systems. The biblical prophets Elijah and Enoch were snatched bodily up into Heaven at the end of their earthly lives, as was Christ. The most heroic of the ancient Greek heroes hoped to walk the Elysian Fields after death, if the gods so decreed, and the bravest Norse warriors killed in battle were likewise conveyed to Valhalla.

Modern Christianity sometimes seems ambivalent about the nature of an afterlife. There is an acceptance that the dead continue to develop. People used to believe in purgatory followed by heaven or hell on the Day of Judgement, some time in the future. In these relatively more gentle times there is hope of salvation for all and progression for the soul.

According to traditional spiritualists, the soul eventually wakes up in 'Summerland', a world created by the best desires of the individual. This is, however, a plane of illusion, and is equivalent to, but generally far more pleasant than, the Kamaloca, the second stage of the bardo (illusory) world as described in the Tibetan Book of the Dead. It may be from this level of post-mortem existence that most messages are received from loved ones through channels or **mediums**.

At death, the soul, consisting of the astral body and spirit body, finally leaves the physical body (see **Clairvoyance**). The etheric body survives only three or four days longer than the physical body itself, during which time the soul is said to have the opportunity to review the whole of its past life. The soul then enters Kamaloca, where the past life is reviewed in detail; desires and emotions are re-experienced and the soul may instigate its own cleansing process. This 'suffering' brings purification, after which the astral body to, is allowed to dissolve away. This process entails abandoning the personality, enabling the purified spirit body to rise to the spirit world, where it can start to choose its next incarnation (see **Reincarnation**).

In the afterlife there is an ultimate awareness of eternity. The immediate afterlife is at a relatively low level of the spirit realm and formed from thought material. There we learn to understand space-time in a new way, just as once – as physical beings – we learnt to appreciate earth-space in a visual way. 'Now' becomes equivalent to 'here' and we can 'see' a little distance in the directions of past and present, just as we can see in different directions around us now.

AKASHIC RECORDS

Akasha is Sanskrit for 'spirit ether' or the fifth element and has been described as 'the stuff of Time and Space'. Everything that happens – past, present or future – is noted on the ether, in the Akashic records. This recording is totally impartial and makes no judgement whatsoever. Our past and present actions are said to determine our future actions, and so it is possible for clairvoyants and **mediums** to read these records and tell an enquirer what conscious action will be taken by him or her in the future. With this belief there is a suspension of free will, or conversely free will has operated before it has become conscious.

The Akashic records may be seen as a type of blueprint for the experiences that a soul needs in order to grow towards perfection. Time spent on the physical plane represents only a small portion of the soul's growth, but it is important to get it right. Records need to be kept in order to ensure that this happens, and also that the soul will be given the opportunity to grow in the future.

The Akashic records are like some huge computer data-base, with various options of action that will ultimately reap a particular end result. Occasionally there needs to be a readout of the plan, and of the action, in order to decide on the best course (see **Karma**).

A form of the Akashic record is sometimes used as a means of explaining discarnate entities or **spirits**. The medium or channel taps into the Universal Mind, and any personality that manifests is merely a trace on the record and not an individual with a continuing non-physical existence.

ALCHEMY

Alchemy was at one and the same time the perfection of matter and the perfection of man. The idea that base metal could be transmuted into gold, once perceived as 'perfect' matter, coincided with the search for the Elixir of Life that would enable the alchemist to free himself from the bonds of matter and allow him to exist in a perfected state.

The philosopher's stone for which alchemists searched was to be the catalyst. Using salt, sulphur and mercury and various crude processes and working with fire, they sought to create blackness, whiteness, and redness. In esoteric terms, these are purging, illuminating and perfecting – the union of the human and the divine. The three metals represented body, mind and spirit, with the element of fire being transformative love. Man would have to go through the stages of transformation and integration. Many believe that the actual element they were searching for was plutonium, which is notoriously unstable, and as destructive as it is transformative.

Many of the alchemical writings are thought to be symbolic representations of the esoteric process. Natural man would need to be purged of dross – of old ideas – to receive enlightenment, and to be transmuted into perfect man unhampered by his physical body. Since Jung's work on alchemy and its meaning, this is now an accepted psychological transformation, which incidentally corresponds very closely to the processes gone through in the Eastern systems of growth and spiritual enlightenment.

The elixir of life for which alchemists were also searching is even less tangible. Not enough is known about the interaction of the various systems of the body to prolong life indefinitely. In the last twenty to thirty years much greater understanding of hormones and their interaction has prolonged life without necessarily improving its quality. It is possible that the alchemists of old, particularly **Paracelsus** (see under **People** in this section) – whose main aim was to cure disease – had an instinctive knowledge of the interaction without being able to prove its workings.

One of the other processes which interested alchemists of old was the formation of new life outside the womb. These attempts were known as homunculi and pre-date the idea of test-tube babies by some hundreds of years. Thus, alchemy, which was more intuitive when forming its hypotheses about matter, led directly to scientific experiment, which sets about proving hypotheses as validation of their truth.

ALTERED STATES
Also see **Consciousness**

Everyone recognizes at least two states of consciousness or awareness: being awake and being asleep. Some people divide waking consciousness into two types: normal everyday consciousness, which is relatively automatic and habitual, and a more focused form of awareness in which we are fully conscious of ourselves as effective individuals. Besides these there are other so-called altered states of consciousness. These can be induced in various ways: for example, by taking **drugs** (1), or by unusual mental activity such as **meditation**, going into trance or a controlled state, self-hypnosis, or submitting to **hypnosis** by someone else. Some altered states of consciousness may apparently occur without any deliberate intent on the part of the person concerned, as in cases of **out of the body experiences** or of **possession**.

ANTHROPOSOPHICAL MEDICINE
See **Therapies**

AROMATHERAPY
See **Therapies**

ART THERAPY
See **Therapies**

ASSERTIVENESS TRAINING
See **Therapies**

ASTRAL CORD
See **Silver Cord**

ASTRAL PLANE/WORLD

The astral plane, or astral world, may be explained as another dimension of reality that exists in space with our physical world, just as the astral body and the physical body coexist. We are said to inhabit the astral world during normal sleep and during **out of the body experiences**.

The astral world is sometimes called the inner plane, but is experienced subjectively. It could be defined as the 'subjective world'; that is, an experience by the individual and assumed to take place outside ourselves – the 'objective world' or that which can be observed. Some people recognize the experience that others claim to have had in the astral world as examples of **visualization**, or, in Jung's terminology, **active imagination**. The psychic, mental or astral world is not therefore a world in the three-dimensional sense. The use of the word 'plane' is perhaps an attempt to show this distinction.

Various non-physical entities can be encountered on the astral plane. These include demons and goblins and nature spirits that seem intent on making life difficult and are believed by some to be **thought forms**.

ASTRAL PROJECTION/ASTRAL TRAVEL

'Astral projection' is sometimes taken as a slightly old-fashioned term for what has become known as **out of the body experiences**. There is however a difference, in that OBEs tend to be spontaneous occurrences when unconscious (whether naturally or accidentally), whereas astral projection is a deliberate act that occurs when the individual wilfully projects his or her consciousness to another place. Astral travel, where one is mindful or aware of the process of movement, appears to occur more often during sleep. It is possible to learn the techniques of both astral projection and astral travel.

The process by which either of these occurs is not yet fully understood. Explaining these phenomena involves recognizing that we are surrounded by an electro-magnetic field that contains awareness of ourselves. In times of stress, in OBEs, in sleep and in astral projection, this field becomes detached and is able to be free of the physical body. A truer explanation might be to say that the physical body has 'trapped' our own particular part of the astral plane and that we can 'will' the energy to be free.

The belief that one must remain attached to the physical body, and the fear of not being able to return to it, has given rise to awareness of the **silver cord** that holds the two bodies together and is only severed at death. Human consciousness is so used to experiencing objects in spatial terms that there has to be a suspension of belief – or rather disbelief – before we can be truly free. As fears and doubts reduce there is less need to mentally experience the connection. It is then feasible, eventually, to do away with the idea of an astral double (a **thought-form** of our own body), which is what is used in astral projection.

Technique of Astral Projection

Astral projection can be achieved using various methods. The following is a simple technique involving the four stages: the thought process, or, more properly, the intent; imagining the process; imaging; and achievement.

It is easier to start with projection around the physical plane. The intent has to be firmly held in mind to begin with, so let us assume that we wish to visit a friend. We then imagine travelling towards and being with our friend, envisaging her face and body, and holding that image. We can then imagine, or sense, what environment she may be in and at this stage it is possible to record information for later checking; we may look at what our friend is doing, or for physical proof such as recognizing pictures or ornaments. Often we are able to bring back information we could not possibly have known at the time. We have achieved success when we experience a different feeling from the one that accompanies imagination. This feeling will be specific to each individual. Sometimes we will not know that we have succeeded and the only proof will be that our friend was conscious of a presence.

With practice we can become more proficient and move on to other dimensions. However, it needs to be stressed that it takes time to perfect the technique even on the physical plane.

When we are ready to move to other realms and levels of **consciousness**, we need to be aware of the inherent dangers there are in dealing with energies we do not fully understand. In OBEs or near death experiences it is as though a door has blown open, allowing us to glimpse another room. If we train ourselves to astrally project, we are giving our 'selves' the key to the room and must use it wisely. If we use the suggested technique and the visualization of a door, we have the ability to alter our state of consciousness at will and therefore to deal sensibly with our activities. The benefits of being able to access spiritual knowledge and information can, if we will it to be so, enhance the way we live in the here and now.

Astral projection can ultimately bring us closer to others and to a greater understanding of how to live with grace and dignity. While it may initially be an interesting pastime, it is also a learning tool that needs to be used with care and with respect for the privacy of others.

ASTROLOGY

Also see **Splenic Chakra** in Section Three,
Eastern Astrology, under **Divination** in this section,
and **Astrological Counselling**.

Man has long watched the skies and used the changes seen in them to measure time. The seasonal changes were once marked by the longest and shortest days (the solstices), and by the times when night and day were the same length (equinoxes). He created a simple calendar to tell him when to plant crops. Soon he realized that certain phenomena in the skies coincided with events on earth. Eventually, these parallels were considered to be omens or portents and were embellished into myths. The earliest astrologers kept meticulous calendars and complete records of celestial movements, and soon began to affix significance to the position of these planets against certain constellations in the sky. It is said that the three magi knew of the birth of Christ because they were astrologers as well as astronomers.

Through the centuries astrology has dealt with the charting and interpretation of the cycles and movements of celestial objects. When astronomy and astrology split, astronomy became the scientific branch, astrology the intuitive. Now, through the use of computers, calculations that once took months for mathematicians to perform by hand can now be done in seconds, and the positions of planets can be computed to hundredths of a degree. The interpretation part is another matter, relying on centuries of richly embroidered legend and mythology.

Astrology deals with ten planets. Eight of these are similar to the earth's planets: Mercury, Venus, Mars, Jupiter, Uranus, Saturn, Neptune and Pluto. The other two are the Sun and the Moon, neither of which is strictly a planet, but astrologers generally include them in the 'ten planets'. If you think of yourself as being at the centre of a vast circular stage you may see all ten planets moving around you in the same direction, from your right to your left. Each of the planets is dancing at its own speed. The faster planets circle the stage several times a year, while slower planets take much much longer.

The Planets

The planets represent different cosmic forces that affect basic human character traits and various urges and needs. They provide the energies that drive the physical, emotional, mental and intuitional sides of ourselves. These energies are modified by the planets' positions in the zodiac, and by the relationships between the planets. Various characteristics are associated with the planets, which may be grouped as follows:

Personal planets – those that deal with the here and now

Sun	Identity, purpose (Individuality)
Moon	Feeling, responsiveness (Personality)
Mercury	Intellect, communication (Mentality)
Venus	Attraction, harmony (Affection)
Mars	Energy, assertion (Initiative)

'Growth' planets – those that affect long-term inner urges

Jupiter	Enthusiasm, adventurousness (Expansive)
Saturn	Caution, restraint (Conservative)

Transpersonal planets – those that affect generation issues

Uranus	Independent, intuitional (Originality)
Neptune	Inspirational, mystical (Sensitivity)
Pluto	Regeneration, obsession (Control)

The Significance of Signs:

Aries	Outgoing	**Taurus**	Conservative
Gemini	Versatile	**Cancer**	Emotional
Leo	Authoritative	**Virgo**	Exacting
Libra	Helpful	**Scorpio**	Determined
Sagittarius	Optimistic	**Capricorn**	Cautious
Aquarius	Independent	**Pisces**	Impressionable

Every sign falls into a group of signs, either fire, earth, water or air. Ancient astrologers associated each element with temperaments.

Fire Signs   Aries, Leo, Sagittarius:
Enthusiastic, courageous, passionate, impulsive.

Earth Signs   Taurus, Virgo, Capricorn:
Practical, materialistic, conservative, inhibited.

Air Signs   Gemini, Libra, Aquarius:
Intellectual, enquiring, searching.

Water Signs   Cancer, Scorpio, Pisces:
Emotional, sensitive, placid, susceptible.

These four groups of signs combine two major fundamental approaches to life: active and passive. The fire and air signs make up the active or masculine signs, while the earth and water signs make up the passive or feminine signs.

There are four signs in each group of Qualities which are cardinal, fixed or mutable. They suggest the basic kinds of activity a person will be engaged in – getting things started, keeping them going or steering them in different directions.

Cardinal Signs	Aries, Cancer, Libra, Capricorn: Initiating, enterprising, ambitious, domineering.
Fixed Signs	Taurus, Leo, Scorpio, Aquarius: Determined, conventional, organizing, dogmatic.
Mutable Signs	Gemini, Virgo, Sagittarius, Pisces: Adaptable, imaginative, tutorial, critical.

AURA
Also see **Aura Therapy**, under **Therapies**

The aura is the energy or force field that extends beyond the physical body. It is composed of very subtle electro-magnetic currents. Some people can have a profound effect on delicate instrumentation simply by standing near it, while others are adversely affected by stormy weather conditions, getting headaches and other aches and pains. Many clairvoyants and mediums see or sense the aura as a band of light around the individual; some will sense this as white light, while others will perceive the aura as containing many colours. No two people will perceive the aura in the same way.

The aura has also been described as the etheric body, which is only perceived by those with trained sight (see **Clairvoyance**). It is, in fact, relatively easy to learn how to 'see' auras – have someone sit in front of a white background (a white sheet or similar material will suffice), then look at them through half closed eyes. It is possible to see the corona – initially as a yellowish/white light – around the shoulders and head. Some might say that this appears because the eyes are out of focus. This is true, but the action also allows you to see beyond the physical. With greater proficiency it is possible to see colours in the light. These correspond to the colours of the **chakras** (3). The blending of the colours indicates certain physical, mental and spiritual conditions. Traditionally these are:

- Brown and reddish yellow: strong emotions of an animal nature.
- Red streams: violent anger, passion.
- Dark green clouds: injured dignity, self-doubt.
- Brighter reddish-yellow and green: the more delicate emotions.
- Green: thinking, consideration.
- Rose-pink, light violet: noble sacrifice, spiritual love.
- Blue: devotional, healing.

Brighter shades are more active, paler shades more passive. Most **healers** and **mediums** tend to develop their own interpretations of colour within the aura.

Auric Healing

The depth and tone of the various colours seen can be used to diagnose certain conditions. The healer's abilities can then be used to help the individual to draw in energy to help clear the condition (see **Colour Healing**). Alternatively the healer uses her own ability to make use of available energy to effect a closing of the aura. Often in cases of disease the aura is perceived as being incomplete; in other words, disease can often be recognized before it actually manifests in the physical body.

AURICULOTHERAPY
See **Therapies**

AUTOGENIC TRAINING
Also see **Therapies**

Autogenic training is probably most suited to those individuals who suffer from illnesses associated with stress, such as colitis, high blood pressure, tension headaches and ulcers. Briefly, it is a system of self-**hypnosis** which uses a series of formulae to enter the **hypnagogic** (half-awake/half asleep state) where the individual has most access to material from the unconscious self.

Following the work of Oscar Vokt, who discovered that many of his patients were able to use self-hypnosis to achieve **relaxation** after he had hypnotized them, J. Schultz developed a number of formulae in order to help the individual enter a hypnotic state induced by passive concentration. During this passive concentration the client is asked to observe her breathing pattern, or other bodily functions, and to repeat statements designed to create calm and peaceful conditions. She is helped to relax even more deeply by instructing herself to experience warmth and heaviness in various parts of the body. When really deep relaxation is achieved, incidents from the past are recalled until a pleasant state is experienced. This state is subsequently used as an 'anchor' to be recalled when good feelings are needed, until the process becomes automatic. Unwanted behaviour patterns may be dropped, and **affirmations** used to reinforce the self-esteem that replaces them.

AUTOMATIC WRITING

Automatic writing is a phenomenon that arises during the development of mediumship (see **Medium**) or channelling. It requires the medium to be in a light trance or altered state of **consciousness**. There are two types of automatic writing, both of them equally valid.

The first requires a clean sheet of paper, a pen and tremendous patience. The individual holds the pen lightly and concentrates on putting themselves in a receptive state. Most channellers will have developed their own technique for this – perhaps through breathing or withdrawal of external awareness. Often nothing happens for some time, although the individual may find her mind begins to become very focused. Random marks, words or phrases then tend to be scribbled without the medium's assistance and often the pen appears to be moving of its own volition. (At this time the scribblings can be very similar to the writings of schizophrenics.) Often what is being written bears little resemblance to the individual's normal way of expressing herself. Gradually the writings begin to make more and more sense and can often be in the style of a deceased writer or other creative artist. Many mediums and channellers confess to not knowing whether it is a discarnate spirit that communicates or a split-off part of their own personality.

The second kind of writing, and perhaps nowadays the most often experienced, is what might be called inspired writing. This happens when the recipient appears to be listening to inner dictation and writing it down (see **Inspiration**). Sometimes this seems to be happening at a very fast rate, faster than normal dictation speed. Often ideas not consciously accepted by the recipient are expressed. This phenomenon is often experienced as a sort of side effect of clairaudience, though which is the primary skill is unclear.

Automatic writing is one of the **psychic abilities** which benefits from regular use. It used to be said that by making oneself receptive at a regular time, the **spirit** entities would know when to communicate. However, it is just as likely that the self-discipline necessary to attain this state makes one more receptive to communication anyway (see **Altered States** and **Discipline** (1).

AVERSION THERAPY
See **Therapies**

AYURVEDIC MEDICINE
Also see **Therapies**

Ayurveda, meaning the 'science of life', is the traditional medicine of India. It has been practised in that country for over two and a half thousand years, and is beginning to achieve popularity in the West. Some of the texts on which it is based described the cells of the body, operative techniques and how infection is transmitted long before these were recognized in the West. The training for the Ayurvedic system is long and thorough (three and a half years plus three years' post-graduate study to achieve full qualification), and also covers many subjects taught in Western medicine. Considerable progress has been made since the early 1970s to upgrade standards and to achieve consistency in registration.

The Ayurvedic system is a truly holistic method of healing. According to the system there are five elements which need to be considered, and in this it is similar to **Chinese medicine**. These are earth, fire, air, water and ether. Additionally, there are three basic qualities – or dispositions – that must be balanced within the individual and according to the environment. These are rajas (active), tamas (passive) and sattva (unifying). Treatment can be with **breathing** techniques, **diet**, **exercise**, **herbs**, **massage**, surgery, urine treatment or yogic cleansing techniques (see **Crown chakra** in Section Three). Diagnosis involves taking a personal history, using astrological information, observing the condition of the physical body and checking the quality of 32 pulses within the body.

Cross-fertilization between modern allopathic and traditional Ayurvedic medicine might provide some solutions to patient care within the West. Siddha medicine, which incorporates the use of minerals in treatments, and Unani, which incorporates Graeco-Arabic theories, are both offshoots of Ayurvedic medicine.

B

BACH FLOWER REMEDIES

The Bach flower remedies heal by harmonizing the subtle energies within the individual. These subtle energies are affected by negativity and disharmony, resulting in **psychosomatic (1)** problems. Where energy becomes blocked the Bach remedies assist in re-establishing a correct flow which then allows healing to take place.

Edward Bach, whose meticulous research led to the development of this principle of healing, wrote in 1934:

'The action of these remedies is to raise our vibrations and open up our channels for the reception of the Spiritual Self; to flood our natures with the particular virtue we need, and wash out from us the fault that is causing the harm. They are able, like beautiful music or any glorious uplifting thing which gives us inspiration, to raise our very natures, and bring us nearer to our souls and by that very act to bring us peace and relieve our suffering.

There is no true healing unless there is a change in outlook, peace of mind, and inner happiness.'

Bach claimed that two basic errors are the cause of disease:

● The first is that the mortal personality does not act in accordance with its soul – that part of us which is immortal. There is a mismatch between the understanding of its life-purpose at a soul level and the intention at a personality level. The personality misinterprets the 'messages' it receives. Positive characteristics can thus become destructive and negative.
● The second is that the personality deliberately acts against the information it receives from the soul. It is as though a block is purposefully being used to prevent the individual from acting in his or her best interests.

Thus Bach healing works in two different ways. Firstly, to put right an imbalance between the physical and the spiritual, by lifting the vibration of the physical. Secondly, to make the spiritual vibration and the soul's purpose available to the personality.

THE REMEDIES

Below is an alphabetical listing of the plants used in Bach remedies, together with the symptoms or spiritual malaise that each may be used to alleviate, and the potential for transformation that the user may experience. Only the active principle of each plant, the essence, is extracted for use in Bach remedies, not the oils. This ensures that the remedies act directly on the inner problem, not on the symptoms. The remedies provide a simple method of self-healing based on perceptiveness and clarity. Often the individual can work with the principles and the changes that take place, rather than there being a conflict of interests.

AGRIMONY

Key symptoms: Attempts are made to conceal torturing thoughts and inner restlessness behind a façade of cheerfulness and freedom from care.
Potential: Even temper; discernment; objectivity.
Genuine inner joyfulness.
The trusting optimist, the untiring peacemaker.
Capable of integrating the less pleasant aspects of life.
Problems are seen in the right light.
Able to laugh at own worries, being aware of their relative unimportance.
Awareness of unity in diversity.

ASPEN

Key symptoms: Inexplicable, vague fears, apprehensions; secret fear of some impending evil.
Potential: Able to enter into more subtle planes of consciousness and as a result gain insight into esoteric and religious lines of thought.
Access to higher spiritual spheres. Feels attracted to these spheres and fearlessly sets out to explore them regardless of difficulty.

BEECH

Key symptoms: Critical; arrogant; intolerant. Criticizing without any understanding of the views and situations of others.
Potential: Mental acuity; able to grasp the different patterns of human behaviour and individual development.
Good diagnostic faculties.
Tolerant and well grounded in life, recognizing unity in diversity.

CENTAURY

Key symptoms: Weak-willed, over-reaction to the wishes of others, good nature easily exploited; can't say 'No'.
Potential: Knows when to say 'Yes', but also able to say 'No' if necessary.
Able to integrate well in groups, while preserving own identity.
Wisely giving service following own inner objectives.
Able to live life in accordance with own true mission.

CERATO

Key symptoms: Lacks confidence in own decisions.
Potential: Intuitive and capable of enthusiasm; curious; eager to learn.
Able to gather information, organize and use it.
Happy to pass on knowledge.
Good co-ordination of abstract and concrete thought.
Accepts guidance of inner voice, trusts in self and stands by own decisions. Acts wisely.

CHERRY PLUM

Key symptoms: Fear of letting go, of losing control, of losing one's mind; uncontrolled outbreaks of temper.
Potential: Courage, strength, spontaneity.
Able to penetrate deeply into subconscious and integrate the insights gained there into everyday life.
Connected to a powerful reservoir of spiritual strength.
Able to come through great physical and mental torture without harming the soul.
Open to great spiritual insight; able to recognize a true life goal and make advances in development.

CHESTNUT BUD

Key symptoms: Repeating the same faults over and over again, because experiences are not digested and not enough is learnt from them.
Potential: Mentally flexible; a good learner.
Mentally active; also learns by observing the behaviour of others.
Follows life events with attention, taking note particularly of all that is negative and of own errors.
Attention is always focused on the present and the experiences it offers; inner gain.
Able to see self and faults as others see them.

CHICORY

Key symptoms: Possessive, excessively interfering and secretly manipulative. Demanding full support from those around, lapsing into self-pity if unable to get own way.

Potential: The archetypal 'eternal mother'.
Gives great love and attention in caring for others.
Gives without expecting or needing anything in return.
Warm, kind, sensitive; secure.
Gives security and a sense of protection to others.

CLEMATIS

Key symptoms: Daydreamer; thoughts always elsewhere; pays little attention to what is going on around.
Potential: Has control of thought-world, and is daily finding new interest in the real world, because the connections between these different worlds and the deeper meaning connecting them is understood and accepted.
Purposeful in bringing creativity to fruition, for example, as an actor, writer or designer.

CRAB APPLE

Key symptoms: Feels unclean, infected; self-disgust. Gets stuck in details.
Potential: Generous; little things will not upset composure.
Sees things in their proper perspective.
A sense of the overall picture.
Recognizes unresolved issues and is able to transform them.

ELM

Key symptoms: Temporary feeling of inadequacy; overwhelmed by responsibilities.
Potential: Inherent altruism; follows inner calling.
Above-average gifts; great potential.
Natural leader; positive; great sense of responsibility.
Self-assured and confident; responsible and reliable.
Unshakeable conviction that help will always come at the right moment.
Ready to attempt the impossible if it is a matter of overcoming difficulties relating to the whole.
Able to see problems in their proper perspective.

GENTIAN

Key symptoms: Sceptical, doubting, pessimistic and easily discouraged.
Potential: Ability to live with conflict.
Conviction that if one has done one's best there will be no failure.
Certainty that problems can be overcome.
Unshakeable confidence despite difficult circumstances.
Ability to see 'the light in the darkness' and to convey this feeling to others.

GORSE

Key symptoms: Hopelessness; utter despair; an 'Oh, what's the use' attitude.
Potential: Convinced that all will come out right in the end.
Able to accept own destiny.
Realizes that hopelessness impedes the healing process and that 'Everybody has their burden to carry'.
Knows that one should never say 'Never', and may hope.
In milder cases: new hope of a cure arises, and this is the first step towards recovery

HEATHER

Key symptoms: 'The Needy Child' – self-centred; obsessed with own troubles and affairs; constantly needs an audience,
Potential: The sympathetic adult; great empathy.
A good listener, interested partner in discussion.
Able to enter completely into the concerns of another or something that needs to be done.
Radiates strength and confidence.

HOLLY

Key symptoms: Jealousy, distrust, feelings of hatred and envy.
Potential: Living in inner harmony, radiating love.
Profound understanding of human emotions.
Able to take pleasure in achievements and successes of others, even when having own problems.
Has a sense of the 'scheme of things' and is able to acknowledge people on their terms.

HONEYSUCKLE

Key symptoms: Longing for the past; regrets over the past; not living in the present.

Potential: Has a living relationship to the past but is living in the present.

Has learnt from past experience but does not cling to it.

Able to preserve what was beautiful in the past for the present.

Able to bring the past back to life; e.g., as a writer, archaeologist or historian.

HORNBEAM

Key symptoms: Weariness; mental exhaustion; procrastination.

Potential: Lively mind; clear cool head; likes variety.

Sure of being able to master the tasks ahead even if they appear to be beyond one's power.

IMPATIENS

Key symptoms: Impatient; irritable; excessive reactions.

Potential: Quick thinking and acting.

Independent minded.

Above-average gifts.

Patience, delicacy of feeling.

Gentleness, empathy and understanding for others.

Able to use gifts diplomatically for the benefit of all.

LARCH

Key symptoms: Expecting to fail due to lack of self-confidence; inferiority complex

Potential: Is realistic in tackling things.

Perseveres even when there are setbacks.

Able to assess situations objectively.

MIMULUS

Key symptoms: Specific fears that can be named; shyness, timidity; afraid of the world

Potential: Fine character; sensitive.

Has grown beyond anxieties, able to face the world with cheerful equanimity.

Personal courage; understanding for others in a similar situation.

MUSTARD

Key symptoms: Periods of deep gloom and melancholia suddenly appear and disappear for no apparent reason.

Potential: Inner serenity; cheerfulness and stability on bright or cloudy days.

OAK

Key symptoms: The fighter exhausted and brought to his knees who, nevertheless, struggles on bravely, never giving up

Potential: Endurance, reliability, steadfastness, strength, common sense. Able to stand great stress exceedingly well.

Overcomes all of life's vicissitudes with courage.

OLIVE

Key symptoms: Extreme physical and mental fatigue.

Potential: Great strength and vitality.

Relies on inner guidance during periods of stress, and is thus able to cope cheerfully even with extreme demands.

PINE

Key symptoms: Self-reproach; guilt feelings; despondency.

Potential: Admits own faults but does not cling to them.

Feels genuine regret rather than guilt; able to forgive self and forget.

Deep understanding of human nature, particularly human feelings.

Shares the burdens of others, but only if this is meaningful.

Great patience, humility, simplicity of heart.

True understanding of the Christian concept of salvation.

RED CHESTNUT

Key symptoms: Excessive concern and worry over others.

Potential: Ability to radiate positive thoughts of security, well-being and courage in difficult situations.

Able to provide a positive influence and guidance for others from a distance.

Able to keep a cool head in emergencies; able to cope mentally and physically.

ROCK ROSE

Key symptoms: Extremely acute state of terror and panic.

Potential: Heroism; able to 'grow' in emergency and crisis situations and to mobilize almost super-human powers.

Acts for the benefit of others regardless of possible risks to self.

ROCK WATER

Key symptoms: Hard on self; strict, rigid views suppressing inner needs.

Potential: Open-minded idealist; able to let go of theories and principles when confronted with new insights or deeper truths.

Does not allow self to be influenced by others. Knows that the right insights are to be found within at the right time.

Able to bring great ideals to fruition.

Joy in life and inner peace – a natural example to others.

SCLERANTHUS

Key symptoms: Indecisive; erratic; lacking inner balance; opinions and moods change from one moment to the next.

Potential: Power of concentration and determination.

Maintains inner balance whatever the circumstances.

Versatile and flexible, able to integrate more and more potential.

Makes correct decisions instantaneously.

Presence soothing to others.

STAR OF BETHLEHEM

Key symptoms: After-effects of a frightening experience at some point in life; may be physical, mental or psychic in origin.

Potential: Inner vitality, clear mind and inner strength.

Able to adapt nervous system well to energy changes.

Facility to make quick recovery.

SWEET CHESTNUT

Key symptoms: Feelings of absolute dejection, and of having reached the limits of endurance.

Potential: Was lost and has found self again; phoenix rising from the ashes.

Has recognized that a crucial change is possible; the inner journey has started.

Able to believe again; personal experience of God.

VERVAIN

Key symptoms: Over-enthusiastic in supporting a good cause. Strains energies; highly strung, possibly fanatical.

Potential: Stands up for ideas, but also allows others the right to their own opinions.

May allow self to be converted to another view by cogent arguments in a discussion.

Sees things in a wider context.

Able to use energies effectively and with love for a worthwhile end.

The 'torch-bearer', effortlessly able to enthuse and inspire others and to carry them along.

VINE

Key symptoms: Dominating, inflexible striving for power.

Potential: Wise, understanding leader; beloved teacher who has natural authority, 'good shepherd'.

Able to delegate and place leadership qualities in the service of a greater task.

Helps others to help themselves and find their own way.

WALNUT

Key symptoms: Difficulties in adjusting to periods of transition in life. Wants to resist powerful influences and follow own true ambitions.

Potential: The pioneer who remains true to self.

Follows own life goal unswervingly despite adverse circumstances.

Open and unprejudiced towards the new.

Recognizes the laws behind the changes that occur.

Immune to outside influence and open to inner inspiration.

175

Able to free self from the shadows of the past.

WATER VIOLET

Key symptoms: Inner reserve; proud withdrawal; feeling of superiority in isolation; little emotional involvement.

Potential: Charming, gentle with tactful reserve.

Independent attitude; equable; calm.

Capable, competent; often superior to others.

Self confident, knows who one is.

Comfortable with self; likes to be alone.

Generally has life well in hand.

Moves through life quietly, beautifully and unobtrusively; possesses inner dignity.

Often speaks in a low, polite and insistent voice.

Tolerant attitude – live and let live.

Never interferes, even when views issues differently.

Seen by others as a well-balanced, independent-minded person.

Acts in humility, love and wisdom.

Able to create an atmosphere of calm confidence and tranquillity.

WHITE CHESTNUT

Key symptoms: Cannot get rid of unwanted thoughts; mental arguments and dialogues.

Potential: Balanced state of mind.

Clear and calm thoughts.

Solution for every problem comes up of its own accord from a calm mind.

Able to use powers of thought constructively.

WILD OAT

Key symptoms: Indefinite regarding ambitions; dissatisfaction because a mission in life has not been found.

Potential: Ability to recognize own potential and develop it to the full.

Wide range of talents; able to do many things well, even successfully to do several jobs simultaneously.

Able to follow a higher guideline and bring things to completion.

Has clear ideas and ambitions and will not be deflected.

WILD ROSE

Key symptoms: Apathy, lack of interest and ambition; resignation; life one long paralyzing routine.
Potential: New, vital interest in life.
Ability to follow the inner laws of life happily.
Lives in a feeling of inner freedom and flexibility.

WILLOW

Key symptoms: Unspoken resentment, bitterness; 'poor me' or 'victim of fate' attitude.
Potential: Positive attitude, taking full responsibility for own fate.
Recognition and acceptance of the connection between one's thoughts and external events.
Knows there is a law called 'as within so without' and one may therefore attract positive or negative events; constantly makes use of this principle.
Instead of a 'victim' becomes 'master' of own fate.

RESCUE REMEDY

This is a specific against deep trauma, such as an accident or witnessing or taking part in something unpleasant, and ensures speedy restoration of the energy balance. Rescue remedy is a combination of five of the basic Bach Remedies. These are Star of Bethlehem, Rock Rose, Impatiens, Cherry Plum and Clematis.

BATES METHOD
See Therapies

BIOCHEMIC TISSUE SALTS
See Therapies

BIOENERGETICS
See Therapies

BIOFEEDBACK TRAINING
See **Therapies**

BIOTHERAPY
See **Therapies**

BODIES
See **Clairvoyance**

BODY AWARENESS

There is a belief that the body mirrors in itself certain difficulties, problems and tensions. In Chinese medicine, for example, certain areas of the body correspond to particular emotions and spiritual difficulties, and so rather than merely curing physical symptoms it is considered better to treat their cause by working holistically.

Listed below are various areas, features and organs of the body together with the emotional problems or characteristics associated with them. An understanding of these correspondences may help us to change attitudes and behaviours in a positive way. (The entry on **psychosomatic** illness (1) may give the reader additional insights.)

Right side

The right side of the body represents the masculine energy within us. This is the extroverted side and incorporates the drive that carries us forward into new things. Problems in this area might indicate a difficulty with a relationship with a man, or a difficulty in making a decision to move forward. It is for you to decide whether the difficulty lies within you or is reflected outwards in your external life. There may be a difficulty in being open and giving to others as well as to yourself. Rigidity here can indicate rigidity of thought or ideas. Physical pain showing up in the right side of the body can be caused by over-exertion in some area of life, perhaps in the physical realm but also on an emotional or spiritual level.

Left side

The left side of the body represents the feminine energy within us. It is the more intuitive, introverted part that allows us to be passive, and to receive from others. It also involves our inherited perception of the feminine, reflecting relationships with our feminine side and also relationships with the women in our life. Problems in this part of the body might indicate some unresolved conflicts in any of these relationships. There is an inability to receive fully from other people, and an inappropriate expression of feminine energy. Physical pain can suggest inhibition of creative expression, because you are not responding to your intuition.

Top half (waist upwards)

The top half of the body signifies the way we express our selves within the everyday world. It is the more outgoing, sociable side that deals with the emotions and the senses. It is also the tactile side and the side that deals with interpersonal relationships. Problems in this area might indicate difficulty in fitting into the world or into a chosen way of life. A body stance with the top half thrust forward often suggests an assertive approach to life. Rigidity in this area can indicate a degree of repressed aggression.

Bottom half (waist downwards)

Also see **Base** and **Splenic chakras** in Section Three

The bottom half of the body represents the contact that we have with the earth, and how we give ourselves stability and strength. Through being able to be self-supportive we become balanced and independent. Problems in this area might indicate an inability to be emotionally self sufficient. Pain and rigidity in this area can also suggest a need for both physical and emotional support.

Ankles

Also see **Legs** – under **Base Chakra** in Section Three

The ankles can be ambivalent in their meaning. They represent the capacity to support oneself and all aspects of stability and balance. However, this balance is best achieved by an ability to be flexible and to be prepared to move in order to make progress. You need to be aware of your ability to adapt and deal with the changes which life brings. Problems in this area can often be traced back to an inflexible attitude, or an inability to support yourself in some way. It is more than likely that there is resistance to some necessary change; you may be feeling unstable, not grounded and somewhat unsure of the direction you should be taking.

Back/spine
Also see **Base Chakra** in Section Three

The back represents strength, stability and uprightness. It also signifies total determination, the ability to support ideas and projects and to accept responsibility for one's actions. Problems in this area might indicate a lack of emotional support or personal support. It could be that you are carrying too much responsibility or, conversely, depending too much on others. Repressed fears can also manifest as pain, discomfort and back tension. A 'slipped disc' can suggest some doubt and fear over one's ability to carry out new tasks. It can indicate the need to stop completely, to reconsider future plans, and to make adjustments accordingly. Lower back pain often indicates issues to do with repressed sexuality or passion, or lack of self esteem. The last mentioned – by association – may also involve financial worries.

Bladder
Also see **Splenic Chakra** in Section Three

The bladder is associated with all aspects of control stemming from childhood. Problems in this area indicate that we are holding back on ideas, emotions or desires that need to be expressed. We are not able to go with the flow of life, and are too frightened to take risks lest we get out of control. Often we may need to eliminate old ideas concerning our abilities and talents. We may quite literally be 'pissed off' because someone has treated us badly, and need to get rid of resentment and bad feeling. Often we may feel ineffective and shy within a situation and want to remove ourselves from the public gaze.

Blood
Also see **Heart Chakra** in Section Three

In the Middle Ages bad temper was thought to be a condition of the blood which could be cleared up by giving the sufferer a dose of sulphur. This 'solution' is somewhat drastic, but it is true that negative thinking can have an effect on blood flow. Whether this is because of changes in the breathing or other physiological reasons is not fully understood. Purifying our thoughts and emotions does seem to have an effect on our overall well-being. Certainly the blood represents joy and vitality and brings nourishment to all parts of the body. Problems in this area might indicate issues to do with selfishness and scepticism.

Bones
Also see **Base Chakra** in Section Three
The bones are primarily the framework and support of our physical structure. Equally they represent the foundation of our emotional and mental structure. The ability to support ourselves, to stand upright in the world is governed by our bones, which show our strength, power and integrity. The bones often give an indication of the earthly lessons we must learn in life, and problems may manifest when there is a lack of internal support, or a lack of personal integrity. There is often the need to be very grounded and solid within our understanding of ourselves and others.

Bowels
Also see **Colon** and **Base Chakra** in Section Three
The bowels are connected with the automatic expulsion of the negative within our lives. Suggesting as they do the end of a process or where something has been used up and can be discarded, the bowels represent our ability to utilize our experiences. The principal problems in this area are constipation (holding back) and refusing to let go, and diarrhoea, where we seem to be in too much of a hurry to get things finished or are unable to absorb information that is being given. Irritable Bowel Syndrome suggests that there is some difficulty in deciding which of these two courses of action is appropriate.

Breasts (female)
The breasts are always strongly connected with a woman's self-image. When, for instance, radical surgery is carried out a woman needs

reassurance that she has not lost her femininity. The breasts symbolize nurturing, loving, giving and all issues to do with motherhood. It is now well understood that cancer of the breasts can be to do with the suppression of emotion. Problems in this area might indicate a perceived lack of respect from others, feelings of inadequacy, frustrated desires to do with childhood and mothering, and also over-concern as a mother.

Colon
Also see **Bowels**, and **Base Chakra** in Section Three
The colon is one of the most sensitive areas of the body, and almost any emotional problem will have an effect on its functioning. Extreme fear, for example, will cause it to empty spontaneously. On a physical level the colon deals with the elimination of that which is no longer necessary. On an emotional level it is associated with issues related to control and material gain. Loneliness, repressed rage, over-controlling attitudes and envy can all make themselves felt as illness in this part of the body. Problems might indicate that one is holding on too tightly to people, material possessions or the past. An ability to deal with feelings of guilt, bitterness and cynicism will often cause physical symptoms to disappear.

Diaphragm
The diaphragm represents the division between the lower, more animalistic self and the higher, more intelligent one. Pain in the diaphragm may represent grief, hypersensitivity, pent-up emotions, obsession with details, worry and anxiety. It is as though the individual cannot achieve a balance between internal feelings and outward reality.

Ears
Also see **Brow Chakra** in Section Three
The ears symbolize the capacity to hear and listen. Problems with them might indicate the avoidance of unpleasant facts and a refusal to hear the truth. There has to be a willingness to be open to the opinions of others, and to be able to listen to life. Lack of enthusiasm for life is sometimes a factor in deafness.

Eyes

Also see **Brow Chakra** in Section Three

The eyes are said to be 'the windows of the soul'. They represent perception and clarity of expression. We all have the capacity to see life and its issues clearly. When we are willing to be open and make contact with other people, we gain through knowledge and experience. Our eyes can often signify our curiosity and our ability to meet the challenges of life. Problems in this area might indicate a refusal to face reality, a lack of motivation and perhaps low self-esteem. There may be a fear of intimacy, or an attempt to protect one's privacy; this may be particularly so in short-sightedness. Sometimes it may seem as though the individual is not able to see beyond the immediate situation, and is more able to find a solution through introspection. Far-sightedness sometimes represents an almost too visionary outlook, with a tendency to live in the future without paying due attention to the immediate situation. Obstacles that may prevent success are often not even considered. The eyes are often affected by problems associated with responsibility.

Face

The face reflects our attitudes to life. The way we feel about ourselves is mirrored in the face, which will show our emotional reactions such as pain, joy, fear and anger. We often use the face as a mask to hide the inner self. Problems in this area might indicate inner conflict and difficulty. For instance, pain in the jaw can suggest holding back on something we wish to express. Pain in the sinuses can be a substitute for the ability to cry.

Feet

Feet signify support and stability and the ability to be grounded and practical. Each of us needs to be able to stand on our own two feet, and above all else to be ourselves. With understanding and a balanced viewpoint we are able to move forward (step out). Problems in this area might indicate that we are out of touch with physical reality, and that we do not have the inclination or motivation to undertake new experiences, suggesting an inadequate grasp on our overall situation.

Fingers

Also see **Hands** under **Heart Chakra** in Section Three

It is with the fingers that we grasp whatever life holds for us and whatever experiences we are searching for. The fingers represent our ability to take responsibility; the giving and receiving of love and creativity, and the ability to 'feel' in the sense of making our feelings tangible. Each digit signifies something specific. The thumb is connected with the conscious mind, and with issues to do with self-control, steadiness of purpose, strength, and will-power. The index finger symbolizes ambition and authority, the ego, pride, judgement, leadership and power; in palmistry, an index finger as long as the middle finger signifies a touch of megalomania. The middle finger is usually taken as representing balance, introspection, philosophy, service, religion and responsibility. The ring finger is said to be connected with the heart and is to do with adaptability, creativity, emotion, relationships and sociability. The little finger monitors mental and physical communication and expression and the subconscious.

Genitals

Also see **Splenic Chakra** in Section Three

The genitals are the seat of sensation and the life-force. The relationship to one's own sexuality and interpersonal relationships is governed by this area. Courage, will-power, achievement and the ability to give and receive pleasure are all initiated in this area. The ability to 'let go', to surrender to life's spontaneity, and also issues of power and assertiveness, belong to this part. Problems in this area might indicate repressed emotions together with other negative feelings, such as guilt, anger and fear. Lack of affection, fear of letting go, of inappropriate relationships may all manifest themselves as trouble in this area, as can the misuse of, or over-indulgence in, sex.

Glands

Also see under each of the **chakras** in Section Three

The glands secrete substances called hormones that keep our whole system balanced and healthy. Initially it was thought that hormones governed only the sexual function, and changes of mood were attributed to imbalances in these – hence the development of the pre-menstrual syndrome. It has now been found that the secretions from the various glands do much more than just regulate the sexual function – they also have a part to play in our use of vitality and our energy. There is also a strong co-relationship between our attitudes and responses to life and these glandular secretions. Problems with the glands might indicate that there are attitudes and beliefs that need to be tackled or that the ability to integrate and balance the totality of experience needs to be cultivated.

Hands/arms
Also see **Heart Chakra** in Section Three
The hands and arms are the physical expression of love. They also represent the ability to take hold of life and its experiences through communication and creative movement. One may 'feel' the way ahead in order to take hold of life, both giving and receiving along the way. However, there may be an unwillingness to feel which in turn produces feelings of insecurity and the failure to give or receive what one is capable of.

Head
Also see **Crown Chakra** in Section Three
The head represents the way in which we view ourselves and think about ourselves, and therefore is the main influence over the rest of the body. The head, hopefully, receives information from other levels of understanding in the body and then uses that information to create a stable and constant life-plan. The issues that we relate to our own conscious thinking – such as decision-making, intellect, faith, and the will to progress – are all integrated through the head. There may be problems when these conscious thoughts do not align with our need for love and knowledge. For example, we may use the intellect to escape from feelings or from a lack of faith in spiritual matters, and to take us in pursuit of material goals.

Heart
Also see **Heart Chakra** in Section Three

The heart is the basis of our real selves – the root of spiritual gain. The expression of love, affection, compassion, desire, and sensitivity for oneself and others – which one is always striving to communicate – is the heart's domain. This is not without its dangers and can produce insecurity, fear of rejection and all that brings with it (heartbreak, loneliness, inadequacy), which in turn lead to a closing down of feelings. The road of self-protection is sometimes an understandable one to take. However, no good can come of it, because insensitivity, arrogance, hate and anger will be the overriding emotions, and these will halt the flow of 'vital love' in the heart.

Immune system
Also see chakras in Section Three, particularly **Crown Chakra**
The immune system is the core of strength, vitality and devotion on all levels – that is, physical, emotional and mental. It also relates to our vulnerable side. Physically, the immune system guards against infection and invaders of the various systems of the body. The importance of a strong immune system cannot be stressed too highly; it is crucial for confidence and enthusiasm in all aspects of life. If our immune system is compromised, our resistance to vulnerability and openness will be strong. We will be very self-critical and negative and ultimately destructive. Maintaining a psychological defence against the power of vulnerability will eventually encourage stress in the body and mind. It is paramount to realize that the one true strength is integrity and openness, and that all other so called 'defences' are just vain attempts to hide from our true feelings.

Joints
Also see **Base Chakra** in Section Three
The joints reflect the flexibility of the mind and body. They indicate the ways in which we handle life's ever-changing moods and circumstances. Once we lose flexibility – for example, in our attitudes and views towards life and other people – we become rigid with cynicism and unwilling to adapt and give ourselves over to life's 'flexible' and unpredictable map. In effect, we will become a 'disjointed' and extremely limited person.

Kidneys

Also see **Base Chakra** in Section Three

The kidneys signal how able we are to 'go with the flow' and in turn let life 'flow' through us, at the same time as flushing out all that is negative and oppressive. This flushing out is important as the kidneys are very sensitive to emotional stress, particularly stress within relationships. The kidneys will mirror a person's tensions and anxieties, in whatever shape these may take, by way of resistance leading to malfunction. Degrees of anger and indecision, emotional stress and pain, and tunnel vision are indicated by kidney trouble.

Knees

As with the joints, the knees represent flexibility in one's attitude and mind. Through this comes a willingness to progress in life, while encouraging a stable grounding – which is important when adapting to life's experiences. Problems in the knee area could indicate a resistance to change and an unwillingness to adapt.

Legs/thighs

The legs, quite literally, move one forward through life, grounding and supporting along the way, as well as promoting strength and power – all crucial when dealing with life's pressures and problems. If one feels unable to move forward due to, say, a lack of strength – or one feels unsupported – this will often manifest as a problem in the legs. There can also be a lack of initiative.

Liver

Also see **Solar Plexus Chakra** in Section Three

The liver is the great worker in the body, and corresponds with our emotions. Therefore, any stress or feelings of despair, indeed most negative emotions, will affect the liver. Anger, envy and bitterness can all lead to problems in this organ.

Lungs

Also see **Heart Chakra** in Section Three

The lungs, by association with the heart, mirror the inhalation of 'life breath' – that is, love, openness and inspired thinking. Problems here may well be rooted in relationships. Stress, anger, resentment, selfishness and anxiety are all possible triggers for problems here. Apathy and lack of appreciation are all associated with the lungs. Grief is also held within the lung area.

Lymphatic system

The lymphatic system has strong associations with water, and reflects our ability to go with the flow. It allows life to flow through us, to get rid of what is unnecessary and help the flow of emotional energy. Feelings of confusion or being overburdened or restricted in some way usually indicate a problem with the lymphatic system. Unresolved emotional issues can often be resolved by working with this area.

Mouth/jaw/tongue

Also see **Throat Chakra** in Section Three

These are the channels through which we express our spiritual and emotional views and feelings, and take in and acknowledge new information and new ideas. There is much creativity in the spoken word, and coupled with the power of thought it can either destroy (negative) or heal (positive). Problems will emerge through tension and unexpressed feelings which, in turn, lead to anger and defiance. Gossiping, lying and complaining will all lead to tension in the area of the mouth and jaw – hence the term 'hard faced'.

Muscles

The muscles are the primary manifestation of all that is physical; we express our needs through our muscles, using strength and willpower to induce movement and progression. Lack of energy and an unwillingness to progress are signified by muscle fatigue. Problems with the muscles may occur when one is being too overbearing.

Neck

Also see **Throat Chakra** in Section Three

The neck is the channel through which our feelings manifest into expressed thoughts and words. Our ability to be flexible is related to the neck – being able to see questions from different angles. Neck problems may suggest stubbornness or stiffness in our views on life; communication problems may also arise which may lead to a lack of sensitivity ('brass neck').

Pancreas
Also see **Solar Plexus Chakra** in Section Three
The pancreas is our balancing organ: it absorbs information and helps to share out equally our capacity to give and receive love. Too much of one and not enough of the other may cause an imbalance within the entire body. The list of concerns affecting the pancreas is lengthy: worry, anger, bitterness, confusion, uncertainty; these may be directly related to abandonment or self-pity, or an inability to deal with beauty – that is, the beauty of life and life's pleasures.

Shoulders
These, not surprisingly, relate to responsibility, as Atlas would testify – 'having a lot on one's shoulders'. The shoulders also, together with the heart and the arms, are associated with our expression of love. Problems here would suggest that responsibilities are seen as an encumbrance – an affliction – with regard to someone else's demands. They may also indicate a lack of self-esteem and a feeling of insecurity in romantic matters.

Skin
Also see **Skin** entry in Section One
There is an interrelationship between skin and how we see ourselves, our self-image; that is, what we want to be and what we are, which are often poles apart. Our individuality is also related to our skin. Problems here are to do with frustration, perhaps at our lack of individuality, perhaps at a lack of achievement.

Stomach
Also see **Solar Plexus Chakra** in Section Three
The stomach, literally, takes in and digests life's experiences. The

stomach recognizes what is important and can be dealt with, and what isn't important and can't be dealt with (indigestion). A tendency towards a critical attitude where one may condemn others – and oneself – may arise. Fear, worry and a repression of feelings leading to emotional upsets are the concerns here – literally, the stomach churning. For those who suffer with their stomach, some degree of caution may be needed when selecting food.

Throat
Also see **Throat Chakra** in Section Three
The throat is our creative and expressive centre. As we have seen (under **Mouth**), the spoken word and communication are powerful tools. The throat is the verbal pathway for mind and heart expression. Problems may arise if one is scared of expressing feelings or if one's creative potential is not being fulfilled. The fear may be of either success or failure. There is much energy and power in our speech; therefore negative words will have the effect of inducing illness throughout the body. Equally, positive words will heal and protect.

Torso
Also see **Splenic**, **Solar Plexus** and **Heart Chakras** in Section Three
The torso deals most especially with our unconscious feelings. The organs in the body most likely to be affected are the lungs, pancreas, bladder, heart, stomach, spleen and lower body. Again, unexpressed feelings or suppressed emotion (i.e., fear, hatred and jealousy) will surface as problems in the torso.

Uterus
Also see **Womb** under **Splenic Chakra** in Section Three
The uterus is the outlet for new and creative angles in life; i.e., the birth of a new idea. For women, the uterus can indicate their relationship to men. For both men and women, sexuality is the issue. The uterus deals directly with sex and relationships. Difficulties such as holding on to the pain of the past or guilt regarding sex are the problems to look out for.

C

CANDLES
See **Magic**

CHANTING

Chanting is a form of prayer and glorification used by many religions to enhance an act of worship. It can consist of a meaningful phrase repeated over and over using words, tones or musical notes. Sometimes it is accompanied by musical instruments such as drums or gongs, sometimes not. It is often used to focus the individual's mind on one particular idea, concept or ceremony and can be used to bring about a change of awareness.

One simple chant would be to use the sound of your own name, repeating it rhythmically until you achieve a sense of tranquillity or centredness. (There is a belief that the name one is given at birth contains within its meaning the lesson one needs to learn in life. Thus chanting in this way would link one to one's essential purpose.)

A variation on this would be to use a Holy name, whatever is appropriate with your own belief system. By and large a three-syllable chant works best, because it links in with the essential nature of the number three, and vibrates with body, mind and spirit. Various phrases and words of meaning can also be used, such as Aum – the sound of creation, Om Mane Padme Hum or Nam Myo Renge Kyo ('I devote myself to the Mystic Law of the lotus' – i.e., cause and effect). Gregorian chant is possibly one of the most beautiful forms of chanting. Using particular cadences, it brings a sense of peace to chanter and listener alike.

CHARISMATIC HEALING
See **Therapies**

CHEIROLOGY
See **Therapies**

CHINESE MEDICINE
See **Therapies**

CHIROPRACTIC
See **Therapies**

CLAIRVOYANCE

Clairvoyance is 'clear seeing' and is akin to the clarity and simplicity with which a child perceives his world as he first ventures away from his relationship with himself and his immediate surroundings. As children at this stage of development we learn or are forced to monitor the emotional input from other people and to decide what is an appropriate response to that input. At the same time we begin to have a sense of our own ability to give out emotionally and spontaneously. Very often we learn by degrees that our spontaneity can be threatening to others. We respond by tending to push down the natural response and uprush of energy. This distorts our perceptions to a greater or lesser degree, and leads to a loss of our natural clairvoyance.

Clairvoyance aims to get back to that spontaneity and unmonitored response, enabling us to perceive the needs, wants and desires of others more clearly so that those requirements can be met. In order to do this it is imperative to learn how to relax and how to be relaxed (see **Relaxation**) - they are not necessarily one and the same thing. To be relaxed we have to learn how to trust our own reactions and be receptive to the reactions of others. The clairvoyant does not reject images and information, however odd they may seem. For one thing, they may have relevance to the sitter. For another, the mind has a fund of archetypal images whose symbolism will become apparent the more often the technique of clairvoyance is used.

In order to develop clairvoyance and other psychic skills it is worthwhile trying to understand the way in which our perception changes as we uncover the different layers of our selves. Each layer or body carries with it certain understandings and skills which become useful as tools to help us deal with the spiritual and physical aspects of our lives.

Traditionally, there are seven bodies or states of awareness and changes of consciousness occur as we move between them.

Leaving aside the first body, the physical, we will look in detail at the others.

The etheric, the state between energy and matter, which is the energy necessary for the physical tissues and organs to exist. The etheric is closest to the physical body and extends approximately two inches beyond it. Seen clairvoyantly, the etheric body appears as a web-like film which is in constant motion. It can be observed by positioning your subject against a white background and observing the pulsation as the light moves within the band of energy around the head and shoulders. You should focus slightly in front of or behind your subject.

The emotional body is associated with feelings and extends between one and three inches beyond the physical body. It is seen as coloured clouds which vary according to the confusion or clarity of the emotional state. During therapy the tones will often clear as the patient comes to terms with her emotions.

The mental body extends up to eight inches from the physical body and appears as a yellow light around the whole body. Different colours superimposed on this body represent the emotion connected with the mental processes. The more we concentrate on an idea the brighter and more focused this mental body becomes.

The astral body extends between six and eight inches beyond the physical body. The clouds of colour associated with the astral body tend to be infused within the 'light of love', which is pink. This particular body tends to connect us on a subliminal level with those we care about on the physical realm, and also those who have died. It is this body which becomes uncomfortable when we are in a crowded place, such as a train or a supermarket.

The fifth level echoes the physical aspect of the etheric body but in a more perfect form. It is from this level that **healing** is drawn to recreate perfect health. To the clairvoyant eye it will be seen as an oval layer approximately eighteen inches to two feet from the body. This particular level is perceived almost as a photographic negative.

The sixth level connects us to spiritual ecstasy and to mysticism. It extends about two to two and a quarter feet from the physical body and is seen as an opalescent light. At this level we are capable of creating our own present in the here and now. Some people perceive it as veering more towards gold, while others see it as silver. This connects the love of humanity and of human beings with spiritual love.

Within the seventh body, the strongest and most resistant body of all, our **consciousness** is at one with the creator. This body contains and protects all the other bodies and is composed of what appears to the clairvoyant eye to be pure light. It extends to about two to two and a half feet from the body and is egg shaped. The seventh body connects our past with our future, and encapsulates all our experiences in this life, in previous lives and lives to come.

It is at this level that we create our own future being. Our total experience and whatever connection we have with 'everything that is' can be assessed at this level.

Each body – and work done on any body – can have a profound effect on the other bodies. For example, adjustments made through manipulative techniques on a physical level may release emotions which have been suppressed for years and allow spiritual progress. Realizations which belong to past life trauma may 'cure' a physical problem which has proved resistant to any other kind of treatment, in a way that may seem almost miraculous. In our awareness of our sense of 'at-oneness' we are able to take responsibility for the creation of a world that can be at peace with itself.

COGNITIVE THERAPY
See Therapies

CO-COUNSELLING
See Therapies

COLOUR

Colour offers fruitful insights into ways of achieving harmony within oneself, in others and with others. Believers in Atlantis (see **Lost Continents**) claim that colour was used in healing. Certainly the ancient Egyptians seem to have had an interest in colour. Their temples show evidence of rooms so constructed that on entering them the rays of the sun were broken down into the colours of the spectrum. Certain colours were used to signify status (priests, for example, wore blue and gold) and many of the gods had colours assigned to them. Yellow was associated with Isis, and red with Osiris. In Indian philosophy a specific colour is ascribed to each of the **chakras** (see chart and under individual chakras in Section Three). The Theosophists (see Theosophy under **Religions**) associated the colours of the rainbow with certain functions.

The Meanings Of Colour

COLOUR	MEANING
RED	Passion, strong feelings; love, when mixed with rose
Clear red	Moving anger
Dark red	Stagnated anger
Red-orange	Sexual passion
ORANGE	Ambition, vitality
YELLOW	Intellect, emotion
GREEN	Healing, balance, nurture
BLUE	Wisdom, sensitivity
PURPLE	Mental connection with spirit
INDIGO	Moving towards a deeper connection to the spiritual world
LAVENDER	Spiritual energy; spiritual entity
WHITE	Truth and clarity

Light, which we perceive as white, divides into the colours of the spectrum between the frequencies of ultra-violet and infra-red. Each colour has its own frequency and is known to affect us physically, mentally and spiritually. It is now recognized, for instance, that mentally ill patients are calmer in rooms painted green or blue than in those with colours at the warmer end of the spectrum. Healers have known this for many many years and watch with interest as this knowledge is increasingly applied in everyday life. Much of the experimentation with colour therapy owes its origin to the work done by Theo Gimbel.

As with all forms of therapy, working with colour is intensely personal. However, meanings have been ascribed to various colours (see page 195).

Healing with Colour
Often a healer will need to hold a certain colour that is being channelled through them. Holding a colour means holding one's own 'auric field' throughout a healing. The energy level that one uses must be kept intact, ready for whenever the recipient may need it.

There are various ways of holding colour, for example, in 'auric egg' template healing. (The 'auric egg' is the protective layer which surrounds the energy field and to the clairvoyant eye can appear to be damaged or missing.) It is also possible to hold white light, which contains all colours. This is sixth level healing, which involves a very high frequency. There is also spine clearing, in which colour is passed up or down the spine; and **chakra** charging, in which the colours specific to the chakras are held (see **chakra activation techniques** in Section Three) until each has been energized.

It is very important for the healer to practise a kind of colour acceptance or control exercise, in order to be with the colours coming through at any given time during healing. If this is not done properly it is possible to interfere on a mental level with the colour being transmitted in response to the patient's need, by unconsciously changing the field. One must learn what it is to be 'in' a colour rather than just visualizing it or thinking about it. All the colours of the rainbow are part of a holistic healing process. Every colour has its own effect

The colours used in healing

COLOUR	PURPOSE
RED	Charging the **aura**, burning out tumours, warming cold areas.
ORANGE	Charging the etheric field, increasing sexual potency, increasing immunity.
YELLOW	Charging **third chakra**; clearing the head.
GREEN	Energizing **fourth chakra**; balancing, general healing.
BLUE	Cooling, calming, protecting, healing on a mental level.
PURPLE	Connecting to the spirit dimension.
INDIGO	Opening and developing the third eye.
LAVENDER	Cleansing the aura of negative vibration.
WHITE	Can be used to clear and 'tune up' the electro-magnetic field.
GOLD	Strengthens and charges energy field; increases awareness of divine energy.
SILVER	Strong purification of energy field.
VELVET BLACK	Brings one into a state of grace, silence and peace with God
PURPLE BLUE	Takes away pain during physical work; helps to expand awareness in order to realize task.

within a field, and each colour can be used to energize the chakra that metabolizes that colour. Suggestions on the use of colour in everyday life will be found under the individual **chakras** in Section Three.

Higher frequency colours

GOLD	Connection to one's own concept of God; in the service of humankind, unconditional love.
SILVER	Communication with other dimensions.
BLACK	Absence of light, leading to a forgetting of one's life purpose.
BLACK VELVET	Before the dawn of light; entrances to other realities. The Void.
MAROON	Moving into a spiritual task. Recognizing one's own validity.

CONSCIOUSNESS

Normal consciousness is thought to consist of separate moments of awareness connected by memory. A similar connectedness can be experienced in other types of consciousness, particularly by sensitives who are aware of them and can sense the transitions that occur. Deepening understanding of one's inner being, for example through meditation, makes it possible to change or enhance one's state of awareness. Initially this process may produce a sense of awe, but with practice it becomes natural and habitual according to the situation in which one finds oneself.

A step beyond individual consciousness is cosmic consciousness, a mystical experience through which we begin to understand the significance of belonging to a vast 'Universal Mind', the collective unconscious. This large, group mind links all individual consciousness and is the sum total of all knowledge acquired by man. It is shared racial memories, the inherited unconscious and those archetypal memories that belong to all of us. Only when we reach a certain stage of understanding are we able to access the collective unconscious and develop clairvoyance and other psychic skills. The individual who reaches this stage becomes conscious of both the one and the many, he recognizes order in the universe and realizes that everything 'fits together'. He exists in a heightened state or higher form of consciousness and is prepared to work for the greater good rather than individual success. He does not simply live in the present but becomes conscious of his part in creating a future for the world.

COUNSELLING
See **Therapies**

CRANIAL OSTEOPATHY
See **Therapies**

CREATIVE VISUALIZATION

Creative visualization is a very positive, self-affirming method of transforming one's life. We all have different ways of preventing ourselves from achieving what we want. The use of **affirmation** is one way of influencing our lives so that things happen the way we want them to. A simpler alternative is the technique known as visualization.

Creative visualization is deliberate day-dreaming or focused fantasizing. When day-dreaming we tend to begin with the statement 'Wouldn't it be lovely if.......', and then cancel this out by following up with 'But it will never happen'. The first stage in realizing our dreams is, therefore, to learn not to make negative statements, and indeed to learn not to entertain the thought of failure. Because anything can happen when we fantasize and day-dream, it is important that we do our best to make our visualization as perfect as we can. Here we immediately experience a problem, because what one person may consider perfect another will not. For example, you may decide that one small visualization in complete detail is perfection, while another person may agree that detail is important but feel that the visualization should be expansive. A third person may feel that perfection is the actual manifestation, or occurrence, of their visualization. Each person must learn to understand their own process in this respect.

As a preliminary to creative visualization, it is often necessary to experiment with our day-dreaming and fantasizing and to decide what is comfortable for us. For those of a particularly pragmatic turn of mind, it may even be necessary to learn how to day-dream!

The seven stages of creative visualization are:
● Setting the scene in as much detail as you can.
● Visualizing yourself and others participating in your scenario.
● Refining the detail, rejecting things that are obviously not feasible or are excessive, and accepting and adding additional detail where possible.
● Seeing and feeling yourself participating in your visualization; this is slightly different from Stage Two in that your participation should be possible.
● Testing your doubts and fears. These may range from 'Have I the right to expect this?' to 'Someone will stop me....'. It should encompass a huge range of statements in between, including 'Do I really want this?'.
● Accepting that whatever you are visualizing can happen for you. Giving yourself an acceptable present, both in the sense of a gift and the here and now.
● Taking responsibility for allowing your visualization to happen, accepting the notion that you have, and can have, a sustainable future.

Exercise
Let us assume that you have decided to change your life by finding a new flat in which to live.

Stage One might mean that you decide on a one-bedroom flat. The bedroom is light and airy, quite large with a double bed and fitted wardrobes. Visualize this room in as much detail as you can. Then work in the same way on the living room, kitchen and bathroom, and whatever else you think you require. This might include the area in which you wish to live, the rent you wish to pay, the distance from public transport and other such details. Be as specific as you like, and as fanciful as you dare. Allow your imagination total freedom.

Stage Two suggests that you see yourself enjoying your new environment, perhaps settling in, inviting friends round, and participating. This stage is vitally important because it puts you into the framework, not just observing the flat as something 'out there'. Spend time on this, but stay focused without allowing your mind to wander. If it does begin to wander, bring the visualization back into focus and concentrate again.

Stage Three means that you would need to be fairly rigorous in 'pruning' the visualization. For example, it would be useless having materials that require a lot of upkeep if you hate cleaning. It would be pointless having a large garden if your job often takes you away travelling – unless you visualize a change of job as well! Often your unconscious self will take over at this point and make you more aware of your requirements. At this stage you will tend to move away from what you want to what you actually need.

Stage Four occurs when you are able to experience what it is like to be within your visualization. As suggested previously, it is somewhat different from Stage Two in that you can allow yourself feelings and emotions as appropriate. Often this gives you a flavour of the emotions and feelings you would like more of, and engenders a positive feeling.

Stage Five can feel very strange after such positivity, because it deals with negative feelings. However, it is almost a self-test and reveals those blocks you may put on your own progress, enabling you to deal with them before they occur. Often this stage entails being firm with yourself and refusing to entertain the idea that anything can go wrong, or that it 'can't happen'.

Stage Six is a natural progression from stage five, and entails accepting the new situation. Without being too fanciful you are giving yourself a gift – the here and now that you have created, a present that is acceptable. It is often at this stage that your new flat will begin to appear. Often something approximating to your visualization will be brought to your notice. Some details will differ, and it is up to you whether to accept an approximation or wait for a better materialization.

Stage Seven occurs when you accept the manifestation of your visualization, and create a reality that you are prepared to take responsibility for. You are capable of sustaining the reality without a problem – until the next time you need a new flat!

Working with Creative Visualization

It has taken longer to describe the various stages than it will take you to carry out the process. With practice you will become more proficient at visualization, and will instinctively feel what is possible. In order for visualization to succeed it is necessary to persevere – it is no use visualizing what you want once and simply expecting it to happen.

Creative visualization works by affecting your unconscious, and allowing you to give yourself permission to be creative and often to create. The more you consciously reinforce your own desires, the more they are likely to happen. Thus it is vital to remember that part of the process is visualizing what can be sustained when it does become real. One might visualize a change of employment, for instance, then discover that the hours that have to be worked are impossible. While you are learning the process it is a good idea to set a modest visualization goal but to include as much detail as possible. Attention to detail is one of the keys to successs with any visualization method. The more confidence you have the greater the likelihood of your visualization becoming reality.

Some visualizers like to feel that they are co-operating with their own universe, in which anything is possible. Others may feel that they are drawing desired aims towards them. We each have our own way. Another method of creating an acceptable present is through 'replacement'. In this technique you visualize yourself in your present situation, then in your future situation, and then very quickly replace the former with the latter. Replacement does work, though it requires more confidence than other methods.

If your desire is not fulfilled, the belief that it was not meant for you, or that there is something better, should be of some comfort. Creative visualization should not only be used for the attainment of material desires, however. It has a wider application, to change conditions on a universal level. This involves a huge sense of responsibility and a deep awareness of the issues involved. Group visualization with intent can be a powerful agent of change in the world.

CRYSTALS

The following information is presented in as simple a way as possible for those who wish to explore their personal progress along the spiritual path. The methods given have been proven to achieve the desired results and take you from the acquisition of the crystal (or mineral) through the preliminary phases of preparation to the utilization of crystalline energies. You are encouraged to discover additional techniques relating to you personally.

Choosing a Crystal

'Finding' crystals or being open to them 'finding' you are the best techniques for obtaining the crystals you need. One may acquire them by various methods – for example, buying them, receiving them as gifts or, very occasionally, unearthing them. Because our lives are so full, many of us will *only* come into contact with crystals as gifts or in shops. One relatively common way of 'finding' a crystal is by using the 'first recognition' method:

● Stand in front of a group of crystals.

● Close your eyes.

● Open your eyes quickly and pick up the first crystal you see or the one that attracts you.

● When holding a particular crystal or running your hand over it, you may experience an energy 'reaction', such as a tingling sensation, heat or a flash of light.

At other times you may feel drawn to a particular crystal without knowing why. The crystal may not necessarily be for you, and could be for somebody else (possibly somebody you have not yet met). You can help that person have the crystal by buying it and keeping it until the time comes when you may present it to them.

If you are choosing a crystal for a specific purpose (meditation or healing, for example), you should hold that purpose in mind while choosing. Some people may sense an energy 'reaction' from a certain crystal. This response could, as above, take the form of a tingling sensation, heat or a flash of light.

Consciously choosing a crystal for somebody else is also quite easy. Visualize the person for whom you are choosing, project that visualization on to the crystals and select the one to which you relate. Another method is to close your eyes, visualize the person for whom you are choosing the crystal, and when you open your eyes be aware of which crystal attracts you.

Upon receiving a new crystal it is recommended that a dedication is made. This can be achieved by holding the crystal while consciously thinking that the crystal be used only for good purposes.

Cleansing

You may well feel that you want to clean your crystal, especially when you first receive it. There are many different methods. The following are the most practical:

● Take the crystal to the sea, clean it in sea water, and allow the water to wash over it. The crystal should then be left in the sun where it can 'energize'.

● Put the crystal in commercial sea-salt for at least seven and up to 24 hours, rinse with pure water and 'energize' in the sun. (*Note:* Never use abrasive substances, and ensure that salt is properly dissolved, otherwise it may impair the surface of your crystal and affect its properties.)

● Soak the crystal in salt water for anything from one to seven days. Use approximately three tablespoons of salt to a cup of water – the water must cover the stone. Put the salt water in a glass container with the crystal and leave in a sunny place.

● The following is a cleansing method that has been used for hundreds of years in African and native American cultures. Smudge the crystal with a sage stick or favourite incense; in the latter, let the smoke from the incense engulf the stone.

● Put the crystal in the middle of a large group of crystals or on top of another mineral that is a specific energizer, such as rock crystal, for 12 to 24 hours.

● Clean the crystal in flowing spring, lake, river or tap water, and then energize it by leaving it in the sun. Water is known to be a cleanser and is efficient in cleansing negativity from all known materials.

Reactivating and Programming

There are many ways of 'awakening' crystals, that is, reactivating them

– for example, by sounding prayer or other bells or wind chimes near the crystal. This aligns the energy of the crystal structure so it can be efficiently directed.

Crystals are prepared for programming by charging them. There are several ways of doing this. Below are three of the most common:

● Place the crystal in a large crystal cluster.

● Place the crystal in the centre of a circle comprised of other crystals whose ends are pointing towards the centre.

● Put the crystal in sun or moonlight. Some people believe that the days relating to the summer and winter solstices, the full and the new moon, and the vernal and autumnal equinox are more heavily charged.

Programming a crystal aligns the energy of the crystal to the intent. Using a carefully thought out **affirmation** and directing this to the centre of the crystal is sufficient to programme the crystal.

HEALING STONES

The stones listed below have all been used for their healing properties. It is believed that each stone emits a certain energy that may be beneficial if the wearer is receptive to its powers.

Agate A member of the quartz family, it is available in a range of natural and dyed colours. Agate has general healing properties, and improves self-esteem.

Amethyst A crystalline type of quartz with a rich, purple colour. Its composition aids creative thinking, and is thought to protect against blood diseases, neuralgia, fits, grief and insomnia. It is also a specific against drunkenness.

Aquamarine An attractive clear silicate, containing aluminium and beryllium. The stone varies in colour from a greenish blue to a highly prized deeper blue. Aquamarine is good for the eyes and it helps against nerve, throat, liver and stomach troubles.

Aventurine A quartz stone found in various colours (commonly green), aventurine is good for skin conditions.

Bloodstone Another quartz, but of a dark green colour, flecked with red jasper. Bloodstone strengthens the will to do good.

Carnelian A beautiful translucent quartz, of a red or orange colour. Carnelian makes the voice strong and is recommended for rheumatism, depression and neuralgia.

Citrine Like amethyst this is a form of crystalline quartz, but it has an attractive yellow colour. 'Sherry' or 'brandy' citrine is a deep yellow orange. Wearing citrine may bring greater control over the emotions and help blood circulation.

Coral Not a gemstone, this is the calcareous remains of marine organisms. The colour varies, but pink to deep red are the types most commonly used in jewellery. Coral may help anaemia and bladder conditions.

Emerald This is a precious stone which, like aquamarine, is a silicate containing aluminium and beryllium. The colour is a deep dark green. Emerald improves the intellect and memory; it may also help with some cases of insomnia.

Garnet The name given to a group of gemstones of varying composition. Pyrope garnet contains magnesium and its colour is deep blood red. Almandine garnet contains iron and ranges in colour from orange to purple red. Garnet protects against depression and promotes self-confidence and self-esteem.

Jade A silicate of calcium and magnesium, thought to be beneficial in treating kidney complaints; 'nephrite' comes from the Greek word for jade. The most highly prized stones are green in colour; blue and white jade may also be found.

Jasper A mixed type of quartz which is found in various colours. Red jasper is an attractive type commonly seen. Jasper improves the sense of smell and helps problems with the liver and kidneys and also with epilepsy.

Lapis lazuli A mixture of minerals having a deep blue colour often containing glistening flakes of 'fool's gold'. This is an ancient stone and is recommended for heart and vascular conditions.

Malachite The best examples of this attractive vivid green ornamental stone show banding. The copper in malachite helps with asthma.

Moonstone A silicate containing aluminium and potassium. The stone has a milky sheen, the best stones containing a bluish colour. Moonstone gives inspiration and enhances the emotions.

Onyx A type of agate often stained a uniform jet-black and given a high polish. Onyx aids concentration and is an important healing agent in certain ear diseases.

Opal A hydrated silica that shows a strong play of colours; highly prized for jewellery. Opal helps in lung conditions.

Peridot A silicate containing magnesium and iron. The bottle-green colour has a soft, almost oily appearance. Peridot aids digestion and improves digestive complaints.

Rock-crystal Pure quartz, clean and colourless. This is an important healing stone with general healing properties. It assists the wearer by promoting intuitive powers.

Rose-quartz A translucent quartz, rose-quartz enlivens the imagination and calms the emotions.

Ruby A precious stone, ruby is an oxide of aluminium, coloured red by the presence of chromium. Ruby improves mental ability.

Sapphire The same composition as ruby but with a rich blue colour due to traces of iron and titanium. Sapphire can also be colourless, yellow, or green. Sapphire is the stone of friendship and love. It gives devotion, faith and imagination.

Smoky quartz An attractive crystalline that is smoky grey to black in colour . It is used to bring good luck.

Tiger's eye A quartz mineral in which the crystals are needle-like and reflect the light to give the tiger-eye effect. Tiger's eye is worn for clearer thinking.

Tourmaline A complex silicate containing aluminium and boron. Colours range from pink through to yellow, greens and blue. Tourmaline attracts inspiration, good-will and friendship.

Turquoise An opaque stone given a blue-green colour by the presence of copper. Turquoise is a great protector; this is a good stone to give as a present.

Astrological Crystals
Also see **Crystal Gazing** under **Divination** and, for more esoteric information on the subject, under each of the chakras in Section Three, Journey of a Lifetime.

Many traditions have evolved that attribute certain gemstones to certain astrological signs. There are no right and wrong stones to have, but below is a table that gives the gemstones associated with each sign of the zodiac.

ASTROLOGICAL SIGN	STONE
Aries	Bloodstone, Diamond
Taurus	Emerald, Rose Quartz
Gemini	Aquamarine, Agate
Cancer	Pearl, Moonstone
Leo	Citrine, Onyx
Virgo	Garnet, Sapphire
Libra	Tourmaline, Jade
Scorpio	Black Opal, Ruby
Sagittarius	Topaz, Peridot
Capricorn	Tiger Eye, Jet

| Aquarius | Lapis Lazuli, Amber |
| Pisces | Turquoise, Amethyst |

CURSES

In the West a curse is regarded as a form of superstition. One plausible explanation is that curses have an effect on the subtle body or aura of the recipient, and it is this which creates the problem. The power of thought directed with intent can both harm and heal (see **Absent Healing**). Curses are negative thought directed with a specifically malign intent. When the power of thought is backed up by the power of words or of particular rituals, then the effect can be even more profound. Logic denies the possibility of such an effect, but many people are intuitively aware when negative thought is directed against them.

D

DANCE AND DANCE THERAPY
See **Therapies**

DEJA-VU

Psychologists regard the phenomenon of déjà-vu (lit. 'already seen') as an inappropriate excitation of nerve endings which produces a double image. Another explanation is that the two halves of the brain are not acting in harmony and that an image is received slightly in advance of the reality. However, neither explains the flashback effect, when the perceiver feels that he has been in a particular place as another person. The following explanations of the phenomenon are perhaps more satisfying:

It is believed that the surroundings that induce the feeling of déjà-vu may have been brought to the individual's attention while astrally travelling during sleep or in dreams. In some instances of déjà-vu – for example, when a place is seen as it was centuries ago – the perceiver may need to become aware of past life experiences in order to re-learn a lesson in this life. Finally, experiences in a previous lifetime may overshadow the here and now and cause particular patterns of behaviour or belief in the individual.

DICE
See **Divination**

DIET

One of the easiest ways to change your life is to reappraise the food you eat. By eating more greenstuffs, fresh fruits and vegetables, you are accomplishing two important things. The first is altering the type of energy that is taken into the body and bringing it more in tune with the natural vibrations. The second is giving your body the opportunity to use energy more effectively. Most of the dietary changes that you decide upon should be made gradually and not all at once. It is worthwhile experimenting with the various groups of food to find out what suits your digestive system best. Also, it is never advisable to impose on other people the changes you have decided to make for yourself. If Little Jimmy doesn't like spinach, it won't matter to him that Popeye, or Mummy, does.

The following suggestions provide the basic daily dietary requirements your body needs:

● Fresh fruit or juices at least twice a day.

● Where practicable, salads containing principally greenstuffs twice a day.

● Fresh vegetables, preferably raw or steamed, once a day.

● Eight to twelve ounces of fresh vegetable juice.

● Two ounces of fresh sprouted seeds such as mustard seed, alfalfa, mung beans.

● Four ounces of yoghurt or cultured dairy products, such as crème fraîche and unsweetened fromage frais.

● If lacto-vegetarian, two to four ounces of cheese or one egg.

● Between two to four slices of bread – preferably wholemeal or granary.

● One or two servings of soy protein or, if not allergic to them, nuts.

● Adequate multi-vitamin and mineral supplementation. (Your health food practitioner or pharmacist can advise you on this.)

If you decide to change your diet, do so gradually, introducing each new food at intervals of about a week. Often on making this type of change your body will produce flatulence. This will stop once your system gets used to the new foods, so be patient. You will need to try your new way of eating for at least six weeks before making a judgement as to its success. Hopefully, you will experience a new feeling of vitality and lightness. It is possible that your perceptions will become sharper, colours will become brighter and for a time you may be intolerant of noise. Equally, you may discover that music, books and paintings that you previously enjoyed no longer hold the same interest. You may find that relationships shift very subtly, that you decide to change your job or make some other kind of radical alteration in your lifestyle. These spontaneous changes are totally in order as your own vibration is changing and others become aware of this.

DISEASE

All 'dis'-ease arises from an imbalance. From a holistic practitioner's point of view this imbalance can arise in many ways. For instance, any difficulty experienced on a physical level will have an effect on the mental attitude of an individual, which in turn may affect the emotions, and also spiritual outlook. Conversely, a spiritual difficulty – such as a loss of faith – can profoundly affect a person's physical being, making the healing of wounds or other trauma difficult.

From a holistic point of view, therefore, everything must be considered in order to restore the balance, and each aspect of the disease treated on every level. A slipped disc, for example, would appear to be purely physical in origin, but it may be healed by working additionally on fears and doubts that may have arisen, perhaps from the individual's change in occupation. Depending on which area of the spine is damaged, the slipped disc may be caused, or made worse, by a conflict between the person's principles and those of others around him; also see **Body Awareness** and **Therapies**.

A great deal of relief can be derived if the sufferer – from whatever disease – explores ways of activating awareness of the various imbalances that can occur, possibly by using various complementary therapies. The **chakra** system can help us to identify and deal with the underlying causes of difficulties – see Section Three.

DIVINATION
Also see **Oracles**

Divination was initially an attempt to discover what the divine intent was – that is, what the gods intended for mankind, and therefore for each individual. It was recognized that certain patterns and **symbols** meant different things and, as with the principle 'as above, so below', that the gods' intent could be mirrored or pictured in everyday life.

Hence, symbols were seen in the way that candles burn, or in the way that tea leaves formed patterns, or even in the way that the animal entrails of slaughtered animals fell and could be interpreted successfully. Those people capable of interpreting the simple symbols would tend to develop their **psychic abilities**, and would be able to make intuitive interpretations. The patterns seen in the palms of the hands or in the way that cards fell were gradually discovered to have a common meaning, and from these observations a body of knowledge was developed. This, combined with intuitive interpretation, led to the development of other methods of divination which could more properly be called sciences. This was particularly so when mathematical calculation became involved, as in **numerology** and **astrology**. The **I Ching**, for instance, with its 64 hexagrams (six-line figures), is as complex in its permutations as many of today's modern computer programs.

Today the method of divination chosen will usually depend on whether the diviner is of a scientific or artistic bent. It is often helpful to be able to check one's findings using more than one method, although by tradition the gods (or powers that be) do not like to be questioned continually. Therefore, after a time of protracted use, the pendulum, for instance, may not function efficiently and must be left to rest. As with anything connected to the unknown, certain **rituals** have become associated with divination. Many people now have developed their own set of rituals which are often based on a deeper psychological understanding of older ones. When dealing with esoteric matters, it is always wise to treat the method with respect and integrity.

Candles

Candles can be used in divination particularly to decide how soon an event will occur. The candle is marked off in sections, representing days, weeks or months, and then lit. It is left to burn until it goes out of its own accord, the level the candle reaches giving the answer to the enquirer's question. As can be imagined, this is not an accurate forecasting tool. (See the section on **magic** for a fuller description of the use of candles as spiritual or magical tools.)

Crystal gazing

Crystal gazing has always been a favourite method of divination by virtue of its reliable and convenient form and because it rarely involves the clairvoyant in an unpleasant or distressing experience. The ancients marvelled at the physical properties of **crystals** and various theories abounded. The most commonly held was that rock crystal consisted simply of water that had been subjected to a phenomenal degree of cold far below freezing. Another was that crystals are the result of the solidification of water by intense heat. And a third that crystals were trapped light or energy.

Crystal gazing, or one or other of its allied forms of 'scrying', was used in ancient times as a method of clairvoyance. The ancient Persians were the first crystal gazers. The Greeks used a clear mirror, a practice revived in Europe during the Middle Ages.

The globe first used for scrying was probably made of natural rock crystal, either quartz or beryl. A deep blue or yellowish beryl is particularly favourable to the production of symbolic visions, with clear colourless quartz often yielding the best results. Some clairvoyants prefer an ovoid or egg-shaped mass of glass or crystal instead of a sphere.

Why visions may be seen in crystals has baffled scientists, and no conclusive explanation is available. Perhaps the 'best' one comes from this author's teacher of psychology, who suggested that the crystal heightened awareness by making the nerve endings fire in a different way from normal.

Dice

The use of dice for all manner of games dates back to ancient times. In ancient Egypt, Greece and the countries of the Far East, cubes of wood, metal or glass with their sides numbered from one to six were popular for gaming and as a means of consultation. The opposite faces of a dice always add up to seven, a magical number of manifestation.

Traditionally preparation is very uncomplicated. A circle is drawn in white on the board on which the throws are to be made. Any dice that fall or roll outside this circle are not considered, unless they fall on the floor, when it is an omen of furious argument. Certain rituals are associated with dice throwing:

● Three dice must be used and shaken with the left hand.
● The best time for dice throwing is in the calm of the evening.
● Strict silence must be maintained during the shaking and throwing. (If the same number should turn up more than once, it signifies the coming of important news.)
● To throw the dice so that one remains on top of the other can indicate the need for extreme caution in business, or in dealing with the opposite sex.

Dominoes

Dominoes are interpreted according to the laws of **numerology** and the meanings traditionally assigned to each piece. First of all the pieces must be shuffled and left face downwards then one is drawn and the number shown. Dominoes, as with all divinatory tools, should be treated with respect. Not more than three pieces should be drawn in a single consultation or on the same day, otherwise the 'reading' may be misleading. To draw the same domino twice running strengthens the prediction and indicates almost immediate fulfilment.

Dowsing

Dowsing using a divining rod is also called rhabdomancy. The dowser commonly uses a cleft stick. Many prefer this stick to be of a living material, such as hazel wood, which is thought to be the origin of the magician's wand. Almost anything can be searched for by this method. The cleft stick is held lightly in both hands and the ground (or map, if done at a distance) quartered until the stick dips in a recognizable way.

Although the usefulness of dowsing has been proved many times, no one knows exactly how it works. However, bearing in mind that brain activity is electrical, there may be some interaction between the electro-magnetic fields of the dowser, the rod and the object being dowsed for. Experiments have shown that sensitives are more able to pick up vibrations from people if there is excitement, suggesting that dowsing and **telepathy** share basic principles, and that 'radiations' are not involved.

Dowsing may also be performed with a pendulum, in which case the method is slightly different. The question put by the dowser has to be in a form answerable by a simple 'yes' or 'no'. How the pendulum swings depends on the energy levels within the questioner. For some people a clockwise swing denotes 'yes' and an anti-clockwise swing 'no'. For others a circular motion is 'yes', etc. To test the pendulum (which can be made of any substance, such as crystal, wood, or even metal), a question is asked to which the answer is known: e.g., 'Am I a woman?' or 'Am I a man?' Once the 'yes'/'no' paradigm has been decided, the actual question is then asked. A neutral answer may sometimes be received if, for instance, the question is not answerable by a positive or negative.

It is also possible to dowse for health matters or to decide correct medication, by questioning the pendulum, either over a sample of the material, or even the words written on a piece of paper. This, however, requires an element of trust as much as **intuition**. A pendulum can also give an indication of when to do things; for instance, think about each day of the week, or day in the month, and question the pendulum on each one in turn, as described above, until it reacts positively. Thus, Monday – negative; Tuesday – negative; Wednesday – negative; Thursday – positive; Friday – positive; Saturday – negative/positive; Sunday – negative. So, in answer to the question 'When would it be best to carry out a certain action?' – Thursday and Friday are best, while Saturday is less favourable. Or, first of March, positive, second of March, positive, third of March, negative and so on.

Dreams

Since ancient times dreams have been thought to be prophetic. Dream interpretation is an enormous subject area and certainly too broad to even begin to discuss here. There are as many interpretations as there are dreams. (For those interested in pursuing this further, see my book *10,000 Dreams Interpreted*.) It is possible to solve problems while we are in the dream state, when the sleeping self has the freedom to work them through. Simply concentrate on the problem before falling asleep. When you wake the answer will probably be already formed.

Eastern astrology
Also see **Astrology**

The Eastern zodiac, devised in ancient India and China, operates in a cycle of twelve years instead of twelve months as in the system used in the West. Each year of the cycle is symbolized by a particular animal. A traditional Japanese story explaining how this came about runs as follows: Buddha called all the animals of the world to him. He promised that those who came to pay him homage would receive a gift. They would each be given a year which would thereafter be named for them. Of all the animals in the world, only these twelve came, and they came in this order: Rat, Ox, Tiger, Rabbit, Dragon, Snake, Horse, Sheep, Monkey, Cock, Dog and Boar.

From these twelve symbols our fortune and characteristics may be told. People born in one year may also have characteristics belonging to those born in another. It is believed that there are three phases in our lives and that the fortune of each phase is clearly defined.

I Ching
Also see **Mysticism**

The *I Ching* is recognized in the West principally as a tool for divination, but it is also a book of profound wisdom put together some 3,000 years ago. *I Ching*, which means Book of Changes, is said to contain within it the answer to every question anyone could ever ask. Its rich symbolism offers many meanings and the opportunity for almost anyone to find answers to their problems. Its central idea is the age-old one of how we as individuals can establish order out of chaos.

The *I Ching* can help us to attain serenity and harmony within our surroundings, and may be used as a map towards spiritual awareness.

Divination by this method begins with the throwing of three coins. The way these coins fall (e.g., three heads, two tails and a head) is symbolized by a line which has been given a specific meaning. This act is carried out six times which builds into a hexagram or 'ideagram' which in itself is symbolic. The image formed was given a short explanation by the ancient Chinese which is still in use today. At the moment the coins are thrown, it is as though time stops and is captured, like an image in a photograph.

As with all such systems, the more you use *I Ching* the deeper becomes your understanding of its symbolism and through that, ultimately, a deeper understanding of yourself.

Numerology

Out of numerology mankind developed the laws of mathematics that govern our lives. Many algebraic calculations, for example, were secret formulae used by alchemists and magicians. Chief among the architects of numerology were the Greeks and the Hebrews and, to a lesser extent, the ancient Egyptians.

Numerology is concerned with the reduction of everything under consideration to the form of an arithmetical figure. The figure can then be interpreted by reference to the traditional meanings of numbers. These interpretations date back to the time when man first visualized the interpretation of a number and associated it with a spiritual meaningfulness. It should be understood that figures themselves are merely signs that represent an idea of number and are meaningless in themselves. There are many systems of numerology in existence, but the most widely used comes from an ancient and reliable source and is based chiefly on the nine primary numbers, represented by the figures 1 to 9 inclusive. All numbers greater than 9 can be reduced to one of the primary numbers, except eleven and multiples of eleven. These are the 'master' or spiritual numbers, which have their own interpretation, but can also be reduced to smaller numbrs and give a less difficult course of action.

The most widely known calculation is that of the birth date. Thus,

23 April 1966 would become (2+3)=5+4 = 9 +(1+9+6+6)= 22= 31 (3+1) = 4. This person can then research the meaning of the number 4. Other numerological calculations can be made from the name by assigning a number to each letter.

1	2	3	4	5	6	7	8	9
A	B	C	D	E	F	G	H	I
J	K	L	M	N	O	P	Q	R
S	T	U	V	W	X	Y	Z	

The Oraculum (or Book of Fate)
Also see **Oracle**

Also known as the Sibylline Leaves, this method was said to have been used by Napoleon. It consists of a set of instructions which show the user how to reduce their question to a set of asterisks laid out in various patterns. The answer is divined from these patterns. Difficult to use, it nevertheless allows you to concentrate on the question in hand and may possibly allow the correct answer to surface intuitively.

Palmistry
Also see **Cheirology**, under **Therapies**

Palmistry was first practised in the Orient some 5,000 years ago. Highly regarded by the Greeks, it is referred to extensively in classical literature. Today it is one of the most respected of the divining arts and capable of giving relatively accurate forecasts. The skill of the palmist is paramount to its effectiveness.

Palmistry is a way of interpreting the future, and many clairvoyants use it as an adjunct to their skills. However, it can also help us to make decisions about ongoing everyday matters, such as career moves or changes in lifestyle. The shape of the hand, the length of the fingers, the way the hand is held and its softness and hardness are all taken into account before the lines and marks in the palm itself are interpreted according to given formulae.

The lines on the hand show the trends in life rather than the actual future – they do not necessarily forecast the arrival of the proverbial tall, dark, handsome stranger. Principally, the left hand holds the experiences we are given, or must go through, and the right hand is what we make of them.

Phrenology

Phrenology is the art of reading the skull, and is a branch of **physiognomy**. It was discovered by Franz Joseph Gall, a doctor who practised in Vienna in the 18th century. About 30 organs said to represent the mental faculties were identified. Importance was attached to the relative size and development of each organ.

Physiognomy

Physiognomy is the art and science of reading character from the facial and bodily form. Used in a different way it means the ability to interpret facial or bodily contours with a view to predicting a person's course of action.

Physiognomy was highly regarded by the ancient Greeks who used it as a way of assessing character. They believed that men could be compared with animals in their physiognomy and character. Seventeen animal types were identified, e.g., bull-headed, sheepish, feline, etc.

Playing cards

Playing cards link with the minor arcana of the tarot and have a special place in divination. Frivolous questions will tend to receive frivolous answers, or perhaps nebulous explanations. Cards tend to be used for practical questions and often predict an expected outcome. Various layouts, handed down through the ages, may be used.

Psychometry

Strictly defined, psychometry is the ability to link into the vibrations of an object and read its history. The belief is that most objects are similar to recording machines and pick up the emotions and feelings of their owners or wearers. Where there have been several owners of, for example, a piece of jewellery, the reader must be able to differentiate between the experiences of the various owners. Psychometry makes it possible to evaluate a person's future actions and to link in through the object being read to the **Akashic records**.

It is important that the reader suspends belief and does not allow his or her judgement to become clouded by the emotions – and perhaps problems – touched into. As in **clairvoyance**, images that arise may be symbolic or belong to memory (see **Sitting**). Many sitters prefer psychometry to clairvoyance, possibly because it tends to be the most showy demonstration of psychic powers. Almost any object can be used, from a flower that has been held by the sitter to a strand of their hair.

Runes

Ten years ago few people had heard of runes, an ancient alphabetic script each of whose letters possesses a meaningful name as well as a signifying sound. Runes were employed for poetry, for inscriptions and divination yet never evolved as a spoken language. Little has been written about the runes as a contemporary oracle. The interpretation of the runes for divination in ancient times has long been lost to the mass of people. The passing on of sacred knowledge through initiation was probably practised among the Rune Masters of old. Recently runes have enjoyed a renaissance of interest, with the ancient meanings rediscovered intuitively by **sensitives** and developed as a tool for spiritual advancement.

The runes were last in popular use in Iceland during the late Middle Ages, and were often employed by warriors bent on conquest. From the beginning the runes had a ritual function and were used for divination and evoking higher powers that could influence the lives of people. There were runes and spells to influence crops, love, healing, the weather, the tides, runes of fertility, cursing and the removal of curses, birth and death. Runes were carved on objects in daily use, such as amulets, drinking cups, battle spears and the prows of Viking ships.

By about AD 98 runes were becoming widely known on the Continent, carried from place to place by warriors, tradesmen, merchants and, later, Anglo-Saxon missionaries. However, for this information to be disseminated to other cultures, a common alphabet was required. The alphabet devised became known as *futhark*, after its first six letters. Although later Anglo-Saxon alphabets expanded to include as many as 33 letters, in Britain the traditional Germanic *futhark* is comprised of 24 runes. These were divided into three families of eight runes – three and eight being numbers credited with magical qualities. The three groups, known as *aettir*, were named for the Norse gods Freyr, Hagal and Tyr. Later a twenty-fifth rune – a blank – was introduced and this was included in the traditional 24-rune *futhark*.

The runes are shaken together and then laid out according to accepted patterns. Interpretation varies according to whether the runes are the right way up or reversed.

Tarot
Also see **Throat Chakra** in Section Three
The origins of Tarot cards – who first designed them, where, when and for what purpose – are vague and elusive. However, these cards have been in use for at least 500 years and maybe much longer. The oldest extant tarot deck is that painted for the Visconti Sforza family in Milan at some time between the 13th and 15th centuries.

The Tarot cards are not **occult** – that is, they are not supernatural or magical in the sense that those words generally convey. That may be the reason for their continuing popularity. There is evidence to suggest that in mid 15th-century Europe they were freely available to anyone who could afford them.

Writers on the subject of the tarot have suggested a wide range of sources for the cards. Some claim that their origins lie in the religious rituals and symbols of the ancient Egyptians, others that they come from the mystery cults of Mithras in the first centuries after Christ. Others have cited links to pagan Celtic beliefs or to the poetry cycles of the Holy Grail that emerged in Western Europe during the Middle Ages. The first documented decks of tarot cards appeared in the second half of the 15th century and were painted in Italy. There are three packs of tarot from this time, all of them incomplete.

In the 15th century the word *trionfi* was used in Italy to designate the 22 major arcana. Later this term encompassed the complete deck of cards, comprising the major arcana and the 56 minor arcana.

The minor arcana consist of 56 cards divided into four suits. There is no evidence to suppose that the 22 major and 56 minor arcana derive completely from one original deck of 78 cards. In fact, it is assumed that the figured and numbered cards of the minor arcana were developed independently of, and at a later stage than, the major. There are four suits: swords, wands, cups and pentacles, said to represent the four seasons or the elements of earth, water, fire and air. It has also been suggested that they represent the joys, gains, doubts and fears that every individual faces in life. The four face cards of the minor arcana are the king, queen, knight and page.

In 1500 a complete list of the major arcana, with their names and numbers as used today, was found. When used as a pictorial representation of the 'path' to be followed (or, as some believe, the way in which Isis reassembled the body of Osiris in order to give birth to the Sun God, Horus), it is a representation of the spiritual journey man takes towards Enlightenment. The major arcana are also connected with the Cabbala and the **Tree of Life**.

Tea leaves
Of all the many forms of divination, perhaps the most simple is the reading of tea leaves. Almost anyone who possesses the necessary patience to make a study of the symbols and their meanings can become proficient at it. Although any type of cup may be used, a better result will be achieved if it is a large one with a wide mouth and sides. The inside should be white and without a pattern. The best type of tea to use is China tea, because it produces well-defined pictures.

The enquirer drinks from the cup, leaving about a teaspoonful of liquid in the bottom. The cup is then held in the left hand and moved three times in a circular, anti-clockwise direction while the enquirer concentrates on a question. Then the cup is slowly turned over in the saucer and left there for a minute for the liquid to drain. Any shapes formed out of the tea leaves are then interpreted.

DO-IN
See **Therapies**

DOMINOES
See **Divination**

DOORKEEPER
Also see **Guardian Angel**

In spiritualism, the spirit guide who stays with an individual through-out earthly life is called the 'doorkeeper'. Each person has only one doorkeeper. This permanent guide is a kind of link between the individual and the spirit world and stands on the threshold between this world and the next. The doorkeeper also controls the comings and goings of other guides. Some people prefer to regard the doorkeeper's role as being fulfilled by the individual's own **higher self**, which the personality finds too difficult to recognize except in the guise of another separate entity. It is usually thought that there is a special link between the guide and the individual (see **Group Soul** and **Karma**) and that as part of their own spiritual process these guides have elected not to incarnate as **gurus** but to work as discarnate entities. It is possible to experience these guides through **active imagination**, channelling (see **Medium**), **guided imagery** and **meditation**.

DOWSING
See **Divination**

DRAMA THERAPY
See **Therapies**

DREAMS
See **Divination**

DREAM-WORK
See **Therapies**

E

EASTERN ASTROLOGY
See **Divination**

ENERGY
See **Therapies**

ESSENTIAL OILS

Essential oils have been used since time immemorial for their fragrance and for their therapeutic properties. Unlike **Bach flower remedies**, in which only the essence is extracted, essential oils are the oily perfume component within plants, herbs and flowers. The oils are obtained by distillation or expression.

When used as part of aromatherapy treament the oils produce a twofold effect: immediate mood change and longer term healing. First, the brain receives messages through the olfactory nerves and the lungs which encourage the release of hormones and neuro-chemicals, and thus affects our mood. Secondly, the oils are absorbed directly into the bloodstream via the skin, producing a relatively speedy overall effect on the body. Advice is usually given with a treatment not to bathe for six hours afterwards, otherwise the beneficial effect may be lost.

As a self-help tool, essential oils may be used as a body rub (provided they have first been diluted in a carrier oil, such as almond or other unscented massage oil), in the bath or vaporized in a burner, thus enhancing the effect of a treatment. *Note:* Oils should not be taken by mouth, except under the instruction of a qualified practitioner.

A-Z OF COMMON ESSENTIAL OILS

Essential oils can be uplifting, refreshing, soothing, stimulating or relaxing. Some of the most commonly used oils, together with their effects, are givenbelow.

Aniseed Anise oil is distilled from the dried and crushed seeds of the herb, which originated in the Near East. The oil has a sweet, fresh smell and can be used for cramps, digestive problems and coughs. *Warning*: Because of its fairly high toxicity, this oil is best used only for short periods.

Basil This combines a refreshing fragrance with an uplifting, sparkling effect on body and mind.

Bergamot Extracted from a rare citrus fruit, Bergamot oil is known for its revitalizing, flowery scent, and its relaxing qualities.

Black Pepper The oil is produced by steam-distillation of the dried, crushed fruits of the pepper vine, grown mainly in Indonesia and India. A hot, dry, spicy oil with a deeply warming effect, it is useful for relieving muscular aches and pains, and for stimulating the digestive and lymphatic systems. *Caution:* Black pepper oil must be well diluted before it is applied to the skin.

Cajuput This oil is distilled from a tree that grows abundantly in Malaysia and is used mainly in inhalations for respiratory infections, including coughs, colds and sore throats.

Cardamom Distilled from a tree that grows abundantly in East India and Sri Lanka, this has a warm, spicy aromatic smell. Cardamom has been used in Eastern medicine for over 3000 years as a digestive aid, and in the treatment of nausea, flatulence and diarrhoea.

Cedarwood One of the oldest oils produced (it was used by the ancient Egyptians to embalm their dead), cedarwood has a pleasant, mild, balsamic-woody odour. It is used to treat oily skin, oily hair and dandruff, and also for mucous in coughs and colds.

Chamomile This oil contains a high content of Azulene, and is especially appropriate for people with sensitive skin. Its qualities are soothing and relaxing.

Cinnamon This oil, distilled from the inner bark and leaves of a bush native to East India and Indonesia, has a powerful, warm, sweet-spicy odour. The strongly stimulating properties of cinnamon make it useful for circulatory and respiratory systems. *Caution:* This oil must be well-diluted before use because it can be an irritant.

Citronella Distilled from a type of grass, this has a pungent lemony scent. Its main use is as an effective insect repellent.

Clary Sage A form of the popular garden herb, Clary sage has a distinctively nut-like scent. The oil is warming as well as soothing, and is sometimes used to encourage a feeling of well-being. *Warning:* It should be used with great care, and not during pregnancy.

Coriander An oil distilled from the crushed, ripe seeds of a small herb native to south-eastern Europe. Coriander oil has a fresh spicy scent, is a natural deodorant and aphrodisiac and will stimulate the digestive system.

Cypress Extracted from the leaves of the Mediterranean Cypress tree, this oil has a refreshing fragrance. It is used for invigorating and stimulating the system.

Eucalyptus Obtained from the fresh leaves of the Eucalyptus tree, this refreshing oil has many beneficial properties. It is especially effective at clearing catarrh and mucus from the system.

Fennel Sweet fennel oil is steam-distilled from the crushed seeds of the plant cultivated in Mediterranean Europe. It has a very sweet, fresh smell, similar to aniseed. Fennel is used to treat indigestion and flatulence and is also a mild diuretic.

Frankincense Distilled from the resins that saturate the bark of a small tree found in the Far East, and probably the original 'incense', this can have an elevating and comforting effect.

Geranium Obtained from the leaves of the Pelargonium plant, geranium oil has a fresh, luscious fragrance. If used as a bath oil it produces a cleansing, cooling effect on mind and body.

Grapefruit Expressed from the peel of the grapefruit, this oil is used as a detoxifier and astringent.

Jasmine The most uplifting of all oils, jasmine has a rich, exotic smell. The essential oil can be worn as a perfume, creating a sense of relaxation and enjoyment. It may be used as an aphrodisiac.

Juniper Taken from the berries of the Juniper bush, this oil is well known as an antiseptic. Invigorating and refreshing as a bath oil, it can also be used as a cleanser and toner for oily skin.

Lavender Considered one of the most generally beneficial of all the essential oils, lavender blends well with most other plant essences, adding a softness to most concoctions. Lavender's relaxing elements help soothe away mental and physical fatigue.

Lemon This oil can be used as an antiseptic for the skin. It is well known for its invigorating and fresh aroma.

Lemongrass The oil is obtained from the fragrant everlasting grass indigenous to Asia. It tones and refreshes and is useful for treating skin problems and as an insect repellent.

Mandarin This very sweet-smelling oil is expressed from the ripe peel of the fruit. It is used to treat indigestion arising from gastric problems.
Marjoram Marjoram has a relaxing and calming effect, and is used to aid recuperation after illness.

Melissa The revitalizing and gentle qualities of melissa have been appreciated for centuries; the oil is certainly effective when one is in need of refreshment, and beneficial when treating headaches and nervous asthma.

Myrrh This is distilled from a resin that occurs naturally in the trunks of small trees grown in eastern Africa and Arabia. The oil is amber in colour and sticky. It is used to treat chronic lung conditions and infections of the throat and mouth.

Neroli Distilled from the blossoms of the bitter orange tree, this oil has a refreshing floral smell and is a classic ingredient of high-quality perfumes. It is used to treat depression, anxiety, insomnia and dry skin.

Orange With its uplifting aroma, this pure essential oil has excellent restorative and relaxant properties. It can also have a good effect on dry skin conditions.

Palmarosa Distilled from a grass that grows in India, palmarosa has a pleasantly sweet mildly stimulating floral smell and a regenerative effect on the skin.

Patchouli An oil with aphrodisiac properties, patchouli is distilled mainly in Indonesia, from the dried leaves of a small plant. It has a distinct dry, somewhat woody smell. Oily and problem skin as well as scarring can be treated with patchouli.

Peppermint This is distilled from the dried herb that is native to Europe, although the oil is now mainly produced in the United States. Peppermint is known for its decongestant properties. It is also used to treat many digestive problems, most popularly in the form of a tea.

Pine Pine oil is distilled from the needles and wood chippings of the pine tree. It has a refreshing, sweet, woody smell and is effective in the treatment of respiratory complaints.

Rose An exquisite oil produced from red roses grown in Bulgaria, and more recently in Morocco, rose is a cool and soothing oil and used for treating stress-related conditions and PMT. It is also beneficial for the calming of dry and inflamed skin.

Rosemary Derived from a version of the well known garden herb, Rosemary is used as a cleanser and stimulant for the mind. It is also an effective general pick-me-up. Rosemary can often be used in place of lavender.

Rosewood This particularly light oil has a subtle hint of spice. When used as a bath oil, it helps revive and refresh.

Sage Sage oil is distilled from the herb indigenous to the Northern shores of the Mediterranean. A strongly stimulating oil, it is used to relieve muscular problems, and in the treatment of mouth infections. *Warning:* Sage should not be used during pregnancy.

Sandalwood Taken from the Asian sandalwood tree, this oil is well regarded for its health-giving properties, as well as its musky perfume. Good for treating dehydrated skin, sandalwood is also both uplifting and relaxing.

Tagettes Distilled from a type of marigold, this has a bright orange-green colour coupled with a sweet smell. It is useful for treating foot problems, such as corns. *Warning:* Tagettes oil may photosensitize the skin and should certainly not be used when in the sun.

Tea Tree With a scent similar to eucalyptus, tea tree is a powerful antiseptic and refresher. It can be worked with in different ways and, like lavender, can be used undiluted.

Thyme Thyme oil is a warming and stimulating oil that relieves muscular pain. It has a strong anti-microbial effect and is used to treat many kinds of infections. Thyme oil also strengthens the immune response. *Caution:* The oil must be well diluted before use.

Vetiver Vetiver oil is distilled from the roots of a scented grass grown mainly in India and Indonesia. It has a sweet woody, earthy smell and is calming and relaxing.

Ylang Ylang Considered the strangest of all pure essential oils, its name means 'flower of flowers'. It has a rich scent reminiscent of a mixture of jasmine and almond, and calming, soothing and uplifting qualities. Through its balancing of the masculine and feminine qualities, it has an aphrodisiac effect.

EXORCISM

Exorcism is the removal of 'bad' spirit or negative energy. Extreme emotion leaves behind it disturbed energy, which can be experienced by the living as a **ghost**, or as a negative or malign influence. It can manifest as a force that moves things around or take the form of a spirit possessing the body of another. This latter example is probably the one that most people think of in relation to exorcism.

In times when less was understood about the management of suppressed energy – particularly sexual – such activity could appear as an extreme change of personality and the sufferer thought to be possessed by another entity. If this entity could be driven out, it was thought, then the individual would recover. This driving out was often done by scourging and commanding. Even today, there have been cases where these methods have been used to the detriment of the supposedly possessed. Cases of multiple personality were at one time mis-diagnosed as possession. Nowadays therapeutic techniques such as **psychosynthesis** would be used instead of exorcism.

In cases of hauntings, exorcism is usually carried out by someone who is comfortable with his connection with God or the ultimate – in other words, someone who is not limited in his belief to the physical dimension. Rituals are carried out to allow the spirit to return to its own realm, and to calm the space that has been invaded. An important part of this process is to remove the fear suffered by witnesses, because an unquiet spirit is thought to 'feed off' the disturbed energy.

Poltergeists are also forms of disturbed energy. Such manifestations often occur when there is a sensitive teenager in the house, and occasionally when there has been a birth. It is as though a door has been left ajar through which a wind blows. The door is closed by raising positive energy, through understanding and sometimes exorcism.

F

FAITH HEALING
See **Therapies**

FASTING
See **Therapies**

FELDENKRAIS METHOD
See **Therapies**

FENG SHUI

Feng shui, the Chinese art of placement, is several thousand years old. Pronounced 'fang shway', the words mean wind and water, which are the forces responsible for health, prosperity and good luck. The way of placing objects in different areas of a room or house defines the power within that area. Using the balance of **yin/yang**, the **I Ching** (see **Divination**) and the Five Elements, it is possible to improve well-being and health. Feng shui can be applied with equal success to both living spaces and work spaces. Much better work seems to be done in environments where the principles of feng shui have been applied. The emphasis depends on needs; for instance, the conditions prevailing in a service industry will be different from those in a factory.

FLOTATION THERAPY
See **Therapies**

FREUDIAN ANALYSIS
See **Therapies**

G

GESTALT THERAPY
See **Therapies**

GHOSTS

It could be said that a dead person has truly manifested if a phantom is seen and identified by someone who has no reason to believe that the person is dead. These apparitions often appear to be so solid that they are mistaken for the real person. There is a widely held view among researchers that apparitions of this kind are purely telepathic messages from the person seen. It is more likely that these appearances are a projection of the etheric body of the deceased, which does not fade away until approximately three days after death. An alternative view is that an apparition appearing after a crisis, such as sudden or traumatic death, is the result of out-of-the-ordinary perception - simply ESP – on the part of the perceiver.

While the term 'ghost' is taken to mean any appearance by a dead person, in spiritualistic terms it is more properly the 'shade or residue of an unquiet spirit'. (A spirit is the energy field that is perceived after the etheric body has dispersed.) Most people who see a ghost are totally convinced that it is real on some level, and for some it offers proof of the existence of life after death.

GROUP SOUL

A group soul is similar to a 'spiritual being'. Just as individuals recognize that on a soul level they are part of a greater whole, so a group soul is seen to be part of a greater cosmic being. The principle is that at certain times during the earth's life cycle, a group of souls need to incarnate to fulfil a particular purpose. Some of the energy does not need to incarnate in the earthly sense, but remains connected to those who do in order to ensure the correct 'management' of the incarnated souls at that point. Often, members of the group soul have an instinctive recognition of one another without necessarily understanding why.

Sometimes, a group soul is taken to mean a group of people who share one entity as a **higher self** or spiritual **guide**.

GROUP THERAPY
See **Therapies**

GUARDIAN ANGEL/GUIDE
Also see **Higher Self and Doorkeeper**
It is believed that an entity or guide who stays with you throughout your life on earth is your guardian angel. This is one of the areas in which Christianity and spiritualism generally agree, although there are

differences – the main one being the actual role of guardian angels. Spiritualists see them as their guides and as spirits who have at some time incarnated as human beings. Orthodox religion tends to play down their personification, preferring a direct relationship with God and His messengers. (Angels will not have adopted human form.) It is said our guardian angels are there to lead us back to the path from which we have strayed, and that they represent the voice of conscience.

GUIDED IMAGERY
Also see **Active Imagination**

The technique of encouraging the imagination to experience both archetypal and deeply personal symbols arising from the unconscious has been given various names, for example guided fantasy, directed day-dream, and inner guide meditation. The technique usually begins with deep relaxation, a regular breathing process and the initiation of a passive meditative state or change of consciousness. A facilitator will then describe the outline of, for example, an imaginary journey, always leaving the greater part of it to be formed by the day-dreamer. The purpose of the process is often therapeutic, whether by calling up universal healing symbols or transformative images, so the facilitator who guides the imagery is often a therapist. Frequently the opportunity is taken to 'meet' a helpful guide or being who can be accessed in times of need. This process can be done individually by reading the proposed journey before starting the **meditation**.

Tarot cards and meaningful pictures can also be used as a stimulus for experiencing the inner world of symbolic expression; see the tarot as journey in the Throat Chakra in Section Three. Instead of following a brief description for the guided imagery, one studies the design of the card or painting and enters it to meet, and maybe even talk to, the depicted figures.

GURU

A guru is a spiritual teacher who has the ability to guide the religious seeker in her search for spiritual truth. Initially this was taken to be through the disciplines of yoga, but as Western and Eastern practices come closer together this is not always the case. Part of a guru's spiritual path is to impart learning to others, but only if the pupil or 'chela' seeks knowledge. Humility and honesty are integral parts of this process, because every guru should also be aware of what is learnt from those who seek her out. In every way the guru should epitomize the qualities of the true hermit and recognize that her physical and material needs will be cared for. In today's acquisitive society this can mean the accumulation of considerable wealth. Ideally this wealth should be placed at the disposal of others, or for the greater good. A guru is therefore expected to be an enlightened yogi.

H

HAKOMI
See **Therapies**

HALLUCINATION

A hallucination is the inner perception of that which has no objective or outer reality. It is a subjective – entirely personal – experience, which is usually visual but which can involve all the senses. Initially the recipient accepts the perceived stimulus as coming from something real within the world. (Hallucinations should not be confused with illusions, which occur when we see an object and identify it incorrectly from our memory.)

Hallucinations do not have an external stimulus, and yet the nerve endings are stimulated as though there was. It has been suggested that hallucinations occur when for some reason the normal sensory filtering mechanism in the brain is not functioning correctly. This may be through shock, sensory deprivation, drugs or certain foodstuffs. It is possible that certain psychic or religious experiences can have the same effect, as also can the monotony of motorway driving. Many UFO sightings occur in this state of altered consciousness. Hallucinations are recognized by the medical profession as symptoms of psychosis and other mental illness, but most people who have these experiences are probably not mentally ill.

HALO

In most if not all religious pictures an exceptionally holy person is shown with a halo or disc of light encircling the head. This is thought to be a representation of the **aura**, and to show how different is the spiritual power and wisdom of such people. Its position above the head suggests a state of enlightenment which is not available to the ordinary individual without much study. A halo indicates a state of cosmic awareness and responsibility, a dedication to the creation of a sustainable spiritual future for mankind, and a connectedness with the true meaning of spirituality, on both a personal and a global level.

HEALERS/HEALING

For individual types of healing, see under **Therapies**

A faith healer is usually a member of a religion. The main requirement in this type of healing is the faith of both healer and patient in the power of God to heal. Spiritual healers, however, claim to be channels for healing energies and do not consider it to be of importance whether or not the patient 'believes in healing'. The belief in psychic healing is that the healer's own energy is used in the healing process. Some of these healers also believe that they may be 'contaminated' by the patient's condition, and so perform certain semi-ritualistic actions (such as flicking away the negative energy or the washing of hands) in order to limit such risk.

The Catholic Church initially allowed the laying on of hands by priests while praying that the sick be cured by the Holy Spirit (as the Apostles had done), but this practice was subsequently outlawed. In some non-Catholic religions there has been a resurgence in the practice, with the healers regarded as channels for God's healing power.

HELLERWORK

See **Therapies**

HERBS

Also see **Therapies**

Herbs can be safely used as part of everyday life. They may be used in cooking, room freshening and, by some people, in magic. Various

GLOSSARY OF ACTIONS

Alterative – cleanses and normalizes the system

Analgesic – stops pain

Anthelmintic – clears worms

Anti-inflammatory – stops inflammation

Anti-microbial – combats infection

Anti-neoplastic – inhibits and combats the development of tumours

Anti-pyretic – stops fever

Anti-spasmodic – relaxes nervous tension (which causes colic)

Anti-tussive – stops coughs

Aromatic – highly scented

Astringent – stops discharge

Carminative – moves material through the digestive system

Cholagogic – clears liver and gall bladder

Demulcent – soothes the membranes

Diaphoretic – increases perspiration

Diuretic – increases flow of urine

Emetic – causes vomiting

Emmenagogic – increases the flow of menstrual blood

Emollient – soothes the tissues

Expectorant – expels mucus

Hypotensive – lowers blood pressure

Nervine – acts on the nerves

Parasiticidal – kills parasites

Purgative – cleanses the digestive system

Tonic – revitalizes the system

Uterine tonic – contracts the uterus

Vulnerary – heals injury to the skin

parts of the plants are used, such as the flowers, roots, fruits or bark. Herbal medicines have been used for thousands of years, and indeed today some 60 per cent of the world's population still uses no other kind of medicine.

Herbal medicine

Like all medicines, herbal medicines should be kept out of the reach of children and be disposed of once their expiry date has been reached; this will be marked clearly on the container. They are most effective in preventing disease and in helping to strengthen weakness in the body. There are specific herbs which strengthen and tone specific organs and systems. Self-diagnosis is not advisable and it is suggested that you consult a qualified herbalist or practitioner to ascertain the nature of your problem.

The duration of treatment will vary depending on the condition being treated. For example, osteoarthritis will take some time, while digestive problems should respond fairly quickly. In general, it will take two to three weeks before any significant improvement will be noticed.

There are over two thousand plants that can be used in herbal medicine. If you intend to have a home herbal medicine chest, you should include the following 25 plants, which may be stored as dry herbs or as tinctures.

Aniseed – the dried fruits are used. Its actions are expectorant, anti-spasmodic, carminative, parasiticidal and aromatic. It is best used as an infusion or in its pure oil form (one drop of oil in half a teaspoon of honey).

Black Willow – the bark is used. Its actions are anti-inflammatory, anti-pyretic, analgesic, antiseptic and astringent. It is best used as a tincture or a decoction.

Boneset – the dried aerial parts are used. Its actions are diaphoretic, tonic, anti-spasmodic, and it relaxes mucous membranes. It can be used as an infusion and a tincture.

Burdock Root – the roots and rhizomes are used. Its actions are alterative and diuretic. It can be used as a decoction and a tincture.

Cayenne – the fruit of the plant is used. It acts as a stimulant, a tonic,

THREE SIMPLE HERBAL PREPARATIONS

Infusion Into a warmed teapot put one teaspoonful of the herb or herb mixture for each cup of tea. Add boiling water and leave to brew for 10 to 15 minutes. The infusion may be drunk either hot or cold and may be sweetened with either honey or brown sugar.

Decoction Put one teaspoonful of dried herbs or three teaspoonfuls of fresh for each cup of water in a container. Dried herbs should be powdered, while the fresh material should be cut into small pieces. The container used should be of glass, ceramic or earthenware. If metal is used, it should be enamelled – aluminium should never be used. Add the water to the herbs, bring to the boil and simmer for 10 to 15 minutes. Strain the tea while it is still hot.

Alcoholic tincture Put four ounces of chopped, ground or dried herb into a container that can be sealed tightly. Twice this amount should be used if the herbs are fresh. Pour half a litre of 60 per cent proof alcohol (for example, vodka) over the herbs and close the container tightly. Keep the container in a warm place for two weeks and shake it well twice a day. After decanting the bulk of the liquid, pour the residue into a muslin cloth suspended in a bowl. Wring out all the liquid. Pour the tincture into a dark bottle, well stoppered.

diaphoretic and carminative, and as an antiseptic. It can be used as an infusion and a tincture.

Celery Seed – the dried ripe fruits are used. Its actions are anti-rheumatic, diuretic, carminative and sedative. It can be used as an infusion and a tincture.

Chamomile – the flowers are used. Its actions are anti-spasmodic, carminative, anti-inflammatory, analgesic and antiseptic. It can be used as an infusion and a tincture.

Cleavers – the dried aerial parts and the fresh expressed juice are used. Its actions are anti-inflammatory, diuretic, tonic and anti-neoplastic. It can be used as an infusion and a tincture.

Coltsfoot – the dried flowers and leaves are used. Its actions are expectorant, anti-tussive, demulcent, anti-catarrhal and diuretic. It can be used as an infusion and a tincture.

Comfrey – the roots and leaves are used. Its actions are vulnerary, demulcent, astringent and expectorant. It can be used as a decoction and tincture.

Dandelion – the roots and leaves are used. Its actions are diuretic, cholagogic, anti-rheumatic, laxative and tonic. It can be used as a decoction and tincture.

Echinacea – the cone flower is used. Its actions are anti-microbial and alterative. It can be used as a decoction and a tincture.

Elder – the bark, flowers, berries and leaves are used. Its actions are – *Bark:* purgative, emetic and diuretic. *Leaves:* Externally emollient and vulnerary; internally as a purgative, expectorant, diuretic and diaphoretic. *Flowers:* diaphoretic and anti-catarrhal. *Berries:* diuretic, diaphoretic and laxative. It can be used as an infusion, a juice, an ointment and a tincture.

False Unicorn Root – the dried rhizomes and roots are used. Its actions are diuretic, anthelmintic, emetic, uterine tonic and emmenagogic. It can used as a decoction and a tincture.

Marshmallow -- the roots and leaves are used. Its actions are – *Root:* demulcent, diuretic, emollient and vulnerary. *Leaf:* demulcent, expectorant, diuretic and emollient. It can be used as a decoction, an infusion, as a compress and a tincture.

Meadowsweet – the aerial parts are used. Its actions are anti-rheumatic, anti-inflammatory, antacid, anti-emetic and astringent. It can be used as an infusion and a tincture.

Nettles – the aerial parts are used. Its actions are astringent, diuretic and tonic. It can be used as an infusion and a tincture.

Peppermint -- the aerial parts are used. Its actions are carminative, anti-spasmodic, aromatic, diaphoretic, anti-emetic, nervine, antiseptic and analgesic. It can be used as an infusion and a tincture.

Senna – the dried fruit pods are used. Its actions are cathartic, causing rapid expulsion of the intestinal contents. It can be used as an infusion and a tincture.

Skullcap – the aerial parts are used. Its actions are as a nervine tonic, sedative and anti-spasmodic. It can be used as an infusion and a tincture.

Thyme – the leaves and flowering tops are used. Its actions are carminative, anti-microbial, anti-spasmodic, expectorant, astringent and anthelmintic. It can be used as an infusion and a tincture.

Valerian – the rhizomes and roots are used. Its actions are sedative, hypnotic, anti-spasmodic, hypotensive and carminative. It can be used as an infusion and a tincture.

Wormwood – the leaves and flowering tops are used. Its actions are as a bitter tonic, carminative, anthelmintic and anti-inflammatory. It can be used as an infusion, a tincture or in pill form.

Yarrow – the aerial parts are used. It is diaphoretic, hypotensive, astringent, diuretic and antiseptic. It can be used as an infusion and a tincture.

Yellow Dock – the roots are used. Its actions are alterative, purgative and cholagogic. It can be used as a tincture and an infusion.

In addition to these herbs, it is advisable to have the following in the form of ointments: arnica, chickweed, comfrey and marigold.

Preparation

There are various methods of preparing herbs for both external and internal use. From a holistic point of view, the best way of using herbs is to take them internally. There are numerous ways of preparing remedies for internal use. Those shown below are the basic kinds.

Infusions and Decoctions

There are two ways of preparing water-based extracts: infusions and decoctions. Infusion is perhaps the most simple and common method of taking a herb. Either fresh or dried herbs can be used for this; where one part of a dried herb is suggested, it can be replaced by three parts of the fresh herb.

Infusions are most appropriate for plant parts, such as leaves, flowers or green stems. For the infusion of seeds, resin bark or roots, it is best to grind them into a powder first to make mixing with the water easier.

Decoctions are appropriate when the herb to be used contains hard, woody material. This method ensures that the soluble content of the herb reaches the water. When preparing a mixture containing both soft and woody herbs, it is best to prepare an infusion and a decoction separately.

To sweeten an infusion or a decoction, add sugar directly to the liquid.

Tinctures

Alcohol is often a better solvent than water. Alcohol preparations are called tinctures, as are preparations based on glycerine or vinegar. As alcohol tinctures are much stronger than water-based preparations, dosages are proportionately smaller – between 5 and 15 drops depending on the herb.

Tinctures can be used in a variety of ways, either taken straight or mixed with a cup of hot water. Drops can be added to a bath or used in a compressor mixed with oil and fat to make an ointment. Suppositories and lozenges can also be made by mixing oil and fat.

Vinegar contains acetic acid and this acts as a solvent and preservative in a way similar to alcohol. Apple cider vinegar is recommended for use in vinegar-based tinctures because it contains its own health - giving properties. Synthetic chemical vinegar should not be used.

Glycerine-based tinctures have the advantage of being milder on the digestive system than alcoholic tinctures. However, they are not as efficient at dissolving resinous or oily materials. Although generally better than water-based preparations, because they are gentler on the digestive tract, glycerine-based tinctures are not as effective as alcohol-based types.

To sweeten a tincture, mix three parts of syrup to one part of tincture.

Dry preparations

Commercially prepared dry herbal preparations take the form of capsules, pills and lozenges. The benefit of dry preparations is that their effects are longer lasting than those prepared by infusion and dissolved in liquid form, although these latter begin their action more speedily.

If you wish to prepare your own herbs, be warned that the required plant constituents are not always readily available. The herbs have to be ground into fine powder before use.

There are a number of herbs which, when combined with certain rituals, are reputed to have magical properties. A few are included in the entry on **magic**, although the author accepts no responsibility whatsoever for any outcome!

HIGHER SELF

The higher self is the spiritual self, that which exists beyond the personal. It is the vehicle of true consciousness because it exists beyond the rational and is transcendental, representing faith and higher intention.

Awareness of the higher self is possible in mystical experiences. Through **active imagination**, **guided imagery** and **meditation** we can learn to strengthen the ties between the conscious self and the higher self, bringing the personality into alignment with the soul.

HOMEOPATHY
See **Therapies**

HYDROTHERAPY
See **Therapies**

HYPNAGOGIC

When they are between wakefulness and falling asleep some people are conscious of voices and see mental pictures or visions. These 'hypnagogic' images can seem to invade our awareness without conscious effort. Music may also be heard. Such images and sounds may prove creative and enlightening. The hypnagogic state is regarded by many as a route into the paranormal and information received at such a time is often precognitive (see **Precognition**). Thomas Jay Hudson (see **Absent Healing** and **People**) considered the moments just before sleep and just after waking (**hypnopompic**) as the best times for experiments in sending out healing vibrations.

HYPNOPOMPIC

The sounds and visions that arise during the transitional state between sleeping and waking consciousness (the opposite to the hypnogogic state) are called hypnopompic images.

It is similar to the **hypnagogic** state that occurs just before one falls asleep, and is equally helpful in perceiving and understanding the paranormal. In such a state the individual is highly sensitive to psychic vibration of all sorts. This may explain many precognitive and certain déja-vu experiences.

HYPNOSIS/HYPNOTISM

Since Franz Mesmer discovered, in the 1780s, a state of **consciousness** in which a patient was extremely suggestible, much controversy has surrounded hypnosis. This controversy has ranged from the question of the violation of human rights – whether the hypnotist has the right, either for amusement (as in stage hypnotism) or therapeutically to influence an individual – to whether the information given under hypnotic **trance** is, in fact, valid.

The Bloxham tapes, which were a series of recordings made of past life regressions, were verifiable in part. It cannot be proved, however, whether the individuals concerned were actually present on the occasions they described, or were reading the **Akashic records**.

What is certain is that there are some areas of the personality that are more easily accessible when an individual is in a state of deep relaxation. This state is usually brought about by some kind of repetitive visual or auditory technique. When suggestions are made to a person by a competent practitioner, such goals as the healing of long-standing physical problems (e.g., certain skin conditions), the stopping of habitual behaviour, such as smoking, or the improvement of depressive conditions become possible. Interestingly, it would seem that information, such as telepathic images, which is not consciously available to the subject, becomes more readily accessible through hypnosis.

When investigators have suggested to volunteers that they are in touch with deceased great scientists and philosophers, those volunteers have given information which is out of the range of their conscious knowledge. Whether the individual is indeed in touch with the deceased personality is irrelevant: it would seem that they are in touch with a stream of knowledge not accessible under normal circumstances. It may be, therefore, that clairvoyants (see **Clairvoyance**) and channellers (see **Medium**) are capable of a degree of self-hypnosis in order to achieve the heightened state of **awareness** necessary to help their sitters.

HYPNOTHERAPY
See **Therapies**

I

I CHING
See **Divination**

INCUBUS

Modern psychology classifies incubi as figments of the imagination, delusions or **hallucinations** which are manifested as a response to repressed desires. An incubus was understood to be any demon that disturbed one's sleep by invading the mind or appearing in some offensive form. Later, an incubus was seen as a materialization that appeared to women and had intercourse with them. The corresponding entity for men was known as a succubus. Popular belief held that incubi and succubi were manifested by witches and warlocks.

INITIATION

Initiation is an individual's entry into the tribe, or the passage from one stage of life to another. Most initiations require considerable training. They are always turning points – for example, in Christianity baptism is an initiation representing a rebirth after the cleansing of original sin.

Some initiations, such as those in Mithraism, included ordeals, either real or symbolic. Such symbolism is still seen today in the initiations undertaken by **Freemasons** (see under **Religions and Philosophical Movements**) and members of some **religions**. Certain life experiences that initiate us into different states of awareness are seen as spiritual initiations. By going through them and achieving success in overcoming a particular difficulty, we are able to speed up our own spiritual progress.

INSPIRATION

'Inspire' literally means to breathe in. In the esoteric sense, inspiration suggests breathing in something external to oneself. The artist **William Blake** (see under **People**) was very aware of this external source, and said he worked to a type of dictation. Many **mediums** who practise **automatic writing** are aware of an external presence, and a number of mystics have claimed not to know what they were transmitting or writing. Some poets and writers are aware of their 'muse' as an external source. They will often project this sense of otherness onto someone close to them, almost as though they need to filter the intensity of the experience into something physical.

Inspiration comes to us on a sustained basis, but often not until we have cleared our minds of a certain amount of 'static'. First we must rid ourselves of illusion. This can be likened to a bad filing system, where bits of information, possibilities and probabilities are jumbled up together. When we have decided what is real for us and what is not, we are able to trust our **intuition**. This is the 'spark' that allows us access to a greater awareness, which it then becomes necessary to express.

Steiner (see **People**) believed that inspiration was one of three faculties by which man becomes aware of the world beyond the senses, but that it is secondary to intuition. If we think of inspiration in terms of breathing, it follows that as we breathe in so we must breathe out. Inspiration, therefore, may be regarded as a tool for expressing knowledge.

INTUITION

In one sense intuition means teaching oneself through the use of insight. Many people have likened it to a quantum leap, a huge surge in understanding, and a sharp change in perception. It is as though the mind lies quiescent for a time, and then suddenly is galvanized into action, in a flash producing the answer to whatever conundrum is being considered. Psychologists would have us believe that the unconsious mind takes over the consideration of a problem, and works on it independently of the conscious mind. This is why the awareness that operates in the **hypnagogic** and **hypnopompic** states is so invaluable, because the insight is often caught in those states. These states involve a change of **consciousness**, and are an invaluable tool in creativity. Just as it is possible to train oneself to dream lucidly, it is also possible to harness the energy of these states.

Thinking too hard about the intuitive function seems to block it, because the rational mind is not able to accept the knowledge as valid. It could be said that intuition is the drawing to oneself of information one could not consciously know, but perhaps it might also be said to be a linking with the collective unconscious or with the soul level in order to take correct action. It is part of **clairvoyance**, which we have already defined elsewhere as 'clarity of perception'.

Spiritually, the organ of intuition is the Third Eye (see **Brow Chakra** in Section Three). This is linked to the pineal gland and is said to connect us to all creativity. The pineal gland atrophies in puberty, when the conscious need for survival supersedes an instinctive one. If at this time the young person learns to trust and to use intuition (and learns to trust the process), she should instinctively know how to create an acceptable way of life for herself. If she grows to fear the intuitive process or believes it is invalid, a great deal of creativity will be lost.

The first step in training the intuition is to trust one's hunches. Almost everyone has experienced the feeling of knowing that something is going to happen. The salesman who knows he has made a sale, the mother who knows something is not right with her child, or the lover who senses his girlfriend's withdrawal – all are using intuition.

Secondly, put those hunches on record. Whether you talk about

THE PROCESS OF INTUITION

them to friends or make a note of them does not matter. There is no

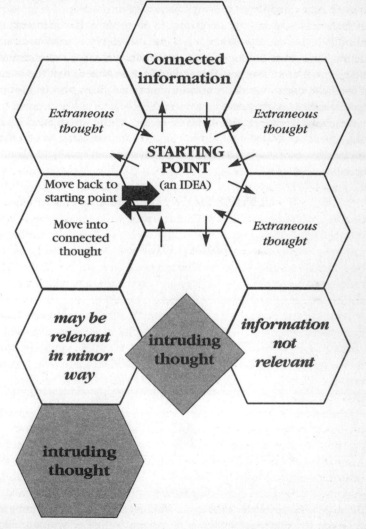

mystique about this; the process simply tells you how many times you get things right and how many times you get them wrong. As with **clairvoyance**, you will gradually be more right than you are wrong and will increasingly learn to trust your intuition.

Thirdly, as your hit rate improves, try to work around the insight. Without trying to rationalize anything, allow your mind to roam slightly away from what you are considerings. If anything comes to mind, note it and move on. Then come back to that thought, allow it to become central and then move on again. The process looks something like the illustration opposite.

Intuition consists of making sense of the whole information available. A well developed intuition is a kind of efficient filing or ordering process that gives you instant access to information you have already received and stored.

IONIZATION THERAPY
See **Therapies**

IRIDOLOGY
See **Therapies**

J

JUNGIAN THERAPY
See **Therapies**

K

KARMA

Karma is a human understanding of the idea that the universe works according to certain principles. It is not the law of retribution but a law of cause and effect. Many scriptures put forward the idea that every action has a reaction and that every reaction requires further action. Put simply, this means 'as you sow, so shall you reap'. If one believes in the idea of reincarnation, this principle carries forward into future lives as actions taken in this life which may go unpunished – or unrewarded – are not squared until the next or subsequent lives.

As we do not know what our future lives hold, it is perhaps prudent to live our present life as best we can, harming no-one and creating as little karmic debt as possible. This is truly the concept of 'do as you would be done by'. There is no judgement in this – all our thoughts, emotions and actions eventually return to us in one way or another.

KINESIOLOGY
See **Therapies**

KIRLIAN PHOTOGRAPHY

Kirlian photography was first developed by two Russian investigators, Semyon and Valentina Kirlian, in the 1930s, as a way of photographing the **aura**. It is said to be able to show imperfections and 'leaks' in the aura and can be used in the detection of cancer and other illnesses. Kirlian photography of the hands of a healer, showing changes in the aura at the fingertips, provides evidence to support the idea that the healing process involves the transfer of energy into the patient. This type of photography has also been used to show the diminution of energy in a plant about 20 hours after it has been picked.

KUNDALINI

Kundalini is a Sanskrit word which means coiled. It is believed by yogis and adepts that the **base chakra** or spiritual centre (see Section Three) is symbolized by a sleeping serpent. Using special techniques such as breathing exercises, sexual discipline, concentration and **chanting**, the 'snake' is encouraged to awake. Energy then rises through each of the chakras until after much practice it finally reaches the **crown chakra** (3). During this process each chakra is activated, giving heightened perception and abilities.

Most teachers and initiates are agreed that the raising of kundalini is dangerous without proper training, although many consider it a necessary part of spiritual development. Kundalini is thought by many to be a figment of imagination and yet it can be experienced as a warmth or power actually travelling up the spine. (The Egyptian head-dress worn by priestesses shows the erect snake that represents Kundalini.)

L

LAYING ON OF HANDS
See **Therapies**

LEFT-HAND PATH
See **Magic**

LOST CONTINENTS

The civilizations of Atlantis and Lemuria are considered to be the lost continents from which all humanity is descended. It is believed that these continents are represented in the Bible by the story of the flood and that both were lost by some cataclysmic upheaval. Lemuria is said to predate Atlantis. Soviet scientists have gathered some physical evidence to support the idea that there was once cataclysm and flood.

Lemurian civilization is said to have communicated telepathically, whereas that of the Atlanteans appears to have been more spiritually based. Despite their meeting with destruction, both civilizations may be seen as blueprints for a perfect order. Looked at symbolically, these continents could be said to have been engulfed by emotional problems, water representing emotion.

LUCID DREAMS

Lucid dreaming occurs in the dream state when we recognize our ability to alter our perception and change an undesirable ending into a better one. When we realize that we have this capability, it need only be a short step to appreciating that we are also capable of bringing about change in our waking lives.

M

MAGIC

There are two forms of magic: that of dedication and service (the right-hand path), and that of personal power and selfishness (the left-hand path). Thaumaturgy – low magic – is brought about using little-known powers of the mind. Theurgy – high magic – is the raising of consciousness deliberately to increase spiritual awareness in accordance with the Divine Plan.

There are three fundamental principles in magic:

● Tapping into the **Akashic records** – this can be done by many competent clairvoyants (see **Clairvoyance**).
● A belief in the limitless power of the magician. The theory is that the magician can achieve anything through the exercise of his will.
● The law of correspondence – that is, a belief that external characteristics correspond to inner qualities.

Within the framework of the art of the magician there stands a great deal of power. Initially, the magician had a special role as an intermediary between God and humanity, a role which is today filled by priests. He also had, and still has, a private function, often working in the background to control cosmic forces on behalf of his fellow man. Control over the natural world for its own sake tends to lead to personal egotism, whereas seeking understanding allows one to act in harmony with the laws of the universe. No-one should be harmed by any of his actions and a natural balance should always be maintained. Most magicians were masculine and thought to be more dispassionate than witches.

Without an **initiation** into the art of magic there can be little comprehension of what it entails. The 'tools' that a magician uses, such as candles, herbs, talismen and so on, have meaning only when they are included as part of the **ritual** of magic. These tools are used variously to change consciousness, to focus the mind and to create an environment within which the laws of nature can act fully.

MAGICAL EQUIPMENT

Candles

When first using candles it is better, as with all techniques, to keep the action as simple as possible. Candle magic is helped by anointing the candle with a good quality oil – olive oil is ideal – which perhaps has been perfumed with appropriate herbs and spices (see below). Rub the candle from the centre upwards (towards the spiritual) and from the centre downwards (towards the earth) for about ten minutes. This helps to focus the mind on the task in hand and facilitates the flow and unification of spiritual and earth energies. The candle is then lit and left in a darkened room. The desired effect should manifest relatively quickly. (*Note:* Care should always be taken never to leave a burning candle untended in a draught or where it can be knocked over.)

The colour of the candle may be chosen to fit in with the overall intent. Preferably it should be solid colour all the way through, and not dipped or merely coated in colour. The following table shows the colours and their corresponding associations:

COLOUR	ASSOCIATION
White	Protection, Purity, Sincerity
Black	Confusion, Discord, Evil
Light Blue	Patience, Tranquillity, Understanding
Dark Blue	Decision-making
Golden Yellow	Communication, Intellect, Strength of Mind
Green	Fertility, Luck, Money
Brown	Hesitation, Indecision
Pink	Integrity, Love, Morality
Red	Endurance, Health, Sexual Love, Strength
Purple	Ambition, Business, Power
Grey	Deadlock, Neutrality
Orange	Adaptability, Attraction, Animation
Lime Green	Anger, Cowardice, Jealousy

Herbs

Also see main entry for **Herbs**

Listed below are herbs that have been used for centuries for various magical purposes. Some are easier to obtain than others, and some appear in more than one group. Research and experimentation is required if you want to ascertain which ones will work best for you. Alternatively, you may wish to purchase your herbs already mixed to tried and tested formulae. Some of the herbs listed also appear in the section on **essential oils** and may be used in an oil burner or as incense. Yet others may be used powdered and crushed, or as teas and tisanes, as with healing herbs.

Note: Most of these herbs are perfectly safe, but you must be prepared to use them only as your retailer suggests. It is most unwise to experiment without expert guidance. For example, some herbs are safe when used as incense but lethal if taken internally.

For protection: Aaron's Rod, African Ginger, Alfalfa, Angelica, Ash Tree Leaves, Balm of Gilead, Basil, Bay Leaves, Benzoin, Bergamot, Betony, Black Cohosh, Bladderwrack, Bloodroot, Boldo Leaves, Calendula, Caraway Seed, Cinquefoil, Cloves, Comfrey Root, Cypress, Dog Grass, Elder Berries, Eucalyptus, Fennel Seed, Flax Seed, Gardenia, Garlic, Holy Herb, Horehound, High John the Conqueror, Kava Kava, Knot Weed, Lily of the Valley, Lovage, Marjoram, Mint, Mistletoe, Mullein, Mustard Seed, Palma Christi Bean (Castor Bean), Patchouli, Purslane, Quince, Rose Geranium, Rowan Wood (Mountain Ash), St Johnswort, Sandalwood, Sea Spirit (Irish Moss), Solomon's Seal, Spikeweed, Stone Root, Vetivert, Woodruff, Wormwood.

For spiritual workings ('Spirit Pullers'): African Ginger, Althea, Anise, Bladderwrack, Carnation, Gardenia, Lemon, Lignum Aloes, Lime, Lotus, Thyme, Violets, Wintergreen, Wormwood.

For luck: Buckthorn Bark, Chamomile, Clover, Dandelion, Dragon's Blood Reed, Frankincense, Heal-All Herb, Honeysuckle, Irish Moss, Job's Tears, High John the Conqueror, Khus Khus, Lotus, Lucky Hand Root, Mistletoe, Myrrh, Nutmeg, Peony Root, Queen of the Meadow, Rose Hips, Rosemary, Sacred Bark (Cascara Sagrada), Sandalwood, Sea Lettuce (Kelp), Seven Barks (Hydrangea), Star Anise, Spearmint, Tonka Beans.

Associated with the black arts: Balmony, Black Pepper, Blueberry Leaves, Boneset, Brimstone (Sulphur), Chicory, Hemlock, Knot Grass, Lemon Verbena, Mullein, Nutgall, Patchouli, Red Pepper, Saffron, Skunk Cabbage, Slippery Elm, Snake Root, Sumac, Tormentilla Root, Valerian, Willow Bark, Witch Grass (Knot Grass), Yarrow.

Aid in legal problems: High John the Conqueror, Buckthorn, Galangal.

Good health and healing: All-Heal (Heal-All), Allspice, Asafoetida, Ash Tree Leaves, Betony, Buckeye, Caraway Seed, Carnation, Catnip, Citron, Coriander, Eucalyptus, Feverfew, Gardenia, Ginseng, Holy Herb (Yerba Sante), Horehound, High John the Conqueror, Laurel, Life Everlasting, Linaloe, Masterwort, Narcissus, Peppermint, Rose Buds, Rue, Sarsaparilla, Sassafras, Thyme, Vervain, Wintergreen.

For general success: Basil, Bergamot, Blue Flag, Frankincense, Grains of Paradise, Lemon Verbena, Mistletoe, Musk, Mustard Seed, Myrrh, Sandalwood, Solomon's Seal, Squill Root, Storax (Styrax), Vanilla, Yellow Dock.

To command/compel/for power: Calamus, Catnip, Cypress, Devil's Bit, Elder Bark, Elm Bark, Fennel, Licorice, Marigold, Polk Root, Poppy Seed, Saffron, Slippery Elm Bark, Smellage Root, Spikenard.

For uncrossing/unhexing/psychic protection: Absinthe, African Ginger, Agrimony, Ague Weed (Boneset), Angelica, Anise, Ash Leaves, Basil, Bay, Benzoin, Betony, Bitter Root (Gentian), Blood Root, Brimstone (Sulphur), Broom Tops, Clover, Cloves, Curry Powder, Dill, Dog Grass, Dragon's Blood Reed, Elder, Five Finger Grass (Cinquefoil), Flax, Fennel Seed, Frankincense, Geranium, Ginger, Hawthorn, Holy Thistle (Blessed Thistle), Huckleberry, Hyacinth, Hyssop, Lilac, Lotus, Low John (Galangal), Marjoram, Mistletoe, Mugwort, Nettle, Pine Bark, Polk Root, Rue, Sage, Sloe Bark or Berries, Spikenard, Tormentil, Unicorn Root, Valerian, Verbena, Vetivert, Woodruff, Wormwood.

For psychic development: Absinthe, Acacia Flowers, African Ginger, Althea, Anise Seed, Betel Nut, Bladderwrack, Buchu Leaves, Calendula, Camphor, Celery Seed, Cinnamon, Cloves, Dandelion, Damiana, Frankincense, Gum Mastic, Heliotrope, Holy Herb (Yerba Sante), Honeysuckle, Hyssop, Kava Kava, Laurel, Lavender, Lilac, Linseed, Magnolia, Mandrake, Mullein, Peppermint, Purslane, Queen Root (Stillingia), Rosemary, Saffron, Wisteria, Wood Rose, Yerba Sante.

For love: Absinthe, Adam and Eve Root, Aloes, Apple Blossom, Archangel, Ash Leaves, Basil, Beth Root, Bittersweet, Black Snakeroot, Cardamom, Civit, Cloves, Coriander, Cubeb, Cumin, Damiana, Deer's Tongue, Dill, Dragon's Blood Reed, Elecampane, Eryngo (Sea Holly), Gentian, Ginger, Grains of Paradise, Heartsease, Hyacinth, Jasmine, Juniper Berries, Khus Khus, Laurel, Lavender, Licorice, Lignum Aloes, Lime, Linden, Lovage, Magnolia, Maidenhair, Mandrake, Marjoram, Mistletoe, Mint, Motherwort, Mullein Leaves, Neroli (Orange Blossom), Orange, Orris, Passion Flower, Pennyroyal, Periwinkle, Quassia Chips, Rose Buds, Rosemary, Rue, Sage, Skullcap, Senna Pods, Southernwood, Spikenard, Sweet Bugle, Thyme, Vanilla, Vervain, Vetivert, Violet, Wormwood, Yerba Mate, Ylang Ylang.

For money: Acacia, Alfalfa, Almond, Basil, Bayberry, Bistort, Buckeye, Chamomile, Cascara Sagrada (Sacred Bark), Cinnamon, Clover, Comfrey, Dragon's Blood Reed, Fenugreek, Galangal, Garlic, Ginseng, High John the Conqueror, Honeysuckle, Irish Moss, Lavender, Lovage, Lucky Hand Root, Mandrake, Mountain Laurel, Myrtle, Nutmeg, Queen of the Meadow, Red Clover, Skullcap, Sea Lettuce (Kelp), Smartweed (Knotweed), Snake Root, Spikenard, Squill, Thyme, Tonka Beans, Yellow Dock.

Talismen and amulets
A talisman is an inanimate object invested with a certain power specifically for the person concerned. Often it is made of traditional materials and according to certain formulae, thus giving it extraordinary potency. Talismen are often used to bring good fortune and avert danger and

give a sense of security to the wearer. The best known talisman is perhaps the cross in its various forms. Perhaps the least understood, except by its wearers, is the pentagram or five-pointed star.

An amulet is a protective device intended to divert evil influences from the wearer but not necessarily to attract luck to him. One of the best known amulets is the 'Hand of Fatima' (the Fatima in question was the daughter of Mohammed), which is said to be an extremely potent image in the protection of material goods.

MANDALA

The mandala – meaning 'circle' – is a sacred shape which signifies the universe in many belief systems. Jung judged this figure to be an important part of psychological wholeness. Characteristically, it is a circle enclosing a square with a symbol in the centre representing the whole of life. It is mostly used as an aid to **meditation**.

The principle it embodies is that one travels from the outer circle (which represents the whole of existence) through the creation of matter (the square) to the centre of existence (the central figure). Finally, one moves back out to take one's place in the physical world again. The mandala is often depicted as an eight-pointed star, and represents both man's aspirations and his burdens. It has also been found that, in the process of **healing**, the symbol occurs over and over again.

The expression of wholeness and yet separateness in this figure moves us into a space which enables us to create a new concept of the principles of existence. By creating and recreating this figure, we move towards and experience a wholeness and tranquillity which would not otherwise be available.

MANTRA

The intense concentration and repetition needed to fill the mind with one concept of whichever God one believes in – coupled with a sense of spiritual union – is a conscious activity designed to achieve a state of restful alertness. The Mantra is the creation of a sound, corresponding to a name or an aspect of god, and is a creative vibration. Often it is three syllables long, and is an aid to becoming closer to the centre of both oneself and the universe. It becomes the personal 'key' to universal knowledge.

Spiritually, sound repeated over and over induces a change of consciousness and awareness. The Mantra permits this to be positive and opens up possibilities for enhanced wisdom and knowledge (see **Throat Chakra** in Section Three).

MASSAGE
See **Therapies**

MEDITATION
Also see **Creative visualization**,
Colour therapy and **Affirmation**

There are three aspects to meditation – concentration, contemplation and dedication.

The Western way of life makes it particularly difficult for the initiate to withdraw attention from the outside world. However, concentration is a necessity if you are to 'still' the mind to achieve inner tranquillity and peace and must be worked at.

Choose a quiet place where you will not be disturbed; if necessary take the phone off the hook. This is your time and you do not want distractions. Sit in a relaxed manner, not necessarily cross-legged, although this is a good position, giving balance and poise.

Technique 1
Close your eyes and become conscious of your own heartbeat. Note its rate. A fast one is usual. Try to slow it down by breathing gently and slowly. At first it will appear to quicken up, but eventually you will discover that you have some control. Sit quietly for as long as you can without forcing yourself, listening only to your heartbeat. When you have reached your limit, gradually become aware of your surroundings again and quietly appreciate them, before resuming your everyday tasks. Once mastered, this technique can be used to good effect, while travelling on public transport, for example, or during quiet moments in a busy day.

Technique 2

A natural extension of the first technique, this one is called 'watching the breath'. Here, instead of paying attention to the heartbeat, one focuses on the breath.

Sitting straight with the head up, place your tongue just behind your teeth. This has the effect of slightly closing the throat, and will produce a slight sound similar to a snore. This breathing is very gentle. On the intake of breath, begin by visualizing the air entering your lungs and body. As you become more proficient you may wish to include the idea that the incoming breathe is recharging your energy, while the outgoing is taking away bodily impurities. A further extension of this exercise is to visualize the air reaching all parts of the body, including the extremities, and again revitalizing and cleansing. You may experience a change of temperature in some parts of the body, or perhaps an energy build-up. This indicates that you have linked with the concept of subtle energy (*prana*). If this occurs, try to circulate the energy more precisely, directing it to other parts of the body. This consciousness of prana will increase with practice, and you may even be able to visualize it as silver threads of light.

Technique 3

Using technique 2, concentrate on the base of the spine and there visualize a pool of energy, or, if it is easier, a pool of light. Visualize this moving up the spine until it reaches the top of the head. Allow it to spill out and surround you. If you are able to sense your own **aura**, feel the energy and light filling it. Sit quietly for as long as it is comfortable before allowing the energy to fall back into its natural position. An extension of this, as you become more proficient, is to reabsorb the energy or light at the base of your spine or first chakra, and to re-circulate it.

Technique 4

As you circulate the light through each chakra, hold the light within each centre and allow it to remain there for a period of time. Hold in your mind the quality belonging to that chakra and then move on. Finally, remain at peace until you need to move.

Technique 5

Sitting as before, place the thumbs and third finger together – this is said to control the ego, and assist in the flow of energy. Close the eyes and focus on the third eye. (The space between the eyes in the middle of the forehead.) Do not let your concentration wander, but remain centred on this point. If stray thoughts intrude, dismiss them and remain focused.

Technique 6

Hold a crystal or other object in your left hand and concentrate on it, right through from its physical qualities to its spiritual aspects. (See individual gems under each chakra in Section Three.) Meditating in this way puts you in touch with the essence of the object.

Technique 7

This technique is similar to Technique 5, except that one remains focused on a concept and not the 'third eye'. The concept might be kindness. Using the same principle as that suggested under **intuition** (see Honeycomb diagram), keep the word 'kindness' in mind and gradually allow your mind to roam around the concept. Each time your mind wanders, re-focus it. Gradually your mind will become tranquil of its own accord, as though it has stopped struggling. When you reach this point, just let yourself be 'with the tranquillity'.

MEDIUM/CHANNEL

A spiritual medium or channel is a person who communicates information from the spirit world and/or from other dimensions of reality or consciousness. He or she is a channel for a spiritual energy that is translatable into speech or automatic writing.

In direct voice channelling or mediumship a completely disembodied voice emerges from an area of the room where the channeller or medium is not seated. This phenomenon is now widely accepted as a manifestation of the combination of energies of several highly developed people present at the sitting. Most mediums work by first making contact with the **astral plane**. This is the dimension where recently departed individuals find themselves. These spirits usually show themselves either as they were towards the end of their lives or as they wish to be remembered. The competent channeller is able to verify the validity of the information being received; one simple way is to test the information in three different ways - the negative or incorrect information, or even a misperception by the medium - does not stand up to questioning three times.

To avoid the dangers of deception on the astral plane, channellers of spiritual energy train themselves to tune into the collective unconscious (see **Consciousness**) to give themselves access to the mental plane as well as the spiritual. Here one is more likely to receive accurate clairvoyance and deeper knowledge of the individual's concerns and difficulties, enabling channelling both to explain the nature of the problem and to resolve it.

A wider range of information than the collective unconscious is also available to the medium. This is the **Akashic records** or the 'Universal Library'. Channelling from this level activates personal responsibility for the world. Working at an even higher level the channeller does not necessarily need words, but may simply allow the transmission of a particularly high vibrational spiritual energy to be used for the greater good.

METAMORPHIC TECHNIQUE
See **Therapies**

MOXIBUSTION
See **Therapies**

MUD THERAPY
See **Therapies**

MYSTICISM

Broadly defined mysticism (from the Greek *myein* - to close one's eyes or one's lips) is a desire to feel at one with God. In order to experience Divine unity, the esoteric aspect - that is, the inner truth -

needs to be experienced for oneself. Only through **initiation** and training, it is believed, can a disciple achieve spiritual awareness and salvation. There are three types of mystical experience: cosmic consciousness, realization of eternity, and union of the soul with God.

Many people have had some kind of mystical or religious awareness of **cosmic consciousness**, although no two individuals will experience it in precisely the same way. Usually it consists of an identification with the cosmos; a sense of being beyond space and time, totally free; a oneness with everything, accompanied by a feeling of universal love and an awareness of being loved by the creator. Such an experience will often lead people to explore religion and the various religious traditions to broaden their knowledge and understanding.

N

NUMEROLOGY
See **Divination**

NATUROPATHY
See **Therapies**

NUTRITIONAL THERAPY
See **Therapies**

O

OCCULT

The word 'occult' quite literally means 'hidden'. There is a great deal of scepticism and superstition surrounding the occult. Many people associate it with anything from theatrical mediums to Satanism and black magic.

Until they were wilfully hidden by those who believe that only initiates have a right to an understanding of the occult (an attitude that is often still in evidence), many occult concepts had a basis in religion and indeed some are still part of the practices of esoteric and religious sects. In his book *An Outline to Modern Occultism*, Cyril Scott defined occultism as 'the synthesis of science, **mysticism**, philosophy, psychology and **religion**'. For occultists the initiation to understanding is the mind. Occultism is seen as simply a recognition of man's hidden powers. As consciousness expands so does happiness, as one progresses from so-called imperfection to a greater awareness of spiritual truths. The ultimate truth is that the physical body simply clothes the immortal soul, a bit like an old coat, and that we are simply depositories and transformers of energy within a universe which is itself simply an expression of that perfect energy. There is a belief that the universal energy is inert until activated by our understanding of that knowledge which it hides.

ORACLE
Also see **Oraculum** under **Divination**

Those who today are called channels, clairvoyants, psychics and **mediums** were known as oracles in Ancient Greece. The most famous oracle of all was undoubtedly the one at Apollo's shrine in Delphi. This Delphic Oracle was said to have originally belonged to Gaia, the earth goddess. The site itself was called 'the navel of the earth' and represented by a marble umbilicus-shaped object which the temple was built to protect.

The gods were contacted through the oracles, who, by virtue of their special powers, were revered and cared for by the community. The most common way for the oracle to work was by what would nowadays be called trance-channelling, although there were other more indirect ways, such as by 'reading' the movement of oak trees.

It is more than probable that the 'communications' of the oracles did not arise out of spiritual awareness. The heightened state of **consciousness** attained by these generally unsophisticated people might be explained by the fact that most temples were situated near an earth fissure and permeated by fumes rising from the volcanic sub-strata.

OSTEOPATHY
See **Therapies**

OUT OF BODY EXPERIENCE

The phenomenon of out of the body experience is known under several names, including separative experiences and Extra Sensory Perception projection, although the best known are **astral projection** and **astral travel.**

In a typical OBE, as they are generally known, the participant is aware of viewing the surrounding environment while being 'removed' from her body. There have been reports of patients who while undergoing surgery have seen themselves being operated on. There have also been reports of patients who have 'seen' parts of a ward or hospital which would not have been visible to them normally. Many people who have had this 'near death experience', as it is called, are subsequently drawn into an exploration of their feelings and beliefs concerning death and the afterlife. Most OBEs are involuntary. A common report from those who have experienced them is of a tremendous feeling of peace or calm. It is possible that an OBE is akin to a peak experience, because it will often occur in times of crisis for the person concerned.

P

PALMISTRY
See **Divination**

PARANORMAL

The term paranormal is now considered to be a more accurate description of occurrences which were previously called supernatural. People with a serious interest in the paranormal are trying to find the universal laws behind the events that are given this label in order to put forward an explanation. Many psychic powers (the development of **clairvoyance** and so on) are now thought to be a natural part of spiritual development, and not as something weird and wonderful that happens outside the individual and separate from her. The build-up of energy which occurs as one develops spiritually can cause certain phenomena, such as the moving of objects, the opening of doors, the turning on of taps, the bending of spoons and so on. These are 'away from the normal', but not necessarily above the natural. Much work done over the last twenty years has made a nonsense of seemingly unalterable laws in the field of physics and other sciences. Happenings that were previously regarded as impossible are now thought possible and even probable.

PEOPLE

In this section an attempt has been made to draw together the names the 'seeker of knowledge' might come across. It is by no means an exhaustive list, but hopefully it provides starting points for the various lines of enquiry into esoteric thought and practice you might wish to pursue.

Adler, Alfred (1870–1937)

Many of Adler's ideas – such as the 'inferiority complex' – are now widely accepted and, to some degree, understood by ordinary people. His main concern, though, was with social problems which, in turn, led him to socialism. Jung was a strong influence on many of his initial concepts. Of his many books, *Understanding Human Nature* is possibly his best known.

Aquinas, Thomas (1227–74)

Certainly the most important philosopher and theologian of the Roman Catholic tradition, Aquinas embraced the philosophy of Aristotle and made it the basis of Roman Catholic theology. He was canonized in 1323 and made a Doctor of the Church in 1567. The study of Thomas Aquinas was made part of all theological teachings in around 1366. In 1880 he was made patron saint of all Roman Catholic universities.

The Aquinas system holds that a level of knowledge is obtainable by reason alone; another level is obtainable by reason for skilled thinkers, and by faith for unskilled thinkers. The highest level, however, is obtainable only by a combination of faith and reason. This system is called Thomism.

Aurobindo, Sri (1872–1950)

Aurobindo was a servant of the British in India until he was arrested for allegedly supporting rebels. During his imprisonment, he had a mystical experience and from then on devoted himself to religion. He sought to interpret Hinduism in terms of evolutionary theory and taught what he called 'integral yoga' – the integration of spiritual and practical discipline.

Aristotle (384BC–322BC)

Born in Greece, Aristotle was sent to Athens at the age of 18 where he worked in close association with the Academy of Plato for some 20 years. Aristotle's logic, known as analytical, sets out the requirements of scientific inquiry and proof. His logic also depends on formal relations and the possibility of discovering principles.

Aristotle was interested in finding the transition in knowledge from sense experience (the things we can know) to the universals (things we understand via intuitive reason). He greatly influenced Western theology (see **Thomas Aquinas**, above).

Bacon, Roger (1214–92)

Roger Bacon was a philosopher and scientist who gained a reputation for diversity and unconventionality with his teachings in alchemy, philosophy and magic. This work led to him being nick-named 'Doctor Mirabilis'. After studying for a time in Paris, he then went to Oxford in 1247 and became a Franciscan. Later, he was imprisoned for heresy and then rejected by the Franciscans, dying soon after his release..

Bacon was linked with the inventions of gunpowder and the magnifying glass, and there was also speculation about his involvement with the microscope and telescope. His writings on maths and philosophy, after initial scepticism, were widely recognized many years later.

Bentham, Jeremy (1757–1831)

Jeremy Bentham – a philosopher and social reformer – is probably best known as a proponent of utilitarianism. His works, *A Fragment on Government* (1776) and *Introduction to the Principles of Morals and Legislation*, argue that the proper objective of all conduct and legislation is 'The greatest happiness of the greatest number'. He also published various works on penal and social reform, and it was in his mind to form 'a poor school'.

Besant, Annie (1847–1933)

Annie Besant's work was wide ranging. She worked tirelessly for women's emancipation, Anglo-Catholicism, and atheism. She was also a great worker for theosophy. Underlying her involvement in all these causes was a passionate interest in the occult.

Besant's life was difficult, including an escape from a strained, unhappy marriage. She worked with Charles Bradlaugh in developing contraception for all women. Though seemingly capable of huge errors of judgement, she nevertheless brought about a number of much needed social changes.

Blake, William (1757–1827)

Blake is best known as one of the most important poets and artists in British culture. A man of great personal contradictions, particularly regarding Christianity, he went on to form his own unique philosophical, symbolic and mythical perspective.

Long an inspiration to individuals and societies in the esoteric movement, his mystical writings – such as *All Religions are One* and *There is no Natural Religion* – were influential in the counterculture of the 1960s and the birth of the New Age Movement, when increasingly people came to search for alternative realities through a spiritual outlet.

Blavatsky, Helena (1831–91)

The founder of the Theosophical Society, Madame Blavatsky was also a huge force in the occult. Her career was extraordinary – ranging from spiritualism to magic and, eventually, to accusations of fraud when it appeared she was performing miracles. Blavatsky discovered the link between the Western and Eastern magical method and found the source of occult wisdom in the Eastern wisdom tradition.

Cayce, Edgar (1877–1945)

Known as the 'Sleeping Prophet' because of his ability to fall into deep trances, Cayce's prophecies, healing abilities and **clairvoyance** have become well known. He is said to have forecast race riots and earth-quakes – prophecies which have only recently come true. In the 1930s he foresaw the end of Communism in the Soviet Union. His medical cures were phenomenal for the time.

Crookes, William (1832–1919)

William Crookes was an eminent chemist and physicist who had a life-long interest in spiritual phenomena. He was only 31 when elected to the Royal Society following his discovery of the element thallium. A lot of his work in psychic research is said to have been either destroyed after his death or fallen into the wrong hands. This confusion has caused modern psychologists to doubt the validity of Crookes' work because there is now no objective evidence to prove his findings. However, most psychologists would agree on its interesting testimony.

Crowley, Aleister (1875–1947)

After a Plymouth Brethren upbringing, Crowley rejected Christianity and went on to become the most famous British occultist of the 20th century. A bisexual drug addict who scorned social convention, he proclaimed himself the Antichrist and took the title 'The Beast'. A poet, novelist and writer of books on magic, he spent most of his life trying to assume the mantle of magician, an aspiration he fulfilled to some extent.

Crowley became interested in the occult while an undergraduate at Cambridge, at the time of a so-called 'magic revival'. In the late 19th century he became a member of the Golden Dawn (together with **W. B. Yeats**) but was expelled for going too far, particularly in regard to his work with young women. Undeterred he formed his own order, known as 'Silver Star'.

Crowley wanted to be called 'The Great Beast' and 'the most evil man alive', though whether he was is open to question. However, a number of people closely associated with him did die tragically – including his wife and child. Crowley himself ended his life in poverty.

Dee, John (1527–1608)

John Dee was a noted scientist and a member of Elizabeth I's secret service. Mystery surrounds his magical activities, which were considered by some to be a cover for his spying. Many people saw him as some kind of impostor, possibly a fraud and dabbler in black magic. Although his life story is quite well known, very little has been done regarding explanation or interpretation of his experiments and conclusions. His various projects and works show him as one of the most exceptional and enlightened of the Elizabethan scholars. As well as being the royal astrologer, he was very knowledgeable in the areas of mathematics, astronomy and navigation.

Descartes, René (1596–1650)

Descartes is the father of modern philosophy. His method is summed up by his famous pronouncement, 'I think, therefore I am'. Realizing the importance of mathematics, he constructed a mechanistic view of the universe and developed metaphysical argument for the existence of God. This he supported with his own form of the cosmological argument. He made radical distinctions between the body and soul, provoking various accusations, including that of heresy.

Conan Doyle, Arthur (1859–1930)

Arthur Conan Doyle was a student of psychic and paranormal phenomena for almost 50 years. In the last 12 years of his life he became a leading exponent of spiritual doctrines and beliefs in the existence of spirit. He did not try to refute the existence of fraudulent mediums, but suggested that there were fewer of these than was commonly believed and that he himself had only come across two or three.

An agnostic, he acknowledged the validity of a number of supernatural phenomena but did not instantly arrive at the conclusion that there is life after death. During his lifetime he also acknowledged the validity of other people's Christian and Buddhist beliefs.

Baker Eddy, Mary (1821–1910)

The early life of the founder of Christian Science is greatly disputed, despite her own autobiographical recollections and various other biographies produced by the Christian Science movement. She founded a church, an international newspaper and through her teachings and several books – one of which sold over a million copies – she managed to influence thousands of people. She also had a reputation as a mental healer (that is, healing of and through the mind), although this is based on a number of dramatic and self-told stories unconfirmed by trained, disinterested observers.

Einstein, Albert (1879–1955)
Einstein radically changed the face of science. His work on relativity laid the foundations for modern physics, and revolutionized the concepts of space and time. Much New Age thought is geared to concepts connected with the relativity of space and time, but perhaps in a more philosophical way than Einstein's scientific approach.

Fortune, Dion (1891–1946)
From an early age, Dion Fortune (real name Violet Firth) showed a sensitive side to people and locations, and it soon became apparent that she had strong psychic ability. A psychoanalyst, occultist and novelist, she was raised in a Christian Science household. In the 1920s she founded her own group, the Fraternity of the Inner Light. Probably her most important book is *The Mystical Qabalah*, written in 1935. A lot of her work related to Aleister Crowley's material on magical writings, and indeed towards the end of her life the two exchanged letters.

Freud, Sigmund (1856–1940)
Hypnosis formed the basis of the early work of the founder of psychoanalysis, only later replacing it with the free association of ideas. He believed that forgotten impressions are the underlying causes of abnormal mental states such as hysteria. He developed the theory that dreams 'are an unconscious representation of repressed desires, particularly sexual'. He wrote many books, including *The Future of an Illusion* and *Moses and Monotheism*, which reflected his strong anti-Christian beliefs.

Galileo Galilei (1564-1642)
The Italian astronomer, mathematician and physicist Galileo

propounded theories on the universality of motion (nothing is ever still) which anticipated Newton's laws of motion. He is often seen as a martyr for science, because of his support of the Copernican theory of planetary motion (with the sun motionless at the centre of the solar system, while the planets, including earth, revolve around it). For this 'heresy' he has brought before the Inquisitors of the Roman Catholic Church and forced to recant.

Gandhi, Mahatma (1869–1948)

The Indian political leader and mystic developed a technique of spiritual and political action which he called *Satyagraha* ('truth force'). He advocated non-violent resistance to British rule and was opposed to modern technology for India.

After spending 21 years in South Africa opposing that government's discrimination against Indians, he returned to his homeland which he sought to free from the grip of materialism. Although a powerful revolutionary religious leader – who used that power for political and social reform – he held no governmental position. Of his many achievements, negotiating with the British in order to establish a new constitutional structure for India – which led to the granting of independence – is probably his finest.

Gandhi's spiritual development included vows of celibacy, and a return to a simpler way of life, as well as fasting, which he used on many occasions as a political device to get his way with the authorities. His concept of a 'soul force' he explained as 'a quiet and irresistible pursuit of truth'. Gandhi was a reformer, although some say he was deluded by his own power. Some of his 'non-violent' campaigns were anything but, although he himself refused to use violence in any form. He was assassinated in Delhi in 1948.

Gibran, Kahlil (1883–1931)

Compared by some to **William Blake**, Gibran was a Lebanese mystic, poet, philosopher, and playwright. His best-known books, which have predominantly Christian themes, are *The Prophet* and *Jesus, the Son of Man*. His paintings have been exhibited all over the world, and his writings have been widely translated. Since his death, there have been claims that the works published under his name were in fact written by a woman. Whatever the truth, these writings contain some of the most thought-provoking poetry in existence and are a continuing source of inspiration to those in the New Age movement.

Gurney, Edmund (1847–89)

Edmund Gurney founded the Society for Psychical Research and went on to become one of the most important early workers in the field of paranormal scientific investigation. His main interest was in hypnotism and phantasms of the living. His work on hypnotism falls into two categories. The first is the theoretical and practical study of the psychological aspects of hypnotism without looking at the paranormal side normally associated with it. The second is a largely experimental study of paranormal associations, for example the telepathic inducement of the hypnotic state, and the actions of people under hypnosis.

Hegel, Georg Wilhelm Friedrich (1770–1831)

The idealistic philosophy of this German philosopher contains various elements. The most influential of these is that reason proceeds from an understood idea to a new and contradictory concept, which leads to a third idea that transcends both earlier concepts. (Imagine a pendulum swinging between two opposites until a point of balance is reached.) The second element is the theory of self-realization by which the 'pendulum' process in the individual leads to a determinate Self which is 'for itself'. The third is the theory of history, a process leading to the forming of the Absolute Spirit which, in every specific age, manifests itself in the 'spirit of the age', informing social and political life, art, religion and knowledge. His system is known generally as Hegelianism and has influenced, among others, Karl Marx.

Hesse, Herman (1877–1962)

This Indian-born German poet and novelist was influenced by Kierkegaard, Nietzsche and Buddhism. The trademark of his work is a desire for experience unaffected by society, and the liberation of thought and behaviour from inherited attitudes. His best known works are *Siddhartha*, *Steppenwolf* and *The Glass Bead Game*.

Hippocrates (?460 BC–370 BC)

Hippocrates was an Ancient Greek physician and the 'father of medicine'. His main body of work is known as the 'Hippocratic Corpus', a collection of about seventy works, believed to have been written c. 450-350 BC. There is doubt as to whether all these writings are by Hippocrates. Plato is said to have contributed some of them, or at least influenced them. The writings, which are the oldest extant on medicine, set out a creed of conduct for medical practitioners – hence the Hippocratic oath.

Not all of Hippocrates' output centred on medicine. 'The Sacred Disease', for example, was a controversial work attacking superstition.

Home, D. D. (1833–86)

One of the most revered mediums of all time, Home was called on to display his abilities by eminent people in all areas of society, from poets to scientists. Remarkably, his reputation remained intact, despite close examination of his work and methods. Indeed, the question of how he performed such feats remains a mystery.

Hubbard, Ron L. (1911–76)

Also see **Scientology** under **Religions and Philosophical Movements**

Hubbard was a well-known writer of science fiction who founded Scientology in 1955 after the publication of his novel *Dianetics: The Modern Science of Mental Health*.

Huxley, Aldous (1894–1964)

A grandson of T. H. Huxley (the main proponent in England of Darwinism), Aldous was a mystical writer and poet who experimented with drugs in order to gain spiritual insight. His most famous work is *Brave New World*.

Ibn Arabi (1165–1240)

Also see **Monism** under **Religions and Philosophical Movements**

Known as 'the vivifier of the religion' and 'The Greatest Sheikh', Ibn Arabi was acknowledged as one of Islam's greatest mystics and poets.

He claimed that everything he wrote was a result of divine intervention. The most widely studied aspect of his work is a doctrine known by Western scholars as Monism. This doctrine suggests that only God '*is*', and the existence of anything else is an illusion.

James, William (1842–1910)
James' father was a follower of **Swedenborg** and his type of mysticism. In 1902 his book *The Varieties of Religious Experience* laid the foundations for the psychology of religion, a subject now taught in schools and universities in order to give an understanding of the individual's need for religious belief. The book also gives an understanding of the need for confirmation of one's experiences. For example, one may reach a certain conclusion about aspects of life, but need confirmation that others think and feel the same way.

Joan of Arc (1412–31)
Joan of Arc's 'heavenly voices' have been recognized as arising from psychic awareness. She experienced clairvoyance and clairaudience and came to believe that her mission was to save France. Her fanatical beliefs, while basically very simple, led to her betrayal and martyrdom by others more sophisticated than she.

John of the Cross (1542–91)
The best known work of this Roman Catholic mystical writer is *The Dark Night Of The Soul*, which shows deep insights into spiritual and psychological states.

Julian of Norwich (1342–1416)
A kind and compassionate nun and mystic, Julian of Norwich is highly regarded by the New Age Movement. Her book *Sixteen Revelations Of Divine Love* extols God's love as the answer to all problems, especially the problem of evil.

Jung, Carl Gustav (1875–1961)
Also see **Active imagination**
The psychiatric concepts of the Swiss-born Jung were initially of a

Freudian nature. In time he developed his own distinct system of psychology. After working closely with Freud, he went on to draw heavily on various esoteric, yogic and alchemical practices. His work also has a good deal of religious resonance, with shades of the occult.

Jung's main concern was with the development of his Archetypal theory (originally a Platonic concept), a collective term for the symbols that appear in dreams. His teaching was that these archetypes are common and available to all of us, but being buried in the unconscious only surface when conscious control is deliberately or inadvertently removed. Thus the monster in dreams signifies our suppressed fears.

His work is presently seen as being somewhat pseudo, in that little can be proved, and is being rejected by many modern psychiatrists.

Kant, Immanuel (1724–1804)

Kant believed that we cannot prove or disprove the existence of God, so religion must be based on faith. He argued that our knowledge of things is controlled by mental structures, which give order to our experiences. His best known work is *The Critique Of Pure Reason*, though some of his other work is probably easier to read.

Kierkegaard, Sorenaabye (1813–55)

Kierkegaard's works have had a profound influence on theology and philosophy in the 20th century through the writings of such people as Heidegger and Sartre. Kierkegaard is considered to be the father of Christian existentialism. His conclusion that 'subjectivity is truth' was the expression of his linking of truth to the existing subject and not to an object.

Koestler, Arthur (1905–83)

Hungarian-born political refugee, prisoner-of-war and writer, Arthur Koestler certainly led a varied life. He wrote a great deal of formative work on parapsychology and creativity. His most famous book, however, is *Darkness at Noon* – a fictional tale of the Stalinist era, and draws on his experiences as a prisoner during the Spanish Civil War.

Always humanistic, he wrote the anti-communist essays, *The Trail of the Dinosaur* and *Reflections on Hanging*. His later works include *The Ghost in the Machine* and *The Case of the Midwife Toad*. He committed suicide (with his wife) in 1983 after becoming terminally ill.

Krishnamurti, Jiddu (1895–1986)

From the age of twelve Krishnamurti was educated by Annie Besant and other theosophists to prepare him to be the next 'world teacher'.

In coming to an understanding of the disciplines and personal standards required by his teachers, Krishnamurti underwent many crushing psychic experiences which created tremendous self-doubt and difficulties for him. After rejecting all religions, preconceptions about Enlightenment, and philosophies, in 1929 he broke away from the Theosophical Society and began teaching a kind of therapeutic concept involving the reconciliation of opposites.

Lee, Ann (1736–84)

'Mother Ann, the word', as she became known, formulated the characteristic tenets of the Shaker movement. These were celibacy, communism, a type of elitism, pacifism, a belief in the coming of the Kingdom of God and the manifestation of spirituality through shaking (hence the name). The Shaker movement flourished when the English-born Lee and seven of her followers emigrated to New York in 1774.

Lewis, C. S. (1898–1963)

A Belfast-born theologian, Lewis went from being an agnostic to **theism** and then eventually moved towards Christianity. He wrote a number of books in defence of Christian values; *The Pilgrim's Regress* is one such example. Lewis' most popular writings are the seven chronicles of Narnia. The second of these, *The Lion, the Witch and the Wardrobe*, has laid claim to being the best children's book ever written. It was not widely known at the time that his writings were informed by his strong Christian and moral beliefs.

Lieh-Tzu (4th century BC)

Lieh-Tzu was a Taoist philosopher who suggested that Hedonism (pleasure is the ultimate good) is the only way to experience life, which ultimately ends in death. Life is to be experienced in full, not suffered.

Leary, Timothy (1920–96)
The American Timothy Leary is best remembered for his anti-capitalist philosophy, encapsulated by his catchphrase 'Turn on, tune in and drop out', which was adopted by the 'hippy' culture of the 1960s. Demonized for his influence on young people and especially for his experimentation with psychedelic drugs, Leary was in fact genuine in his work with the expansion of consciousness. He believed that life should be lived to its greatest potential, and held to that even when he was terminally ill with cancer.

Levi, Eliphas (1810–75)
The Parisian-born Levi was probably the best known of all French occultists. His books, which include *The History of Magic* and *The Key of the Mysteries*, established his high reputation in occultist circles in France and Britain.

Loyola, Ignatius (1495–1556)
A Spanish mystic and religious innovator, in 1540 Loyola founded The Society of Jesus whose members were called Jesuits. This was preceded by years of study which led to a 'vision' of Christ. Loyola and his followers dedicated themselves to the service of suffering Christians, the conversion of unbelievers and absolute obedience to the Pope. Each Jesuit is to carry out to the letter the commands laid upon him.

Luther, Martin (1483–1546)
Born in Germany, Luther was one of the most influential figures in Western Christianity and the architect of the Protestant Reformation. From his study of the Bible he formed his doctrine of 'justification by faith'; that is, if one believes, one is justified in one's actions. The family of Lutheran churches is named after him. He was ordained in 1507 as a Roman Catholic priest and he also taught philosophy. After a

pilgrimage to Rome in 1510, Luther was appalled by the decadence of church leaders and the sale of indulgences (priests would 'forgive' individuals who made contributions to the Church). It was these practices that led him to protest and, in 1517, to his writing of the 95 Theses.

Initially his aim was internal reform of the Roman Catholic Church, but his insistence on scripture alone being the source of authority for the Church was rejected by Catholic theologians, thus beginning a persecution of Luther's followers and the schism that brought the establishment of Protestantism.

Marx, Karl (1818–83)

Marx is remembered principally as the man whose ideas provided a philosophical basis for modern communism, which in its purest form may be a basis for the management of society. Marx himself eventually rejected all forms of religion, feeling that a taught mass belief gives power to some over others. His revolutionary activities led in 1849 to his expulsion from Prussia and exile in England where he was to write many of his works. His most famous work, *Das Kapital*, draws on Hegelian philosophy, despite his rejection of its idealism and advocacy of a proper framework of law (instead of appeals to natural justice) as the instrument of social justice.

Mill, John Stuart (1806–73)

The work of Mill has had a profound influence on both sociology and economics. A philosopher, writer and political activist, his best known writings are *On Liberty* and *The Subjection of Woman* (he was an ardent advocate of women's suffrage). In ethics he was an altruistic utilitarian and his *Principles of Political Economy* is still considered indispensable study material.

Sun Myung Moon (1920–)

Also see **Unification Church** under **Religions and Philosophical Movements.**

Korean founder and leader of the Unification Church, his main work is *The Divine Principle*. His followers are known as Moonies.

Thomas More, Sir (Saint) (1487–1535)

A statesman and humanist, Thomas More was Henry VIII's Lord Chancellor until the King's wrangle with the Roman Catholic Church over his divorce from Catherine of Aragon led to the Act of Supremacy and the transfer of papal powers to Henry. More's opposition to Henry resulted in his imprisonment and subsequent martyrdom. His most famous work is *Utopia*, a representation of an ideal state founded on reason.

Morris, William (1834–96)

A socialist and writer, as well as a craftsman and designer of wallpaper and fabrics, Morris held wide-ranging ideas on social welfare, from better conditions for workers to the right of ordinary people to live in pleasant surroundings. Morris also had connections with the Anglo-Catholic Oxford Movement, and believed in the resurgence of spirituality, in that an individual must discover for himself his own spiritual beliefs and find others who think likewise. He supported the Pre-Raphaelite Brotherhood's rejection of industrial, materialist culture.

Myers, F. W. H. (1834–1901)

A friend of **Edmund Gurney**, Frederick William Henry Myers was one of the founders of the Society for Psychical Research. He was the first Briton to explore the areas of hypnosis and schizophrenia, which up until that time was the domain of European investigators. His two-volume work *Human Personality and its Survival of Bodily Death*, published two years after his death, outlines his views that the personality survives the death of the body. This is still a seminal work in the understanding of spiritualism.

Nichiren, Shoshu (1222–82)

Also see **Buddhism** under **Religions and Philosophical Movements.**

Nichiren was a Japanese Buddhist priest and founder of Nichiren Buddhism. He taught that the *Lotus Sutra* (probably the most important text of the 'Great Tradition' of Buddhism) was superior to all other *sutras* or teachings. The main tenets of Nichiren Buddhism are: 1, the Buddha is eternal; 2, the Buddha's personal enlightenment guarantees the enlightenment of all sentient beings; 3, the lotus *sutra* was given by Buddha to replace all other teachings; and 4, Nichiren is the incarnation of a being through whose torment his followers may obtain salvation.

Nietzsche, Friedrich Wilhelm (1844–1900)

The German philosopher Nietzsche rejected Christianity for its 'slave morality', advocating instead an individualistic morality that would bring about a society led by super-men. He is remembered for his phrase 'God is Dead', which described how man was gradually denying the existence of God. One of the foremost thinkers of all time, his ideas had a profound effect on 20th-century idealogues.

Paracelsus (1493–1541)

Paracelsus was a physician and alchemist who first pursued magical and occultist activities, and then advocated a mystical form of Pantheism. (In this, nature and God are believed to be identical – a belief that is accepted as valid by many New Age thinkers.)

Patanjali (2nd century BC)

A mystic and teacher, Patanjali is acknowledged as the author of the first three books of the yoga *sutras*, which is still today a source of much esoteric yogic belief. He first taught the art of meditation and also the eightfold path (see **Crown Chakra** in Section Three). His *sutras* or teachings are divided into 196 aphorisms or verses presented in four easily assimilable sections.

Peale, Norman Vincent (1928–86)

A popular writer in the 1950s and 60s, Peale was a believer in and teacher of positive thinking, which is now a widely accepted technique within many New Age religions. His most popular book is *The Power of Positive Thinking*.

Piaget, Jean (1896–1981)

Swiss psychologist and pioneer in the study of child intelligence,

Piaget studied zoology but then turned to psychology and became a professor at Geneva University. He is well known for his research on the development of perception, intelligence and logic. He used his own children as case studies, and to postulate the various stages of cognitive progression. Piaget's work on child development has had a profound influence on modern education and on the management of childhood trauma.

He perceived, for instance, that the older child is capable of seeing the intention behind a lie whereas a younger child is not. Between the ages of 11 and 14 the child is capable of abstract thought and can imagine hypotheses and the possible consequences of his and others' actions. *The Moral Judgement of the Child* indicates that rules are socially transmitted and variable from one society to another.

His books include *The Child's Conception of the World*, and *The Origin of Intelligence in Children*.

Plato (427?–347 BC)

Plato held that the physical world is a temporary copy of permanent unchanging reality. (He contrasted form which is authentic and everlasting with appearance which is short-lived and illusory.) This is similar to the belief 'as above, so below', and highlights the concept of the transience of the physical world.

The term 'platonic friendship' has come to mean a non-sexual relationship between two people of opposite sex. The implication in modern-day terms is that such a relationship is somehow less valid than a sexual relationship. However, Plato's concept was that a spiritual relationship could be so deep and meaningful that the sexual act became simply an expression of that spiritual relationship, or that it was in some cases unnecessary.

Swami Prabhupada (1896–1977)

Founder of the **Hare Krishna** movement, Swami Prabhupada decided to become a monk at the age of 58 after many years as a businessman. In 1965, after much religious study, he began spreading the Krishna beliefs.

Rajneesh, Bhagwan Sri (1931–91)
Rajneesh founded a New Religious movement that promoted self-gratification, sexual indulgence and the use of drugs. Despite the fact that the movement did not have roots in any other religion, it gained a particularly large following in the United States in the 1960s. Bhagwan himself was deported to India because some of the practices he advocated were considered immoral.

Rousseau, Jean-Jacques (1712–78)
A radical French philosopher who supported the education of children in his famous book *Emile* while abandoning his own offspring to the workhouse. He was an advocate of deism and had a socialist view of society.

Russell, Charles Taze (1872–1970)
The founder of the Jehovah's Witnesses, Russell developed his own system of biblical interpretation which centred on prophecy. This included a prediction that the world would end in 1914. His followers became known as Russellites, but later split into a number of groups, the best known being the Jehovah's Witnesses.

Sartre, Jean-Paul (1905–80)
A moralist, man of letters, novelist, playwright, but above all a philosopher, Sartre was a leading exponent of **existentialism** (see under **Religions and Philosophical Movements**).

Sartre's main influence, Heidegger, is evident in his phenomenal production of works on self-consciousness, imagination and the emotions. In his first major work of philosophy, *Being and Nothingness*, he describes man as 'a useless passion'. His first novel, *Nausea*, has been called by some the most influential French novel of the century. Unfortunately for his reputation, Sartre is often mis-quoted and his ideas have been misunderstood and for these reasons he has lost some credibility over the last twenty years or so.

Schopenhauer, Artur (1788–1860)
The German philosopher Artur Schopenhauer hated the idealist tradi-

tion of his time, as formed via Hegel – he was also disillusioned with his own life. His major work, *The World as Will and Idea*, reflects the influence of Plato and Kant and is a contemplation on the theory of knowledge and its implications for the philosophy of nature and ethics. He emphasized the active role of 'will' as the creative but hidden, irrational force in human nature, and to this end he influenced both Nietzsche and Freud. Schopenhauer argued that art represented the sole kind of knowledge that was not subject to 'will'.

He came to public attention in 1851, with the diverse essays and aphoristic writings, which were published under the title *Parerga and Paralipomena*. His pessimistic and atheistic view of life influenced **Tolstoy**, Richard Wagner and Thomas Hardy.

Smith, Joseph (1805–44)

The founder of Mormonism, Smith claimed that his work *The Book of Mormon* was translated, with the help of an angel, from hieroglyphics written on golden plates. An open advocate of polygamy from 1843, he was subsequently arrested and then murdered by a mob.

Socrates (470–400 BC)

The teachings of the Greek philosopher Socrates are known to us thanks to the writings of his pupil, Plato. Concerned with the moral improvement of the citizens of Athens, he set himself up to be their guide. The knowledgeable, he believed, could not deliberately err, because virtue and knowledge were as blood brothers. He regarded the soul as the centre of both waking consciousness and moral character. He was very critical of the government and of religious establishments in Athens and consequently made many enemies. He was tried and convicted of corrupting Athenian youth and for religious heresy and given the choice of exile or death. He chose death, by drinking hemlock. His method of enquiry to further knowledge, known as The Socratic dialogue, involves examining the answers to a series of questions.

Solzhenitsyn, Alexander Isayevich (1918–)

The writer Solzhenitsyn is most widely remembered for his outspoken criticism of the Soviet regime in Russia before the fall of the Iron Curtain. His experiences in a forced labour camp, where he spent eight years, were the source of inspiration for his novel, *One Day in the Life of Ivan Denisovich*. His two masterpieces, *The First Circle* and *Cancer Ward*, are satires on the harshness of life in the Stalinist era, and were written after the ban imposed on his work from 1966. Four years after being awarded the Nobel Prize for Literature, in 1970, Solzhenitsyn was deported to the West and eventually settled in the United States. *The Oak and the Calf*, a literary memoir, and subsequent works showed his development as a Christian thinker and are testimony to his faith.

Steiner, Rudolf (1861–1925)

Rudolf Steiner's extraordinary mind revealed a philosophical link between natural science and the world of **spirit**. His ideas took shape in a number of ways and spanned art and architecture, education and agriculture. His interests in science and art led him to the work of Goethe and he was, in fact, responsible for editing Goethe's scientific works. In 1897 he went to Berlin, primarily as editor of *The Magazine for Literature*, but while he was there he also joined the staff of a working men's college. It was at this time that he developed the ability to meditate, a facility which he considered crucial to man's well-being.

A ten-year connection with the Theosophical Society and meetings with its principals, Annie Besant and Colonel Olcott among others, resulted in Steiner becoming General-Secretary to the German branch of the Society. However, in 1909 he broke away from theosophy to found the Anthroposophical Society and a system which explained the world in terms of spiritual science. His theories on the education of children received widespread acceptance, particularly in Britain. His system is concerned solely with general instruction, the children receiving the help they need in order to discover their identity. This education encourages freedom of expression and explores a particular line of inquiry which might lead the individual to self-knowledge through such disciplines as art, mathematics, music and movement.

In the last years of his life Steiner developed and worked on ideas concerning **karma** and **reincarnation**. In 1923 he re-formed the

Anthroposophical Society as the General Anthroposophical Society, which was intended for people outside the original movement who wanted to follow a course of self-development.

Swedenborg, Emanuel (1688–1772)

A well-known engineer and scientist as well as religious thinker, the Swedish-born Swedenborg published many works on a wide variety of subjects, ranging from the animal world to the brain. It was not until the publication in 1745 of *Worship and the Love of God* that Swedenborg devoted himself solely to religious and spiritual questions. His mysticism involved regular, direct communication with heavenly beings. The records of these communications form the basis of his religious writings. Swedenborg had no intention of forming a new sect or religion. He believed that his followers could be of any denomination. After his death, however, the New Jerusalem Church or Swedenborgian movement was established by his followers.

The concept of humanness is a central idea in Swedenborg's work – 'it is only through man's own eyes that he can see God, ... God exists only in the terms that man can see him and ... those terms are human terms'.

Teilhard de Chardin, Pierre (1881–1955)

De Chardin was a Jesuit priest and also a palaeontologist of some renown. His most influential work, *The Phenomenon of Man*, was published after his death. In it he describes the salvation of the world through a fusing of science and religion. This would involve religion reinterpreting itself in terms of evolution and science becoming more mystical.

Thomas à Kempis (1380–1471)

Thomas à Kempis was a German monk and mystic whose *The Imitation of Christ* to this day continues to motivate many towards a life of religious devotion.

Tolstoy, Leo (1828–1910)

Although most famous for his classic novels *War and Peace* and *Anna Karenina*, Tolstoy was also a mystic, social reformer and great thinker who dismissed traditional Christian doctrines in favour of a more rational system. Tolstoy's pre-occupation with the mystical elements of death – his own and the hereafter – made him give up the traditional aspects of his aristocratic lifestyle and wish for a simpler, almost peasant-like existence, and in this he was a forerunner of **existentialism**. (see under Religions and Philosophical Movements).

Vivekananda, Swami (1863–1902)
Vivekananda believed that India could be changed through a new interpretation of Vedanta (the unification of science and religion). This would include, among other things, freedom for women. In 1881 he converted to Hinduism despite many years of studying Western philosophy.

Yeats, W. B. (1865–1939)
With his friend George Russell, a mystic and visionary, the poet and writer Yeats formed the Dublin Hermetic Society. It was through this Society that Yeats met the well-known theosophist Mohini Chatterjee, who taught him the basics of Hindu philosophy, a subject that Yeats continued to study throughout his life.

Yeats was also interested in spiritualism, although he maintained a rigorous attitude. This stemmed not from scepticism, but from the realization that many explanations of phenomena are possible.

Yogananda Paramahansa (1893–1953)
One of the most important spiritual figures of our time, he founded the Self-Realization Fellowship in 1925 with the intention of disseminating the science of Kriya Yoga and the art of spiritual living to attain direct personal experience of God. His *Autobiography of a Yogi* has been translated into eighteen languages and is many people's starting point in the journey towards an understanding of spirituality.

PERI-CONCEPTUAL CARE
See **Therapies**

PHRENOLOGY
See **Divination**

PHYSIOGNOMY
See **Divination**

PLAYING CARDS
See **Divination**

POLARITY THERAPY
See **Therapies**

POLTERGEIST

Poltergeist (from the German 'noisy spirit') activity is not necessarily the work of spiritual agencies and is more likely to be caused by a build-up of excess psychic energy. It often occurs at major turning points in people's lives, such as puberty or after childbirth. In primitive societies it may be that the ceremonies to mark such rites of passage enabled excesses of energy to be discharged without harm to anyone. In Western society less attention is paid to these rites, and so there is more opportunity for poltergeist activity to occur. Around teenagers, poltergeist activity can take several forms. The most startling of these is **telekinesis** – the movement of objects, both large and small. Few people are harmed by such movements, although it can be frightening to be pinned down by a large piece of furniture. Often objects will disappear only to turn up again when least expected; or objects will appear apparently out of nowhere. This phenomenon is known as 'apport'.

Poltergeist activity can often be quietened by very simple techniques. If the disturbance is recognized quickly enough, the teenager can be encouraged to take a glass of water to bed. This performs two, or perhaps three, functions. First, using the law of correspondences (see **Magic**) the young person will feel protected. Secondly the water will act as a kind of early warning system of strange movements. Thirdly, the act of throwing away the water will have the effect of discharging some of the excess emotional energy, because water is said to represent emotion. If the activity becomes more troublesome, the house can be cleared very simply, using a **creative visualization**.

Visualize the house being 'washed' three times: once to remove the physical or material residue, once to remove mental contamination, and lastly to cleanse the spiritual **aura** of the house. After being challenged three times in accordance with magical law the negative or wild energy will not usually remain in evidence. It is worthwhile remembering, too, that such wild energy feeds on fear. A **crystal** such as rock quartz or amethyst will quieten the atmosphere if it is specifically dedicated to that purpose.

POSSESSION

Popularly, possession is understood to be the taking over of a personality by a non-human entity. Sometimes this can be a deceased person, an evil entity or even by another personality or sub-personality of the 'victim'. Possession can also become apparent when someone becomes possessed, or aware of possessing, extraordinary powers in times of crisis. For example, sometimes in accidents feats of strength and bravery are performed which are not normally thought possible.

Possession by a spirit entity is dealt with by **exorcism**. This is when the entity is commanded to return to whence it came. Often this entity will respond to a name which, in occult terms, suggests that the entity has been acknowledged and can therefore be controlled. This corresponds to types of therapeutic work in which the individual is enabled to regain access to certain suppressed parts of his or her own being (see **Psychosynthesis**, under **Therapies**).

Possession may occur through a lack of knowledge and bad practice, and through allowing a weak personality to experiment with hidden (**occult**) knowledge without supervision. It often appears to be spontaneous, although there are those who would point out that, at some level, the individual will have been party – or open – to that possession. When exploring the world of spirit, it is wise to follow an accepted method of development or philosophical thought. Various methods of protection can be used, such as the wearing of a crucifix which has been blessed or mental constructs such as a visualization of light protecting you. One may protect oneself by **prayer**, **chanting** or **music**. Some years ago it was felt unwise to meditate alone in spiritualism, because of the dangers posed by negative energies or spirits, and thus the idea of a development circle was born.

A rule of thumb to follow is that sub-personalities, when recognized as such, should be absorbed or integrated. The influence of discarnate **spirits**, such as **guides** or visiting entities, should be accepted or rejected according to their intent. Many **mediums** or channellers are happy to allow themselves to be controlled or 'possessed' by discarnate entities during a sitting, in order for those present to be given information which would not be available to them under normal circumstances. Such 'possession', however, is only established after a trust has been built up over a period of time between the medium and the discarnate being. Additionally, there needs to be a degree of trust between the channeller and the sitters, because the channeller can be vulnerable during possession. The dangers inherent in this vulnerability gave rise to the so-called 'closed' circle, which requires a degree of spiritual understanding in the sitters, thus enhancing the calibre of energy and power available for use and creating a group mind of intent and therefore an easier connection.

PRAYER

Prayer can be defined as an act of supplication or a polite request. The components of a prayer are said to be acknowledgement of the status of the god, a recognition of a greater power, a request and a promise. Recent research has found that prayer has a healing effect on many illnesses. Experimentation has ranged from 'absent prayer' – praying for people who are not known (see **Absent healing**) to personal prayer for oneself. On the latter level it is suggested that the **relaxation** which is brought about by repetition of a well-loved formula and a stilling of the mind acts in the same way as **stress (1)** management. The levels of adrenaline and stress hormones are lowered, and the so-called 'placebo' effect – an expectation of better health because of one's belief in God or gods – will have a healing effect.

For many of us religion and ritual are ways of tapping into cosmic consciousness, something greater and wiser than ourselves, for guidance. Chanting can also bring about a change of awareness. If one believes that the power of many people linked together is far greater than the power of the individual, group prayer focused on one common aim can have a profound effect.

There are many aids to prayer and worship. The rosary of the Catholic Church is used as a counter for the repetitions of the various prayers, as are prayer beads in other religions. **Mandalas** are an aid to concentration. Pictures or icons of a revered personality, whether Christ, Buddha or a lesser being, are also seen as an integral part of prayer. **Mantras** are different forms of chanting used to focus the mind.

PRECOGNITION

Precognition, prediction and premonition are all aspects of clairvoyance which concern future events.

Precognition is 'having achieved knowledge of impending events without using the normal conscious senses'. In prediction the future event will have been spoken about or noted prior to the event by the person who receives the information. In premonition the information received usually seems to be a warning of danger, difficulty or disaster. For instance, a developing clairvoyant found that before several aeroplane crashes she would dream of hands reaching out towards her. She came to dread such dreams – her distress being that her dream was always too late to change the outcome.

There are many theories as to how these aspects of awareness work. Probably the easist to understand, particularly in cases of premonition, is that we do not actually 'see' the future event but are reacting on some deep level to a psychic disturbance. Another theory is that this same psychic disturbance enables us to access the **Akashic records**, which is something the majority of people are not able to do at will.

Since **dreams** are often one of the ways in which we gain precognitive knowledge it is accepted that a change of **consciousness** is necessary to access this information. An individual will be increasingly able to predict future events the more consciously aware he or she becomes. Often a developing clairvoyant will be able to acquire their own shorthand of symbolism which becomes recognizable to them. In the example quoted above, the woman was able to recognize the symbolism of the hands without being able to identify the location of the mishaps.

PRIMAL SCREAM THERAPY
See **Therapies**

PSYCHE

Psyche comes from the Greek word for the soul. It is perhaps easiest to understand the real meaning of the word by looking at the myth of Psyche and Eros. Psyche was an exceptionally beautiful, but wayward, woman who made the goddess Aphrodite jealous. The goddess instructed her son, Eros (the god of love), to make Psyche fall in love with the ugliest creature he could find. Instead, taking on human form, he fell in love with her. Their story tells of the development and growth necessary for self-understanding and a successful relationship. Only by overcoming her own shortcomings, and undertaking a task apparently beyond human ability, was Psyche finally able to be reunited with Eros in the upper realms.

This story tells us about an elusive part of ourselves which, when harnessed by love and mental discipline, enables us to reach our own deeper selves and access previously unavailable information. In short, achieving this unity brings us into touch with our own souls. Being in touch in this way opens up further possibilities.

PSYCHIC ABILITY

The capacity to be in touch with previously hidden information is what the majority of people understand by psychic ability. Yoga teaches us that these *siddhis*, or powers, will only develop properly as part of our spiritual development. One should not attempt to train specifically in these skills lest it leads to their misuse. The wise pupil will appreciate that psychic skills are tools to enable the individual to be of service to others as well as enabling him or her to live life to its full capacity. Spiritual and psychic development will thus take place hand in hand.

PSYCHIC ATTACK

Many sensitives and channellers fear psychic attack, although correct spiritual development and good practice will make such an occurrence unlikely. The belief is that as the **aura** is an extremely sensitive instrument the subtle bodies can be influenced by **negative thoughts (1)** and misplaced emotion in much the same way that a physical body can be injured. At certain stages of development this is indeed true, but if one believes in the principle of personal responsibility, there will be a certain degree of collusion and an acceptance of victimization on the part of the recipient of such an attack.

A simple way of dealing with such a situation is to use visualization, such as mirroring the ill-will away from oneself. Incidentally, when under any kind of attack one may always mentally ask for Divine justice in the knowledge that 'what goes around, must come around' in due course. Often inaction is as effective as action.

PSYCHIC HEALING
See **Therapies**

PSYCHIC SKILLS

There are many types of psychic skills. The most common are clairaudience (receiving information by hearing), clairsentience (by sensing), and **clairvoyance** (by seeing). People may develop gifts in **healing**, or psychic surgery (operation on the physical body to remove such things as diseased organs and tumours.) Often such people prefer to be known as sensitives. As well as the better known skills there are others such as psychokinesis (the movement of objects), psychic photography (without the use of a camera an image is imprinted on photographic paper) and psychic portraiture (the ability to draw the sitter's spirit **guides** and loved ones). These are all developments which are in keeping with the sensitive's personality, and are often modified or disappear as the individual understands his or her own psyche and reaches for further spiritual enlightenment.

Q

QI

The ancient Chinese held that a vital energy, qi (or ch'i) permeates the whole universe, from minerals, through plants and animals to human beings. This energy increases in concentration and power the higher up the scale of earth-life one goes. Qi enters the human body through the ingestion of food and air, and the etheric body through planetary and cosmic influences. The more subtle the energy taken into the body the more spiritual the understanding of the individual becomes. Qi is comparable to the Hindu concept of *prana*.

R

REINCARNATION

The idea of having to be born – or to exist – repeatedly is one that belongs mainly to Eastern religions. A concept accepted by spiritualists, it seems to arise from the need to feel that we continue to exist in one form or another beyond physical death. Reincarnation explains how the soul learns and relearns lessons on the physical plane. All lessons appropriate to a single lifetime are experienced consecutively and within the structure of man-made time. When these lessons are not properly integrated by the soul it is given the opportunity to relearn the lessons in another way. This happens in order for the soul to be purified sufficiently so that it no longer needs to take on a physical form but can exist in a totally blissful state. The process can take many lifetimes.

To understand reincarnation it is perhaps easier to do away with the concept of man-made time and to think of the soul's existence as being like a wheel. At the centre of the wheel is the real soul, which is part of 'all that is'. Radiating from this are the spokes of the wheel, each of which is one particular lifetime. The more spiritually aware one becomes the clearer are the lessons to be experienced in each life. This knowledge can open the doors of perception to other lifetimes, at which point it is possible to look into other aspects of the soul's experience and become conscious of how each lifetime affects the others. The rim of the wheel connects all these lifetimes. The truly aware individual can often access information from other incarnations.

Some people believe that not all incarnations take place within the physical or earth plane but can occur in other dimensions. Others feel that what appear to be different reincarnations are in fact hidden aspects of our own personalities which have surfaced in order to help us to understand ourselves better. This latter theory does not explain the information that is discovered under regression and which can be verified; see **Hypnosis** and **Akashic Records**.

RELAXATION TECHNIQUES

Many individuals and therapists use relaxation techniques to relieve stress and tension, and so enable and encourage healing. Stress and tension not only raise stress hormone levels, which in turn depress immunity, but can also reduce the blood supply and so disturb normal bodily functioning. Breathing exercises, **massage** and **meditation** are some of the techniques used.

Tape-recorded instructions can show you how to relax the whole body, then how to do this quickly in a number of different situations, and finally how to use relaxation to cope with the onset of feelings of **anxiety** (1) or tension. The exercises teach youl what it feels like to be totally relaxed and where particular centres of tension are.

Regular practice is essential and should be at a settled time of day reserved for the purpose. When you have completed the relaxation exercises, try to imagine herself in a situation where you feel completely calm and contented. The sight and sounds of this situation can then be recreated at will whenever the situation demands it.

The following is a beneficial exercise for when you begin to feel anxious: relax the brows and neck, drop your shoulders and practise slow, regular, shallow breathing. A key word like 'calm' or 'relax' can be used to start the sequence. Exercise such as cycling and swimming may also help to relieve symptoms of anxiety.

RELIGIONS AND PHILOSOPHICAL MOVEMENTS
Abramic Religions

These are religions that accept a creator God. The major ones are Christianity, Islam, and Judaism. They claim Abraham as a role model for their faith and custom.

Adventism
The best known Adventist movement is the Seventh Day Adventists, which was founded in the 19th century by William Miller. He taught that Christ's return was imminent and that a millennial kingdom would be inaugurated.

African Traditional Religions
These religions stress healing and spiritual well-being, and usually express their beliefs through dance and music. In them the role of ancestors is a common theme and the practice of witchcraft widespread. African traditional religions seem not to have been influenced by Christianity, Islam or Hinduism, although these do have their place in the religious framework in Africa. **Ritual** is important, with or without the participation of priests.

Agnosticism
This is the belief that knowledge of a divine being, immortality, and a supernatural world is not possible. People usually profess to be agnostic when they do not wish to be called atheist.

Anglican
An Anglican is a member of the **Church of England**. Anglo-Catholicism is the High-Church movement, sometimes known as the Oxford Movement, within the Church of England.

Anthropomorphism/Anthroposophy
This is the attribution of human characteristics or emotions to God, e.g., God the Father, Son and Holy Ghost. The word anthroposophy (literally 'man-wisdom') was first used in the writings of the 17th-century mystic Thomas Vaughan.

As a spiritual philosophy and set of teachings, anthroposophy was founded by **Rudolf Steiner** (see entry under People). Steiner had started as a theosophist, but he felt that **theosophy** was developing too strong a bias towards Eastern doctrines at the expense of Western faiths. Many of Steiner's teaching were already part of Western occultism.

Arcane School

This is a form of **theosophy**, but differs in opinion as to who is the world saviour.

Asceticism

Religious practices that consist of extreme spiritual exercises based on self-denial and physical deprivation.

Atheism

According to this, God does not exist, the existence of God is not proveable, and therefore there can be no religion.

Baha'i

This faith, which originated in Persia (Iran) in the 19th century, promotes universal peace, the unity of the human race, the removal of prejudices, the essential unity of all religions and prayer for the dead. The movement has spread widely throughout America, Europe, Africa and the East. Although originating from Islamic religion, it is considered heretical by believers of this faith.

Baptist

The Baptists trace their origin to the New Testament but only emerged as an identifiable movement in the 17th century. There is a great diversity of belief and practice within the Baptist Church, although the central core of belief is in the baptism of the faithful.

Buddhism

Buddhism resulted from the enlightenment of Gautama Siddhartha in Nepal in the 6th century BC. From the time of this experience he began to preach a set of disciplines and doctrines called the Dhamma. Buddhism teaches that, with understanding, the individual may be freed from great suffering and illusion. He may attain Samsara – freedom from earthly existence – through right action.

Unlike most other religions, Buddhists do not believe in a surviving personal aspect of human personality nor in the existence of a god or gods. There are a large number of Buddhist schools of thought, ranging from The Great Sangha Party, which dates from about one hundred years after the death of Buddha in 383 BC to Nichiren Buddhism in the 13th century.

Cabbala

The Cabbala is a way of experiencing the divine/human relationship and recognizing the oneness of everything. It is also experienced as a magical system of working. The major written source of information is the Zohar, which emerged in medieval times and is based on the beliefs of Plato, who held that the material world is merely a copy of unchanging forms. According to Plato, the truly aware practitioner and philosopher is able to perceive things from a proper perspective, and to use reason to stabilize the world in which he lives.

Cargo Cults

Where earthly prosperity seems to be a major factor in making converts, the movements are known as cargo cults. They were first discovered in Polynesia where followers of a prophet figure are promised 'cargo' or rewards when the people are freed from repression by a 'new saviour'.

Catholic Apostolic Church

This originated as a charismatic group with a strong emphasis on the imminent return of Christ. Many of the new religious movements in the Third World have been influenced by this movement.

Charismatic Movement

Starting in the 1950s, this revival movement spreads Pentecostal-type experiences (the gifts of the Holy Spirit, especially healing and speaking in tongues). It is a world-wide phenomenon and has brought much of the 'joyful experiences' of non-Western religions into Christianity.

Children of God

Originating in the late 1960s, this group began as part of the Jesus Movement. Members developed charismatic gifts and encouraged prophecy. It developed into a cult, with one of its most highly publicized practices apparently involving prostitution in order to attract potential converts. Mainstream attention was focused on the movement when it became necessary to de-programme members.

Chinese Religions

Traditionally, three major Chinese religions have been identified – **Buddhism**, Confucianism and Taoism. However, this view is challenged today by a much more complex one which sees the Chinese religious tradition vigorously incorporating various other traditions within Chinese religion. The cult of ancestors, **shamanism**, and the 'worship of heaven' are all important aspects of Chinese religion.

Church of England

Also known as Anglicanism or, outside England, as Episcopalianism. Christianity was brought to the British Isles by the Romans in the 4th century. A century later attacks by Anglo-Saxon pagans almost destroyed it, and in the late sixth and early seventh centuries the Italian missionary Augustine of Canterbury began 'reconverting' the natives, starting with King Aethelbert. Until the Norman invasion of 1066, the English Church remained isolated from the ecclesiastical affairs of continental Europe, but by the time of Henry VIII conflict between England and the papacy had reached breaking point and the King used his divorce from the Catholic Catherine of Aragon as a way of detaching England from the Church of Rome, thus instituting a **Reformation** of a different character from that experienced on the Continent. The English Church briefly returned to the Roman fold, under Mary, but her successor, Elizabeth I, restored an independent church that trod a careful path between Catholicism and Calvinism.

In the 17th and 18th centuries the Anglican Church was affected by Deism, whose adherents (including Voltaire, Rousseau, Benjamin Franklin and Thomas Jefferson) believed in an intelligent creator – indicated by the course of nature – that does not guide or intervene. More influential, though, has been the revival in evangelism. This began in the late 18th century when a group of influential Englishmen, including William Wilberforce and Lord Shaftesbury, established the Clapham Sect, which pressed for social reform as well as support for missionary work and evangelical Christianity. In the 1830s the Oxford Movement set in train a controversial revitalization of Anglican rituals. Known as Anglo-Catholics, its clergy revived ceremonial customs and doctrines associated with Roman Catholicism, and advocated a return to spirituality. The movement's concern for social welfare was continued by Christian socialists in the mid 19th century. An awareness of the Church's social responsibilities and a strong strain of evangelism are still to be found in its clergy.

Comparative Religion

The study of comparative religion began with the Greek philosopher Xenophanes in the 6th century BC when he observed that Thracians and Ethiopians depicted their gods after their own image. Writers like St Augustine made acute observations on the differences between religions, but it was not until Darwin's theory of evolution gained popularity in the late 19th century that the serious study of comparative religion began. Many scholars discovered what they saw as links through evolution and religion. During the up-surge of interest in Eastern religions in the 1960s, comparative religion was renamed 'religious studies'. At its most basic, comparative religion teaches that all religions are equal and originate from one reality. However, a problem occurs when we realize that the teachings of the world's major religions are as different as they are similar.

Death of God Theology

This theological movement of the early 1960s was built on the assumption of a continued movement away from a belief in God. It is associated with the British theologian John T. Robinson, then Bishop of Woolwich, whose book *Honest to God* caused a sensation on its publication in 1963. The term was used by theologians in the 1960s to express the reality of religion (a system of belief) in a worldly society.

Eckankar

A New Religious movement founded in 1965 by Paul Tritchell (1908–71), who claimed to be the 971st ECK master and revealer of a long-secret tradition to the world. His teachings included reincarnation, soul travel, and many yogic and occult beliefs. The group he founded split in 1978 after internal differences.

Ecumenical Movement

The name given to the drive by those in the Protestant, Catholic and Eastern Orthodox faiths to unite all Christians. The movement got under way in 1910 and led eventually, in 1948, to the formation of the World Council of Churches.

EST

Erhard Seminar Training was founded in 1971 by Werner Erhard on the basis of spiritual practices derived from Zen **Buddhism** and **Scientology**. The movement, which has described itself by various names, holds intense weekend seminars that are intended to break down the participants' inhibitions and put them 'in touch with themselves'.

Evangelical Movement

Evangelical Christians believe in the inspiration of the Bible, which they regard as the divine rule of faith and practice. They affirm the basic doctrines of the Gospel. Evangelization was initially the spreading of the Christian Gospel. More recently it has come to mean the spreading of any propaganda that creates converts.

Existentialism

Existentialism, broadly defined, is unconditional acceptance by God which enables each individual to have the courage to be. It is 'that which is outside oneself'. The movement emerged shortly before World War Two, and was united by common concerns, motives and emphases. Arising out of the writings of **Kierkegaard**, its most influential exponents were Martin Heidegger, Karl Jaspers and **Sartre**.

The movement began with the belief that Western philosophy is preoccupied with the idea of basic nature – that is, with the universal features of anything – rather than with the particular. Individual essence (one's basic nature) is counted as being more real than existence because it is unchanging. Existentialists believe that Western philosophy is irrelevant because it has obscured truth and not illuminated the reality of human existence. Generally speaking, an existentialist Christian theology argues that the self is a unity of radical freedom and confinement. Faith is an acceptance of this paradox. The decision to be oneself as oneself is the only faith necessary. Individuals who have developed the courage 'to be' have, therefore, embraced the idea of unconditional acceptance by God.

Findhorn Community
The Findhorn Community is one of the most influential New Age communities and sources for modern neopaganism. Founded in 1965, the community ascribed its success to the intervention of nature spirits such as gnomes, fairies and dryads. The community is influenced by, and promotes, various forms of occultism and theosophical thought. The 'games' the community has developed are widely accepted as expanding spiritual awareness.

Freemasonry
The origins of the movement lie in 12th-century Europe. There are two major divisions: the Old Charges, which date from between 1390 and 1400, and the Masonic Word, which is a Scottish institution of unclear origin. 'Speculative masonry', or modern freemasonry, developed in the 18th century. The Grand Lodge was formed in 1717 to co-ordinate other lodges. The origins of most Masonic ceremonies are somewhat obscure, but are believed to have a basis in initiation rituals.

The movement places much importance on social welfare activities, particularly for its own members, and claims to be based on the fundamentals of all religions. The Church of England and Roman Catholics have tended to condemn Freemasonry as un-Christian. Initially connected with the art of sacred construction, it is an international organization whose principles are embodied in symbols, parables and myths. Freemasonry involves a strict oath of secrecy.

Gnosticism
A philosophical religious movement, Gnosticism was popular in the Graeco-Roman world and was expressed through many sects. Gnostic groups were characterized by their claim to possess a secret knowledge

('gnosis') regarding the nature of the universe and human existence. Many people have attempted to show a link between the early Christian Church and Gnosticism, and several New Age groups, through new understanding and knowledge, accept the beliefs of gnosticism.

Hare Krishna Movement

The International Society for Krishna Consciousness was founded in America in 1965. It is one of the most visible and well known of the New Religious movements. Devotees sing, dance, sell records and books or the magazine *Back to Godhead* and wear saffron-coloured robes. The men have their heads shaved, apart from a topknot. Adherents believe that Krishna (an incarnation of the Supreme deity) will lift them up by this when he rescues them at the deliverance of the world. This topknot represents the connection between the spiritual and physical worlds. The theological basis of the movement is the *Bhagavad Gita* (a sacred text) as translated by their master.

Harrist Churches

In 1913-14 a revival based loosely on Methodism was established in West Africa in response to the preaching of the 'prophet' Harris, who prophesied the arrival of Bible teachers. In 1924 the long-awaited teachers arrived in the form of Protestant missionaries. Today the Harrist churches form a large family in a number of different church groups. Harrist theology is broadly orthodox, although deeply influenced by the experience of colonialism and African culture.

Hinduism

Hinduism began as a diverse group of religious traditions, consisting of numerous cult movements, beliefs, ritual practices and the caste system, which seemingly have little in common apart from their origin and location within the Indian sub-continent. In the 19th century, these traditions were reinterpreted to form a unified whole and the basis of a national religion. Included in this were the doctrines found in the Upanishads, the Vedas and popular devotions to gods such as Vishnu, Vasudeva and Siva. In this interpretation the religious history of India was given as a combination of earlier Vedic and Brahmanical religions, mediated by priests or Brahmins and representing the triumph of a great tradition, Vedanta, over thousands of local traditions. 19th-century interpreters recognize five periods in the development of Hinduism. 1, The early, or Vedic, religion. 2, The Upanishadic period. 3, The classical period – lasting from 500 BC to AD 500 during which it is claimed Hinduism acquired its now distinctive form. 4, The medieval period, which saw the evolution of the Bhakti – devotional – cult. 5, The modern period, when Indian intellectuals attempted to grasp the impact of Western thought coupled with British domination.

In attempting to understand Hinduism, it is important to realize that very little evidence, except passing observations by Buddhist – and later – Muslim scholars, exists before the 18th century, and that the earliest copies of Hindu scriptures are no older than 15th century. Hindu thought had a profound effect on the originators of **theosophy**.

House Church Movement
The House Church Movement traces its beginnings to the New Testament, where Christians, as a dissident group, are depicted as meeting in people's homes. This would give it the status of a sect rather than a church. The modern movement originated in Ireland in the early 19th century, giving rise to the growth of the **Plymouth Brethren**. It is, however, a highly varied and diverse movement. In the 20th century Brethren-inspired groups emerged in China and Japan, before returning to Britain and North America, where the movement gained a new momentum during the 1980s.

I Am Movement
A New Religious movement of theosophical origin, the I Am movement was founded by Guy Ballard in North America during the 1930s. The movement's ascended masters, of whom St. Germain is probably the best known, do not belong to Eastern thought but are based firmly in the West. This can appear to give the movement a very American character. Belief in the **occult** and the significance of the correct use of **colour** to produce serenity are important aspects of the teachings of this movement.

Inca

Much of what is known of Inca religion comes from Spanish sources, which seem to have regarded it with some trepidation. The Incas appear to have worshipped a creator God who had no name but was given a series of titles. A number of other deities were also worshipped, open-air ceremonies were held in large areas and temples were used to store ritual paraphernalia. Many priests served the religion, which involved large public ceremonies and constant sacrifice. Human victims, mainly women and children, appear to have been sacrificed in times of crisis.

Islam

The followers of the prophet Mohammed believe that theirs is the final and perfected religion. Essentially, the word 'islam' means giving oneself over to God and renouncing any other object of worship. When written as 'islam' it signifies surrender to God, but when it is written 'Islam' it denotes the religion established by Mohammed in the 7th century AD. Muslims are expected to observe five basic religious duties: the recitation of the creed, praying five times a day, fasting during the month of the festival of Ramadan, the payment of a religious tax, and pilgrimage to Mecca at least once in their lifetime. On current estimates there are over 200 million Muslims in the world.

The poetry of Islam's holy book, the *Qur'an*, is considered to be the first miracle. The second is the early conquests by the Muslim armies. Mohammed is said to have been the last of the prophets. His followers were confined to Arabia, although after his death large areas of the world, including Damascus, Jerusalem and the Persian capital, were conquered. Attempts were also made to invade Europe, but the Muslims were defeated in France.

Islam makes no distinction between religious and civil law, or what Christians term Church and State. As a result, life is shaped by religious law based on the *Qur'an*. One major point of conflict in Islam is that of the role and rights of women. It is argued that Islamic women have always been allowed to own property and that they have a much higher status than Western women. This appears to be true in formal terms, but some may question its practice.

Jainism

This highly conservative movement stresses asceticism and holds beliefs similar to those of **Buddhism** and **Hinduism**. It dates back to the 8th century BC, although some scholars have traced its founding to Mahavira in the 6th century BC. Its main creed is that the universe is a never-ending chain of heavens and hells to which all beings are bound by **karma**. Liberation from this chain is only possible through ascetic practice.

Jehovah's Witnesses

Founded by **Charles Taze Russell** (see under **People**) in the late 19th century, Jehovah's Witnesses are highly rationalist **Adventist** pacifists. Originally the sect combined interpretations of biblical prophecy, pyramidology and other esoteric teachings in order to foretell the end of the world. Evolution, orthodox Christian beliefs and the incarnation of Christ were all rejected in favour of a deistic theology.

Judaism

Ancient Judaism is the religion of the Hebrew Bible, which declared a bond between God and the people of Israel. The Jewish people experienced the salvation of God around the time of their exodus from Egypt. At Sinai, the bond was made with the nation, the law granted and worship established. A passage from tribal leadership to kingship then came at the hands of Samuel.

A united cult followed under King Solomon with his construction of a temple in Jerusalem. However, the unified nation soon divided into Northern and Southern kingdoms after his death, with the temple and Jerusalem remaining in control of the Southern kingdom. In 722 BC the Northern kingdom was conquered by Assyria and subjected to exile. In 587 BC the Southern kingdom was conquered by Babylon. During the Hellenistic period (300-63 BC), Hellenism influenced Jewish thought and the theocratic state gave way to a Commonwealth. Judaism became radically pluralist, with some groups seeking to be faithful to their vision of traditional conventional beliefs, while others pursued Hellenistic influences. The end result was, on the one hand, a liberal interpretation of law, and on the other, a radical adherence to purity. Multiformed Judaism was brought to an end with a revolt against Roman rule which resulted in the loss of Jerusalem and the destruction of the temple in AD 70. This point marks the emergence of Rabbinic Judaism, in which the Jewish people sought a new focus to restore their faith. The main motive of Rabbinic Judaism is the quest for underlying meaning and ethical action in Jewish life. The Law, formulated from the Rabbinical teachings written down in the Mishnah and the interpretation of biblical text (Midrash), replaced the temple and sacrifice as the centre of Jewish worship.

In the Middle Ages Judaism flourished in Europe, and soon developed a sound tradition of philosophy and mystical experience. It influenced the intellectual development of Christianity and Islam, while uplifting both European and Arab cultures.

Modern Judaism represents the offshoots that developed since the 18th century as a direct response to the Enlightenment as well as Jewish liberation in Europe. The important expressions of Judaism are: reformed Judaism, which seeks to accommodate traditional Jewish beliefs within the modern world by adopting a rational liberalism and rejecting Messianic expectations; orthodox Judaism, which seeks to modify accommodation with modernity, stressing ritual practice and tradition; Hasidism, which grew up during times of persecution in Eastern Europe during the 18th century, and suggests a mystical relationship to God.

Liberal Protestantism

Liberal Protestantism can be traced back to the 19th-century German theologian Schleiermacher, who emphasized the necessity of theological relevance. It became an umbrella movement for a wide range of religious thought, and was especially popular in America in the 1920s and 1930s. Its characteristics are an eagerness to discard old orthodoxies, confidence in the power of human reason guided by experience, belief in freedom and in the social nature of human existence, and faith in God's benevolence.

Local Church

Local Church is a highly controversial religious movement which is strongly influenced by the theology of the **Plymouth Brethren**. It has been accused of heresy by other Christian movements, which question its interpretation of the incarnation and the Trinity.

Lorian Association

A tangent of the **Findhorn** community, the Lorian Association was founded in California in 1973, initially to promote New Age ideas such as trans-channelling.

Manichaeism

Manichaeism was founded by Mani, a 3rd-century Iraqi religious prophet, in Persia. He taught that there are two warring principles in the universe: good and evil. A synthetic religious system, Manichaeism incorporates elements of **Buddhism**, Christianity and **Gnosticism** and also has a complex cosmology involving light particles in the realm of darkness and their liberation by the father of light.

Methodism

In 1739 John Wesley started a society in London to promote evangelical Christianity. In 1784 he and his followers broke from the **Church of England** in order to establish their own church, which developed as a Christian revitalization movement and made a significant impact on the missionary movement in the19th century. Methodism is still marked by strong social concerns, and recently has tended to encourage liberal theology to move away from its revivalist roots.

Mormons

Mormons are members of the Church of Jesus Christ of Latter Day Saints. They claim to represent true Christianity as restored on earth by the ministry of Joseph Smith (1805–44).

Smith was called a prophet after centuries of apostasy (the abandonment of the principles of a religion). The movement's characteristics are shaped by the doctrine of continuous revelation. Among the Mormon's various doctrines is the belief that God has a human body, and that believers eventually become gods through the law of eternal progression.

Nation in Islam in the West
This radical black New Religious movement founded in 1930s Detroit highlighted the evil of white oppression and claimed the existence of black space people who would eventually restore the glory of the black race. The group later moved in a more orthodox Islamic direction after the disappearance of its founder, W. D. Fard, in 1934.

Native American Religions
The religious traditions of Native Americans are diverse and complex. Although a number of these religions hold beliefs in common, many have developed their own unique perceptions, understanding and practices. These religions were documented by early missionaries such as James Mooney and Alice C. Fletcher. However, the work of **Jung** and Joseph Campbell seemed to encourage suppositions regarding mythology and ritual practices, which in turn led to a rash of, some would say uneducated, 'expositions' of Native American sacred traditions.

Natural Theology
Natural theology attempts to construct a doctrine of God without any appeal to faith or revelation, using a basis of reason and experience. It is argued that, in principle at least, it is possible for philosophers to prove the existence of God – to some extent. It is also argued that everyone has some sense of deity, and that traces of God's being appear in the created world. Since Adam and Eve's Fall from Grace, various human transgressions have made it necessary for God to move us by special revelation if we are to know him.

New Age Movement
The Movement grew out of the so-called counter-culture that arose in the1960s as a reaction to Western values. This pursuit of alternative realities (through drugs and the study of Eastern religions) paved the way for the promotion of a new philosophy based on a synthesis of Eastern and Western thought. The New Age Movement continues to gain acceptance today, possibly due to its influence on the creative and artistic community.

Orthodox Church

The Orthodox Church – also called the Eastern, Greek, or Graeco-Russian Church – is a 'family of churches' found mainly in Eastern Europe. Although administratively independent, all Orthodox churches acknowledge the honorary primacy of the patriarch of Constantinople and reject the claims of the Pope. Orthodox churches are distinguished by liturgical tradition, a theology founded on the Nicene creed, a Christology emphasizing the incarnation, an understanding of salvation that stresses the restoration of humans to the divine life, and a form of worship distinguished by the use of icons.

Peyote Cult

A religious revitalization movement, the Peyote cult swept through a number of North American Indian tribes in the late 19th century and is still found today. The cult combines traditional practices and beliefs with others derived from Christianity. The central sacrament of the cult is the use of mescaline (taken from the peyote cactus) as a hallucinogenic drug.

Plymouth Brethren

The Plymouth Brethren were one of the most influential and respected New Religious movements of the 1830s. Eventually the Brethren split into a number of different sets, including the extremist Exclusive Brethren and the more moderate Open Brethren. Despite their small size, the Plymouth Brethren have had a tremendous influence on modern Christianity.

Puritans

The Puritans arose in the 16th century as a Calvinist party within the Church of England. They were a much misrepresented religious movement popular with the lower and middle classes. They emphasized preaching, pastoral care and the authority of the Bible. The Puritans also put much emphasis on education and the improvement of life for ordinary people. Their persecutution before and after the English Civil War of 1642–48 caused many to flee to America where they were to play a significant role in the shaping of religion there.

Pyramidology

Pyramidology is now a feature in the growth of many New Religious Movements. In some quarters it is regarded as a science. Pyramidologists use the measurements of the pyramids, especially the Great Pyramid at Giza, as a means of making predictions and interpreting prophecies. The information received by practitioners is made available to them by the high-frequency energy believed to be generated by the pyramids. Used properly, this energy can enhance meditation and the regeneration of certain objects.

Quakers

The Quakers (also known as The Society of Friends), arose in the 17th century as a result of the preaching of George Fox. His first believers were called Friends In Truth, but quickly acquired the name Quakers because of the trembling that accompanied their worship. They emphasize the leading of the Holy Spirit, which means a rejection of the Sacraments, an insistence on plain speech and dress, and a rejection of all forms of art. The Quakers are strongly pacifist, and have been very active in social reform and, in particular, education.

Rastafarians

A Jamaican religious sect, Rastafarians believe in the divinity of the former Ethiopian emperor Haile Selassie. Indeed, many followers refuse to believe that he is dead. The movement has some political overtones and, controversially, regards the smoking of marijuana as a sacrament.

Reformation

The term 'Reformation' has now come to mean any religious movement that reforms a pre-existing tradition to restore its purity. Traditionally, though, it refers specifically to the reform movement within the **Roman Catholic** Church in the 16th century. This began suddenly in Germany in 1517 when **Martin Luther** (see under **People**) posted his 95 theses on the church door at Wittenberg. Luther's attacks on the doctrines of the Church of Rome lead to the creation of independent churches, which renounced the claims of the

Papacy and sought to return to a form of Christianity based on the authority of the Bible.

Restoration Movement

Similar to **Reformation**, the Restoration Movement is a type of revitalization movement which seeks to revive a religious tradition by returning it to its original state of purity. The term also refers to an American religious movement arising in the 19th century which appealed for Christian holiness, a return to the teachings of the New Testament, a belief in Christian unity and a strong commitment to the authority of the Bible. Recently the term has been adopted by various Pentecostal groups who are seeking to both return vitality to the church and inspire Christians to expand their own particular society within modern culture.

Roman Catholic Church

This is the Christian Church, headed by the bishop of Rome, who is called the Pope. All Catholics accept the Gospels of Christ's Apostles (Luke, John, Matthew and Mark) and the Church's interpretation of them. The nature of Roman Catholicism has been shaped by the doctrinal statements issued by the Pope and the Vatican Councils. One of the most contentious of these is the doctrine of papal infallibility, issued in 1870. The liturgy of the Church is based on a belief in the Sacraments, which are channels of 'grace' flowing from God to the believer. There are seven sacraments: communion (the Eucharist), baptism, confirmation, holy orders, penance, matrimony, and anointing of the sick (also known as extreme unction). (Baptism, communion and matrimony are the only sacraments recognized by most Protestants. Grace, they believe, is conferred through faith, not the sacraments.) The main form of worship is the Mass, at which believers receive the sacrament of the Eucharist, in imitation of Christ's taking of bread and wine at the Last Supper.

Confession has played a central role in Roman Catholicism. In the 16th century it was linked to the doctrine of purgatory, and led to the trade of indulgences in exchange for forgiveness, a practice that eventually led to the **Reformation**.

Romanticism

In the late 18th and early 19th centuries a reaction to the rationalism of the Enlightenment was discerned in art, literature, music, philosophy and religion.The watchwords of Enlightenment thinking, reason and order, were dirty ones to the Romantics, who preferred instead to give free rein to the senses and the emotions. Reality, according to the Romantics, was to be found through feeling and spiritual illumination. The impact of Romanticism on religion has been considerable. In the United States, for example, it encouraged transcendentalism and an interest in Eastern religions.

Salvation Army

The Salvation Army is probably one of the best known and most widely admired Christian organizations in the world. An evangelical Christian movement, it was founded in the East End of London in 1865 as the London Revival Society. The principal aim of its founders, William Booth and his wife Catherine, was to give material and spiritual help to the poor. The movement became the Salvation Army in 1878 and is run along military lines. The Army provides shelter for the homeless and meets other social needs of the underprivileged. A firm, but non-moralistic, stance is taken against alcohol and other forms of abuse.

Scientology

Scientology is a controversial therapy based loosely on a New Religious movement. The founder, Ron Hubbard, aims to apply religious philosophy in order to recover spirituality and increase individual ability. Originally called Dianetics, this philosophy maintains that humans, and the human mind, are capable of resolving problems by becoming their own saviours and thus releasing their inner spiritual being. Scientology uses the language of science to promote a Western version of yogic religion and supports this with the mythology found in Hubbard's various science fiction novels. Scientology has received some bad press, with allegations of payments to celebrities who agree to promote it.

Shamanism

The central feature of Shamanism is the control of spirits by a **Shaman** who negotiates between this world and the spirit world. Shamanism is found among hunting peoples and presupposes a belief in a multiplicity of spirits and the survival of the soul after death.

Sikhism

Sikhism evolved out of a number of Indian movements which sought unity between **Islam** and **Hinduism**. The first Sikh guru, Nanak, established a community of Sikhs. He preached the unity of God and taught the centrality of Bhakti-type devotion (see **Crown Chakra** in Section Three) using the repetition of the divine name.

Spinal Tap

This small New Age religious cult was formed in 1983 following the success of the motion picture *This is Spinal Tap*. The cult promotes, as does the film, unified thinking and encourages symbolic bondings of 'fire and ice'. Cult members also believe that we are all spiritually linked to Stonehenge.

Followers would often hold vigils to conjure up, or 'tap' into, the spirits of its gurus, Nigel Tufnel and David St. Hubbins. This would often include repeated renditions of specially written prayer songs, such as the controversial 'Sex Farm'. The cult was dubbed 'none more black' in 1985 after the death of one of its members in a bizarre gardening accident.

Sufism

The origins of this enigmatic movement within Islam are unclear. The name comes from the Arabic for wool, and this is reflected in the fact that early Sufis wore coarse woollen clothing in protest against what they saw as the decadence of the Caliphate (an Islamic concept of a ruler under which religious and secular realms are united) in the 7th and 8th centuries. Sufism emphasizes a love of and devotion to God. Although influenced by Christianity, there is wide agreement that Sufism reflects a genuine flowering of inherent spirituality within Islam.

Taoism

Taoism is a Chinese religion which developed from Shamanism, magical cults, and a combination of mystical elements within the philosophy of Lao Tzu and Chuang Tzu. Its original aims were to realize happiness and prolong life through unity with the Tao, by practising non-activity, non-interference and humility, renouncing force, pride and self-assertion. The various techniques used include alchemy, some health and dietary rules, a Chinese form of yoga and the worship of powerful deities.

Theism
Theism is the belief in one's own personal God, one who is the lone creator of the universe and all existence. This one unified being is the source of the cosmos and the power that continues to be active in it.

Theosophy
Theosophy is a mystical tradition propagated by the Theosophical Society, which was founded in New York City in 1875 by spiritualists **Helena Blavatsky** (see under **People**) and Henry Alcott. It is a form of Monism (a belief in one reality) that teaches spiritual evolution and seeks spirituality through mystical experience based on finding esoteric meanings in the sacred writings of the world.

Transcendentalism
Transcendentalism arose out of Unitarianism in the 1830s. It preached extreme individualism and liberalism and also a pantheistic view of God; the doctrine that all things and beings are modes, attributes or appearances of one single reality, hence nature and God are believed to be the same. Transcendentalism encouraged mysticism and an interest in yogic religions. It was very popular in 19th-century America, and contributed to the rise of many New Religious movements.

Unification Church
This Korean New Religious movement was founded in 1954 by an engineer, Sun Myung Moon. The principal document of the movement is the 'Divine Principle', which describes its rudimentary teachings. The theology of the sect is one of the most extensive found in any of the New Religious movements. It consists of a systematic attempt to interpret the

Bible from the perspective of Korean thought, based on Confucian and Buddhist philosophy with insights gained from Korean Shamanism (see **Shaman**).

Vedic Religion

This is the religion of the ancient Aryan invaders of India as found in the *Rig Veda* and other Indian literature. It is rich in myth and ritual, and involves gods, sacrifice and heroic deeds.

Voodoo

Much misunderstood, this Afro-American religion with West African roots is spiritual in nature. Its rituals involve sacrifice and firedances by priests or priestesses who are 'possessed' by various gods to become spiritualist **mediums**. It is practised in Brazil, Cuba and parts of North America.

Witchcraft

Witchcraft is a diverse system of beliefs and practices involving supernatural effects to influence human affairs. Since the Enlightenment, witchcraft has been regarded as an irrational belief system. However, the system of thought informing it does follow an intelligible pattern. In the West, popular belief in witchcraft died out during the 17th and 18th centuries, only to be revived in the late 19th by occultists as a form of ritual magic.

Modern witchcraft is a relatively influential New Religious movement based on a select mix of Masonic ritual, Eastern folk culture and yogic religion.

Zion Christian Church

The Zion Christian Church (also known as the ZCC) is an African independent church which, with at least 3 million members, is the largest sect in Southern Africa. Basically orthodox in theology, it is nonetheless **charismatic** – that is, it believes in the manifestation of the gifts, such as **healing**, **speaking in tongues** and the prophecy of the Holy Spirit. The Church expresses its emphasis on healing and prophecy through traditional black cultural symbols.

RITUAL

There are many different kinds of ritual, ranging from the mating habits of animals, through obsessive behaviour in neurotics to established forms of religious behaviour. Most rituals are carried out in the belief that something will happen.

In animal mating rituals a particular response is called for from the recipient; for example, a peacock will display his tail feathers in the expectation that the peahen will accept his overtures.

In neurotic behaviour, such as obsessive hand-washing, the individual is not free to continue with further activity until the obsessive action has been completed to his satisfaction.

Religious ritual takes place so that the observer is comforted by familiarity, while the priest or priestess has a deeper knowledge of the hidden significance of his or her actions. These actions are carried out in the knowledge, for instance, that the particular order of performance will bring about a desired result.

Magical ritual (see **Magic**) is believed to have an effect on particular aspects of the universe and bring about a required result. To use a common example, the magician may light a candle in order to use the element of fire, while a priest may light a candle as part of a **prayer** ritual. Both actions are the same, but the intent is different.

Ritual is not simply an expression of tension or aggression, or necessarily a belief in the potency of that ritual. It is, however, designed to evoke a particular emotion, and, especially in either religious or magical ritual, a greater sense of the infinite. Rituals are often used to reinforce beliefs. The early churches, for instance, adopted many pagan rituals in order to give some continuity to the changes of belief they introduced. Rituals are used by various societies to acknowledge status. What is appropriate in one culture may not be acceptable in another. An Inuit, for example, would ritually offer his wife as a sleeping partner to an honoured guest. This would not necessarily be appropriate to the businessman from London who *is* the honoured guest.

Without the appropriate knowledge one would not consider the deeper significance of the various rituals one performs automatically. To use the symbolism of the lighting of a candle again, a host may automatically place candles on the dinner table and will have no trouble lighting these as part of his own ritual of preparation. However, he may have great difficulty in lighting a candle with the intent that the candle will draw financial gain towards him, an action that would give no problem to a practitioner of magic. He would possibly also have difficulty in lighting a candle on an altar in church, whereas he may not have difficulty in lighting a candle in front of a statue of a saint - one would be the action of a priest the other that of a supplicant. If these rituals were combined into one, and our host treated the dinner table like an altar, it would bring about prosperity and a wider meaning to the dinner party.

ROLFING
See **Therapies**

RUNES
See **Divination**

S

SEANCE
See **Sitting**

SELF
Also see **Meditation**

The self is the part of us that is considered to be above the humdrum concerns of the everyday personality (lower self). It guides us and supports us when needed. The Upanishads (yogic texts) say that we must all be at one with the self and God, or there can be no way of reaching our true goal. 'The self is everything and everything is the Self - the self is the source of all virtue. ... The self is eternal and immortal, the one without a second.'

There is a need, as in the teachings of Hinduism, to meditate on the self, to bring the conscious self or 'I' in line with the **higher self** in the **superconscious**.

SHAMAN

Nowadays most people think of Shamanic practices as originating from North America and the North American Indian, but this is not wholly true. There are many Shamanistic practices in such wide-ranging places as South America, China, Japan and Australia. All of them have a number of things in common.

Originating from the Tungus People in Siberia and also related to the Indian Samana (meaning 'monk'), the Shaman (or poet, magician, philosopher and priest – these days he can be any one of these or a composite of them) is a kind of mediator between the different levels of reality. With the use of rhythmic music or psychedelic drugs, the Shaman gains entry to these other levels. He can travel down into the underworld, or his soul can rise up to the sky, bringing messages back on his return.

It has to be said that generally Shamans were male, though it is known that certain tribes in the Philippines adopt a female Shaman. (By linking with the intrinsic awareness and intuition which every woman has and allowing the instinctive use of ritual, many modern women are adopting Shamanic practices and thereby allowing inner freedoms to surface.)

Although Shamanic practice is more fragmented than it was, it is important to note that the Shaman has always been the religious centre of a community. He is the healer, as well as the convoy of the souls of the dead.

SHIATSU
See Therapies

SILVER CORD

The Silver Cord is a type of umbilical cord that links the subtle bodies together. Which **chakra** it extends from depends on the awareness of the individual, but most often it is the solar plexus. Many **mediums** and clairvoyants (see **Clairvoyance**) have witnessed the Silver Cord severing from the physical body on death. Also known as the psychic cord, it has a pulsating energy which is traditionally experienced as silver although other colours have been seen.

SITTING

When an individual or a group of people wants to contact someone from 'the other side', they go for a sitting (or séance, from the French) with a **medium**, channeller, or clairvoyant (see **Clairvoyance**). It is usually assumed that the sitters expect communication from the spirit or discarnate entity. Although it should always be possible to make contact in some form, this may take some time. Success will depend on whether the spirit wants to be contacted and on the proficiency of the 'seer'.

Certain conditions are considered more favourable than others for success. The atmosphere should be relaxed and happy; often music helps the proceedings and makes them harmonious.

The images that the 'seer' receives can be a situation that both the spirit entity and sitter has experienced. The situation is often seen from the spirit's perspective and so may need interpreting by the sitter. The communicating entities may show themselves in several ways: for example, how they see themselves, how they want to be remembered, how they are most likely to be remembered by the sitter, or in a way that gives information to the **medium** or channeller. In one case a spirit showed itself wearing a green dress. The sitter had no recollection of a green dress, and this was in fact a kind of shorthand for the medium, to represent love and knowledge. It is important that no information is dismissed because this may be relevant, if not in the present then in the future. Interpretation can take some time.

Because a good deal of energy is used both by the controlling medium and by the discarnate entities, there can often be sharp changes in temperature, either in the air, or in the sitters themselves. This can be lessened by instigating a few quiet moments at the beginning of the sitting in order to create a focus of energy.

SIXTH SENSE

The sixth sense is an old-fashioned term for what are now known as the intuitive senses. These come into play as the individual becomes more aware of the wider implications of his or her own spiritual development.

SOUND THERAPY
See **Therapies**

SPIRIT

Spirit is a term to describe all non-material states of being. In essence, the soul is taken to be perfect, and the spirit is the expression of that perfection. The two are similar, but not the same. The spirit connects the soul and the physical, and could also be called the Higher Mind.

Many people become confused between the idea of soul and spirit. It is perhaps easier to think of the spirit as being that part of us which still has connection with the physical. We become aware of its gifts and powers when we reach a certain stage of psychic development. We then become aware of the soul as that part of us which is unchanging – that which belongs to God or the Ultimate.

SPIRITS

On separating from the physical body after death the soul is known as a spirit, or spirit entity. All entities which are active on levels of being other than the physical are known as spirits.

Non-human entities, such as angels (who have not incarnated – been born – physically) and demons, which are thought forms with malevolent intent, are also known as spirits. In the classical world there were various types of human spirit. The spirits of the dead, *manes,* were divided into separate parts. Whereas *shades* were in Hades, an earthbound part of the spiritual being, in the form of the *lemures,* might well haunt places known to them while alive. Everyone had a personal guardian spirit, called a daemon. The *lares* were the spirits of ancestors, and the *penates* were protective spirits; see **Guardian Angel** and **Doorkeeper**.

There has been recognition of a kind of 'hierarchy' of spirits. There are two forms of spirit – high and low. The low spirits are those who have passed over but still retain their connection with the physical realm. Some may be earthbound and not able to progress at this time. Others undertake to assist an individual to progress spiritually on the earth plane as part of their own development – their task is to guide the earth plane. Those spirits who have deliberately put their own progress on hold are known as Bodhisattvas in the Buddhist belief. The higher order of spirits seem to show more concern for the individual and for wider issues; also see **Possession**.

The dominant religions are very suspicious of the idea of spirit communication, mainly due to the possible enticement of the individual to relinquish his responsibilities and follow whatever 'they' say. Another reason for this suspicion is the supposed unreliability of spirits. The belief is that, particularly in the case of the recently departed, there is essentially no proof that they are any wiser than the living. However, most people who seek this sort of communication are after reassurance of continuing existence rather than guidance.

SPIRITUAL ENERGY HEALING
See **Therapies**

SPIRITUAL SCIENCE

As **Rudolph Steiner** said, 'To the study of the spiritual processes in human life and in the cosmos, the term "spiritual science" may be given'. This term is sometimes used by occultists to refer to **occult** teaching, as for example in **theosophy** and **anthroposophy** (see **Religions and Philosophical Movements**).

SUPERCONSCIOUS MIND

The superconscious is an area of the unconscious mind which has been largely ignored by conventional psychology. There is a link, though, between the superconscious and the use of **trance**. It is believed that **psychic powers** are energized by retracting **consciousness** from the external world and focusing awareness in the superconscious.

Within the realm of the superconscious is the source of higher feelings: unselfish love, genius, or the states of contemplation, illumination and ecstasy. In this realm are the potentially higher psychic functions and spiritual energies. It is the domain of the real **self**. There are many different conditions of consciousness, and different ways of focusing it. Altering perception to use the superconscious enables us to grasp other realities, without being distracted by the everyday world or our own emotions.

SYMBOLISM

Jung defines a symbol as 'a term, a name or even a picture that may be familiar in daily life, yet that possesses specific connotations in addition to its conventional and obvious meaning.' It is, therefore, something that has a deeper meaning than its obvious one. By searching for the deeper meaning we widen out into other possibilities of interpretation. Some may be personal, some archetypal – belonging to a greater collective **consciousness** – and others relevant only within the knowledge of a particular culture. Often these symbols are used to represent concepts which may be difficult to understand fully. For instance, the crucifix with the figure of Christ on it signifies the meaning of a multitude of beliefs and ideas inherent in the cross itself and also symbolizes the sacrifice and the agony undertaken by Christ on behalf of others. The form of an animal symbolizes those aspects of the personality that we equate with 'lower' types of life and that we must understand and come to terms with. Different cultures handle these aspects in different ways.

Both personal and archetypal symbolism occur side by side in **dreams**. You should ask yourself 'What does this mean *to me?*' before asking 'What does this mean?' Our unconscious is a rich repository of symbols and symbolism which it uses as tools to make us aware of the deeper meaning of life.

Knowing and recognizing our own symbols helps us to tap into a higher stream of consciousness more readily, and thus widen our spiritual knowledge. **Meditation** helps us to unlock the door to our unconscious, and in doing this a new language needs to be mastered. In the early stages, before one reaches a state of complete tranquillity, symbols form this method of communication.

Symbolism is used also by clairvoyants (see **Clairvoyance**) and **mediums**. Often this can be of a personalized type. For instance, to one reader the word 'Peter' heard psychically may signify betrayal – unless, of course, a Peter is known to the sitter. Many mediums have used symbols to denote time periods. For instance, daffodils might suggest spring, a bucket and spade holidays, and so on.

Perhaps the best illustration of symbols and symbolism is the **I Ching** (see under **Divination**). Each trigram (three-line figure) used is an evocative symbol itself. When combined they build into a different pictogram, to be interpreted more fully.

SYNCHRONICITY

'Synchronicity', which means quite literally 'together time', is the name given to meaningful coincidences – with the connotation that it also gives an explanation for them. Random chance or chaos does not have an obvious pattern, whereas synchronicity does. It is a cluster of things occurring within a short period of time.

It was Jung (see under **People**) who in 1930 came up with the idea of 'a synchronistic connective principle'. However, his book on synchronicity, subtitled 'An Acausal Connecting Principle' was dismissed as meaningless. It was an attempt to explain paradox. Drawing on his interest in the **I Ching**, Jung identified a type of coincidence that was not just the result of unplanned events. At any given moment an action in physical reality, such as tossing coins, mirrors the psychological situation. They are inter-connecting occurrences but do not cause each other; they are both aspects of a greater reality. Jung suggested that we are able to grasp this greater situation which 'transcends space, time and causality' – hence the concept of 'as above, so below'.

Synchronicity also suggests that the mind may interact with the rest of the universe and affect events. In essence, it is possible for us to influence events by our attitude: people with a negative attitude may 'attract' bad luck, while those who are more positive will do the opposite.

T

T'AI CHI CH'UAN
See **Therapies**

TALISMEN
See **Magic**

TAO/TAOISM
See **Religions and Philosophical Movements**

TAROT
See **Divination**

TEA LEAVES
See **Divination**

TELEKINESIS

Originating from the researcher Charles Richet, telekinesis is another term for psychokinesis (PK) and defines various forms of movement by spirit agency. The word was coined with the development of physical mediumship (see **Medium**) in the late 19th century to indicate 'certain supernormal movements of objects' (F.W.H. Myers). Table-turning (in séances), levitation and apport (the appearance of objects 'carried from another place') are all forms of telekinesis.

TELEPATHY

Telepathy – mind to mind communication – is accepted as normal in simple 'unsophisticated' society. It is accepted as perfectly normal that when one person is not able to contact another physically the latter can be reached mentally. It is only when Western society attempts to apply scientific reasoning that telepathy becomes something of wonder. Many people have had the experience of thinking of someone only to be contacted by them shortly afterwards, or have had someone finish off a sentence for them when there was apparently no way they could have known what was being thought about. Experiments in telepathy are notoriously difficult to prove except by the statistical analysis of correct identification of pictures, or of cards.

Experiments have been carried out where both the 'sender' and the person receiving are in carefully controlled laboratory conditions. The sender attempts to transmit to the receiver an image of the picture or symbol they have been given. The success rate is considered high when the results are greater than pure chance. Experimenters have noted a displacement effect in some subjects where the receiver correctly identifies a card that is the next or next but two card to the one being transmitted. When there is a degree of consistency in these results, telepathy is deemed to have taken place.

Experimentation and statistical analysis do not always show the full effect of telepathy, which could be described as an intuitive skill. The mother who wakes moments before her child indicates distress is probably acting telepathically. Someone instinctively knowing that their partner is returning early from work is acting telepathically. The therapist or counsellor who is aware of a client's difficulty is also acting telepathically.

Opinions differ as to whether telepathy is an altered state of **consciousness** or not. For some people it is so natural – simply a knowing – that it does not seem that consciousness has changed. Others must make a considerable effort to achieve telepathy. What is certain is that what seems to have been an ancient gift will in the future become an enhanced tool of communication.

THALASSOTHERAPY
See **Therapies**

THERAPIES

This section brings together and deals briefly with many of the therapies, both well-known and otherwise, which the seeker of information may come across. You will also find expanded entries for some of them in the main body of this section. These are marked with an asterisk*.

Absent healing*

Many people believe that by the use of concentrated thought, prayer, meditation, visualization, or other forms of focusing to channel their energy, healing can take place even though the recipient is not present. This power, which comes not from them but from God or some other spiritual power, is not in their control; they are simply being used as a conduit.

Acupressure

Acupressure is rooted in Taoist philosophy, and is older than acupuncture. Specific acupuncture points will respond to pressure and relieve the symptoms of certain problems – for example, pressing the temples can relieve migraine. You can use this Chinese medical technique as a self-help technique or by consulting a therapist.

Acupuncture

According to Chinese theory, energy flows in channels – known as meridians – throughout the body. Symptoms may be cured by inserting fine needles into particular points in the skin and manipulating them. Stimulation or calming of these acupuncture points rebalances the energy. Initially it was thought that only needles could be used, but in the hands of skilled practitioners these points can be stimulated by electricity, fingertips, heat (moxibustion), magnets or staples.

Alexander technique

The Alexander technique, developed by Australian actor F. Matthias Alexander to overcome a problem he had with his voice, concentrates on helping people correct their posture, movement and balance. In learning to recognize how we may be sitting or standing badly, or not using specific groups of muscles correctly, we can free ourselves from unnecessary muscle tension and the ill-health that stems from it.

Anthroposophical medicine

The philosopher **Rudolf Steiner's** (see under **People**) belief in the human being's need to be treated holistically lies behind the artistic, spiritual and scientific insights of anthroposophy. Treatments include special medicine, homeopathic remedies, essential oils, art and music therapies, counselling, rhythmic massage, and a system of movements (performed in rhythm with the spoken word) called euryhmthy.

Aromatherapy
Also see **Essential Oils**

The essential flower oils are extracted from plants and flowers by various methods, and are used to treat illness and promote well-being. Some oils are absorbed by the skin during massage, or their vapour absorbed through the breathing passages. It is important to receive this therapy under professional guidance – essential oils are potent entities that can produce unwanted side-effects if used incorrectly or inappropriately.

Art therapy

Negative and suppressed emotions can undermine health, and this is where art therapy can be used as a release mechanism. An art therapist works with the **colours** and shapes in the patient's paintings, helping her to express her feelings and make sense of what's going on. This type of therapy has been of great assistance in helping abused children to express and come to terms with their feelings.

Assertiveness training

Assertiveness can improve relationships, increase self-esteem and make people feel better about themselves. Learning to communicate what you think, feel or want is very valuable in a controlled and yet supportive environment. Assertion training can, therefore, be an important aid to well-being in that it teaches the individual how to create the circumstances in which expression is devoid of fear.

Astrological counselling
Also see **Astrology**

The positions of the planets at the moment of our birth are said to give some idea of the type of people we could become. Using those positions, a competent astrologer can help an individual to move towards self-understanding and to cope with situations. An understanding of why we have acted in a certain way enables us to make intelligent choices, to change our lives and get the best out of any situation.

Aura therapy

The **aura** is a kind of force field around the body. It is not necessarily seen by everyone but, for those who can see it, different colours symbolize different conditions. A good counsellor is able to tell by the tone and depth of colour of the aura what is going on in an individual's life. Healing can be brought about by the healer helping the individual to adjust the force-field and the intensity of the colour.

Auriculotherapy

Auriculotherapists regard the ear – which some say mirrors the curled-up foetus – as a microcosm of the physical body and use the 200 or so acupuncture points in it to treat the areas of the body to which they are connected. A type of **acupuncture**, it is often used to help people break habits, such as smoking. It can also assist in the treatment of emotional difficulties.

Autogenic training*
This teaches six simple, effective, well-researched mental techniques which can be used to achieve deep relaxation and let go of a habitual response to health. Akin to **meditation**, autogenic training helps to create well-being.

Auto-suggestion
Also see **Affirmation**
Quietly, calmly and in a relaxed frame of mind, you can use this form of **hypnotherapy** or **meditation** on yourself by repeating a particular statement perhaps 20 times a day. Auto-suggestion helps bring about a more positive attitude.

Aversion therapy
Aversion therapy was popular in the 1960s and 1970s as a way of treating socially unacceptable types of behaviours. It is based on the idea that if an unpleasant experience is associated with that behaviour often enough the patient will attempt to change his or her behaviour. While it achieved some success with easily influenced people, other patients found it all too easy to return to old habits after the aversion therapy had ended.

Ayurvedic medicine*
This ancient Indian system of medicine, which embraces the physical, emotional and spiritual aspects of health in its treatments, exists alongside orthodox medicine in the sub-Continent. Practitioners try to discover a person's in-born disposition. They believe health is controlled by three forces: VATA (influencing the central nervous system), PITTA (affecting digestion and the body's chemistry), and KAPHA (governing tissue fluid). Careful pulse and voice diagnosis are part of the routine assessment. Treatments include breathing

exercises, mineral supplements, **meditation**, **yoga** and herbal medicine.

Bach flower remedies*

Dr Bach was a doctor and homoeopath who developed a whole system of subtle healing around his belief in the healing properties of flowers, particularly of what he called those 'of a higher order'. Dr Bach represented the remedy as a healing light entering the mind and body.

Bates method

Dr. Edward Bates, an American eye specialist, believed that one could prevent eyesight from failing with old age and could improve impaired vision. He developed seven exercises which help the eyes to remain in good condition. These include splashing the closed eyes to improve circulation; blinking frequently for lubrication; covering the eyes with the palms of the hand for relaxation; and at regular intervals focusing alternately several times at objects three inches away and at arm's length. Bates practitioners advise on **diet**, techniques to improve the co-ordination of eyes and brain, and memory, imagination and perception training.

Behavioural therapy

Behavioural therapy is literally an attempt to help people to change their behaviour into something that is acceptable and achieves better results. The therapy is wisely used in the desensitization of **fears** (1) and **phobias** (1). Rigorous monitoring indicates what the patient is doing 'wrong', enabling her to change that behaviour. It takes at least six weeks for the subconscious to accept change.

Biochemic tissue salts

Nutritional biochemistry is the treatment of health problems with twelve homeopathically-prepared mineral salts: calcium fluoride, calcium phosphate, calcium sulphate, iron or ferrous phosphate, potassium chloride, potassium phosphate, potassium sulphate, magnesium phosphate, sodium chloride, sodium phosphate, sodium sulphate and silica oxide. It was developed by a German physician, biochemist and physicist, Dr. W. H. Schüssler, who claimed that an imbalance of naturally-occurring tissue salts could cause illness. While this process has not been scientifically validated, the salts are used by naturopaths, homeopaths and medical herbalists.

Bioenergetics

Bioenergetics is a body/mind therapy that tackles problems on the premise that the body internalizes tensions and produces difficulties in posture, breathing and movement. For instance, an unhappy childhood could later result in problems with the spine and hunched shoulders. Bioenergetics aims to retrain the body and therefore release the old problems, allowing them to be dealt with.

Biofeedback training

Biofeedback training can enable those with high levels of stress to consciously deal with the results of that stress. The patient first learns to monitor stress levels by means of a machine that measures electrical impulses and then control those levels through the use of **relaxation**, **visualization**, and **breathing** techniques, all of which have a beneficial effect on the nervous system. Biofeedback training can lower blood pressure, cure migraines, reduce anxiety and prevent pain in tense muscles and bones.

Charismatic healing
Also see **Spiritual Healing**

Many Christians believe that people of special power have a particular gift for healing ill-health through **prayer** and the power of the Holy Spirit. This gift is believed to be given by the grace of God.

Cheirology

This ancient art uses the shape and lines of the hand to gain insight into the self and individual patterns of health. The hand is said to represent a map of our inner condition. Some of the definitions of cheirology are drawn from Buddhist philosophy and the techniques used in it are slightly different from the interpretations of palmistry.

Chinese medicine

This ancient form of medicine encompasses **acupuncture**, **acupressure**, **herbalism**, **moxibustion**, **reflexology**, **do-in** and **t'ai chi**. Practitioners of Chinese medicine regard good health as harmony between **yin** and **yang**. This is achieved by balancing the **energy** that flows between the seven energy **chakras** (see Section Three) to the body's organs and systems. Practitioners pay particular attention to the tongue and various pulses; these pulses are not the same as those identified in Western medicine.

Chiropractic

After medicine and dentistry this is the world's largest healing profession. The word 'chiropractic' means 'done by hand'. Chiropractors rely mainly on their sense of touch to detect badly aligned joints. Treatments include muscle-relaxing techniques and joint adjustment manipulation, which, in some cases, can lead to dramatic improvements in walking and movement.

Clinical ecology

Also see **Allergies** and **Depression (1)**

The idea that sensitivity due to environmental factors, such as power lines, pollution and food additives, can cause illness in people is becoming more acceptable. Treatments include avoidance or desensitization (giving the sufferer minute doses of the substance responsible for the problem).

Co-counselling

In this type of counselling, which originated in the United States, two people take it in turns to be first 'counsellor' then 'client'. It is used where conventional therapy may have no effect – for example in cases where the individual dislikes the idea of therapy. Each person is allowed the same set amount of time to discuss difficulties. Listening and communication skills are important if the therapy is to be effective.

Cognitive therapy

This form of psychotherapy can be done either individually or in a group. Cognitive therapists aim to help people move out of the pitfalls caused by negative self-image, by changing their habits of remembering, thinking and interpreting what others say.

Colour therapy
Therapists in this field use **colour** to treat illness via direct light, as well as by asking people to imagine particular colours in their mind's eye. Therapists identify the colour of the **aura** with the aid of ESP (extra sensory perception) while also assessing the state of the seven **chakras** (3) by stroking the spine.

Counselling
Counselling provides an opportunity to talk about life and to express and accept feelings. It is a way of exploring emotional discomfort in order to be more at ease with the ups and downs of life. Techniques used in counselling include crisis management, goal-setting and practice in changes of behaviour.

Cranial osteopathy
This is a specialized form of osteopathy where the bones of the skull are very gently manipulated to correct any malalignment in the body following on from, for example, a difficult birth, dental work or injury. Practitioners believe that badly aligned bones in the head, face or jaw can be responsible for conditions such as headaches, high blood pressure and loss of balance.

Crystal healing
Some healers believe that **crystals** release blocked energy, rebalance the energy centres and contain healing power. When used in healing, crystals are placed over an affected area or on an acupuncture point.

Dance and dance therapy
Also see **Anthroposophical Medicine**
Dancing is a way of exercising and raising the spirits. The symbolic and rhythmic movements of dance can enable people to express feelings

which may be buried too deep to talk about. Thus, dance therapy can help emotional problems.

Do-in
Pronounced 'dough-in', this is a Chinese system of exercises and do-it-yourself **acupressure**, which if used regularly is said to prevent illness and promote a healthy flow of energy.

Dolphins
Swimming with dolphins has apparently healed a number of people from emotional and spiritual stress, and has become a subject of much discussion. Whether the excitement of a new and thrilling experience does the trick, or some other force is at work, no-one yet knows. It is felt by some that the dolphin's instinctive recognition of distress has a therapeutic effect.

Drama therapy
In this form of group psychotherapy an individual re-enacts a difficult, personal experience by choosing 'actors' from the group to represent the other people involved. Afterwards, the therapist encourages everyone in the group to talk about the experience in the hope that repressed feelings will be released, facilitating new patterns of behaviour and response, and helping to restore emotional health.

Dream-work
The **symbols** and feelings in a dream are generally considered to come from the unconscious mind. Though we hold some symbols in common, which are called archetypes, specific symbols have particular relevance for each individual. Identifying these symbols through dream-work can help us make sense of our dreams, as a possible aid to self-awareness and the unravelling of emotional difficulties.

Energy
Also see **Qi**
Many healers and therapists explain health and ill-health in terms of the

energy flow in and between the body, mind, and spirit. An imbalance of these energies is said to cause ill-health. High and low energy states are part of our normal and necessary cycles of high and low physical, emotional, spiritual and intellectual energy. Good therapists, of whatever discipline, are able to balance these energies successfully.

Faith healing

A firm belief in the art of **healing** may help in the cure various diseases. Different people define faith in different ways, but 'Faith' is usually construed as being a belief in the healer's power, or in divine power sent through the healer, or directly to the person themselves. Whatever the explanation, faith healing is a recognized form of healing.

Fasting
Also see **Crown Chakra**

Naturopaths sometimes advise a period of fasting to treat a variety of disorders, such as arthritis, food allergies and high blood pressure. A fast can last a few hours or one or more days, depending on individual needs. Whatever the requirements, when fasting it is always advisable to drink plenty of liquids.

Feldenkrais method

This is a mechanically-based body therapy based on the ideas of engineer and physicist Moshe Feldenkrais. He believed that some people suffer from pain and physical damage to their body because many of their movements are awkward. He suggested that the part of the brain controlling these movements can be 're-programmed' by practising more efficient versions – almost going back to the way in which young children learn to walk and move. The effect of these movements is augmented by physical pressure and manipulation by a therapist. The therapy can help people who have had a stroke, as well as those with cerebral palsy, spinal disorders, back-pain and muscle injuries.

The Feldenkrais method is taught in two ways. Awareness through movement is taught with a teacher verbally leading a class through a lesson. Functional integration is a term used for an individual session where the teacher will guide the pupil's body through touch and gentle manipulation. Benefits of the method are not confined to the body. Feldenkrais felt that physical movement and posture can have a profound effect on the mind and emotions. By changing negative physical patterns, the state of mind that produced them can be changed too.

Flotation therapy
Several health and fitness centres now offer the opportunity to float in a bath containing a solution of Epsom salts kept at body temperature. The solution is only ten inches deep and is so concentrated that no effort is needed to stay afloat. Floating can bring about a state of extreme relaxation of both mind and body which aids meditation and can help people with high blood pressure, insomnia, and other stress-related problems, as well as those with spiritual difficulties.

Freudian analysis
Sigmund Freud (see under **People**) is best known for his theories on sexuality. Freudian analysis is developed from the principle of free association and aims to get at an underlying problem by means of taking it back to its roots. **Dream** analysis and similar techniques are used in this form of **psychotherapy**.

Gestalt therapy
The German word *Gestalt* can mean 'figure' or 'character'. This kind of psychotherapy is practised in groups or on a one-to-one basis. The intention is to help people re-experience and accept 'shut-off' memories and feelings that are locked in their unconscious mind and may be causing emotional or physical disease. Gestalt therapists aim to help people achieve their full potential by allowing the suppressed part of the individual to expresss itself and reveal how that individual may be preventing his or her progress in this life.

Graphology
The study of handwriting is thought to give a reasonable indication of various personality characteristics and traits. In some cases graphology is

used in combination with counselling to enable people to know themselves better and to unlock hidden talents and strengths.

Group therapy
Various types of counselling and psychotherapy are done more effectively in groups. One or more therapists usually facilitates the work of the group, but much of the work is actually done by the members of the group inter-acting with themselves and the therapists. The idea is learn through sharing experiences. Group therapy is used to help in cases of bereavement, smoking and drug or alcohol addiction, among others.

Hakomi
A gentle body-mind therapy developed in the United States. The name is Hopi Indian for 'Who are you?' Combining techniques from several other therapies, such as deep **massage**, it aims to promote self-awareness and increase the options available to us in daily life.

Hellerwork
This complex form of integrative bodywork incorporates manipulation of the sheaths of connective tissue around muscles, exercises and discussion of how our attitudes, beliefs and feelings can create tension.

Herbalism
Also see **Herbs**
World-wide, preparations made from plants constitute the commonest form of medical treatment. Herbalists say that an extract from a plant is more effective than the 'active ingredients' isolated by pharmaceutical companies. Side effects are possible, but rare, because most plants are balanced in such a way that the various constituents inter-react and work with one another. Today, many people are turning to herbalism as a way of counteracting the side-effects associated with conventional drugs. Herbal preparations have been particularly successful in the treatment of eczema and other skin disorders.

Homeopathy
Homeopathy is based on the notion that an illness can be cured by

administering minute doses of a substance which in larger doses would cause similar symptoms to those of the illness. Diluting the substance is said to increase its healing potential. Symptoms treated homeopathically often get worse before they get better.

Hydrotherapy

Water can help many health problems. A very important aspect of hydrotherapy is temperature. Warm water dilates blood vessels, relaxes muscles and joints, and promotes sweating. Cold water tightens blood vessels, reduces superficial inflammation and congestion, and encourages blood flow.

Exercise and massage in water, hot or cold compresses, ice packs, cold wraps, baths with mineral salts, bran or seaweed, warm water baths (in which to give birth), hot and cold sprays, Turkish baths and saunas are just some of the many forms of hydrotherapy used by naturopaths and other therapists.

Hypnotherapy

A general misconception is that hypnotherapists work by inducing a full hypnotic trance. This is not the case. Most help the patient to relax physically and mentally into a tranquil state of mind, then suggest ways in which insight can be gained and change brought about. Hypnotherapy can help stress-related disorders, smoking and alcohol **addictions**. **Auto-suggestion** could be termed the do-it-yourself variety of this technique.

Ionization therapy

An ionizer is a machine which releases a flow of negatively charged ions. City air and air in centrally heated homes and offices which are furnished and decorated with synthetic materials contain few negative ions and make some health problems worse than they should be. Using an ionizer can improve conditions such as **asthma**, bronchitis, hay fever, insomnia (see **Sleep (1)**) and **depression**.

Iridology

This is a branch of therapy which uses the state of the iris of the eye as a diagnostic tool. As the feet in **reflexology** reflect other parts and organs of the body, so do the various sections of the iris. Iridology is often used in conjunction with other alternative therapies.

Jungian therapy

Freud's theories about sexuality caused the Swiss psychiatrist **C. G. Jung** to break with him and go on to develop his theory of analytical psychology. Jung was especially interested in working with dreams and symbols, and with what he called 'archetypal' ideas, said to be part of humankind's shared, inherited unconscious store of memories. Therapy or personal growth work based on Jung's ideas can be very rewarding. *Also see* Freud and Jung entries under **People**.

Kinesiology

Also known as 'touch for health', this therapy is based on the belief that each group of muscles is related to other parts of the body. Practitioners learn about the state of the body by the way muscles respond to tests. They treat problems with massage of sixteen pressure points said to be associated with specific muscle groups. The channels between pressure points, muscles and other areas are the same as in **acupuncture**. Kinesiology is used to discover food sensitivities and allergic reactions.

Laying on of hands

With this form of healing the hands are placed on or just above the person, or the part of the body to be healed. Christians lay on hands to channel healing energy, or power, from God. Spiritual healers regard it as transferring healing power from themselves or from an external spiritual source.

Massage

Various techniques are used to stimulate or relax body and mind, and to treat specific problems such as muscle tension. Massage is effective in relieving stress and the disorders arising from it; it is beneficial, for example, in aiding recovery from heart attack.

Massage takes various forms, each form depending on the

complaint: sometimes gentle, rhythmic stroking movements are used, as are **essential oils**. It is based on the strongly human instinct to hold or rub a place that hurts. This instinct to use the hands as instruments to assist healing has been formalized into set patterns and types of movement. Massage is often used in conjunction with **osteopathy** or **chiropractic** in maintaining the posture of the body. The four main movements are:

Effleurage – a stroking movement that soothes the patient and relaxes the superficial muscles in preparation for stronger movements. Effleurage may be stimulating if used vigorously.

Pettrisage – this involves kneading, rolling and squeezing the tissues, much as one kneads bread.

Friction – used deeply with small circular movements against the bone, with the intention of releasing specific areas of tension and blockage.

Tapotement – movements are stimulating and designed to tone and strengthen the muscles. Cupping, hacking, flicking and clapping should be followed by effleurage movements.

Massage has a wide area of application, but there are a number of contra-indications. It should not be used in the acute inflammatory stage of arthritis, or any other condition in which inflammation is present.

Meditation*

The meditational state is one of relaxation and tranquillity of mind and body. Regular meditation can help relieve **anxiety**, stress-related disorders, such as high blood pressure and **depression**, and can boost **confidence**, creativity and concentration.

Metamorphic technique

Gentle massage of the feet, hands and head are used in this technique, which aims to help people come to terms with long-standing physical and emotional problems. The originator, Robert St. John, believed that the feet represent movement and energy, the hands action, and the head thought. He also suggested that many physical and psychological problems develop before birth, and that these are reflected in parts of the foot (particularly the 'spinal' areas recognized by reflexologists).

Moxibustion
In this form of acupuncture, needles are warmed with a 'cone' of burning Moxa leaves, or a roll of leaves is burnt over the skin, which is protected with salt or ginger. Moxa is mugwort (*Artemesia vulgaris*).

Mud therapy
Mud is used in spas and health farms, either in bath water or applied directly on to the skin. It contains major minerals and trace elements, vitamins, natural antibiotics and other constituents, depending on its source. Some of these enter the body and may be responsible for the beneficial effects that are felt.

Music therapy
Also see **Sound Therapy**
Listening to, or making, music helps us recognize or express deep feelings. Working with music can help people with movement and breathing problems. Music therapists use the sounds, rhythms, harmonies and patterns of sound and silence to help physically, emotionally and mentally disabled people, both adults and children.

Naturopathy
Naturopaths help people improve their general health as a means of enabling the body to resist ill-health or cure specific problems. Therapies include: a healthy **diet**, **fasting**, dietary supplements, **hydrotherapy**, **herbal medicines**, **homeopathy** and **counselling**. Naturopaths deal with problems as disparate as **arthritis**, ulcers, viral infections, **anxiety** and tiredness (1).

Neuro-linguistic programming
This is defined as 'the art and science of personal excellence'. Founded by John Grinder and Richard Bandler in the early 1970s, it is a science because it is a method and process for discovering patterns of behaviour which lead to high achievement. It is an art because it allows for the modelling of this behaviour by others in education, business and counselling.

Nutritional therapy
Also see **Diet**

A type of therapy practised by dieticians, naturopaths and some doctors, this aims to correct illness caused by nutritional deficiencies, to restore the balance of a previously unhealthy diet, and to treat some people with amounts of nutrients that in some cases would be considered excessive. The links between diet and disease are increasingly being revealed.

Osteopathy

Osteopaths treat mechanical problems of bones, joints and ligaments, the nerves and muscles which move them, and the soft tissues around them to encourage the body to heal itself. They use manipulation and **massage**, and advise on how to avoid **stress** (1) and strain. Low backache and neck pain are the main areas of pain treated by osteopaths. Other conditions that can be helped are tension headaches, sports injuries and early osteoarthritis. The founder of osteopathy, Dr. Andrew Taylor, had studied engineering as well as medicine and felt that many problems in the body, including disease, could be caused by musculo-skeletal disturbance. Later practitioners have recognized the connection between the spiritual and physical.

Peri-conceptual care

This aims to optimize the health of both potential parents in the months leading up to conception, and to ensure that the pregnant woman has the best information on how to look after herself and her baby in the early weeks of her pregnancy. Attention is paid to **diet**, water, air, as well as the home and work environment.

Polarity therapy

Dr Randolph Stone, the founder of this therapy, believed that most disease is caused by disturbance or blocking of the life energy. He taught that good health depends on 'polarity relationships' between the five energy centres and the parts of the body. Polarity therapists release and rebalance this energy through **diet**, teaching rocking and stretching **yoga** exercises, bodywork, and **counselling**.

Most of the work in polarity therapy is manipulation to balance the energies. This is sometimes done by the therapist placing each hand on different parts of the body to facilitate the flow of energy between them. Three types of pressure can be applied: positive, which moves energy; negative, which unblocks energy; and neutral, which is soothing. Also natural, cleansing foods are eaten in order to strengthen the body's own resources by expelling toxins from the system.

Prayer*
Christians use this to heal sickness through the power of the Holy Spirit. The **healing** may be of part of the body, mind or spirit or of all three. It is believed that the timing of the healing is in God's hands, i.e.,'Thy will be done'.

Primal therapy
A type of **psychotherapy** in which a person is helped to remember traumatic experiences during birth, infancy or childhood. The theory is that if emotional pain is unbearable, it is suppressed. Reliving these experiences allows people to free themselves of the burden. Primal scream therapy, using the founder Janov's techniques – which mirror a baby's first intake of breath – is considered to be too traumatic. It did, however, give rise to rebirthing, which concentrates on breathing techniques and a more physical expression of the trauma. This type of therapy is favoured by followers of **Rajneesh** (see under **People**).

Psychic healing
Also see **Psychic Ability**, **Psychic Attack** and **Psychic Skills**
Healers use their psychic ability to 'tune in' to a sufferer. Many claim to see an **aura** which tells them about a person's past, present and even their future. Others see a picture or hear a message, or sense a particular smell. Much is learnt through the use of **intuition** and of ESP. Therapists then make use of healing energy according to their own beliefs to help people make changes and choices.

Psychosynthesis
In this therapy, a facilitator helps a sufferer to bring out the various

aspects of the latter's personality. These aspects are understood as sub-personalities which are worked with and given self-expression.

By exploring our inner assortment of roles, and their diverse means of expression, it is possible to achieve a harmony between the various elements of our being and ultimately to develop a stronger sense of identity. In practice there are some basic sub-personality groupings that are common to most of us. Recognizing these configurations allows patients to work with aspects of their personality that they both like and dislike.

Psychotherapy

Psychotherapy can help people deal with relationships differently, get more out of life, and cope with crisis. It can also be useful in **psychosomatic illness** (1).

Unresolved traumatic events or difficult situations in the past can influence self-image, feelings and behaviour. This 'unfinished business' can be dealt with through remembering, learning to deal with the feelings, and changing behaviour. There are many methods, including listening and interpreting, role-play, painting, **dreamwork**, bodywork and family 'sculpting'.

Pyramid healing

Scientific experiments show that being inside a pyramidical structure has an effect on the electrical activity within the brain. It also seems to make some people sleep and feel better. Pyramid power, while one of the most ancient forms of **energy** work, continues to be investigated. Many New Age practitioners believe that complex geometric structures enhance the earth's energy.

Qi gong

Qi is the Chinese name for the life energy. Qi gong (pronounced *chi gung*) is a healing art based on exercises said to build up *qi*. Used as a physical discipline, it is the forerunner of **t'ai chi** and can be practised on an individual basis. When someone has built up their own *qi*, they can heal others by allowing their *qi* to flow through their hands to the patient via the various acupuncture points.

Radionics

Radionic practitioners 'tune in' to a patient via a sample or 'witness', such as hair. Next they determine the body system affected by seeing how a pendulum reacts when each system is thought of in turn. (Using a pendulum in this way is one aspect of **dowsing**.) Next the practitioner determines the location of the problem, the cause and the remedy. Treatment involves setting the dials of an instrument box according to how the pendulum has moved, and perhaps placing a **homeopathic** remedy next to the witness, then 'broadcasting' it or projecting the vibration. Sometimes cards showing the location, cause and cure, or a colour, are placed in the box. Radionics is usually practised in the absence of the sufferer, who may be given dietary and lifestyle advice. Scientists regard radionics as a form of **absent healing**.

Reflexology

This form of ancient Chinese medicine/therapy is based on **zone therapy**, which divides the body into ten zones. Energy is said to move within a zone. Congestion and tension can impede its free flow and cause ill-health. Pressing with the fingers on part of the foot corresponding to one zone affects other areas of the body in that zone by releasing the blocked energy.

Research has shown that reflexology was also known to some primitive African tribes, the American Indians, and the early Egyptians. It was rediscovered in the early 1920s by an ear, nose, and throat consultant, Dr William Fitzgerald, although the main pioneer was a nurse, Eunice Ingham, who toured the US lecturing and training students. One of her students was Doreen Bayly, who returned to England and introduced the method in the 1960s.

When reflex treatment is given, the hands, and particularly the thumbs, are used. The thumbs are kept in contact with the foot as much as possible. Results should become evident after about three treatments, and a course of six to eight treatments is usually recommended.

Conditions such as migraine, sinus trouble, back problems, poor peripheral circulation and tension can all be helped by this therapy. After treatment some people may feel tired or in some cases have a form of 'healing' crisis, such as a cold or a skin rash. These are short-term effects as the body seeks to rid itself of toxins. There are certain instances when this treatment should not be used, e.g., heart trouble, thrombosis, shingles, or pregnancy.

Reiki
Also see **Laying on of Hands** and **Spiritual Energy Healing**
'Reiki' is Japanese for 'universal energy'. Reiki therapists lay hands on their clients and claim that through contacting and channelling this energy, healing is caused by an activation and acceleration of the person's own healing power.

Rolfing
Poor posture was said by the American Dr Ida Rolf to lead to many problems. She devised a system of massage and manipulation of the muscles and connective tissue called 'rolfing'. Its aim is to re-align the body.

Structural integration is based on the premise that the shape and contour of our body is a dramatization of our experience. Life events and stresses impose distortions on the body, which, over time, are set into the connective tissues. The therapy is a deep form of **massage**. The masseur applies his weight through fingers, knuckles, and often elbows. Ideally, the body should show a symmetry between left and right, when looking face on. When looked at from the side, one should be able to draw a straight line from the bottom of the ear to the ankles which should pass through the middle of the shoulders and middle of the hips. If the body is not in alignment, extra energy is needed to maintain equilibrium.

Shiatsu
This Japanese therapy, which aims to balance energy by redistributing it, is similar to Chinese **acupressure**. Fingers, thumbs, and sometimes forearms, elbows, knees and feet are used to press on points called 'tsubo' along the body's meridians. Based on the ancient theories of traditional Chinese medicine, it also incorporates modern knowledge of anatomy and physiology. The treatment, which is received fully clothed,

THERAPIES

aims to balance the body's energy (or *qi*) via the traditional **acupuncture** meridians and involves additional holding and stretching techniques. The treatment is felt to be relaxing, invigorating and humane.

Sound therapy
Practitioners assert that each part of the body has a particular resonance and benefits from sounds with similar vibrations, but reacts adversely to unharmonious sounds. Ill-health, they suggest, makes the parts of the body vibrate at different frequencies. Sound waves of appropriate vibrations are believed to restore healthy frequencies and are used in some hospitals for various conditions, including those affecting bones and muscles. **Voice therapy** is a type of sound therapy.

Spiritual energy healing
Many spiritual healers believe they channel power from outside themselves to the patient. The patient does not need to believe in this power. Healing can be practised by **laying on of hands**. Alternatively it can be done at a distance, and aims to strengthen the person's own healing ability, perhaps by expanding spiritual potential.

This type of healing, while being less overt and therefore less spectacular than others, is nevertheless the most efficient and encompasses all other forms. There is direct spiritual contact between the essential energy available to a well-trained healer (both his own and all other available energies) and the depleted energy of the sick person.

The healed spirit of the patient then makes use of that energy to effect a cure on the physical plane or possibly a transition to a more spiritual state. This is understood as a learning experience. There may be either physical, mental or emotional discomfort. Healing occurs on the appropriate level for the individual, releasing him or her from further distress. With this method of healing the physical energy loss from the healer is replaced by **meditation** and **prayer**.

Contact healing was until fairly recently believed by many orthodox religions to be the province of priests and ministers and in some cases this is still so. However, with increased interest in Eastern religions and mysticism, many more people are found to have this power.

T'ai chi ch'uan

This series of dance-like movements and postures – which grew out of **qi gong** – is based on Buddhist and Taoist philosophy. The belief is that complete control of one's movements allows one to practise the martial arts, such as aikido and judo, without violence. Learning and practising t'ai chi is said to benefit self-awareness, posture, co-ordination, **relaxation** and health.

Thalassotherapy

Using sea water to promote health and well-being is an ancient pastime. Formalized in a clinic setting as a form of **hydrotherapy**, it can involve sea-water baths, mineral-rich seaweed poultices or baths, **floating**, swimming, or exercise in a swimming pool of sea water.

Transactional analysis

This type of psychotherapy was developed by Dr Eric Berne in the 1970s as a way of explaining the negotiation that goes on between the three different ego states in any personality: the parent, the child and the adult. By learning to understand the script or games we play – with ourselves and others – we are able to become better integrated individuals.

Transpersonal psychotherapy

The term 'transpersonal psychotherapy' covers a wide area. It has its roots in both Eastern and Western religious traditions. It also arises from Abraham Maslow's work on peak experience and the psychology of what he called 'self-actualizing' people.

The self – the organizing central principle – goes beyond the personal sense of 'I' or ego, and is seen to include not only a personal sense of being but an awareness of the collective and universal. This 'self' unites the different parts of the personality in an experience of wholeness. Crises are not therefore seen as illnesses or even problems, but part of the process of the individual becoming more aware. **Dream-work** symbols, **guided imagery**, fantasy and **meditation** are used in sessions as well as methods of **Gestalt** (a dialogue between the client and a part – or parts – of himself in which the client acts out that part).

Visualization
Also see **Creative Visualization**

Therapists and individuals can use their imagination to visualize pictures to aid healing. These may be relaxing scenes (to help with **relaxation**, pain relief and to lower blood pressure) or parts of the body (focus healing power). Visualization can also reinforce positive feelings.

Voice therapy

We can use our voice to feel better by expressing emotion. **Prayer** and singing give us extra-special voice and can release feelings. Some therapists use **chanting**, **mantras** or particular ways of making sounds to help self-understanding, to develop potential and to release tension.

X-tra

Laughter (the extra component) is said to be the best therapy of all, and researchers maintain that a sense of humour makes people healthier. Qualified 'laughter therapists' include comedians, cartoonists and anyone, including ourselves, who can make us laugh. Laughter has been proven to increase the circulation, relax muscle tension and may leave us mentally more alert.

Yoga
Also see **Crown Chakra** in Section Three

'Yoga' is the Sanskrit word for 'union', and implies the union of mind, body and spirit. There are therefore many different types of yoga. Most people who learn yoga concentrate on the static exercises and disciplined breathing of hatha yoga as an aid to relaxation and general wellbeing. Yoga seeks to develop the 'inner spiritual light' or 'divine principle hidden in the personality' through **meditation**. Many of its principles derive from Hindu philosophy.

Zone therapy

This was the original term for **reflexology,** but some therapists still call themselves zone therapists to this day. They use finger therapy to work on the pressure points of the ten 'zones' or 'energy channels' said to run through the body.

THOUGHT-FORMS

It has long been accepted that thought is a powerful force. Thought is used in **healing** and in **prayer**, and also in 'ill-wishing' someone.

Thought-forms are not easily accepted by the rational mind but should be noted. Some thought-forms can be very beneficial (for example, those created by meditation and music), but there are other types which can be malign. People who practise magic are capable of creating elementals in the form of protective devices. However, if enough negative energy is absorbed, these elementals may adopt an existence of their own to the detriment of the individual.

Certainly at some stage in our development it becomes necessary to face a negative thought-form, whether one's own or someone else's. A simple banishing technique according to one's own belief system is usually enough to send it back 'to whence it came'. Such an experience raises awareness of our own potential negativity, and the existence of what **Jung** (see under **People**) called the Shadow – all those parts of ourselves which we most dislike.

TONGUES, SPEAKING IN

This is often labelled 'dissociation' – that is, speaking in another language whilst in **trance**. This language is mostly an unintelligible or unknown (a form of xenoglossy). Speaking in tongues usually occurs when mystics reach a state of ecstasy, when their devotional outbursts are filled with emotion.

Many of the charismatic movements are noted for their speaking in tongues, although the validity of the phenomenon is disputed. Physics also have the faculty, which, it is believed, may coincide with the development of the **Throat chakra** (see Section Three).

TRANCE

The trance state has fascinated people since time immemorial. It is an altered state of awareness, brought about by an external agency such as a hypnotist, or drugs. In the case of mediumistic trance, it is the relinquishing of control of one's personality to other spirit entities in order that they may impart information. It does need to be understood that each of the resulting states of **consciousness** is totally different. A hypnotic trance is in no way the same as a mediumistic one. While there may be a degree of self-hypnosis in the latter, there has to be a conscious decision to allow the 'controlling entity' to take over one's personality.

Each **medium** or channeller will experience the displacement, or dissociation as the psychologists would call it, differently. By and large there are three distinct states, termed light, medium and heavy control. In the first, the controlling entity is separate from the channeller, and in the author's experience appears almost to be dictating what needs to be said. In the second the controlling entity moves closer to the medium, and some overshadowing takes place (see **Transfiguration**). The medium may take on some of the mannerisms of the guide or discarnate entity, but is still aware of what is going on. In the state of 'heavy' control the discarnate spirit takes over, and uses the channeller's voice and other mannerisms as its own. In this state there has to be trust between channeller and spirit, otherwise the channeller's natural fear will form a barrier. If the channeller is willing, she can train herself to leave the body entirely at this point, to experience a state bordering on ecstasy. This facilitates control by the entity, and enables the channeller to experience a connection with the ultimate more fully, although some channellers regard it as escapism.

At any stage during such work the medium is in a very sensitive state, and any loud noise or unexpected touch can be detrimental. It is perhaps this which differentiates trance from other states of altered consciousness, and perhaps indicates that at this point the medium is working from the subtle body (see **Clairvoyance**) and not the physical.

TRANSACTIONAL ANALYSIS
See **Therapies**

TRANSFIGURATION

When a **medium** or channeller takes on the physical appearance of a deceased person (as seen in the film *Ghost*): this is known as being overshadowed. Transfiguration, however, sees a much more extreme change than overshadowing, the channeller often taking on the mannerisms of the deceased or spirit entity.

Similar changes can take place during **prayer** or deep **meditation**, when the **aura** becomes visible and is seen as a kind of inner light within the person.

TRANSPERSONAL PSYCHOTHERAPY
See **Therapies**

TREE OF LIFE

'The Tree of Life extends from above downwards, and is the sun which illuminates all'. (*The Zohar*)

According to the Cabbala there are ten attributes of God; these are known as the Sephiroth. Together they make up the Man of Light, or the Tree of Life – the link between the planetary and the ethereal worlds.

Kether	Crown
Chochmah	Wisdom
Binah	Creative intelligence
Chesed	Kindness, mercy
Gevurah	Justice, severity
Tiphareth	Beauty, harmony
Netzach	Triumph
Hod	Splendour
Yesod	Foundation
Malkuth	Kingdom

These ten attributes are called the Major Paths of Wisdom. All have archetypal significance. The progression from one path to another can be seen as a step on the road of self-discovery.

There is also an eleventh position, which represents ultimate knowledge – a point of great transformation and a higher realm of understanding. The cabbalist reaches this stage via the other ten.

Tree of Life

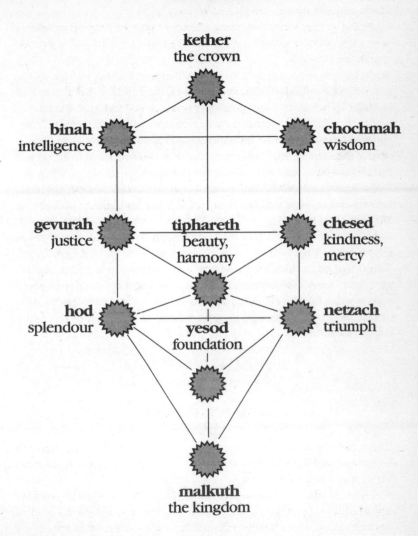

V

VISIONS

What are visions? – apparitions? hallucinations? figments of the imagination? Some would say that visions are all these things. But we should
consider the external circumstance – was there an external stimulus or
was there not? When someone sees a vision without the help of hallucinogenic drugs it would indicate that the spontaneity of the vision is
part of the experience – that the mind has allowed itself to transcend
its normal conscious barriers in order to impart information. When the
vision is part of an artificially induced change of consciousness, it is the
external stimulus which has removed the barriers, giving access to a
different state of reality.

Consciousness can be changed through trauma, as in near-death
experiences, through emotional states as well as through drugs.
When the experience of a vision has a profound effect on the
perceiver, particularly if the information received is directive in some
way, it will often be classified as a vision. Religious experiences such
as Our Lady of Lourdes and the appearance to St Teresa of the Angel
are of this nature.

VISUALIZATION
See **Creative Visualization**

VOICE THERAPY
See **Therapies**

X, Y, Z

X-TRA
See **Therapies**

YIN/YANG

According to Chinese philosophy there are two balancing forces at work within the universe – the negative female (Yin) and the positive male (Yang). These are seen as complementary attributes. In the yin-yang symbol, the pak wa, each part, positive and negative, contains an element of the other, thus:

YIN		YANG
negative		positive
passive		active
female		male
receptive		creative
dark		light
shadow		sun
night		day
winter		summer
cold		heat
soft		hard
wet		dry

YOGA
See **Therapies** and **Crown Chakra** (in Section Three)

ZONE THERAPY
See **Therapies**

JOURNEY
OF A
LIFETIME

INTRODUCTION

When we as adults decide that we are going to change our life, it is often because we discover that we do not know enough about ourselves and the world we live in. We become curious about the gaps in our knowledge and want to take things further. The process of exploration becomes a journey and a search for knowledge. We need information on an intellectual level and need to be able to filter that information and compare and contrast it with information we already have. We have to reassess knowledge and make it fit our way of life. Making life changes requires a great deal of courage and persistence. These are the qualities that develop through an understanding of why we act as we do.

In terms of personal development, when we are learning about ourselves and how to function effectively, we need some sort of structure to help us make sense of all those things we must learn and remember. Self-development mimics the path that a child follows in growing up and in learning confidence, competence and creativity.

The journey you will be embarking upon in this section of the book is of the chakras, which constitute our spiritual universe within.

UNDERSTANDING THE CHAKRAS

'Chakra' is the Sanskrit word for wheel, the wheel being a powerful symbol representing the various circular motions or patterns of life. Other names for the chakras are lotuses or *padmas*.

The chakras – or spiritual centres – evolve naturally in line with the physical and spiritual development of a person. That is, they open up according to an increase in knowledge – hence the image of the open lotus. Everyone has a physical body and other more subtle bodies capable of being 'bonded'. The chakras act as a kind of bridging device between the two.

Information and teachings about the chakras can be found in many spiritual traditions, but most especially in **Hinduism**, beginning with the Upanishads (see **Religions**). There are four texts in these writings which specifically deal with the locations and symbolic attributes of the chakras.

Energies associated with each centre vary according to the chakra. The base and sacral chakras are linked with the physical body. The next three are more closely linked with the subtle bodies – the solar plexus with the lower activity of the **astral body**, and the heart and throat with higher, more intellectual activity. The crown and brow centres are linked with spiritual life.

The Western mind often prefers to group the chakras into a lower triad (group of three) associated with the personality, and a higher spiritual triad with the brow centre acting as the focus of integrated personality. In this grouping each centre in the triad is said to receive the transformed energies from the lower triad; the heart from the plexus, the throat from the sacral, and the crown from the base.

Many spiritual traditions share a common belief that the human body receives sustenance from the cosmos in a form such as Pneuma – or *prana* – and that this energy gives power to the psyche and life to the body. The energy is drawn in, converted and transferred through specific centres in the body. This same concept is seen in Tibetan **Buddhism**, in **Taoist yoga** (2), and was also seen in the Western alchemical tradition (see **Alchemy** (2)). Just as today **crystals** (2) and gems are associated with each chakra, so previously metals and the planets were given similar correspondences.

The renewed interest in Eastern religions and concepts of life has led to a re-awakening of a knowledge of these spiritual centres, and additional correspondences have been discovered. These include the physical systems and organs of the body, along with the endocrine glands. The health of each system can often be judged by clairvoyants, who are capable of viewing the chakras. There is even a correspondence in the way that a child develops and the development of the chakras.

It is from the base chakra (Muladhara), at the bottom of the spine, that the **kundalini** (2) power rises up the etheric spine – also known as the Sushumna.

The Sacral centre, Svadhisthana, is concerned with sexual power and our view of ourselves.

CHART OF SPIRITUAL CENTRES AND THEIR BASIC MEANINGS

Chakra	Music Note	Colour	Meaning	
Crown	B	Violet	Spirituality (creativity)	
Forehead	A	Indigo	Spirituality (objectivity)	
Throat	G	Blue	Wisdom	
Heart	F	Green	Self-knowledge	
Solar plexus	E	Yellow	Emotion	
Splenic	D	Orange	Relationship with others	
Base of spine – sexual	C	Red	Self-image	

Altered state of consciousness (self) and spirit	Altered state of consciousness (others)	Main problems	Age
Power (passive)	Inertia (power used actively or passively)	Ambiguity and illusion of life	16/17 yrs
Sexless entity, space	Healing	Loss of spiritual direction	14 yrs
Ability to speak or otherwise; sage (Chinese, Tibetan etc.)	Options of action	Futility; 'Why me?'	10/11 yrs
'Library' of religious beings	Information – e.g., guides, beginning of trance	Self-control; world pain; intolerance	8 yrs
Appearance of spirit form (friends, relatives, doorkeeper)	Awareness of 'lost' relatives; emotional trauma	'Supermarket shouts'; inability to close down	4/6 yrs
Vulnerability (openness)	Tension in relationship	Extreme sensitivity to others; view of self	2 yrs
Heightened sense of awareness	Physical difficulties	Sexual identity	9 mths

The third chakra is the solar plexus (Manipura). It is situated below the level of the shoulder-blades on the spine and just above the diaphragm below where the ribs divide at the front of the body. It is concerned with the personality and the ego; it belongs to the lower triad of chakras and transmutes energy from the physical level to a higher vibration.

The heart centre (Anahata) governs the heart, the blood and the circulatory system. It is through this chakra that we radiate love, charity and self-sacrifice. The emotions are felt both on a personal and transpersonal level.

The throat centre (Vishuddha) is concerned with the spoken word, and also the search for truth, wisdom and knowledge. It also gives the ability to remain silent when necessary.

The brow centre (Ajna) is associated by some with the pineal gland, and by others with the pituitary. It is highly sensitive to light and vibrations. Activation of the brow chakra brings about heightened perception and increased psychic ability.

The crown chakra (Sahasrara) is at the top of the head. Assigned by some to the activity of the pituitary gland, and by others to the pineal (the reverse of the brow chakra), it is the highest of the seven main chakras. Its function is to energize the other centres and bring about union with the divine, thus bringing spiritual illumination. It is a focus for **meditation (2)**.

Altered states of consciousness

As you become more familiar with each of the chakras, an expansion in awareness will occur as each one becomes activated. Often as perception is enhanced the **consciousness (2)** of spirit form is also enhanced.

On the base and sacral centres one becomes more conscious of the 'inner being', of the people one meets. We may simply realize that we are more sensitive to them, and the physical difficulties they may have, or we may be aware that there is some kind of tension in their relationship structure. This is not true clairvoyance, but is the growth of empathy – a 'being together' with another person, being on their wavelength. At this stage, too, we may also become aware of the presence of spirit, without necessarily being able to identify who it is.

As the solar plexus chakra begins to open up, the individual will often be able to identify the spirit entity that is making its presence felt. Often it is friends or relatives who have passed over, and who have been known either to us or those we are with. It is likely also that we will become aware of the emotional trauma of people around us. This can be quite difficult to handle. For this reason, it is important that anyone who is choosing the path of spiritual development learns about themselves, their own emotional make-up and how to handle the input of emotion from other people. They must learn how not to get 'sucked in' to other people's emotional trauma. Such a state should simply be noted as belonging to the other person or spirit entity and not taken on by the individual.

As the heart chakra begins to grow and expand, we become aware of the vast amount of knowledge available to us. Often in dreams or in meditation the sense of being in a huge library and of being in contact with other discarnate religious beings – such as monks, nuns, priests or religious leaders – occurs. At the same time we tend to become conscious of information of which we could have no previous knowledge. This is a perfectly natural stage of development. Depending on an individual's basic religious belief, this information may come through a **guide** or **guardian angel** (2), or simply 'float' into the consciousness. When using this increasing **clairvoyance** (2), the individual may also become aware of a distinct change in consciousness. The reaction may be physical – as in a change of temperature – or mental as in a kind of widening of perception.

When the throat chakra is ready to open up, one often finds oneself motivated to speak out, sometimes without feeling the need to monitor what is being said. It is as though the knowledge is more readily available, both as to what options of action may be open to you, and also to the people you are with. Trying to monitor at this stage can be counter-productive, because the rational mind will often deny the intuitive awareness. Provided you take care to make a dedication that no-one will be hurt by any action whatsoever of yours, and that everything is for the greater good, you will be able to trust your own judgement. Along with this ability to speak out comes a knowledge of when to remain silent. At the same time you will often become aware that the spirit entity which is communicating with you is some kind of wise person, perhaps a Chinese sage or a Tibetan monk. This is not a figment of your imagination. It simply indicates that you are beginning to become aware of more philosophical ideas and universal truths. Often, if you are so-minded, exploring the culture and traditions of your communicating entity can be tremendously rewarding and thought-provoking.

When the 'third eye' or brow chakra begins to open there is an awareness of the ability to be much more objective and dispassionate. The student at this stage can become aware of the ability to bring healing to others, and often of the most appropriate way in which this can be done. Intuitively he or she will 'know' what alternative therapies will be most applicable and should also be aware of when conventional medicine can be used successfully. He will be conscious of himself as a conduit, or channel, for spiritual energy and may feel that in some way he plays no part in the process of healing. Clairvoyance and other psychic skills which develop at this stage will tend to be geared towards making the world a better place in which to live. By taking responsibility for your actions, you can maximize the potential to use their talents properly. By becoming more conscious of the fact that you are not simply a member of the human race, but are part of a greater whole, you will be able to widen the perception beyond immediate surroundings or circumstances. If one is aware of spirit form, it is that of the asexual entity, often perceived as an angel. Communication with these beings tends to be much more on a vibrational level, rather than through speech or thought.

The crown chakra connects one to true spirituality and creativity. Beyond rational understanding, words and descriptions are inadequate to describe the state of awareness that belongs to this chakra. One becomes aware of true inertia – that is, power which can be used actively or passively for other people. On a personal level the awareness is of power and energy 'which passeth all understanding'. It is the blissful state known by many names, such as Nirvana, Samadhi and so on, and is an appreciation of the idea that we are all part of a greater whole. It is an entirely passive power, although it has within it the awareness that anything is possible. Experienced as a spiritual energy which has been described as pure light, pure energy and pure power, it is the point from which all manifestation and creativity is possible. The crown chakra allows us to create a future that is sustainable and in which we can all share. The realization that we are responsible not only for the here and now, but also for the future of the universe, enables us to continue the quest for perfect peace and tranquillity.

Difficulties

Each spiritual centre has certain difficulties which must be understood if progress is to be made. Roughly they approximate to the same problems that a child encounters as he or she grows towards maturity.

When working with the first chakra, problems to do with gender issues and how one handles one's own sexuality and sensuality often come to the fore. If these issues have not been worked with before, it can be something of a shock to realize that one is a highly charged person with needs which have been suppressed or forgotten. The ability to take pleasure in one's own physical body can seem slightly bizarre until one realizes that this echoes the growing awareness the child achieves as he or she begins to become a viable human being.

The second chakra brings a sensitivity to other people's view of you. There is also a difficulty in being able to balance your own internal sense of self with the information from others. As the growing child must deal with the frustrations of lack of understanding, so the spiritual seeker must come to terms with relationships with other people.

The third chakra is to do with the reception of emotional input from other people. One problem can be the inability to close down, and to filter the information coming at you. It is at this time that crowds can become a nuisance, and for instance travelling by public transport can be painful, as too many impressions impinge on your psyche. This is very similar to a child's struggle as he or she ventures out beyond the confines of the family and tries to take in all the information which is needed to grow into an emotionally stable human being.

The fourth chakra problems arise from difficulties with self-control. Often development of this particular chakra highlights just how difficult it is to maintain emotional stability in the light of what we feel to be injustice. Because this spiritual centre connects with love and compassion, we can become very intolerant of what might be called 'world pain'. This means that issues such as racial or sexual inequality can exercise our minds quite considerably. This became very obvious in the 1960s and 1970s when, for example, such injustices as apartheid in South Africa were the focus of vociferous protests.

The fifth chakra, in highlighting wisdom and communication, can give a problem with futility. We may ask the question 'Why me?' This can range from 'Why has this happened to me' through 'Nobody is listening' to 'What have I done to deserve this?' The problem is that we are in touch with the innate wisdom and awareness which we all have, without being able to put it into words so others can understand. Also the energy behind this can build up to such a pitch that our beliefs may appear fanatical and even frightening to other people

The sixth chakra problem can manifest as a loss of spiritual direction. Because this centre is to do with clarity of vision and objectivity, the very vastness of our perception can cause problems. It can seem as though our options of action have been denied us, or that there are so many avenues to explore that we are incapable of being able to make choices.

Approaching the seventh chakra brings us to a whole new concept of reality. The ambiguity of life and the illusions under which we have been existing must fall away, to enable us to live entirely according to spiritual principles. It can be frightening to realize that we have in effect been living a lie. We are capable of living a life in which the spiritual is glorified by matter, but we must also be aware of the paradox of matter glorified by spirit. It is for us to decide which is more truly our way.

Having treated the chakras in a general format we can now move on to considering each chakra individually. This has been approached in a slightly unusual way in that the information has been kept as pragmatic as possible so that your exploration can begin from your own practical starting place, and not from esoteric knowledge.

CHAKRA ACTIVATION TECHNIQUES

Tradition and experience have shown that the chakras are extremely sensitive to vibration. By adopting a way of life which allows us to activate the chakras in the correct way, we are able to create conditions which make the qualities and lessons of each chakra become a natural part of our growth. Below are some simple suggestions, using natural ideas and materials, to help in the activation of each spiritual centre.

● Live your life with absolute honesty and complete integrity.

● Eat fresh fruit and vegetables that are rich with the corresponding colours of the chakras. (See **colour** (2) and individual chapters on the chakras.)

● Fast occasionally (abstain from solid food) for short periods, provided you do not feel you are endangering your health (see **Crown Chakra**). This is an excellent way of cleansing and assisting the body and also helping to bring about fresh psychological insights and spiritual revelations.

● Make use of the vibrational power of **sound**, **colour** and **crystals** (2).

● Use the power of **prayer**, **meditation**, **visualization** and **affirmation** (2).

● While meditating, visualize the colour of each chakra saturating and balancing the part of your body with which it is associated. Attend to each of the seven chakras from the base of the spine to the top of the head. This is a good exercise to do during a long train or bus journey.

● Put clear quartz crystals in your drinking water. This is said to help restructure the crystalline properties of the water and to aid the energizing of personal consciousness. A crystal can be placed within filtered water, or in a glass of water overnight. This should, of course, be removed before drinking the water.

● When lying flat, place either the appropriate gemstone (see **Crystals** (2)) or a clear quartz crystal on each of the chakra points on the body. It is believed that by enhancing the positive flow of energy throughout the mind, body and spirit, this technique will help to clear emotional blocks.

● Visualize your body as being completely empty. As you breathe in imagine that your whole body is being filled with colour. Work through the colours of each chakra – the colours of the rainbow. Each colour gradually replaces the last. Finally, fill your whole body with white light, before gradually allowing your awareness to return to your surroundings. This has the effect of energizing the whole body, mind and spirit. Initially, some colours will be more difficult than others, but it will become easier as you become more practised.

● Become more aware of your breathing. 'Conscious breathing' helps to align the body, mind and spirit. As you breathe, imagine and feel yourself to be inhaling and exhaling through a given chakra point. This will charge that chakra and the surrounding organs with vital life-force. This can be done while going about your daily business or relaxed in a comfortable position.

● Often sleeping outside on the ground in a natural place can 'recharge' the batteries. There are places of power on the earth's surface which are considered to be the planet's chakras. Try sleeping with your head facing north, to align with, and become charged by, the Earth's electro-magnetic force.

● Use the relevant types of yoga and exercises to charge and activate the chakras.

● Work at consciously expanding your expression of unconditional love, compassion, gratitude, forgiveness and creativity. Use your imagination. You have the ability within you to create an acceptable present and a sustainable future.

Finally, service to others will aid the opening of the chakras in a natural and non-forceful manner, as will caring about the world you live in.

THE
CHAKRAS

In order to make this section easy to use, information on working with each aspect of the chakras is given alphabetically. Because the chakras form a holistic system, it is possible to work with different aspects on the same chakra or indeed the same aspects in different chakras at any one time. For example, you could work simultaneously on the colour in base chakra and the problems which arise on, say, fourth chakra.

ROOT OR BASE CHAKRA

Location: Base of the spine (coccyx)
Colour: Red (secondary, black)
Diet/Foods: Proteins (but meat and dairy products not recommended). Red fruits and vegetables
Element: Earth
Functions: Gives vitality to the physical body. Life-force, survival, instincts
Gems/minerals: Ruby, garnet, bloodstone, red jasper, black tourmaline, obsidian,smoky quartz
Glands/organs: Adrenals, kidneys, spinal column, colon, legs, bones
Negative qualities: Self-centredness, insecurity, violence, greed, anger. Overly concerned with physical survival. Tension in the spine. Constipation
Positive qualities/lessons: Matters relating to the material world, success. The physical body, mastery of the body. Grounding, individuality, stability, security, stillness, health, courage, patience

Every human being forms an image of him or herself at a very early age. As we grow and mature this image will often change outwardly, but there will always be some vestige of our initial view of ourselves. It is amazing how our basic survival instincts and the way in which each of us handles our life force become fixed very early on. A child with a well developed survival instinct will thrive, whereas a child with a less firm hold on physical life will do less well. When a baby is sick, how often has it been said, 'He was a fighter, but couldn't seem to thrive'.

The more a baby learns to appreciate the physicality of its own body, the better image it will have of itself. One way of giving a baby a good self-image is through gentle massage. The baby learns to appreciate its own body, and to take a delight in itself. It is for this reason that a baby does not *have* to be corrected if it uses its hands to explore both itself and its surroundings, unless it is putting itself in danger.

A baby also learns about itself from others around it, and learns what is 'good' and what is 'bad' in their eyes. As it learns to be more appropriate in its actions, and receives positive feedback, it develops greater and greater self-confidence. Recent research has revealed that children of mothers who work full-time probably do less well and are less capable academically than the children of those who work part-time. It is thought that encouragement sets the tone for the later development of potential.

In terms of embarking upon the path of personal development, we need to be able to realize that potential. We need first of all to know what are our individual strengths and what are our weaknesses. Sometimes a weakness can be exploited so that it becomes a strength. Often the harder we have to work at overcoming something, the more skilful we become. The more skilful we become, the more effective we become. The more effective we become, the more confident we become, and we finally finish up having overcome our own obstacles to progression.

COLOUR

Every colour has a particular vibrationary impact on the spiritual system, and this is most often experienced through the chakras. A whole body of knowledge and expertise has been built up over the centuries to do with the use of colour. It would seem, however, that the assignation of the colours of the rainbow to each chakra may be a later Western addition to an already existing system. The Western mind can easily comprehend the symbolism of red being a forceful strong colour – full of life and vitality. This is the colour assigned to the base chakra, which is situated at the base of the spine, and deals with gender issues and self-image. While working on, and increasing your knowledge about, this particular area it is often valuable to introduce that colour into your environment. This can be done in many ways through furnishing, pictures, clothes and other small ways. Because it is such a strong colour it is probably wise to make these introductions gradually, particularly if you share your environment with someone else. Introduce the colour on a more personal level to begin with and experiment with what it does for you. It is the colour of passion in all its forms, not just sexual passion, although it is probably not by accident that women's underwear in this colour is seen as erotic and sexy.

Black is usually accepted as this chakra's secondary colour, particularly through its association with the hidden or **occult** (2). Black is often thought of as being negative, but actually contains the potential or possibility for every colour.

DIET AND FOODS

In accordance with the principles of colour set out above, foods associated with the base chakra are coloured red; for example, strawberries, red apples, tomatoes and cherries. Many foods can have a sensual element to them in the right situation. Many foods reputed to have aphrodisiac qualities are actually high in vitamins and minerals. For example, oysters have a high zinc content – which is important in the production of semen. Protein foods for the repair of bodily tissue, and for use as building blocks, are important, although it is advisable to keep red meats and dairy foods to a minimum. A diet rich in organic produce and health foods is helpful.

ELEMENT

Each of the chakras or spiritual centres is ruled by one element. In the case of the base chakra, that element is the earth. This represents grounding, stability and security. When perceived as the Earth Mother (with which we all need to develop a very deep connection if we are to evolve and develop our talents fully) the symbolism is one of nourishment and fertility. This leads to a relentless creativity. The earth thus represents matter brought into being, the universal symbol for which is the square. In Chinese religion the colour for this symbol is yellow although in Western belief it is red. The animal associated with the element of the earth is the tiger, and it is perhaps significant that as the earth's resources become depleted, that magnificent animal stands in danger of becoming extinct.

FUNCTIONS

We have to learn at a very basic level what motivates and also what demotivates us. Once we have assessed our own personal needs and goals, we can set about fulfilling them. If material security is one of our needs, then we must find the maximum way (for us) to achieve this. If a beautiful body is our aim, then we must find the motivation to maintain that. Many of the recent teachings about success are to do with how we deal with our self-image. This is why exercises in **creative visualization** (2) and in **affirmation** (2) work so well on this level.

One very good exercise to help ground our aspirations is to use a collage of our daydreams to make them more tangible. Gather together pictures cut from magazines or small objects which represent what you want and paste them onto strong card to create a picture. For instance, if your dream is of a cottage in the country, you might paste up a picture of such a cottage, along with some rose petals, a small square of carpet and so on. While creating your picture, concentrate hard on each object, and see yourself in your dream scenario using the objects you have represented.

There are many people who would suggest that concentration on material gain is not in keeping with spiritual advancement. However, it is worth while remembering that humankind's basic need is for survival and that developing the base chakra will help us to be in the right place at the right time. If our physical needs are met, we can then concentrate on spiritual ones.

GEMS AND MINERALS

Bloodstone is normally green with flecks of red. It awakens and normalizes the vibrations in the base chakra and helps to align this with the navel, sacral and heart chakras. The message is to be in the here and now, and gives the opportunity for revitalization of the physical, mental and emotional bodies. Bloodstone has been used in the treatment of kidneys and intestines. It is good for neutralizing toxins in the body, and thus eliminating them.

Garnet (particularly the variety known as pyrope) is concerned with the protection of both the base and crown chakras. It stabilizes the grounding force of the base chakra, and stimulates warmth and gentleness in order to make contact with the creative side of oneself. Garnet itself is an excellent stone for treating disorders of the spine and at the same time enables the free-flow of energy from the base to the crown chakra.

Jasper (Red) helps one to be protected against negativity and to be grounded to Mother Earth. It helps us to learn to progress and keeps us focused on the correct goals and aspirations.

Obsidian provides a connection from the base of the spine to the centre of the earth. It is an excellent grounding stone and helps to disperse a dislike of one's physical form. Black obsidian, particularly, is used to aid the body to rid itself of disorders. Red obsidian stimulates the physical energy and balances the male/female energies.

Quartz (Smoky) helps to focus one's attention in the here and now, and to ground through the base chakra. It enhances stability and in healing can be used to ground the vibration and prevent 'healing crisis'. It is said to be able to activate creativity in business, and is also known as the stone of co-operation. It can stimulate unification of the various drives within teamwork. It also facilitates the regulation of fluids in the body.

Rhodolite, a form of garnet, is often used to initiate the raising of **kundalini** (2).

Ruby, often more properly assigned to the heart chakra, is an excellent shielding stone, providing protection from **psychic attack** (2). It is said that as long as one retains a piece of ruby, wealth will never go away. Ruby is also said to promote dreaming and therefore to stimulate a connection with practicality and spirituality.

Tourmaline (Black) can be used for the stimulation and balancing of the adrenal glands, and stimulation of the reflex points associated with the lower back. It also activates grounding between the base chakra and the centre of the earth, thereby enhancing one's physical well-being. It protects against negative or difficult spirits.

GLANDS AND ORGANS

Each chakra is associated with the physical systems of the body, and the energy which is developed as a child grows is directed principally to those glands and organs which are ruled by the particular chakra.

When as adults we choose to develop and understand ourselves in a more spiritual way, we are often able to make adjustments in our make-up. We are able to go back and revitalize those aspects of ourselves which may not have been given enough attention during the growth process. In the case of the base chakra the energy will be directed to:

Adrenal glands These are found just above the kidneys, and consist of two parts. The first – the outer cortex – produces three groups of hormones in response to messages from the pituitary gland. The first group deals with the balance between salt and potassium, and the second affects the metabolism of glucose, amino acids and fat. The steroid hormones maintain the essential building blocks in the body, and control inflammation. The third group are the sex hormones, the balance of which decides whether we are biologically masculine or feminine.

The adrenal medulla produces adrenaline and nor-adrenaline, which are our physiological responses to stress. If this stress response is inhibited (which is often the case in emotional situations), a difficulty somewhere else in the body may be experienced which can lead to chronic illness and exhaustion.

From a spiritual perspective it can be seen that the adrenal glands deal with our ability to be present within the here and now, and to maintain our hold on our physical being, as well as handling our emotions in an appropriate way.

Bones The bones are a finely developed system designed to give a working structure to our physical being. We do not give much thought to this structure, until something goes wrong with it, when we realize how important it is. From a physical perspective, by the time we come to work with the base chakra it is probably fair to say that we are likely to need to do more maintenance than growth. By giving careful consideration to the needs of this structure, the right balance of mind can be established, and it can be appreciated that the body is there to be worked with and not punished.

Colon The colon deals with the utilization of what we have, and with the elimination of what we have 'used up'. Processing as it does the elimination of that which is no longer necessary, it also addresses issues related to material gain. We need to understand that we are capable of making room for new things in our lives, but can sometimes only do this by a kind of peristalsis – moving material by rhythmic movements on and out. The colon is one of the areas of the body most susceptible to both external and internal influences, and almost any problem of an emotional nature will have some effect on its performance. When you are able to deal with feelings of guilt, bitterness and cynicism, difficulties with the function of the colon may disappear. Spiritually, the colon suggests our ability to take in and properly digest the information we have on a physical level, and our ability to sort and make use of it.

Kidneys The kidneys, which are part of our elimination system, regulate the fluid levels within the body. They act as a filter although they are often described as excreting water. Their prime function is to conserve in as good a balance as possible the fluid necessary for the maintenance of good health. Much of the work that the kidneys do is geared around the salt/potassium balance. This balance is vital for the individual's maintainance of a proper hold on physical life. While most people think of diuretics as getting rid of excess fluid, in fact they are used to try to achieve this balance. The kidneys are also involved in the production of a hormone called renin, which is part of blood pressure regulation.

Spiritually, therefore, the kidneys signify our ability to filter the good from the bad, and to regulate the very delicate balance between our physical and emotional selves. Any difficulty in the kidney area might be traced back to the need for a clear-eyed appreciation of our capabilities.

Legs In old illustrations of satyrs and devils the legs were always pictured as muscular and large to symbolize the animal nature of these creatures. These legs also represented the essential hold that is necessary in the here and now for the enjoyment of life and its sensuous pleasures. The legs are used to motivate one and move one forward in order to make progress through life, and indicate a sense of rightness. Not only do they hold within them the potential for movement, they also help us to stand properly. Often this act of standing is crucial, particularly in, for instance, the martial arts, where movement is not only forward but in any direction. Thus the legs can suggest the act of standing our ground in the face of adversity. If for any reason we are unable to move forward, we may need to look to our support systems to find the ability.

Spinal column The spinal column signifies structure and support. While it is thought of as one entity, it is in fact made up of an arrangement of many bones which are designed to fit together to support the physical body. It also protects the spinal cord, which carries the nerve fibres for almost every part of the body. So, in terms of working with the awareness that the first chakra brings, it is important for us to pay attention to the health of the spine, not just for now but also for the future. Good diet can guard against diseases which were once thought inevitable. Exercise helps to maintain flexibility and prevent rigidity and degenerative diseases, therefore helping us to maintain a positive hold on life.

HERBS

Borage acts as a restorative agent on the adrenal cortex, which means it is good for stress (both internal and external). It may be used over a period of time as a tonic for the adrenal glands.

Broom is a valuable remedy for low blood pressure and for cases of water retention due to weakness of the heart. It is a diuretic which helps kidney function by increasing the efficiency of the heart.

Couch grass may be used in urinary infections and to soothe irritation and inflammation. It is of value in the treatment of enlarged prostate gland, kidney stones and urinary gravel.

Dandelion is a very powerful diuretic, and a natural source of potassium. It is ideally balanced and is often used as a liver tonic. It can be combined with couch grass or yarrow.

Liquorice has a marked beneficial effect on the endocrine system and particularly on the adrenal glands in diseases, such as Addison's disease.

Marshmallow is very soothing in cases of mucous membrane irritation, and the leaf is particularly good for urinary gravel and urethritis.

Meadowsweet has an action similar to aspirin because of its salicylic content. It is therefore useful for pain associated with the skeletal system.

NEGATIVE QUALITIES

Problems on the level of the first chakra which can manifest physically are tension in the spine and constipation. Tension is often a rigidity which reflects our inflexibility and **fear** (1), and constipation is usually seen as a withholding, or holding back, of our energy. When the adrenal glands are implicated the life current can be poor, and help may need to be given to enable the individual to enjoy life again.

Emotionally, we may be overly concerned with our own physical survival. There may be a 'devil take the hindmost' attitude which is self-centred in its insecurity. **Greed** and **violence** (1) are negative aspects of this area of development, and often arise from fear.

Spiritually the problems may manifest as a dislike of the present situation, a wish not to be present on the earth plane or even a hearty dislike of one's fellow man. This type of difficulty can only be dealt with by appreciating that one has been born to live this life to the full and with as much enjoyment as is humanly possible.

POSITIVE LESSONS AND QUALITIES

Most of the 'lessons' which are associated with the base chakra are connected with self-image and confidence. Until we know and understand are own capabilities, we are not even able to think of progressing to a more spiritual self. We must learn to be patient with ourselves and others, because the process of working towards spirituality cannot be speeded up. It is a spiritual law that problems are presented to us again and again until such times as the lessons have been internalized. Just as we reach what we think is an awareness of our idiosyncrasies, we are presented with them in a different way. We have to have the courage to be prepared to be set back many times until we know we have got it right. If self-confidence is knowing that one can trust oneself, the experiences we go through as we work with the first chakra lay the foundation for good work as we expand in spiritual awareness.

Our first responsibility is in maintaining the physical body which we have given ourselves. This body is, if you like, the temple from which we work. It houses all that we hold dear, and therefore requires maintenance, just as a temple would do. This can mean anything from the discipline required to **exercise** (1) properly, to ensuring the right input through **diet** (1,2) and vitamins. Mastery of the physical body is not suppression of its physical needs, but a proper use of them.

When working with the first chakra, we need to know what are our needs for stability and security. Mostly these will be to do with material gain, but may also be connected with our need to nurture both ourselves and other people. A warm **aromatherapy** (2) bath, for instance, can be both nurturing of ourselves and helpful in dealing with physical **stress** (1). First chakra work can bring out a realization of our connection with the earth and with other people who have incarnated at the same time or with the same level of awareness as ourselves.

EXERCISE FOR GROWTH

To help you decide what is important to you, here is a short checklist. Number your choice of personal goals from 1 to 11 in order of priority.

1) LEADERSHIP To become an influential leader; to organize and control others to achieve community or organizational goals.

2) EXPERTISE To become an authority on a special subject; to persevere to reach a hoped-for level of skill and accomplishment.

3) PRESTIGE To become well-known; to obtain recognition, awards or high social status.

4) SERVICE To contribute to the satisfaction of others; to be helpful to others in need.

5) WEALTH To earn a great deal of money.

6) INDEPENDENCE To achieve freedom of thought and action; to be one's own boss.

7) AFFECTION To obtain and share companionship and affection through immediate family and friends.

8) SECURITY To achieve a secure and stable position in work and finances.

9) SELF-REALIZATION To optimize personal development; to realize one's full creative and innovative potential.

10) DUTY To dedicate oneself totally to the pursuit of ultimate values, ideals and principles.

11) PLEASURE To enjoy life; to be happy and content; to have the good things in life.

SPLENIC CHAKRA (SACRAL PLEXUS)

Location: Lower abdomen to navel area
Colour: Orange
Diet/Foods: Liquids, orange fruits and vegetables
Element: Water
Functions: Procreation, assimilation of food, physical force and vitality, sexuality
Gems/minerals: Amber, carnelian, citrine, coral, gold calcite, gold topaz
Glands/organs: Ovaries, testicles, prostate, genitals, spleen, womb, bladder
Negative qualities: Over-indulgence in food/sex. Sexual difficulties. Confusion. Jealousy, envy, desire to possess. Impotence, bladder problems
Positive qualities/lessons: Giving and receiving emotions, desire, pleasure, sexual passionate love, change, movement, new ideas.

Health, family, tolerance, surrender. Working harmoniously with others

The second chakra is situated in the abdomen, below the navel, but above the sexual organs. At the back of the body it corresponds to the sacral area and hence is also known as the sacral chakra. The Sanskrit word is 'svadisthana' which means sweetness or 'one's own place'. Physically this centre affects the flow of fluids in the body and therefore its element is water. In some of the older Indian writings the home of **kundalini** (2) is thought to be the second chakra, not the first.

In working with this chakra it is sometimes necessary to sort out what for you is a correct attitude to sexuality and relationships. Primarily, there is a need to develop a good relationship with yourself before progressing to one with other people. Perhaps the biggest difference between the development in a child and an adult is that in the latter case relationships are generally of our own choice rather than of necessity.

The young child forms an image of itself, and needs to develop the confidence to relate to other people. Initially, this is in order to have its own physical and emotional needs met. Gradually the child realizes that it is capable of meeting the needs of others. This realization is also gained by developing the second chakra. At first, we are only interested in satisfying our own needs in a rather selfish fashion. These needs can be either sexual or emotional. Later however, in the course of relationships with other people, we recognize our responsibility to meet their needs.

COLOUR
The colour associated with the second chakra is a deep vibrant orange. Orange is a colour that is simultaneously both softer and more vibrant than red. In the 1960s and 1970s when 'free love' was being explored as a concept, orange was widely used as a background colour to many psychedelic experiences. As relationships become more sophisticated and genuinely more open, this colour appears to be becoming much more popular.

In terms of personal use this colour may be quite a strong one to manage, but, like other colours, it can be introduced as an accent colour in personal accessories and jewellery as well as in furnishing one's immediate environment. In personal clothing the introduction of such a vibrant colour can actually help to brighten a depressing day. Often the instinctive use of the colour we choose to wear can give an inkling as to what sort of a day it is likely to be. It might be useful to have what could be called a 'rainbow drawer' of accessories to help you identify your strongest and weakest areas. Orange contains the qualities of both red and yellow, and interestingly most people can find an orange tone or shade to suit them.

DIET AND FOODS

In order to work successfully with the second chakra it is important to pay attention to the liquid intake. Fruit juices, particularly from citrus fruits, can help to cleanse the body, and working with the kidneys and bladder can ensure the removal of toxins from the body. To this end at least one and a half litres of liquid should be drunk everyday, preferably not as tea (except for herb teas) and coffee. Contrary to popular belief, under normal circumstances such a quantity of liquid will not harm the body but will flush out the various systems to ensure maximum health. Chinese medicine states that the colour and smell of urine can give information as to one's general health, and daily examination may be a practice to be recommended. Many foods can give urine a particular smell, and dark urine may show that some difficulty is being experienced by the body in dealing with water balance.

Foods with an orange colour are helpful when working with the second chakra. These include many fruits and vegetables but not foods which are coloured with tartrazine or other artificial colourings. Many people are sensitive to such colourings, which may be a factor in allergies and conditions such as **hyperactivity** (1) in young children. A reasonable diet at this stage would consist of meals containing a high percentage of both fruit and vegetables. Alternative health practitioners have long advocated at least five portions of fruit and vegetables per day – at least one of which can be fruit juice. This is now becoming accepted practice among nutritionists and dieticians. At least one meal a day can usefully be composed of only alkali-forming foods, such as fruit.

ELEMENT

The element of water is the one that is taken to rule the sacral chakra. It symbolizes the flow of life, energy and emotion, and also represents the source of all potential. Physically, this element is associated with energy and blood circulation. Esoterically, it is a symbol for death and rebirth. Often in dreams water appears as a symbol of the emotional self and also of the Great Mother. Murky waters often represent the chaos and confusion of the physical world, whereas clear water signifies the fountain of life and the movement upwards through joy and the energy of **kundalini** (2).

FUNCTIONS

The functions associated with this second or sacral chakra are, firstly, the assimilation of food, and secondly the physical force and vitality of the body. There needs to be a degree of understanding as to how food is assimilated in order to create the vitality for life to be fun. From the point at which food enters the mouth – and carbohydrates are broken down for easy absorption – to the point at which, all goodness extracted, the body eliminates that which it does not need, some very complex interactions take place. Constipation, for instance, is not in itself a disease but may be a symptom of some underlying problem. This could be a diet which is not appropriate for the person concerned or on a mental level the continuing holding back of appropriate emotional responses. Whatever the cause, often the individual needs to retrain the intestines to enable the contents of the bowel to be moved, as well as learning how to let go both mentally and physically.

Correct diet is an important aspect in developing spiritually as well as physically, and simple suggestions are given within each of the chakras as to appropriate diets on each level of awareness. It is perhaps important to recognize that the appreciation of food is also based in the sensuous and sensual pleasure that food can give us. Many aphrodisiac foods, for instance, give pleasure through texture and shape rather than their composition. This sensuousness and sensuality is an important part of the joy that one takes in forming relationships with other people. Just as the child's body awareness through the first chakra is important on an individual level, so the joy taken through the sense of touch and closeness with someone else is vitally important on second chakra.

The human urge has always been to perpetuate the species, with the intent of continuing one's life essence beyond physical death. Having sex with procreation in mind turns the act from a simple appreciation of another's body into an acknowledgement of that person's potential for being a possible partner in creating a new being and continuing the family line. A true understanding of this is important in relation to the second chakra.

GEMS AND MINERALS

Gems and minerals assist in helping one to be in contact with levels of higher spiritual knowledge. By focusing one's own personal energy the crystal magnifies and enhances one's ability to be in connection with universal energy. Meditation can be enhanced by the use of **crystals** (see technique under **Meditation** in Section Two) and it is also possible to protect oneself through their use. Some people think that minerals can help neutralize harmful chemicals and energies. Healing can also be enhanced by their use.

Crystals and gems which will help the second chakra reflect the basic colour of orange, but there are certain crystal energies which work specifically on this spiritual centre by themselves.

Gems which assist the second chakra are:

Amber This is usually golden to yellow-brown in colour and has the facility to allow the body to heal itself by transmuting negative energy into positive. It provides the energy to help one to choose or to create choices. It has also been used as a symbol of the renewal of marriage vows.

Carnelian Usually red or reddish brown, it is used to protect against **fear**, **envy** and **anger** (1). It also helps to balance the emotional state with the inner condition. It is useful for work with the first, second, third and fourth chakras and can also increase physical energy and creativity. Often used in the treatment of neuralgia, pollen allergies and colds.

Coral comes from the sea and is generally black, pink, red, white or blue in colour. It signifies rational thinking and a calming of emotions. It may also help with **imagination** and **intuition** (2) and can be useful if you are trying to understand mysticism. It can be used to strengthen the bones of the body as well as the circulatory system and is sometimes helpful in the treatment of spinal disorders.

Gold topaz This mineral helps one to understand the inter-relationships occurring within various aspects of a particular situation. It is said to help in dealing with one's relationship with the universe. Golden topaz is useful for activating and stimulating the first three chakras and can be used to attract people towards one; this should not be used selfishly, but can be used for friendship and business.

GLANDS AND ORGANS

The bladder is the depository for the liquid waste materials that have been filtered out of the blood by the kidneys. Only a comparatively small amount of water sufficient to dissolve those waste materials is held in the bladder. However, because the bladder is such a sensitive organ, disease can occur when it is out of balance. Under normal circumstances the bladder, working in conjunction with the kidneys, flushes through the correct amount of solvent. However, such things as urinary infections, cystitis and urethritis can cause distress and upset the balance. Spiritually, the bladder represents the repository for those concepts, ideas and problems which we need to eliminate as belonging to the past. Failure to eliminate such things can lead to a back-flow of energy which can poison and harm.

The genitals, and the whole of the area associated with them, deal with the hormones which decide whether we are primarily male or female, and with our ability to procreate. Because sensitivity is so closely associated with whether we are active or passive, penetrative or receptive, the secretion of hormones plays an important part in deciding how we use that sensitivity.

The testicles in the male and the ovaries in the female deal with the secretion of testosterone and progesterone respectively. It is this balance which can so easily be upset when there are problems in a relationship and lead to problems with libido.

Just as uterine cancer or cancer of the cervix is possibly one of the biggest fears a woman can experience, fears of problems with the prostate gland can frighten any man. The prostate gland is a small gland situated behind the perineum, just in front of the rectum. Because it is both hidden from view but also relatively close to the surface of the body, inflammation and infection can be a problem. Fearing the worst many men with a problem in this area will ignore it in the hope that it will go away. Fears over sexuality and sexual potency can prevent one from seeking medical advice. One fear that grows is that relationships will be affected by prostate difficulties. Spiritually, the prostate holds a man's sense of his own masculinity and power.

The womb is considered by many to be the seat of femininity. A woman's right and ability to have children is epitomized in this very small muscular 'bag' which can enlarge to hold and nurture the living embryo. Spiritually, therefore, it represents woman's ability to carry future life until it is strong enough to exist on its own.

HERBS

The herbs mentioned below are helpful in the management of problems associated with the second chakra:

Bearberry is antiseptic and astringent and has an effect on the urinary system, which it soothes, tones and strengthens. It is also helpful as a douche in vaginal ulceration and infection.

Beth root contains a natural precursor of the female sex hormones, and has a normalizing effect on the body. It is thus both an excellent tonic for the uterus and a regulator of blood flow.

Chaste tree This herb has the primary effect of stimulating the pituitary gland, especially its progesterone function. It has a reputation as both an aphrodisiac and an anaphrodisiac. The best use of Chaste Tree is in calming the activity of female sex hormones, and it is therefore useful for pre-menstrual stress. It is beneficial during menopausal changes, and can also aid the body in balancing itself after the use of the birth control pill.

Couchgrass is used in urinary infections such as cystitis, urethritis and prostatitis. It is also of value in the treatment of enlargement of the prostate gland.

Horsetail acts as a mild diuretic and is often used in the treatment of bed-wetting and incontinence in children. Often used with hydrangea in the treatment of prostate troubles, it is an excellent healing agent.

Hydrangea While diuretics are often thought of as dealing only with water retention, they can also be considered as a balancing agent in the general scheme of things. Thus, urinary stones (the formation of mineral deposits) can be the result of problems elsewhere in the body. Hydrangea can be used for such problems, but its most important use is in the treatment of an inflamed or enlarged prostate gland.

Motherwort is useful in stimulating delayed or suppressed menstruation, particularly when there is anxiety or tension present.

NEGATIVE QUALITIES

Common negative qualities that are associated with the second chakra are the over-indulgence in food and sex. Additionally, bladder disorders and difficulties such as impotence can often can be dealt with by careful consideration of what needs to be eliminated from one's life in the first instance, and how powerless one feels in the second. Treating bladder problems with herbs appropriate to this area may lead to a recognition that one needs to flow more with the current of life. Another problem that can arise is difficulty associated with sexuality. The sexual act is probably the most important recognition of our ability to relate to other people. Learning how to accommodate our fears and doubts about our own validity can be difficult enough without also having to accommodate similar fears and doubts in others. Recognizing our own vulnerability and handling that knowledge can be the most difficult problem to accommodate, although ultimately one that can be turned into a strength. It can also be a very painful process. Becoming open to someone else requires a degree of honesty that can be difficult to achieve. Jealousy, envy and possessiveness are all emotions which have to be handled sensitively by both parties, and need bringing out into the open. Some techniques for working through conflicts that can arise are given below.

POSITIVE QUALITIES AND LESSONS

Perhaps the most important quality to develop through the second chakra is that of working harmoniously with others. Interestingly, a knowledge of astrology can help in creating harmonious relationships. While most people understand the principle of the sun sign (where the sun was at the moment of birth), and how people of different sun signs can relate to one another, it is worth while taking into account the position of other planets as well. Thus, someone having a secondary planet (Mars, Venus, for example) in Aries is likely to get on well with someone whose sun sign is Aries. A competent astrologer will be able to cast your natal chart for you. The accompanying table gives an idea of the interaction that the various astrological signs have with planets in the other signs. 'Planets' here means not just your sun sign but also other planets such as Moon, Venus etc.

Other qualities associated with the second chakra concern personal health, particularly when associated with physical intimacy and certain lifestyles. Understanding the second chakra can improve one-to-one relationships and enhance the decision making which goes towards making commitments to other people. Inevitably, family relationships which need to be handled sensitively also can be helped through the use of the second chakra. The art of tolerance so necessary in handling such interactions can then be extended beyond the family circle. Tolerance consists of understanding people's often hidden motives for things they do and say. Knowing when to let go of a cherished principle or ideal for the sake of harmony can show real progression.

The giving and taking of pleasure and handling sexual desire are all aspects which gain vigour by developing the sacral chakra. This means that more energy is available for the positive aspects of relationship – such as mutual enjoyment, sharing and caring – rather than it tending to be wasted in arguments and difficulties.

Because one is more secure within one's own relationship with oneself,

PLANETARY RELATIONSHIPS

Planet in	Collaborates with	Conflicts with	Associates well with	Wary of
Aries	Aries, Leo, Sagittarius	Cancer, Libra, Scorpio	Gemini, Aquarius	Taurus, Virgo, Pisces, Scorpio
Taurus	Taurus, Virgo, Capricorn	Leo, Scorpio, Aquarius	Cancer, Pisces	Aries, Gemini, Libra, Sagittarius
Gemini	Gemini, Libra, Aquarius	Sagittarius, Virgo, Pisces	Aries, Leo	Taurus, Cancer, Scorpio, Capricorn
Cancer	Cancer, Scorpio, Pisces	Aries, Libra, Capricorn	Taurus, Virgo	Gemini, Aquarius, Sagittarius, Leo
Leo	Aries, Leo, Sagittarius	Taurus, Scorpio, Aquarius	Gemini, Libra	Cancer, Virgo, Capricorn, Pisces
Virgo	Taurus, Virgo, Capricorn	Gemini, Pisces, Sagittarius	Cancer, Scorpio	Aries, Leo, Libra, Aquarius
Libra	Gemini, Libra, Aquarius	Aries, Cancer, Capricorn	Leo, Sagittarius	Taurus, Virgo, Scorpio, Pisces
Scorpio	Cancer, Scorpio, Pisces	Taurus, Leo, Aquarius	Capricorn, Virgo	Aries, Gemini, Libra, Sagittarius
Sagittarius	Aries, Leo, Sagittarius	Gemini, Virgo, Pisces	Libra, Aquarius	Taurus, Scorpio, Cancer, Capricorn
Capricorn	Taurus, Virgo, Capricorn	Aries, Cancer, Libra	Scorpio, Pisces	Gemini, Leo, Sagittarius, Aquarius
Aquarius	Gemini, Libra, Aquarius	Taurus, Scorpio, Leo	Aries, Sagittarius	Cancer, Virgo, Capricorn, Pisces
Pisces	Cancer, Scorpio, Pisces	Gemini, Virgo, Sagittarius	Taurus, Capricorn	Aries, Leo, Libra, Aquarius

there is more confidence in the expectation that intimate relationships will have meaning and excitement. This also means that there is additional energy available to accomplish meaningful changes and movement and to accommodate new ideas and innovative ways of thinking.

EXERCISE FOR GROWTH

The skills involved in conflict resolution, no matter what the conflict is, are the fundamental skills of active listening and assertiveness, coupled with the ability to negotiate. There are four factors which need to be identified if such a problem is to be resolved.

● Identifying the difficulty
What are the issues?
Who are the interested parties?
Who cares?
What are their, and your, views?
Where are they coming from?

● Breaking down the conflict into areas of agreement, disagreement, and irrelevancy
Break the conflict into smaller manageable areas
Agree what you agree on
Agree areas of dispute
Negotiate on the above

● Power issues
Be aware of who is more powerful and in which areas. Develop strategies for changing those power bases to your own advantage

● Develop negotiating skills
Knowing when to concede a point
Knowing how and when to improve suggestions
Breaking deadlocks
Handling and making threats
Reaching agreement

Relationships can provide very fertile ground for conflict. Resolving conflicts quickly and efficiently can enhance any relationship. Understanding your own style of dealing with conflict and that of others can create 'oneness'.

In any conflict there are two points of difficulty: concern for self and concern for others, both of which need to be balanced. Set out below are five main styles of dealing with conflict. None of these is better than the others; each has advantages and disadvantages. Some will be more useful in certain situations than others. The main point is to be able to use them all. Here is a list of common phrases:

COMPETING	COLLABORATING `
(forcing)	(problem solving)
I am not prepared to change my position	Let's work together on this
	What do we agree on?
I'm, sure I'm right	Let's find some common ground
I know best	
Do as you are told	How can we solve this?
My view is clearly the most rational	I think .... what's your view?

COMPROMISING
(sharing)

Let's find a quick solution
Let's split the difference
I suggest we meet halfway
Let's be satisfied with ....
Let's both compromise a little

AVOIDING (withdrawal)	ACCOMMODATING` (smoothing)
I have no comment Let's leave it for now I don't want to discuss it That is outside my brief What problem? I can't take responsibility for	I concede that point I agree with you there I will do as you say I don't want to offend you What can I do for you? I'm glad we agree

Managing relationships is not something people like to think about, and yet it is probably the skill that is most often used in our personal life and beyond. At rock bottom the human being likes to feel good. Problems on the second chakra can arise initially from the child's perception of whether he feels good about himself or as a result of his response to other people feeling good about him. As a young child the perception is very innocent – either co-operating with others makes him feel warm inside, or he senses other people's approval or disapproval. As an adult working and developing the qualities belonging to the second chakra, the perception is that the individual must learn to understand and manage his own reactions as well as those of other people.

SOLAR PLEXUS CHAKRA

Location: Above the navel, below the chest
Colour: Yellow
Diet/Foods: Starches, yellow fruits and vegetables
Element: Fire
Functions: Vitalizes the sympathetic nervous system. Digestive process, metabolism, emotions
Gems/minerals: Amber, citrine, gold, gold topaz, tiger's eye
Glands/organs: Pancreas, stomach, liver, gallbladder, nervous system
Negative qualities: Taking in more than one can assimilate and

utilize; too much emphasis on power/recognition. Anger, fear, hate.
Digestive problems
Positive qualities/lessons: Will, personal power, authority, energy,
self-control. Radiance, warmth, awakening, transformation, laughter,
immortality

'Solar plexus' translates as the 'centre of the sun'. Its position in the
body is above the navel but below the diaphragm. Traditionally
perceived as the nerve centre which receives its energy from the sun, it
is the main nerve centre in the body. It is also the spiritual centre which
is connected with the emotions. In terms of childhood growth, it corresponds to the age of about six years. At this point the child has begun
to venture out into the wide world away from the family, and is becoming aware that other people can – and will – have an influence over her.
The child is in a position to take in information but perhaps not to
discriminate between what is correct and what is not. This distinction
has to be learnt through practice, and in terms of spiritual development
it is one of the most important aspects of growth associated with the
third chakra. One learns to discriminate between the immediate uprush
of emotion – and getting 'wound up', the reaction – and the need to
apply self-control to enable one to give a more considered approach:
that is, to apply the differing aspects of one's nature appropriately.

A six-year old can form the impression that he is responsible (or to
blame) for everything that goes wrong in the lives of the people
around him. This has a great deal to do with the innate, innocent
recognition of the power available to the individual, and can often
translate itself into an abuse of power in later life. On a more positive
note, the child who is confident and outgoing at six will handle difficulties in later life more positively and with greater success than the
less confident.

COLOUR
The colour associated with the solar plexus is yellow, representing
warmth and light. A clear yellow, this vitalizes the digestive system
and also represents analytical thought and the potential for intellec-

tual ability. It can range in hue from a deep orange-yellow through to a yellow-green. Clairvoyants are known to be able to assess the emotional state of a client through concentrating on this chakra. It is probably the most difficult colour to introduce into one's surroundings and personal effects, because the particular shade of yellow has to vibrate to one's own internal colour range. Some yellows, for instance, appear to drain energy while others very obviously have a vitalizing effect. If a calming energy is needed the colour may be closer to green.

DIET AND FOODS

Foods appropriate when working with the third chakra are those of a yellow colour, such as bananas, melons, apricots, lemons and some apples. Grapefruit and grapefruit juice can also be included in this group, as can so-called white cabbage. Starchy foods are particularly important at this level. Wholegrain foods are an important source of complex carbohydrate. They also contain vitamin B, iron and trace elements of magnesium and folic acid. The last-mentioned is now known to be important to the unborn child. If one slice of bread is taken as one unit of complex carbohydrate, equivalents can be found in two ounces of cooked cereal (such as rice), four ounces of ready-to-eat cereal, and two ounces of cooked pasta.

At one time a great deal of the bran and germ of cereal foods was removed because it was thought to be harmful. In fact, fibre is a necessary part of the diet and provides a buffer against the overuse of junk foods. Nutritionists have now discovered that there is both insoluble and soluble fibre; the latter is useful against heart attacks and conditions of high cholesterol. Oats are high in soluble fibre, so the Scottish custom of a plateful of porridge – or indeed, the modern-day one of muesli – has a helpful place in the diet. Insoluble fibre, found in other grains and vegetables, is of use in intestinal conditions in that it helps peristalsis (the muscular movement of food through the large and small intestine).

It is perhaps necessary to mention a problem which appears to be increasing; that of intolerance to wheat products. Bread that is not gluten-free, muffins, cakes and pancakes, for example, can cause bloating and other digestive problems in some people. If wheat is identified as being difficult to digest, or coeliac disease (an inability to digest gluten) is present, care must be taken to substitute other carbohydrates such as rice, millet and other grains. Each individual will need to experiment to find suitable substitutes for their own system.

For those who can tolerate wheat, some further equivalents might be two wheatmeal biscuits, five cream crackers, or one 6-inch tortilla. Starchy vegetables also have a carbohydrate content, and quantities and sources equivalent to one slice of bread are two ounces of baked beans, two and a half ounces of sweetcorn (one small corn on the cob), six ounces of parsnips, four ounces of peas, one small white potato, four ounces of mashed potato or two ounces of sweet potato.

FUNCTIONS

As well as functioning as a regulator of emotions, the solar plexus is intimately connected with the digestive process and the metabolism of food in the body. Thus, the connection between the emotional state and one's intake of food is very strong. Many people who are emotionally upset will suffer from eating disorders such as **anorexia nervosa**, **bulimia**, or comfort eating (1). Others find it impossible to eat, and at this point, it is perhaps worth reverting to liquid 'meal replacement' foods. This allows the whole system to take a rest, but also means that in reverting to liquids one is using nourishment applicable to the **Splenic chakra**.

The third chakra also vitalizes the sympathetic nervous system. This is the system which keeps us functioning automatically. Often when people 'went into a decline' in Victorian times it was because they had lost the will to live. When one is sufficiently emotionally distressed to lose the will to live, working with the solar plexus chakra can reactivate the sympathetic nervous system to the point where it again functions automatically. As more is known nowadays of the psychological reasons for 'losing one's place in life', much useful work can be done jointly by alternative therapists and conventional medicine.

GEMS AND MINERALS

Amber Primarily yellow-brown in colour, although some amber contains red or green shades. Amber turns negative energy into positive, allowing the body to heal itself. It aligns the ethereal energy to the physical and emotional bodies and thus helps to purify the body, mind and spirit. It has an effect on all the chakras, but helps in the manifestation of one's desires. It has been used in the treatment of the kidneys and in bladder disorders; also see **Splenic chakra**.

Citrine ranges in colour from yellow to golden brown. It energizes and opens up the navel and solar plexus chakras and directs the energy necessary to enhance the physical body through creativity and decisiveness. It also helps to make clear intellectual and emotional problems, stabilizes the emotions and dispels anger. It can help with the digestion and circulation of the blood as well as improving sight.

Gold helps to improve the character via learning and lessens the impact of traumatic situations. It balances the energy fields and helps to eliminate conflicts within the ego. It also helps to deal with problems of responsibility and combats **depression** and **inferiority** (1). It deals with self-reproach and calms anger. As a homeopathic remedy it helps with problems of self-image.

Gold topaz stores up energy and thoughts and is useful if one needs to be recharged. It boosts the state of relaxation and peace, and creates lightness within the spirit. It allows one to see the connectedness of all things, and creates faith in universal matters.

Tiger's eye includes in its colour range red, brown, black and blue. It is helpful for those seeking clarity. As well as assisting the base chakra, it also contains an energy which helps, through the solar plexus chakra, to enhance the psychic and intuitive processes. It produces soothing energies and creates a calmness which facilitate enjoyment of life. Tiger's eye has been used in the treatment of intestinal problems, such as diverticulosis. Its use can also strengthen the spinal column.

GLANDS AND ORGANS

The glands and organs associated with the third chakra are those which deal with the assimilation of food and also those which deal with the production of sexual hormones. The pancreas is mainly concerned in the breakdown of protein, fat and carbohydrate. It is a large gland situated near the kidneys which releases digestive enzymes to neutralize acidic juices in the stomach. The Islets of Langerhans are endocrine cells which produce two hormones – part of the management of glucose and fatty acids in the body.

The blood sugar will rise after the eating of a meal. When it does, insulin (the first hormone) is released which then inhibits the liver's glucose production, at the same time inviting the usage of glucose by the tissues of the body. The second hormone that is produced, glucagon, has the opposite effect to insulin in the liver and increases glucose levels. An imbalance of these hormones in the blood will result in either a too low or too high level of sugar.

Difficulties with the pancreas include pancreatitis, which is a painful inflammation of the pancreas when the digestive enzymes attack the pancreas itself. It can sometimes arise through excessive alcohol intake. The other disease of the pancreas is diabetes mellitus, which is a problem with excessively high blood sugar levels. The symptoms are weight loss, thirst, an increase in the volume of urine, and possibly coma. Diabetes is often managed through diet, which should be tailored to the individual's needs.

The principal task of the stomach is to prepare food for processing by the small intestine. This is done by mixing the food with hydrochloric acid and enzymes within the stomach. Problems of indigestion which can cause pain, wind, heartburn and other symptoms can be caused by irregular eating, eating the wrong food, over-loading the stomach, and eating without proper chewing. These are problems of food management which can lead to more serious conditions such as gastritis, inflammation of the stomach lining, or a gastric ulcer.

The gall bladder serves to act as a reservoir for bile which is secreted by the liver. Traditionally, the 'bilious' individual is believed to be harbouring some bitterness which is difficult to eradicate. There may also be problems over making decisions that will carry one forward. There used to be a saying among medical practitioners that cholecystitis (inflammation of the gall bladder) was seen mainly among women who were 'fair, fat and forty'. This is no longer so, and because much more is understood about stress and the body's production of cholesterol, problems with the gall bladder need not always be managed by surgery. The production of gall stones can be prevented by a reduced intake of fat (except olive oil) and an increase in fibre intake.

The nervous system clearly shows the connection between the physical and psychological aspects of our body. The physical body mirrors stress within the nervous system, and vice versa. The main problems that have a psychological basis and manifest in diseases of the nervous system are **stress**, **anxiety**, pre-menstrual tension, **hyperactivity**, **depression** and insomnia. Examples of the neurological diseases which arise from problems within the nerve tissue itself are migraine, multiple sclerosis, neuralgia and shingles. This last disease is actually a viral problem which needs treating by dealing with the whole immune system. Without this total treatment it tends to be hard to cure.

HERBS

There are a number of conditions and diseases which are associated with the nervous system – for example, high blood pressure and coronary disease within the circulatory system; asthma, hayfever, and coughs within the respiratory system; peptic ulcer, flatulence and dyspepsia within the digestive system; thyroid problems, and endocrine disorders within the glandular system; and within the reproduction system various problems regarding menstruation. These conditions can be aided enormously by strengthening the nerves and toning the entire system. Below are some herbs which may be useful in treatment.

Nervous System

Damiana is very good for strengthening the nervous system, and also has a reputation as an aphrodisiac (the leaves and stem are the most helpful part) and as being generally good for the hormonal system.

Hyssop has a number of uses mainly due to its anti-spasmodic actions. It can be used for coughs and colds by virtue of its diaphoretic qualities, and in cases of anxiety and hysteria because of its qualities as a sedative.

Kola nut is excellent as a short-term stimulant for the nervous system. It is generally accepted that once normal health – and thus correct functioning has been regained – the nervous system does not need much further help. However, kola may be used to treat nervous debility and general weakness, most specifically for nervous diarrhoea. It can also be used for **depression** (1) and in some cases of migraine. Kola has also been known to aid in the treatment of **anorexia** (1). (Also see **Bach flower remedies** in Section Two for further information.)

Skullcap, probably the best-known herb-tonic for use with the nervous system, works well with **damiana**. An excellent antidote for nervous tension, it also revitalizes the central nervous system, and thus can be used in cases of exhaustion and depression. It is also regarded as useful in the treatment of epilepsy.

Valerian, like hyssop, has sedative and anti-spasmodic uses. It is best known as a sleeping aid, but it can also be used safely in the reduction of tension, anxiety and hysteria. As an anti-spasmodic it can be used to help conditions of cramp, intestinal colic and period pain.

Vervain relieves tension and stress.

Liver and Gall Bladder

Blue flag By working through the liver (the principal detoxifying organ in the body), this herb can be of use in the treatment of minor skin disorders, eczema and general spots and blemishes. It can also be used to help treat bilious constipation.

Balmony acts as a tonic for both the digestive and absorptive systems and is another excellent herb for dealing with liver problems. It can also be used to treat gall stones, jaundice, and inflammation of the gall bladder.

Vervain, as well as being beneficial to the nervous system, is also good for the gall bladder as a hepatic remedy.

Wahoo helps remove liver congestion, and therefore assists the digestive process. It can be used in the treatment of jaundice, gall bladder problems and congestion due to stones. It can also help constipation when this is associated with the liver and with skin problems (again, if the liver is involved).

Note: Any malfunction related directly to the liver or the gall bladder can be helped by a diet in which fats and fatty foods are kept to a minimum and alcohol is drunk only in moderation.

Stomach

Aniseed When taken internally, this can provide relief from griping, intestinal colic and flatulence. It is also very beneficial in cases of bronchitis, especially if there is a persistent cough. By itself the oil can help control head lice.

Comfrey is an excellent external wound-healing herb and can also be used to help gastric ulcers, hiatus hernia and ulcerative colitis. As with **aniseed**, it can be used in the treatment of bronchitis and irritable coughs.

Fennel is specifically a stomach and intestinal remedy which can help relieve flatulence and colic whilst also revitalizing the digestion and appetite. Fennel can also increase the flow of milk in nursing mothers.

ELEMENT

The element of fire represents transformation, purification, power and strength. Just as the disc of the sun represents universal energy, fire or flame signifies the unseen energy that is in all existence. Energy manifested as fire or flame thus symbolizes spiritual power and force and is a representation of divine energy or of the soul. Many clairvoyants perceive a flame leaving the body at death.

Both fire and flame can be ambivalent – they are either divine or demonic, creative or destructive, positive or negative – depending on the circumstances. (Fire must consume in order to give warmth, so is destructive in order to be positive.) Light and heat may also correspond to the intellect and the emotions – both represent truth and knowledge. Baptism by fire restores purity through association with the idea of passing through fire to regain Paradise, to be reborn. In earlier times, torch bearings at weddings and fertility rites represented the regenerative power of fire. **Symbols** (2) of fire are the upward pointing triangle, lion's mane, swastika and sharp weapons.

In **alchemy** fire is the central element as unifier and stabilizer; in **Buddhism** it is wisdom (2). In Chinese religion flame signifies the presence of divinity; in Christianity it represents martyrdom and religious fervour. In **Hinduism** (see **Religions**, under Section Two) it represents transcendental light and knowledge and the vital energy of wisdom. In Islam fire and flame are light, heat, divinity and hell.

NEGATIVE QUALITIES

On a physical level the negative qualities and difficulties that occur are often to do with digestion. If such problems are dealt with holistically, we may also have to deal with emotional blockages. Feelings of **anger**, **fear** and **hate** will often have to be faced before we can utilize this chakra's energy appropriately. The issues of personal power can mean that, through fear, we create situations where we try to have power over people rather than helping them to have the power to accomplish their own wishes. It is at this level of awareness that the words 'After all I've done for you' are experienced.

Another problem experienced at this level of understanding is that of taking in more than one needs or can utilize. On a physical level, this can be seen as greed, but may also be experienced as possessiveness – taking in too much of another person's energy, or as a type of fanaticism soaking up other people's negativity to the point where one harms oneself. A slightly more subtle version of this could be called 'psychic vampirism', which occurs when one's own personal energy is so low that one leaches energy from others. In those who have developed the healing ability, or other ways of maintaining a high energy level, there need be no problem but for others less experienced a degree of exhaustion can occur. Many of us have experienced visits from a friend which leave us feeling drained and exhausted.

POSITIVE QUALITIES AND LESSONS

The main quality associated with the solar plexus chakra is that of personal power. Just as children learn how powerful they can be once they have ventured into the outside world, adults too, when working with the third chakra, begin to understand how to use their own energy to achieve success. The recognition that we can make things happen if we will it can be quite frightening. It is this ability which can be used in **creative visualization**, in **prayer** and in **chanting**, depending upon one's belief system (2). It is as though by making our needs known, we register an emotional involvement or investment in what we are trying to create.

Ideally, creativity is a combination of emotion and objectivity or vision. Attempts to create from a purely emotional point of view, therefore, may not initially be successful. Working with the third chakra teaches us a great deal about positive and negative emotions. Using personal power to create a negative situation can be quite harmful to all concerned – including the perpetrator. For this reason, one of the other qualities which needs to be developed when working at this level of understanding is that of self-control. This means that we need to understand the principle of reacting to a situation and then responding. We may react, for instance, to someone's harsh words about our conduct with anger and distress. If we lash back, we have allowed the reaction to take us over. On consideration, we may realize that there is some justification for the other person's comments. A suitable response might be 'You are quite right, what can we do about it?' In this way, we have exercised self-control, and have also taken personal authority for making necessary changes.

Another quality associated with the solar plexus is our own ability to create a personal warmth towards other people. When we are conscious of our own personal power, we are not threatened by needing to come forward to welcome other people into our personal space. A very wise man once suggested that if everybody was prepared to go more than halfway to meet other people there would be fewer problems in the world.

The transformative power of the sun is recognized as an agent for growth. So also is the transformative power we all have within our solar plexus chakra. It is through this chakra that we take in information from other people, and with warmth and love can transform it into an energy to be given back to others. An equally transformative energy is that of laughter. The solar plexus chakra is the seat of true joy. This is not some highly esoteric concept, but pure enjoyment of our surroundings, our abilities and the world we live in. By awakening to a deeper meaning, we can find more depth within ourselves and an ability to relate to other people without being 'needy'.

EXERCISE FOR GROWTH

The solar plexus is the level at which we move from being totally self-involved to reaching out to other people. Not only do we reach out as we have done on the second chakra level for relationships with individuals, we also reach out to others in the hope that they will fulfil our personal – or individual – emotional needs.

These needs can be divided into three areas:

Inclusion – Do we belong or not?
This category is about being able to be with others.
People with a strong requirement to be included need to feel part of a group in most areas of their lives; they tend to dislike acting on their own. People with average needs can be part of a crowd but are equally happy to be by themselves should the situation demand. Those with low needs want less contact with others and prefer not to take part in group activities. They are often extremely uncomfortable in group situations.

Control – Do we like being in control, or being controlled?
This area is to do with being prepared to be in a leadership position or, alternatively, wanting to be told what to do.

Those with high control needs will usually try to take control whether or not it is appropriate for them to do so. They have a great deal of difficulty in taking second place. People who are ambivalent about control will take control when necessary, particularly when they feel competent about their own abilities, but will relinquish authority if they feel others are more able. Those with low needs frequently need to be told what to do in quite specific ways.

In unstructured groups people will tend to fall naturally into their own style, resolving conflicts along the way. In structured situations which require teamwork, people may, while gravitating naturally towards fulfilment of their emotional need for control, sacrifice their own style for the sake of the team. A good team manager will recognize each individual's strengths and weaknesses.

Affection – Are we trusting of and receptive to other people, or closed to warmth and affection?
This category refers to how much an individual is prepared to trust others and whether they can be receptive to affection from others. Those with high needs for affection will form relationships within groups which will tend to be friendly, open-hearted and intimate. An individual with low needs for overt affection will create relationships which are more detached and reserved.

By being fully aware of the range of emotional needs, difficulties can be handled and individual requirements met. Assess your own needs with the help of the table below, indicating whether you consider them to be a high, moderate or low priority in your life.

	INCLUSION	CONTROL	AFFECTION
What I express to others			
What I want from others			

Monitor your behaviour for a period of one month to six weeks to ascertain whether your initial assessment was correct.

HEART CHAKRA

Location: Centre of the chest
Colour: Green (secondary, pink)
Diet/foods: Green fruits and vegetables. Vegetarian
Element: Air
Functions: Anchors the life force from the **higher self** (2). Blood. Circulation. Energizes the blood and physical body with the life force
Gems/minerals: Emerald, green and pink tourmaline, malachite, green jade, green aventurine, chrysoprase, kunzite, rose quartz, ruby
Glands/organs: Arms, circulatory system, heart, hands, lungs, thymus gland
Negative qualities: Heart and circulation problems; emotional instability. Repression of love, imbalance
Positive qualities/lessons: Balance, compassion, divine/unconditional love, forgiveness, group consciousness, oneness with life, understanding, acceptance, contentment, harmony, openness, peace

By the time he is about eight years old the child is coming to terms with the fact that he has a part to play in a life beyond the home. He is becoming more aware of himself as a human being and is in the process of learning how to develop self-control. Often around about this time, the child can become very intolerant of those circumstances and situations he does not yet understand. He also becomes aware of emotional, mental or spiritual pain experienced by others. He is becoming aware of what he can and can not do to help in situations (competence), and at this time he often reviews how he has learnt in the past. He becomes more aware of his need for information and is often curious to discover how things work.

Body Care

The question of self-discipline is one that is likely to arise when you are considering self-awareness. There is no need for harsh discipline, but firmness. The word discipline originates from the word 'disciple' and suggests a follower, and self-discipline therefore means following oneself. This then means that we are in a position to do what we perceive as being important to us.

The practice of skin brushing (see under **Functions**, below) helps the body to function effectively, and this requires a degree of self-discipline. Any activity that helps in the elimination of toxins will allow us to function at peak efficiency. Aerobic activities will be particularly useful. Swimming is a sport that uses those areas with which the heart principally deals. You will need to work within your own capacity to gain the best out of your pastime, but equally will need to push your boundaries and tolerance a little harder each time.

COLOUR

The colour primarily associated with the heart is green, and its secondary colour is pink. In your process of growth it will often be helpful to have these colours, and the beneficial vibrations they give, in your environment. You could, for instance, ensure that there are always green plants or pink flowers in your room; that you perhaps have a green cushion; that you wear green or pink, even if it is just a scarf or handkerchief. If you have consciously introduced the colour, you are constantly aware of it and it is therefore working for you on a subliminal level throughout the day. The particular green that is best to use is one that reflects the colour of nature and of the plant kingdom. Plants are balancing agents (among the qualities of the heart), so the combination of plant and colour can help us to achieve balance within ourselves.

DIET AND FOODS

At this particular stage of awareness, a vegetarian **diet** (1, 2) often becomes an acceptable alternative to junk food and heavy proteins.

Foods that have particular relevance to the heart chakra:
Cabbage is reputed to have a cleansing effect on the system, and thus strengthens the heart.
Coriander (also known as Chinese parsley) can be used for healing headaches, and is also thought to increase one's ability to love.
Cucumber has a normalizing effect on the heart because of its slightly

diuretic effect. Traditionally, it is supposed to hinder lust and promote fertility.

Lettuce has a soporific effect and can be used to prevent seasickness.

Spinach helps to regulate the blood because it is iron-rich. It does, however, have to be combined with other foods, such as eggs, for it to be effective in this way.

ELEMENT

The element governing the heart and lungs, air, has the characteristic of dryness and serves to lighten conditions around itself. When the various symbols for air are incorporated into decoration or into one's everyday life, the vibration (atmosphere) is raised and connections can be made that allow one to develop the qualities necessary for growth. The geometric symbol for air is the circle or the arc. In Chinese symbolism air is portrayed by the blue or green dragon, and in the Greek/Roman system by the chameleon. In Hindu and Buddhist symbolism, air is depicted as the crescent.

FUNCTIONS

Physiologically the heart – placed as it is in the centre of the chest – is the pumping centre of our being. In terms of our physical growth and well-being, it has responsibility for the circulation of the blood, the health of the thymus gland, the correct use of our arms and hands, the intake and output of air and the efficient functioning of the lungs. Blood represents the nourishment of life and brings vitality to cells, tissues and organs. Ensuring the efficient circulation of the blood is obviously one way in which we can improve our lives. The simple physical expedient of skin brushing aids circulation and helps us towards greater bodily efficiency. Skin brushing consists of using a rough sponge, cloth or loofah and literally brushing towards the heart. The implement should be dry and the strokes fairly firm. Brushing towards the heart means downwards from above the heart and upwards from below the heart. Thus brushing the legs should be done from the ankle towards the thigh. This helps remove debris from the skin and toxins from the blood.

When we feel dull and sluggish it may indicate lack of enjoyment and enthusiasm and also a degree of scepticism about our right to be happy. Our thinking can have a direct effect on our blood supply. We may find that selfishness and unresolved issues cause problems with the way our bodies function. It is known that the correct diet can enhance our feeling of well-being. Some suggestions for cleansing are given below, under **Herbs**.

GEMS AND MINERALS

Working with gems and minerals can have amazing effects on you and your personality if you choose to make use of the energies available. The particular gems and crystals associated with developing self-awareness are:

Chrysoprase opens and activates the heart chakra and encourages compassion. In assisting the process of self-acceptance, it encourages the integration of body, mind and spirit and allows a non-judgemental attitude. It does not allow either a superiority or inferiority complex, and when used in business encourages faithfulness to a principle. It is also reputed to heal a broken heart. On a more practical level, it is thought to help the body assimilate vitamin C and help with heart problems.

Emerald is said to help facilitate domestic bliss and successful relationships. It has the ability to enhance loyalty, both to oneself and to others. In activating the heart centre, it helps bring harmony into all areas of life and focuses any action into the right action. In this way it allows one to remain centred and in control in the midst of life's hurly-burly. In **meditation** (2) it enables one to go deeply into the meditation and still maintain objectivity. In **healing** (2) it assists in spinal disorders and in problems with the lungs and heart.

Jade (particularly green) brings a realization of potential and helps one to focus on one's life purpose. Often known as the dream stone, it is supposed to release suppressed emotions through dreams. It is also reputed to allow one to manifest dreams and ambitions. By allowing an understanding of the needs of others, it helps one to give wise advice and also to prioritize the needs of the day. Used in healing to assist in the treatment of heart disease, it also helps in the treatment of the kidneys and the spleen. Giving confidence and self-reliance, it enables one to live a long and fruitful life.

Kunzite activates the heart chakra and aligns it with the **throat chakra** and the **brow chakra**. Activating loving thoughts and communication, it helps in the expression of all forms of love. Kunzite can be used to remove and protect one from negative energies, and allows the owner to be both innocent and mature at the same time. By helping the individual to remain calm in the midst of external chaos, it focuses on internal balance. During **meditation** it stimulates creativity and **intuition** (2). In **healing** (2) it strengthens the heart muscles, deals with circulatory disorders and lung problems and helps in the management of **stress** (1).

Malachite is said to be the stone of transformation, helping to change situations for the better. It allows one to let go of negative experiences that might impede spiritual progress. By clarifying the emotions, it allows the user to obtain a balance between needs, wants and requirements and clears the way for progress. By helping one to take responsibility for one's actions, knowing they are the right ones, it stimulates the ability to live life more fully. In healing, malachite can be used to help treat **asthma**, and **arthritis** (1) and other bone problems. It is also used to cleanse the cellular structure and enhance the immune system.

Rose Quartz is often used in helping people to open up to the potential for love in all its forms. Working on the principle that you cannot love others if you do not love yourself, it allows you to achieve peacefulness and calmness when dealing with your own emotions.

Ruby – See **Base Chakra**.

Tourmaline (green) has the effect of allowing openness and love on the heart chakra. It helps with visualization of the link between the centre of objectivity (the third eye) and the love (heart) chakra. It has the qualities both of compassion and of creativity, and acts to inspire creativity and achieve success and prosperity. From a healing point of view, green tourmaline is reputed to enhance one's knowledge of **herbalism** (2). It also balances the thymus and the ductless glands, and can work to clear problems with masculine energy.

Tourmaline (pink) is a good stone to use during periods of growth and change, since it facilitates the processes associated with learning to love. Particularly geared toward the process of universal love, it promotes peace and trust as well as understanding. From a healer's point of view, it is excellent in realigning the body in preparation for healing. It can be used to treat skin disorders as well as those of the heart and lungs.

GLANDS AND ORGANS

Hands and arms The hands and arms represent the ability to take hold of life, to cope with everyday problems and to grasp opportunities that may be offered. They also suggest the capacity to give and receive love. Problems with the hands and arms may indicate a difficulty in expressing what one is really feeling.

Thymus gland This butterfly-shaped gland sits behind the breastbone. It regulates the auto-immune system and plays an important part in the formation of blood cells (T cells). Problems with the thymus gland may indicate a difficulty in remaining grounded and in touch with physical reality.

HERBS

There is often a sense that to 'clean up one's act' we should be using more natural ways of healing ourselves. The action of herbs and how to use them is covered fairly extensively in Section Two. *Note:* A qualified herbalist should always be consulted for the precise action necessary to help ourselves.

The following are efficacious herbal inner cleansers and purifiers:

Balm has a tonic effect on the heart and circulatory system. It causes mild dilation of the capillaries and relieves flatulent spasms. It can also be used in cases of mild depression.

Comfrey is an impressive wound healer and is a powerful healing agent in bronchitis and irritable cough, when it soothes and reduces irritation and helps with expectoration.

Hawthorn berries are among the best tonic remedies for the heart and circulatory system. They will help the heart to function normally, either stimulating or depressing its activity depending on the condition.

Lily of the Valley has an action equivalent to foxglove, without the toxic effects. It helps the body with breathing difficulties associated with congestive heart conditions.

Lime blossom is a relaxant that can be used in cases of hypertension and nervous tension. It can also help to relieve the symptoms of migraine.

Mistletoe quietens, soothes and tones the nervous system. It reduces the heart rate while strengthening the peripheral capillaries. Recent research appears to suggest that it *may* have some anti-cancer properties.

Motherwort is a specific for over-rapid heartbeat where it is brought about by anxiety and stress. It may be used in all heart conditions associated with anxiety and tension.

Passionflower, an anti-spasmodic, is used in cases of asthma where there is much spasmodic activity and associated tension.

Valerian is a relaxant and sedative. It is effective in promoting restful sleep and in enabling one to deal with tension brought about by worry.

NEGATIVE QUALITIES

Gout, gangrene and varicose veins can be viewed as indications of 'stuckness' – perhaps we are not entering into a proper flow with life, not allowing our energy to flow with love. Gout can sometimes indicate the crystallization of a too rigid attitude. Thrombosis may suggest an inability to remove a thought or behaviour pattern that stops us moving forward.

Lung problems are often to do with holding on to grief – sometimes grief that has long been buried. Heart problems may be associated with the inability to let go of old hurts within relationships, or even with difficulties in allowing love into your life. Sometimes the need to take on someone else's pain, in the mistaken belief that it will help, can cause difficulties. It is worth while reminding those who are healers that this can sometimes be a problem for them if they do not develop the correct objectivity in their healing practices (For 'cleansing' techniques, see the visualization at the end of this chakra.)

One worthwhile consideration when dealing with difficulties in the heart area is the possibility that one may be carrying 'family **karma**'(2). This occurs when there is a known difficulty within a family – perhaps an inherited tendency to heart problems. If this is looked at as a difficulty in coming to terms with love, there is a way of breaking the pattern of illness. What has to be broken is the belief that we must necessarily suffer in the same way as our parents. Often it is worth while working with a therapist skilled in such work to come to an understanding of how the patterns repeat themselves. It is important to approach such work with a completely open mind, and in a spirit of forgiveness – nobody is to blame for the establishment of such a pattern.

POSITIVE QUALITIES AND LESSONS

The mental qualities that are necessary as we move toward greater self-awareness will begin to develop of their own accord as we take more care with our diet and better care of our bodies.

The first quality we need to develop is one of balance and discrimination. Self-awareness is to do with achieving a balance between what we can do and what we can not without giving ourselves a hard time. It is about exploring our inner dimensions and comparing and contrasting the huge areas of knowledge we have access to – if we are prepared to make the effort – with what we already know. Much of this can be achieved through the practice of **yoga** ((2) see under **Therapies**). Many people in the Western world think of yoga in terms of an odd discipline that entails going to class once a week and standing on one's head. Properly used yoga can – and will – change your life. There are many types of yoga, but the one we are most concerned with at this particular level of awareness is Hatha Yoga (see **Crown Chakra** in this section for further information).

Other qualities we need to develop are those of unconditional love, acceptance and forgiveness. These are all attributes that can be developed as we learn to utilize our capacity for love. As part of a balanced approach to life, we must first learn to forgive ourselves for what we may perceive as our faults. Once we have done this we may learn to forgive others for their faults and difficulties. We can afford to be tolerant of their idiosyncrasies when we appreciate that they are undertaking their own journey of self-discovery. It is not for us to be judgmental about them. In accepting them as they are and not trying to change them, we are able to allow them the dignity of being themselves. By being able to acknowledge them as themselves, it becomes possible to love them unconditionally and with compassion. If we are then able to develop an openness with them, we ourselves can be at peace in the knowledge that we are making our best effort to enhance the quality of life for everyone. If harmony is established in our own surroundings, it cannot help but make the world a better place.

EXERCISES FOR GROWTH

At this point in your development it is sensible to deal with unfinished business. Ask yourself if there is anything in your life that you feel you have not finished off. A course you started but did not complete? Can you complete it in a different way? Think carefully about it. If you can, finish it off. If you can't, let it go.

Is there anyone against whom you bear a grudge? Think about it, think about them and let it go. Speak to them in your own mind. If necessary, write them a letter, so that you feel you are communicating with them. (There is no need to actually send the letter – this action is for you, not for them.)

The following questionnaire is best done with the help of a sympathetic friend. It is designed to make you think about who you are, what you want and perhaps why. You will find a number of incomplete statements. Complete the first statement by telling your partner as much or as little as you want. Your partner should listen to what you say without verbally responding. In turn your partner should complete the statement, and then you too should listen without responding. If you wish, you may time the activity. When this process is complete, move on to statement 2 and so on. If no friends are available, complete the questionnaire by yourself, writing down your answers. Don't look ahead to the other statements – concentrate only on the one being discussed. Be as revealing as you like – it is entirely up to you to decide how much to say. Stop this activity whenever you (or your partner) wishes to do so.

WHEN YOU ARE READY, BEGIN:

- My name is

- My job is

- My age is

- I live

- I was born in

- My previous jobs included

- To me, being a woman/man is

- My marital status is

- Children

- My parents

- My friend/s

- My hobbies/spare-time activities

- At this very minute, I feel

- Ideally, this time next year

- In the long term, my ambitions are

- The trouble with life at the moment is

- My idea of an ideal holiday would be

- Things that I find very difficult are

- If the worst came to the worst in 12 months' time

- The sort of things I worry about are

- What this country needs is

- My religious beliefs are

- To me, being black/white means

- My secret fears are

- My feelings about you are

- My feelings about myself are

When you have finished this activity, reflect on it. How did you feel? How open and revealing were you? Were you more open about some types of issue than others?

Visualization technique

After having performed a particular task, perhaps having reassured someone of your love or having channelled healing energy, it is worth while visualizing yourself in some element that flows. You could, for instance, visualize yourself on a windy hilltop and allow the wind to blow away the last vestiges of distress or difficulty. Feel yourself revitalized by the power of the wind, then return to the ordinary everyday world. As an alternative visualization, you could use white light or visualize yourself standing under a waterfall and allowing yourself to be cleansed.

THROAT CHAKRA

Location: Throat area
Colour: Sky blue
Diet/foods: Blue/purple fruits and vegetables
Element: Akasha/ether
Functions: Speech, sound, vibration, communication
Gems/minerals: Aquamarine, azurite, blue topaz, celestite, chryso-colla, kyanite, lapis lazuli, sodalite, turquoise
Glands/organs: Thyroid, parathyroid, hypothalamus, throat, mouth
Negative qualities: Communication/speech problems. Knowledge used unwisely. Ignorance. Lack of discernment, depression, thyroid problems
Positive qualities/lessons: Power of the spoken word. True communication. Creative expression in speech, writing and the arts. Integration, peace, truth, knowledge, wisdom, loyalty, honesty, reliability, gentleness

On reaching the age of ten or thereabouts the child is beginning to express himself properly. It may be somewhat unsophisticated, but such expression is essentially very honest and innocent. Unfortunately, a great deal of this innocence is lost as the child matures into adulthood, and on deciding to undertake any kind of personal development it is often this chakra which requires a great deal of work. Such is the belief that one must guard one's speech that many people experience great difficulty in developing the idea of not monitoring what they say.

Creativity is another quality which should be developing significantly as the child grows. Often there is confusion over what creativity really is. Essentially, it is the best use of one's talents, and it is this quality which will eventually be developed during work on the throat chakra.

COLOUR
The colour associated with the throat chakra is sky blue. Generally

considered to be a healing colour, it can be used to project a healing ray at specific parts and organs of the body. Where there are difficulties within the area of communication this colour can shift the blockages. Sky blue, when used for instance for furnishings in business environments, can create an atmosphere suitable for negotiation and bargaining. It is perhaps worthwhile remembering that, in creating a particular ambience, colour can be used in many ways. A light filter composed of a sheet of coloured glass can be used unobtrusively within many situations.

DIET AND FOODS
While ideally the foods which feed this chakra belong in the blue/purple range, it is obviously difficult to be specific in recommending foods with a pale blue colour! However since the thyroid gland requires iodine, seaweeds and kelp are an important addition to the diet. Fish and seafood also help with the vitamin and mineral balance within the body.

Food Combining When one recognizes that some kind of specific discipline actually helps in life management, it is often good to learn ways of following our own leanings. Developing habits which help us to get the best out of life can be painful at first, but later can support us in maintaining good health. The discipline required in food combining is initially quite hard, but as one begins to remember the various combinations – and at the same time experiences an improvement in health, it becomes worth while.

Food combining, which used to be called the Hay System (after its founder, Dr William Hay), broadly consists of meals which do not combine carbohydrates (starches, such as grains, bread, cereals, potatoes, and sugars) with protcins (mcat, fish, cheese, poultry) and acid fruits. The reason for this is that proteins require an acid stomach for digestion whereas carbohydrates require an alkaline stomach. The Hay system suggests that alkaline-forming foods should make up three-quarters of one's diet and acid-forming foods one quarter.

The table below shows how many common foods can be correctly combined. Protein foods are in column one, neutral foods in column two and carbohydrate foods in column three. Neutral foods can be combined with either proteins or carbohydrates. Only the foods listed in columns one and three cannot be combined.

PROTEINS	NUTS	CEREALS
Meat of all kinds: beef, lamb, pork, venison	All, except peanuts	Wholegrain; wheat, barley, maize, oats, millet, brown rice, rye
Poultry: chicken, duck, goose, turkey	**FATS**	
Game: pheasant, partridge, grouse, hare	Butter	Bread – *100 per cent wholewheat*
Fish of all kinds, including shellfish	Cream	Flour
Eggs	Egg yolks	Oatmeal – *medium ground*
Cheese	Olive oil	
Milk – *best with fruit and should not be served with meat*	Sunflower seed oil	
Yoghurt	Sesame seed oil	
FRUITS	**VEGETABLES**	**SWEET FRUITS**
Apples	All green and root vegetables except potatoes and artichokes	Ripe bananas
Apricots *(fresh and dried)*	Asparagus	Dates
Blackberries	Aubergines	Figs
Blueberries	Beans	Grapes
Currants *(black, red, white)*	Beetroot	Papaya – *if very ripe*
Gooseberries	Broccoli	Pears – *if sweet and ripe*
Grapefruit	Brussels sprouts	Currants
Grapes	Cabbage	Raisins
Kiwis	Calabrese	Sultanas
Lemons		

		VEGETABLES
Limes	Carrots	Potatoes
Loganberries	Cauliflower	Jerusalem
Mangoes	Celery	artichokes
Melons *(best eaten*	Celeriac	
alone)	Courgettes	**MILK AND**
Nectarines	Kohlrabi	**YOGHURT**
Oranges	Leeks	*only in moderation*
Papayas	Marrow	
Pears	Mushrooms	
Pineapples	Onions	
Prunes	Parsnips	
Raspberries	Peas	
Satsumas	Spinach	
Strawberries	Swedes	
Tangerines	Turnips	
NB: *Plums and*		
cranberries are not		
recommended		
SALAD DRESSINGS	**SALADS**	**SALAD DRESSINGS**
French dressing made	Avocados	Sweet or soured
with oil and lemon	Chicory *(endive)*	cream
juice or apple cider	Corn salad	Olive oil or seed oils
vinegar	Cucumber	Fresh tomato juice
Cream dressing	Endive	with oil and
Mayonnaise *(home-*	Fennel	seasoning
made)	Garlic	
	Lettuce	
	Mustard and cress	
	Peppers, red and	
	green	
	Radishes	
	Spring onions –	
	scallions	
	Sprouted legumes	
	Sprouted seeds	
	Tomatoes – *uncooked*	
	Watercress	

	HERBS AND FLAVOURINGS Chives Mint Parsley Sage Tarragon Thyme Grated lemon rind Grated orange rind **SEEDS** Sunflower Sesame Pumpkin **BRAN** Wheat or oat bran Wheatgerm	
SUGAR SUBSTITUTE Diluted frozen orange juice **FOR VEGETARIANS** (but not recommended) Legumes Lentils Soya beans Kidney beans Chick peas Butter – lima – beans Black-eyed beans	**SUGAR SUBSTITUTE** Raisins and raisin juice Honey Maple syrup	**SUGARS** Barbados sugar Honey – *in moderation*
ALCOHOL Dry red and white wines Dry cider	**ALCOHOL** Whisky Gin	**ALCOHOL** Lager Beer

A food combining diet is suggested at this stage of development so that one appreciates the practice necessary not just in taking care of the body but also in laying down the foundation for later good health. In thinking carefully about what we put into our systems, we are able to concentrate more fully on our spiritual development.

ELEMENT

The fifth chakra is located in the throat area, and is governed by the element of ether or Akasha. Fire, earth, air and water are *physical* elements, whereas the fifth element, ether, has to be understood on a much more subtle level. Ether could not be researched until an understanding of electro-magnetic fields had developed. It was discovered that each object or class of objects – such as stones, animals and humans – has its own surrounding force field, which is measurable.

It is now accepted that ether is vital to life and is associated with the sense of touch. Ether may be thought of as a 'substance' or 'atmosphere' which provides a bridge between the material and the mental. It is more of a philosophical concept which represents the whole space/time continuum, or the boundary between our own recognized duality of space and time and eternity. It is appropriate that the spiritual centre associated with the ephemeral quality of correct communication and wisdom as well as speech and sound should be connected with such a substance. The idea that this Akasha holds the records of all that is, was or ever shall be – past, present and future – is therefore apt (see **Akashic records** in Section Two).

FUNCTIONS

Perhaps the most important function belonging to the fifth chakra is recognition of the power of the spoken word. Our feelings, emotions, knowledge and wisdom are all conveyed by the spoken word. As we develop the throat chakra, an understanding of what truth really means will emerge. Developing our own style of expression and our appreciation of the arts, such as poetry, film, theatre and music, leads to a much wider acknowledgement not only of our own culture but also of others.

GEMS AND MINERALS

Aquamarine ranges in colour from light blue to green. Known as the 'stone of courage', it can aid intellectual response and the ability to 'be prepared'. It also activates and cleanses the throat chakra, facilitating a higher level of communication. It can be used in the treatment of swollen glands, and is good for the eyes, teeth and bone structure. Aquamarine helps chakra alignment, balancing the structure of the physical and ethereal bodies, and thus helps in the development of spiritual awareness.

Blue topaz stimulates the throat chakra, and therefore helps communication. It assists in bringing the body, mind and spirit into line with the universal force. Its healing qualities include dealing with the loss of the sense of taste and also in the healing of wounds and skin problems. Blue topaz may also help one's overall view of life, as it allows a clearing out of any arrogance.

Celestite Its range of colours includes blue, red and red-brown. It is useful for enhancing mental activities and helps to rationalize thought to enable one's innate wisdom to be expressed. Celestite is helpful for **astral travel** and **clairvoyance** (2), particularly with the articulation of 'messages' received, and assists in the aligning of universal energy by clearing out and tuning up the chakras. It is a good stone to have around on bad days, especially if you are worried or have feelings of claustrophobia. An excellent healing stone, it can be used for eye disorders, hearing and digestive problems, and may also be useful for balancing out mental dysfunction.

Chrysocolla Colours range from blue to green and occasionally brown to black. At the throat chakra it gives strength and balance in communication and expression, and highlights the wisdom of silence. It helps through this to revitalize the base, navel, heart and solar plexus chakras. It promotes inner strength, physical vigour and helps to release negative emotions. In healing it helps one to realize what is needed on an individual level in order to attain perfect health, and enables perception of what the earth requires to replace its resources. It has been used in the treatment of blood and lung disorders, and also helps to balance blood sugar.

Kyanite A varied colour range including grey, black, blue, white, green and yellow. Kyanite is one of the best atunement stones, because it does not retain negative energy. It aligns all chakras as a matter of course. Conscious direction will open the chakras and enable the energy to be used to help the emotional, spiritual and ethereal bodies. It brings a calming effect to the whole, but is particularly beneficial to the throat chakra. It helps communication and psychic awareness, rids one of anger and frustration and helps mental awareness. Kyanite is used to treat problems with the muscles as well as the glands and throat.

Sodalite The colour ranges from dark blue, green-yellow through to lavender blue and can even be colourless. It is a very good stone when used in groups because it promotes solidarity and friendship within the circle. It encourages self-esteem, self-trust and trust in others. Sodalite is helpful in the treatment of digestive disorders, calcium deficiency and in problems involving gland metabolism.

Turquoise strengthens and aligns all the chakras and brings all energies to a higher level. In particular it stimulates the throat and heart chakras, leading to a higher level of communication in arguments which become highly emotional. Turquoise cleanses the energy centres and the physical body and so is very good for enhancing spiritual awareness. A healer of the spirit, it brings a soothing energy which leads to peace of mind. It has been used in the treatment of headaches, but in fact helps strengthen the entire body.

GLANDS AND ORGANS

Hypothalamus The precise details of how hormones are balanced indicate a very complex process. The activity of the hypothalamus is controlled by a type of negative feedback situation, where if a hormone is over-produced the whole system reacts by a compensatory decrease until balance is restored. The hypothalamus co-ordinates the nervous and endocrine systems (also see **Brow Chakra**) and monitors the body's metabolism. The pituitary gland responds to the activity of the hypothalamus, which either stimulates or inhibits the secretion of its own hormones.

Mouth From a physical point of view, problems with the mouth and tongue can often be dealt with by balancing the intake of vitamins and minerals. From a slightly more esoteric standpoint one needs to be aware that the mouth is the vehicle for sound and that quite literally physical problems in this area may reflect a difficulty in putting our thoughts into words. Since the mouth and throat are so intimately connected, problems in one are often reflected in the other.

Throat Physically, the throat and the area surrounding it can be extremely vulnerable. It was problems with his throat which led **Alexander** (see under **Therapies** in Section Two) to develop the body-balancing technique now practised by many actors and musicians. Traditionally sore throats, problems with the tonsils, and possibly with the adenoids, mean that we should look at our communication skills and our ability to express ourselves properly. Connected as the fifth chakra is with wisdom, it is suggested that problems in this area might be relieved by speaking out when necessary and keeping silent when it is politic to do so. Tension in the throat area can often arise from suppressed emotion, so the individual needs to decide whether work on the third chakra is more appropriate or work on the fifth. The **Bach flower remedy** (2) agrimony can often relieve problems in this area.

Thyroid The thyroid gland is a regulator of metabolism in the body. This gland affects both our state of mind and our mood and is in turn affected by them – continual stress, for example, can create problems here. The gland requires iodine to function properly, and there are many parts of the world where natural iodine (found principally in seaweed) is not present. A lack of this essential mineral causes an enlargement of the thyroid gland known as goitre. This condition may also be due to an over- or under-active gland.

The two main thyroid hormones should ensure that the metabolic rate remains constant. When the gland produces too much of these hormones (becomes over-active) weight is lost, the appetite increases and the body burns up food much faster than normal. There is also restlessness, **anxiety** (1) and tension. When the thyroid gland is under-active, lethargy and apathy often occur, as can a tendency to **depression** (1).

Spiritually, bearing in mind that the fifth chakra is associated with the ability to express oneself properly and wisely, the thyroid gland monitors the efficiency of our self-expression. Suppression of correct communication can lead to difficulties, as can unconsidered speech.

HERBS

Bugleweed is useful for treating over-active thyroid glands, especially where the symptoms include tightness of breathing and palpitations. This herb will also aid a weak heart where there is an associated build-up of water. It can also ease irritating coughs.

Nettles strengthen and support the whole body. Although well known as a diuretic, they are also high in vitamin C and therefore aid the body's metabolism.

Oats are one of the best remedies for stress, a condition that is often associated with an under-active thyroid. They are often used in cases of depression associated with such a condition.

Wormwood is principally used as a bitter agent to stimulate and invigorate the system. Used with Bladderwrack (seaweed), it can help in the management of an under-active thyroid.

NEGATIVE QUALITIES

Physical problems associated with the throat area are continual sore throats and those difficulties associated with the thyroid gland. Sometimes these can be helped by some of the yoga postures or *asanas* designed to help this area; for example, the plough or the fish, which can be found in any good yoga book. Problems belonging to the throat area are often those to do with speech. A stutter or stammer, for instance, may be thought of as a difficulty in the connection between the brain and the vocal system. There are, in fact, different types of stutters and stammers and a great deal of information can be gained by listening to the type of speech defect. Problems in communication can be very different from speech defects and many people are conscious of not being able to articulate their thoughts clearly. Working with the fifth chakra can sometimes improve this.

When working with the fifth chakra, one can often become

conscious of the amount of knowledge and wisdom made available. One difficulty is a problem of discernment. There is a tendency to 'cast pearls before swine' rather than giving knowledge only when it is asked for. The individual needs to recognize that a little knowledge can indeed be a dangerous thing.

POSITIVE QUALITIES AND LESSONS

The qualities of honour, reliability and compassion are also learnt when developing the throat chakra. Compassion in this sense means knowing what to say in order to bring peace and tranquillity to other people. Another lesson to be learnt is knowing how to integrate the inner spiritual self with the demands of the outside world. Learning how to find the correct words to have the maximum impact is one of the developments of this knowledge and awareness. When you achieve this others will recognize that you are 'coming from the heart' and yet have access to a higher level of wisdom. The Buddhist concepts of right thought, right speech, and right action belong to this particular area.

EXERCISES FOR GROWTH

At this particular level of understanding, exploring the journey of the major arcana (principal cards) in the Tarot gives an interesting insight into the **psyche (2)** and is more appropriate than techniques.

Below are brief explanations of the meanings of the cards. One technique to follow is to form a circle of the numbered cards and place the Fool in the centre. The Fool at this point represents you as you start your journey of exploration. Contemplating each card in turn, and what relevance its meaning has in your life at present, may help you to come to terms with, and understand, the way that you yourself handle life's 'little problems'.

Another way of using this 'journey of a lifetime' is to select 10 cards from the 22 major arcana and to spend time looking not just at the meaning of your own personal cards, but also at the connection between each card and the next. For instance, drawing the Hermit next to the Wheel of Fortune might suggest the loneliness that one encounters at various stages of change which will ultimately lead to success.

The Fool

This card shows a traveller ignoring the small animal below that seems to be attacking him. Over one shoulder is a stick from which hangs a bag. He carries a walking staff to help him on his way. This card is the only un-numbered card and in a sense is like the joker, the wild card, in ordinary playing cards, a character without rules or definitions, without an agenda in the world.

In fortune-telling the Fool suggests lack of thought, carelessness, which can lead to degradation. Reversed, the image can suggest insanity.

Lack of thought can also come from innocence, carelessness from not being weighed down with worldly concerns. The Fool travels light.

Associations: The simpleton; the Shakespearean wise fool; in the Cabbalist Tree of Life the fool traces the path between Kether (the crown) and Chochmah (wisdom).

I. The Magician

This card shows a man standing, left arm holding a wand raised to the heavens, right arm lowered towards the earth beneath him. In front of the figure is a table on which, among other things, are the cup, coin and sword, the other symbols of the minor arcana. His hat is shaped like the symbol for infinity.

In fortune-telling he represents the inquirer (if it is a man), and when reversed suggests that he is at odds with the world. If the inquirer is a woman, this card suggests a change of position.

This is man, upright, distinct from beast by having mind and spirit; being part of heaven and earth; capable of infinite possibilities and of shaping the world; of making things manifest; of using words. This is generally positive and creative, but can suggest trickery and manipulation.

Associations: Logos; the Trickster or Mountebank; Hermes/Mercury; Adam, the first man; in the Cabbala he traces the line between Kether (the crown, beginning, word) and Binah (creative intelligence).

II. The High Priestess

This shows a seated woman holding an open book; behind her is a veil. She is sometimes shown wearing the three-tiered papal crown.

The book suggests the book of wisdom, the veil suggests that which is hidden.

In fortune-telling this card can represent the female inquirer. The card represents mysticism, hidden or secret knowledge and occult science. Reversed, it suggests unhappy consequences as a result of occult science.

She is the card of unconscious intuition and knowledge, the veil of the soul, wisdom and clairvoyance, with a suggestion of morality.

Associations: Isis, keeper of hidden mysteries, of the secrets of life, death and resurrection; the female pope; in the Tree of Life she lies between Kether (crown) and Tiphareth (beauty, harmony, incarnation).

III. The Empress
This shows a woman seated face on, wings coming from behind her back. She wears a crown and holds in one hand a sceptre with a globe and cross (the alchemical symbol of antimony, the state of near perfection) and in the other a shield depicting an eagle (symbol of royalty and the spirit).

In divination she represents woman, mother and domestic happiness; the female life-giving force. Reversed, she suggests infidelity, inconstant love leading to stagnation and sterility.

She is the feminine ruler, life-giver, counsellor, open to all, practical and decisive.

Associations: Demeter; Hera; aspects of Isis. In the Cabbala she is the link between Binah (creative intelligence) and Chochmah (wisdom).

IV. The Emperor
A man is seen in profile, crowned and seated, usually on a throne, one leg crossed over the other. In his right hand he holds the sceptre, crowned with globe and cross, as does the Empress, and in front of him is the shield with the image of the eagle.

In fortune-telling this represents man in his positive aspects: willpower, authority, strength and courage. Reversed, it shows the softer aspect: benevolence, clemency and pity.

He is the embodiment of masculine power and authority in worldly matters, coupled with intelligence and sensibility, though with the danger of abusing power and becoming tyrannical. (The ideal archetypal father/husband in the proverbial 2.4 family with the Empress as wife.)

Associations: Zeus/Jupiter; demiurge of Platonic philosophy; in harmony with the Great Bear. In the Cabbala he links Yesod (foundation) and Netzach (triumph).

V. The Hierophant

A man seated between two pillars, holding an ornate staff in his left hand, right hand raised in mid-air (to bless or to emphasize). Before him kneel two smaller figures.

In divination he represents wisdom, intelligence, asceticism and inspiration. Reversed, he suggests craftiness and guile.

He is the teacher. Like the High Priestess, he knows the mysteries, but is the conscious word of self-knowledge and spiritual power, the marriage or union of earthly and heavenly principles. His danger is fanaticism, intolerance and bigotry.

Associations: The Pope; Christ; Logos. In the Tree of Life he runs on the masculine side between Chesed (kindness) and Chochmah (wisdom).

VI. The Lovers

In the centre stands a young man between two women, one with her hand on his shoulder, the other with a hand on his heart. Above, framed by the sun, Cupid/Eros hovers with an arrow ready to fire.

In divination this card represents love, youthful indecision, hesitation and instability. Reversed, it suggests broken romance, inconstancy and heartache.

It is the card of choices, and of temptation. It implies inexperience, a putting to the test of learnt ideas, but it gives no indication of who or what to choose. It represents dilemma.

Associations: In the Cabbala Tree of Life the Lovers is the path between Binah (creative intelligence) and Tiphareth (harmony and beauty).

VII. The Chariot

This portrays a man facing head on, riding in a canopied chariot drawn by two horses. The man wears a crown and breastplate and carries a sceptre; on either shoulder is a mask, one taken to represent Unim and the other Thummin, and the horses are often shown pulling in slightly different directions.

This card symbolizes triumph, success and victory. Reversed, it suggests discouragement, quarrels or defeat.

The chariot and horses suggest a harnessing and controlling of forces, the triumph and advancement of spiritual nature over physical nature. Following the Lovers, this card suggests the successful balancing of alternatives, and progression, though there is always the danger of overriding ambition or headlong haste.

Associations: Apollo's chariot in its heavenly orbit, Buddha's chariot drawn by a white ox. In the Cabbala its number associates it with Netzach (triumph), but more properly it is the movement between Binah (creative intelligence) and Gevurah (strength).

VIII. Justice

Justice is portrayed as a woman face on, sometimes seated between two columns, holding in one hand a sword and in the other a set of scales. She represents impartiality, balanced judgement, integrity and arbitration, but when reversed suggests bad judgement or legal trouble.

While the scales represent balance and order, the sword represents the power to enforce fairness, judgement and discipline. There is always the danger that the latter could be misused and lead to constraint or intolerance with the scales uneven.

Associations: Athena; Anubis weighing the souls of the dead. In the Cabbala, Justice links Gevurah (strength) and Tiphareth (beauty, harmony).

IX. The Hermit

This shows an old man, wearing a cloak and walking with a staff. He carries a lantern before him, lighting the way.

The card suggests the need for prudence and wisdom, and perhaps watchfulness and caution against hidden enemies. Reversed, it suggests excessive caution or timidity.

The lantern is a symbol of truth and wisdom. The fact that the old man is walking and the lantern is shaded by his cloak suggests the need to search for such wisdom, yet he carries his own light and thus indicates that the wisdom or truth is his own. The hermit is an isolated character with none of the trappings of worldly acquisition. His isolation may derive from loneliness, fear, poverty or despondency.

Associations: The notion of the hermit or pilgrim is common to all religions. The card corresponds to the Hebrew letter teth *which is the ideogram of a serpent swallowing its own tail, unending wisdom; the hermit's staff is reminiscent of the rod of Aaron. In the Tree of Life the hermit links Chesed (kindness, mercy) with Tiphareth (beauty, harmony).*

X. The Wheel of Fortune

This shows a wheel rotated on its own axis by an unmanned handle. On the rim of the wheel are three creatures, part animal, part human. The one at the top, resting on a platform, is sometimes likened to the Sphinx. The other two cling to the rim of the wheel, the one on the right facing upwards and the one on the left facing downwards.

This card illustrates that good and bad luck are equally possible; that fortune is always changing, so if the card is in a good position it is favourable, but if reversed or badly placed it suggests unlucky influences.

The card of chance, it shows the cyclical nature of the universe, and the inevitability of change.

Associations: The Tibetan Wheel of Life, the Zodiac, the Rosicrucian Rota Mundi. Some regard the symbolism of this card as deriving from the Egyptians, associating the ascending and descending figures with Horus and Set and thus the eternal balancing of good and evil. In the Tree of Life it links Chesed (kindness, mercy) with Netzach (triumph).

XI. Strength

A young woman (sometimes an androgynous figure) wearing a crowned hat shaped in the symbol of infinity stands holding open the mouth of a lion or beast.

This card represents strength and courage, and promises success to those who can direct their natural gifts and willpower. Reversed, it means fruitless striving and dissipated energy.

The beast is subdued by gentleness and intelligence and this implies the channelling of brutish instinct and strength through inner spiritual strength. In that sense the card represents both forms of power and can, badly placed, suggest fury and despotism.

Associations: The lion in most cultures is associated both with primitive strength and with majesty and justice. In the Tree of Life, Strength links Gevurah (strength, in the feminine column) and Chesed (kindness, in the masculine column).

XII. The Hanged Man

A man is suspended upside down, hanging by one leg, the other crossed behind him. The pole from which he hangs is supported on either side by two trees; the sap 'bleeds' where the branches have been cut. In some images his hands are tied behind his back, but he never appears tortured.

In fortune-telling this card represents self-denial and sacrifice and perhaps trials or vicissitudes. When the card is reversed, this sacrifice may be wasted or it may warn of accident or violent death.

The sacrifice of the man is voluntary and suggests a deliberate suspension of the material world, lack of concern for the physical. While this brings inspiration and regeneration, it also means that material life is blocked, and badly placed it can suggest masochism, apathy or paralysis.

Associations: Christ; martyrs in general. In the Tree of Life it is the Path between Gevurah (strength) and Hod (glory).

XIII. Death

A skeleton, smiling grimly, wields a scythe, scattering limbs, hands, heads, and leaves.

In fortune-telling this card is usually seen as portentous, threatening loss and if it is reversed it may be more sinister, possibly suggesting illness or death.

However, as the leaves among the scattered limbs imply, death is a part of life and regeneration and this card suggests change rather than literal death, an end of one part of life and therefore also the beginning of another. It is a form of transition, possibly liberation and transformation, which may not be bad, though it may engender fear. The card can also suggest inflexibility, a reluctance to change.

Associations: The 'Grim Reaper'; the card is numbered 13, traditionally an unlucky number. In the Tree of Life it links Tiphareth (beauty, harmony) with Netzach (triumph), and thus suggests transcendence.

XIV. Temperance

A young woman, with wings coming from her back, stands on the earth, pouring water from one jug to another.

This card represents vitality, life, fruitfulness and balance, restraint. It can fore-tell a rich marriage. Reversed, it loses the restraint and the vitality can become restlessness and dissolution.

Water has always been associated with the source, life, creation and ablution, new life. The flowing of life suggests harmony, communication and equilibrium, but equally it suggests the possibility of stagnation and apathy if the card is badly placed.

Associations: The cups can be associated with the chalice, the Holy Grail; water is source, regeneration and also emotion. In the Tree of Life temperance links Tiphareth (beauty, harmony) with Yesod (foundation).

XV. The Devil

A naked figure with bat-like wings, and horns coming from his head, hovers or stands above a circle. His feet are cloven and he holds a staff or sceptre in his hand. Tied to that by ropes from their necks stand two naked figures, also with horns, tails and pointed ears. (Interestingly, this arrangement of a central figure and two human figures is echoed in the cards for the High Priest, the Lovers, the Sun and Judgement.)

This forebodes temptation, potentially fatal if it is not resisted, and implies weakness, lack of protection and possibly illness. Reversed, it suggests the temptation is from a malign source and is difficult to resist.

This card is associated with base instincts, especially of a sexual nature. The two chained figures represent enslavement to carnal, instinctual desires. However, base instincts are animal and therefore neither good nor bad. The magnetism of such instincts has power and potential which can be positive. It is the card of passion or perversion.

Associations: Pan; Baphomet of the Templars; Lucifer, angel of light become angel of darkness. In the Tree of Life this card links Tiphareth (beauty, harmony) with Hod (glory).

XVI. The Tower

This usually depicts a tower, its top blown off by lightning or flame. It is surrounded by circles (coins) falling from the ruin and shows two people, upside down, falling out of the building. (Sometimes the flame is a green ear of corn bursting out from the top of the tower.)

In fortune-telling this portends a sudden calamity, change or ruin. Reversed, it bodes lessener ills. If placed near the suit or pentacles, it can suggest an unexpected legacy.

This is the card of 'hubris' or 'pride-before-a-fall'; the destruction of man's constructs, the breaking down of established order. However, out of the destruction of the old a new world can begin, hence the ear of corn in some depictions. The two figures represent the complete reversal of previously held belief.

Associations: The Tower of Babel, and man's aspiration to reach God; earthquakes; sudden revelation; the blinding flash of inspiration. In the Tree of Life the tower links Hod (glory) and Netzach (triumph).

XVII. The Star

This card shows a naked woman, pouring water from two jugs into the river at which she kneels. Above her are eight stars and beyond her, amidst the hills in the distance, is a bird on a tree.

This is the card of hope. Water is poured into the land, symbolizing the regeneration of the source of life. Reversed, this card suggests difficulties, loss and lack of hope.

Reminiscent of Temperance, the Star suggests a flow of life on a large scale, not simply a balance of nature. It is the first card to portray the cosmos. The woman's nudity implies a oneness with the world around her.

Associations: Isis and the rejuvenation of the Nile; Eve in paradise; stars as gods; The Qu'ran and Hindus thought of bird as soul; river of life; In the Tree of Life the Star links Chochmah (wisdom) with Tiphareth (beauty, harmony).

XVIII. The Moon

In the centre of the card is a moon radiating over a flowing river. On either side of the river is a tower before which a dog is baying. In the river is a crayfish.

Traditionally in fortune-telling the moon suggests deception, obscurity and concealed dangers. Reversed, it suggests the inquirer will come to grief through his own duplicity.

The moon waxes and wanes, controls tides and cycles and is associated with the mysterious feminine. The river suggests emotion, the unconscious, the deep, while the dogs suggest the mediators between the physical and psychic worlds; the crayfish devours the corrupt and regenerates the river. So while the moon suggests obscurity, it is also the door between the unconscious, inspiration and prophecy.

Associations: The River Styx and the dog that guards it; Hecate, Isis, Artemis. The Tree of Life the moon links Netzach (triumph) with Malkuth (the kingdom).

XIX. The Sun

Two half-naked people play in front of a wall, the sun above them radiating a golden glow.

This is a happy card, signifying peace, contentment and possibly a happy marriage. Even when reversed, it still bodes well.

The sun is a source of light and power that enables growth and embodies a joy of life. As the moon represents the unconscious self so the sun is the vital, energetic self. However, the figures are contained within a wall, and this suggests not only self but happiness on an earthly plane.

Associations: Apollo; Ra; Atum, the creator, Osiris; all peoples have worshipped the sun in some form. The two figures are sometimes associated with Castor and Pollux. In the Tree of Life the sun is the path between Hod (glory) and Yesod (foundation).

XX. Judgement

In this card an angelic figure blows a trumpet, calling the figures below to account.

In divination it represents a judgement of what has gone before – that we must take account of past performance before deciding on a future course of action.

This is the card of the Day of Judgement. On an earthly plane we must be our own judge, and be able to give good accounts of who we are and what we have been. Our past deeds must be looked at and justified in the light of our present knowledge before we move on.

Associations: The Resurrection; eternal life; the angel of doom. In the Tree of Life it is the way between Hod (glory) and Malchus (the Kingdom).

XXI. The World

In this card a figure stands barefoot, with only one foot connected to the earth, within an enclosing wreath (sometimes the ourobos, the symbol of infinity). The figure is either female or hermaphrodite. Surrounding it are the symbols for the four seasons, Earth, Fire, Air and Water, or, according to some interpretations, the Bull, the Lion, the Man and the Eagle.

From a divinatory point of view, this card represents ultimate success and a well-regulated life.

In spiritual terms it suggests a completion. The trials and tribulations of the journey have been overcome, and the individual is now able to take his position in the cosmic dance. He has attained a state of unity and is within the world but not of it.

Associations: Creation; completion; the cosmic egg; achievement. In the Tree of Life it is the final movement from Yesod (foundation) to Malkuth (the Kingdom).

BROW CHAKRA ('Third Eye')

Location: Centre of the forehead, between the eyebrows
Colour: Indigo (dark blue)
Diet/foods: Blue/purple fruits and vegetables
Element: Light
Functions: Vitalizes the lower brain (cerebellum) and central nervous system. Vision
Gems/minerals: Azurite, blue tourmaline, lapis luzuli, quartz crystal, sapphire, sodalite
Glands/organs: Pituitary gland. Left eye, nose, ears
Negative qualities: Lack of concentration. Fear, tension. Headaches, eye problems, bad dreams. Overly detached from the world
Positive qualities/lessons: Soul realization, intuition, insight, imagination. Concentration, peace of mind, wisdom, devotion, perception and duality

The brow chakra, also known as the 'third eye', is connected with the faculty of insight, intuition and soul realization. It is placed in the centre of the forehead and, according to myth, is the last vestige of the eye of the Cyclops, the one-eyed giants. The eye was said to be sensitive to the vibration of light. Nowadays it is recognized that this vibration plays a part in the correct functioning of the hormones and the brain, for instance in Seasonal Affective Disorder.

The sixth chakra corresponds to growth around the age of fourteen to sixteen. At this time the child is coming to terms with physical changes, but more importantly with changes in responsibility. Decisions need to be made which lay the foundations for the future and yet the teenager does not have enough information to be able to make a coherent decision. For the teenager, the here and now must be important because, in addition to coping with the life he or she has experienced to date, sense also has to be made of the world at large. The development of the sixth chakra in the individual is very much akin to this process, as it becomes increasingly apparent that there is a much wider world beyond the confines of their own knowledge. The individual needs to learn to cope with information on spiritual matters and also be able to incorporate that information into everyday life.

Just as the developing teenager becomes conscious of a degree of duality in life, and becomes aware of the pull of both sexuality and of spirituality, so the individual must decide which aspect of being to focus on. At this stage the teenager often becomes aware of the need for some system of belief, and may explore **religion** and **philosophy** (2). This exploration can become fanatical and time-consuming and not leave much space for the development of proper relationships. Thus, the spiritual side of existence receives an inordinate amount of attention. Conversely, sex and sexuality can become inordinately important at this stage. In the development of the third eye (which is where the dual aspects of **kundalini** (2) terminate) the individual recognizes the dual impulses within the self. Initially the perception may be that only spirituality or sexuality can be pursued. Only later is it realized that both spirituality and sexuality are different aspects of the same energy.

COLOUR
The colour associated with the Third Eye is a deep indigo – blue verging on violet. This signifies the search for and attainment of one's spiritual purpose in life. It is a very strong colour which does not suit everybody. However, because it is also an effective healing colour, when working on an intellectual level it can be used in directed healing. Here the healer visualizes the colour and then directs that colour towards, for instance, whichever part of the body needs healing. It can also be used to create a healing environment, by using a

light filter on a lamp. (A simple way to do this is to drape the lamp with a coloured scarf – taking care, of course, not to place the scarf in such a way that it may cause fire.) On a personal level, it is possible to introduce indigo quite unobtrusively into the environment. Use a small amount in personal jewellery or trimming ribbon or in other small ways to raise your vibration.

This colour can also create a protective field against the harmful unknown and deepen perception in meditation. One way to learn to still the mind is to visualize a deep indigo sky initially filled with stars, each of which signifies a subject to be considered. Gradually eliminate each star until only peace and tranquillity are left.

DIET AND FOODS

The deliberate inclusion in the diet of foods in the indigo colour range will help to enhance the growth of perception. Such foods are blackberries, bilberries, plums, purple broccoli, purple onions, beetroot and dark grapes.

Many of these foods are also easy on the digestive system. A light diet can be of benefit when developing **psychic** (2) powers, partly because it does not overload the metabolism, freeing up the energy needed in such activity. Should the individual wish to develop **clairvoyance** (2) or channelling, meals should be eaten at least an hour before practising such skills. Often after using clairvoyant or psychic skills, the appetite can increase. It is wise to use fruit rather than sugary foods.

Many special diets are suitable for this level of understanding. One such is the macrobiotic diet, which consists mainly of using grains (such as rice) and vegetables flavoured with natural seasonings.

FUNCTIONS

The Third Eye (or Ajna chakra as it is also known) is the sixth of the seventh chakras. In Sanskrit, Ajna means 'to know and to perceive'. This is the main function of this chakra. By deliberately developing it, the perception is widened from one's immediate surroundings to a much wider viewpoint. This encompasses the idea that the spiritually aware individual commands her own universe. Life is under control of a higher level of **consciousness** (2). In other words, it is possible to make things happen within the here and now. A side effect of this awareness is the development of psychic powers, such as **clairvoyance** (2) and clairaudience (2). These are *ways* of achieving true perception rather than actually *being* true perception in themselves.

On a physical level, the energy of the Third Eye vitalizes the cerebellum. This is the part of the brain which governs the automatic functioning of the body such as breathing. It also governs the central nervous system and the energy that is required for the nerves to respond to basic impulses.

GEMS AND MINERALS

Azurite Known as the 'stone of heaven', azurite ranges in colour from light to deep blue. By developing objectivity and clarity of vision, it enhances creative ability, self-confidence and helps with problems of indecision. It aligns the chakras and provides a strong link between the physical body and the ethereal. In **meditation** (2), it provides a relaxing quality which in turn allows us to travel deeper into the inner being while maintaining contact with the psyche. It has been used in the treatment of toxin clearance and circulatory problems, and, where there is malformation, in spinal alignment.

Blue tourmaline (particularly dark blue) Used to activate the Third Eye, it assists with the communication of psychic and intuitive awareness. Disorders of the eyes and brain respond to dark blue tourmaline. Light blue tourmaline can be used to treat disorders of the lungs, throat and thyroid, particularly where these are connected with difficulty in communication.

Lapis lazuli A deep blue colour, this stone is said to have been around since time began. It energizes the brow and throat chakras, thus leading to unification of all the chakras. It helps with awareness and intellectual capacity, as well as the intuitive and psychic aspects of the individual. It helps in depression, and is also said to bring happiness within relationships. It can be used for the treatment of throat, bone marrow and thymus problems, as well as to relieve insomnia and dizziness.

GLANDS AND ORGANS

Pituitary Gland In some quarters the pituitary gland is associated with the crown chakra, although this assertion has led to some disagreement because the pineal gland is said by others to have this distinction. Because the pituitary gland is so closely associated with our ability to exist on a physical level, it seems to be more appropriate to assign it to this chakra.

The gland is very small and is found at the base of the brain just above the roof of the mouth and behind the bridge of the nose. It is considered by the medical profession to be the most important gland in the body. Known as the master gland, it rejuvenates and provides spiritual energy for the whole body. This energy has actually been experienced during meditation as a dew-like liquid, and is considered to be a blessing, although its true significance is open to conjecture.

The rear part of the pituitary acts as a storage house for significant hormones used, among other things, in triggering childbirth and the nurturing response, and in regulating water retention. The hypothalamus - which is the co-ordinating centre between the endocrine and the nervous systems - works in conjunction with the pituitary gland to release twelve separate hormones which effect the repair of body tissue, sleep patterns, sexual maturity and temperature control. The other part produces hormones which direct and monitor the functions of other glands in the body as well as stimulating, or inhibiting, the production of its own hormones. The hormones produced by this gland have a profound effect on all other systems of the body, as well as hormonal production by other glands.

Eyes Seeing and perceiving are two different skills. Seeing is more properly a process of recognition - of shape, colour and composition. We quantify and match what we see with other known images and can, in the process, make mistakes in identification. The 'higher' aspect of perception is also closely connected with the eyes. Perception is the ability to see 'all round' something, whether a problem or a concept. It is therefore more holistic than just simply seeing, and requires clarity of thinking.

Nose The nose is the organ which is most closely associated with memories. It is well known that smells can trigger off emotions, whether it be the smell of freshly baked bread which evokes grand-mother's kitchen, or the smell of burning motorcycle oil calling up a family outing. The nose will also identify whether a smell is good or bad, and is also activated during courtship, in the recognition of attrac-tive sexual smells. In working with the higher aspects of **psychic skills** (2), smells are experienced as a reality. Many clairvoyants and **mediums** (2), for instance, will identify a spiritual entity through smell. **Ears** The more spiritual development when working with the sixth chakra is being able to differentiate between the art of hearing and the art of listening. Hearing is the ability to differentiate between various sounds and make sense of them, while listening is being able to under-stand what is being communicated. These two things are not always one and the same.

NEGATIVE QUALITIES
On a purely physical level, problems can arise with the eyes, the ears, and the nose (such as a bad attack of catarrh). Headaches can also be a problem, but at this level of awareness can often be dealt with by **creative visualization** or by the use of **colour** (2).

Perhaps the biggest problem associated with the development of the sixth chakra is the one humorously called being 'a space cadet'. Because one has become aware of the huge potential available in developing the gifts of this chakra, there is a tendency not to be grounded within one's own reality. It is as though one is existing in a state of unconnectedness with the earth – as though one's feet were six inches off the ground. This can lead to a lack of concentration on things in hand and result in bad dreams. The cause may be that one is receiving too much input and is not able to process it properly. This can be dealt with by deliberately choosing familiar but creative activi-ties, such as gardening, sculpting, cooking and so on.

Another difficulty can be the danger of becoming detached from the world. While in Eastern philosophy detachment from earthly desires can be seen as an advantage, becoming too detached from the world in which we exist can mean we become alienated from our loved ones and, indeed, from reality itself. This can lead to the feeling that nothing matters any more. At this stage of development also, fears which have been suppressed or denied may well bubble up from the subconscious and should be dealt with before attempting to progress any further. In any case, these problems will in themselves prevent progression, so it becomes necessary to establish ways of dealing with them before they occupy one's mind totally. If they are not tackled, there is a danger of them taking over, which may lead to confusion and intolerance.

POSITIVE QUALITIES AND LESSONS

The third eye brings about the development of **intuition** (2), insight and imagination. Intuition can be described as a teaching of the self and an inner knowing. It suggests that as one increases in confidence and becomes objective, certain realizations can take place. By and large this tends to apply to oneself initially, and only applies to others when one is proficient in using this awareness. When this proficiency has been acquired the phenomenon is more properly termed 'insight'. Insight can range from very simple recognition of another person's state to a much more complex awareness of why a particular person is reacting in the way he or she is. For example, initial recognition that a person is not able to make a decision at a particular moment may be followed by the understanding that from childhood this person has not properly been allowed to make decisions and has come to rely on others to decide what is his best course of action.

Taken to its highest awareness, insight can become more of a revelation – a revealing of the *meaning* behind people's actions, needs and desires. One then becomes conscious of the weight of responsibility such awareness bring. The psychic skills that develop naturally as one works with the third eye cannot be taken lightly.

Powers of concentration develop strongly while working with the brow chakra, and the ability to remain focused on the task in hand becomes enhanced. Recognizing one's 'place in the world' and the necessity to remain centred in the present – within the here and now – brings considerable peace of mind. In this state of consciousness the recognition is that the future will take care of itself. The enhanced perception allows one to use one's wisdom while being conscious of the duality that exists in each of us.

EXERCISES FOR GROWTH

Look at aspects of your personality as though each of them is a member of a board of directors of which you are the chairman.

Who is on your board of directors? These may be personalities such as publicity promoter, financial director, managing director and so on. Use your imagination.

Are you happy with them?

Where do they fit on the Chakra Chart? What qualities and lessons are these sub-personalities reflecting? For instance, your financial director may be learning how to deal with lessons appropriate to the fourth chakra – how to give.

Which three fears are associated with self-image?

Take one of these and play 'because' until you come up against a 'block' or vicious circle, for example:

1. I feel rejected because I am different.
2. I am different because....
3. What are others hearing in what I say?
4. Do I really believe this?
5. Fear busting – What? Where? Why? When? How?
6. What does the fear feel, look, sound like? Give it a tangible image – e.g., a blob, brambles, a black cloud.
What do I need to do to handle it? For example, make it
smaller, blow it away
What do I think/feel about it?
7. Which of these last can I change?
8. Recognize that self-image and sexuality are closely connected
9. Do I use sexuality to reinforce and/or fight against rejection?

Look at your relationships:

● With yourself – Do you like yourself? Which bits do/don't you like?

● With others – Why do we need relationships? How do we use them? – to support us or put us down?

● Patterning - what scripts have you been given or written?
Are you, for instance, victim/helper or persecutor/helper?
● Work with a friend and speak for five minutes on who you are
and what you feel capable of; get your partner to write these
down. Change over and do the same for your partner and then
have five minutes each on what you hope for the future.
● Would your future be different if you were of the opposite sex?
● Can you incorporate those desires in your own plans?
● Who on your board of directors decides what your future will
be?
● What is your relationship with others - same sex/different sex?
● How do you want these to change?
● List three things you would like to change.
● Which one do you think you *can* change now?
● Does this move you into a comfort or a discomfort zone? - an
area which makes you comfortable/uncomfortable to think about

Confidence is an inner certainty that somewhere or other on an inner
level one is 'right'. A child very often learns that he is not always right
but sometimes does not know why. He may have been accused of
brashness or precociousness, 'clever dickness', or not knowing what
he is talking about. The child then learns to monitor what he is about
to say, but very often does not use his innate wisdom and clarity of
perception. Fear then replaces spontaneity and the ability to express
oneself unconditionally is lost. Lack of confidence learned and
accepted in a child can cause tremendous difficulty later on and often
in very particular circumstances. If this stage runs into the confusions
of puberty, there is often difficulty in one-to-one relationships. If this is
compounded by a problem with self-image which has been present
since early childhood, the child then begins to doubt himself and to
articulate only those things with which he feels comfortable.

One way to deal with the residue of fears arising from childhood is
to use the game of word association at as quick a rate as is feasible.
This is not with any idea of psychological testing, but simply to allow
self-expression through words to come more naturally. Another way is

to 'brainstorm' and allow all ideas to come to the fore. It is often advisable to use a tape recorder when doing this so that even if we cannot express our ideas as fluently as we would ideally like, we will at least capture them.

Wisdom is essentially the ability to know when to speak and when to remain silent. As children we are taught to speak only after having thought, but in actual fact the natural process is much more the ability to deal with the uprush of forthrightness and awareness in ourselves and to weigh the options, as to whether to remain silent or to speak the information we have. Several types of fear are associated with this process.

- The fear of not articulating properly.
- The fear of not understanding or of not being understood.
- The fear that one's emotions will get in the way.
- The fear that the other person will not have patience with you.
- A combination of any or all of these.

Planning for success:
One necessary quality when developing the sixth chakra is that of being able to look objectively at a situation in order to make progress. Below are two different ways of planning for and implementing success. The first is much more 'free-fall' and simply requires that you ask yourself some questions. It is suggested that you write down the answers so that later you will have a record of how far you have progressed. The questions are:

Context
What is the situation at the moment?
Objective
What I want to do is...
FACTORS
The things that will help or hinder me are –
1.
2.
3.
Etc.

Planning and implementation

This is what, when and how I will do the things necessary for me to achieve my objectives

These are the people I will involve

Evaluation

I know I will have been successful by

1.

2.

3.

Etc.

Six-Month Plan

The Six-Month Plan takes into account all aspects of personal and career development, and can be seen to follow the same pattern as the chakras. By constructing the plan you will achieve a clear analysis of your goals in all aspects of life.

Completing the chart will enable you to evaluate your competence in managing whatever you discover to be the most important elements of your life. You will consider your life from various standpoints, which may not, at first sight, appear to be relevant. This process will give you an overall view of your current circumstances, and clearly indicate the progressions that are necessary for you. You will then be able to incorporate these progressions into a carefully considered plan of action.

This plan of action does not remain static throughout the six months. As you achieve the shorter term objectives, and therefore greater skills and confidence develop, the longer term aims will expand. This will result in more awareness of your own motivation, and thus in greater effectiveness.

As an immediate clarification of your current direction, the Six-Month Plan is unparalleled. However, it is recommended that you commit yourself to a regular re-appraisal. Consistent input, using the timing guidelines built into the plan, results in an increasingly effective forward-moving route to personal success and efficiency.

SIX-MONTH PLAN

	1 day	1 week	1 mth	3 mths	6 mths
IDEAL					
POTENTIAL					
WISDOM					
SELF-KNOWLEDGE					
EMOTION					
RELATION-SHIP					
SELF-IMAGE					

CROWN CHAKRA

Location: Top of the head
Colour: Violet
Element: None applicable
Diet/Foods/Herbs: Simple foods and herbs providing *prana*
Function: Union with the divine
Gems/Minerals: Calcite, chrysoberyl, fluorite, quartz, spinel
(all stones are clear)
Glands/Organs: Brain, cerebral cortex, pineal gland, whole body
Negative Qualities: Alienation, duality
Positive qualities/lessons: Bliss, responsibility, silence

The image given to the seventh chakra is that of a thousand-petalled lotus. These petals represent the cosmic energy that the individual is capable of receiving. Unlike the other chakras the seventh chakra has no element assigned to it, nor does it rule any sense or sound. The crown chakra represents spiritual purity and enlightenment and is often seen as a halo of light around the head of those who have achieved this degree of development. In any system of spiritual development the individual is working towards liberation from physical being. This is often experienced as a void or 'nothingness' and is almost impossible to describe because it is such a completely individual experience. It is an experience which occurs only at this particular level of development and has no set structure.

COLOUR
The colour associated with the seventh chakra moves in vibration from the indigo of the 'third eye' to the clear violet of the crown. The experience of this level can only partially be indicated in words, descriptions and concepts. The violet vibration is the purest before that of white light. The use of violet as an aid to spiritual development has to be from a point of understanding that this colour simply widens one's ability to unite successfully with the divine. It is not an easy colour to live with, unless it is used as an accent colour, because its vibration is so strong.

As with all the other colours it should only be introduced gradually, both to find out what effect it will have on you and also what effect it will have on the environment.

Violet focuses the mind on spirituality and right spiritual action, but for some people it can be quite depressive.

Many people when meditating will use either white light or violet light as a focus. Used in this way, it is very calming and soothing and can promote a sense of peace and tranquillity. It also alerts one to the spiritual potential there is in all things.

FUNCTION

The function of the seventh chakra is to unify the individual with the universal spirit. The philosophy is that it is possible to be one with All, that each of us can achieve unity of the human with the divine, leading to Moksha or Nirvana. This can be achieved through the practice of yoga – the root of the word 'yoga' means 'union'.

The aim of yoga is to achieve a union with one's true self. Those people who attain the state of Nirvana, or a state of bliss, are able to see themselves in all things and all things in the self. In order to achieve this state, the individual must achieve control and self-discipline.

Yoga is closely associated with Hindu and Buddhist teachings (see under Religions in Section Two), but its insights and revelations are universal.

Believed to have been in existence since the second millennium BC, its main tenets are contained in the *Bhagavad Gita*, estimated to have been written around 300 BC. Although meditational techniques are crucial in yoga, forming the bedrock of the discipline, there are a number of paths in yogic training and self-discipline that can be followed as a way of activating the seventh chakra, depending on the person. These are:

● Karma – good work, right attitude. This entails dedicating oneself to a life of service to others. By having a philosophy which means that every action undertaken is carried out with joy, one lives one's life as effectively as possible. One exists in the knowledge that what one does will have its own effect – that good comes from good and evil from evil. There is no need to harm anyone or use negative vibration. It is truly living life, being accountable for each and every action. It also means that past misdeeds are recognized and accounted for in whatever way is appropriate.

● Jnana – the gaining of knowledge. This is the way of the scholar. By right study and the seeking of information, the chela (pupil) learns the discipline of philosophical thought and is able to understand the reasoning behind this. He is able to instigate a line of enquiry, and often, through the use of intuition, is able to achieve a union with the divine.

● Bhakti – personal devotion. Through the knowledge of one's own ability to love comes the knowledge that all things are lovable. The omnipotent (all-powerful) is within everything and everything is part of the divine. Through our own personal devotion and living a life of contemplation of the divine and its myriad meanings, we come to love each expression of the divine. Through that great love, we are therefore devoted to every manifestation of divine energy.

● Raja – the use of mental process, of the mind and the will. Raja yoga is in some ways the most disciplined of the yogas, because it requires strong and directed self-discipline. Through discipline of the will comes an understanding of the way in which the mind works. In understanding that the mind is a servant of our being rather than a master, we gain control over our mental processes. We are then able to bring our being into a fit enough state to use the mental processes to attain yoga.

Prior to achieving proficiency in any one or all of these yogas, an understanding needs to be gained of the sutras (or writings) of **Patanjali** (see under **People** in Section Two). This means learning about and practising the following:

Hatha yoga – the attainment of good physical health through posture (asana), senses (pratyahara) and breathing (pranayama). This is probably the best known form of yoga in the West, and the one that most people start with in their quest for spiritual development.

The asanas are specially adopted physical postures, the use of which stimulates not only the physical body but also the more subtle bodies. For instance, there is an *asana* known as the Plough in which first you lie flat on the floor, face up, and then bring both legs – slowly and keeping them straight – over the head to form the shape of an old-fashioned plough. This exercise stimulates the spine and helps to normalize the thyroid gland, and also helps to unblock difficulties in communicating with others.

Control of, and working with, the physical senses enables us to be in touch with the inner self and to become much more aware of our *hara* or inner power. Working with the breath – said to carry the power of life – enables us to remain healthy and also to make the best use of our available physical resources.

Mantra yoga – prayers (2) and incantations to aid meditation. Each chakra has its own specific sound. In ascending order, these are:

First Chakra	O (as in hope)
Second Chakra	Vam
Third Chakra	Ram
Fourth Chakra	Lam
Fifth Chakra	Ham
Sixth Chakra	Om, described as the sound of creation. This is achieved by putting three sounds together. These are A (pronounced Ahhh), U (pronounced oo oo oo), and M (hummed mmmm).
Seventh Chakra	No sound, achieved by allowing the mmm... of Om to die away to nothing.

Chanting (2) these sounds work through the use of sound vibration as a way of raising **consciousness** to balance and cleanse the spiritual centres.

Laya yoga – this stimulates the **kundalini** (2) using both Hatha and Mantra yogas. Combining these disciplines is an extremely powerful way of achieving Nirvana. The raising of Kundalini is a specific discipline in itself.

There is an internal development within yoga which **Patanjali** (see under **People** in Section Two) divided into eight stages:

● Yama – *no violence, no coveting, stealing or receiving gifts*

- Niyama – *cleanliness, resistance of desire, recognition of God*
- Asana – *posture and various hand positions* (mudras)
- Pranayama – *breath control*
- Pratyahara – *control of the senses*
- Dharama – *concentration*
- Dhyana – *contemplation*
- Samadhi – *spiritual ecstasy*

The core of yoga teaching and physical practice is not to feel strain, but to eventually reveal a natural physical and mental strength. There is balance and poise in yoga which leads in itself to spiritual mastery. When one moves into a position it is done gently and is held for as long as possible without discomfort, then the position is released slowly whilst relaxing and breathing abdominally. When one becomes proficient in yoga, a position may be held for longer and therefore eventually need only be performed once in a session. Many practitioners, however, perform each posture at least three times on the basis that it affects first the body, then the mind and lastly the spirit.

Body Care

Tension plays a large part in most people's lives, and yoga can help relieve headaches, indigestion and general aches and pains more quickly than, say, the hour or so medication might take to work. Rejuvenation is the key word in yoga. For example, stretching and bending the spinal vertebrae increases circulation to the spinal cord which then influences the central nervous system. It is accepted by many that our spiritual well-being is closely associated with the spine. This being so, a greater mental balance and higher levels of energy can be achieved through exercising the spine.

DIET AND FOODS

By the time one reaches a level of development which encompasses union with all things, a specific kind of diet is not necessarily appropriate. It is more than likely that your own body will give you the information that you need to nurture it properly. This may include brief periods of fasting – general advice is that it is not sensible to fast for longer than 48 hours unless practised at it, or unless the fast is supervised.

Certain foods can be used deliberately to help one to balance the demands of today's lifestyle with maintaining union with the divine. Many of the entries below can also be used while working on the other chakras but are included here as part of a total way of eating holistically.

Natural laxatives In today's hectic society there is a danger of relying on snacking and junk food for nutrition which unbalances the digestive system. In some cases it may become necessary to use a pharmaceutical remedy such as laxatives to achieve balance. However it is unwise to regard their use as a long-term solution because reliance on them may result in a permanently sluggish system. There are many natural laxatives which when combined with yoga exercises – such as the abdominal lift – can help to bring relief naturally.

Some natural food laxatives are: blackberries, dark molasses, olive oil, wheatgerm, bran, horseradish, yoghurt, milk, honey and bananas.

Natural diuretics Water retention is a problem for many people. It can be caused by a number of factors, including poor diet, too much sugar and hormonal changes. As with laxatives the overuse of chemical diuretics – such as water-releasing pills – can aggravate the problem. A common misconception associated with water retention is that one should cut down on fluid intake. This is not the case, as the body needs plenty of fluids – such as water and fruit juice – in order to work efficiently.

An imbalance between sodium and potassium is thought to contribute to the problem of water retention. Many chemical diuretics actually lead to this imbalance. Water retention can be avoided by using natural diuretics such as linoleic acid, which can be found in vegetable oils. A diet which contains all the basic amino acids (thereby ensuring a correct protein intake), as well as iron and vitamin B6, can help. Natural diuretics are blackcurrant leaves – which can be made into a tea – chicory, dandelion, parsley, and lemon and barley water.

Natural tranquillizers A lack of vitamins and minerals – particularly

NATURAL BEVERAGES

HERB TEA	COMPLAINT
Anise seeds	Intestinal and gastric disorders
Balm	Headaches, sleeplessness
Basil	Fatigue
Caraway	Flatulence
Celery leaves and seeds	Rheumatism and arthritis
Chamomile flowers	Colds, sleeplessness, jangled nerves, menstrual pains
Dandelion leaves and root	Constipation, liver and kidney problems
Dill seeds	Flatulence, unsettled babies
Elder flowers and leaves	Colds, chills, fevers
Fennel seeds and leaves	Coughs, indigestion
Ginseng	Lack of energy
Hawthorn flowers	Nervous stress
Lavender	Headaches, fainting
Licorice root	Bronchitis, gastric ulcers
Lime flowers	Flu, chills, colds
Marjoram leaves	Aching joints, digestive ailments
Mint leaves	Nausea, gastritis, flatulence
Nettle leaves	Arthritis, rheumatism, bladder complaints
Raspberry leaves	Menstrual disorders, morning sickness
Sage leaves	Coughs, sore throats
Senna pods	Chronic constipation
Thyme	Colds, indigestion, chest infections

calcium – has been suggested as one cause of 'nerves'. There are also various yoga positions and breathing exercises which may be useful. Natural relaxants are magnesium, vitamins B1, B2 and B6, calcium, lecithin, vitamin F and vitamin D.

Natural liver tonics The liver is one of the most sensitive and over-used organs of the body. It plays a part in all physiological processes and any dysfunction in the body will be reflected in the liver. Likewise any difficulty with the liver will have an effect on the other systems of the body.

Artichokes can be used to stimulate the liver, promote the flow of bile and to lower cholesterol in the blood. This three-way action is unusual, in that plants do not commonly act on both the liver and cholesterol at the same time. There are many French recipes which use the various parts of the artichoke.

Beetroot is used to keep the blood in good condition. Its liver-cleansing properties are used, particularly on the Continent, against jaundice, hepatitis and other liver conditions. There is a fermented beet juice drink which can be prepared which preserves all the properties of the beet in a particularly digestible form.

Olives can have a marked effect on the constitution, particularly when used as oil. In Mediterranean countries they are often used in the treatment of liver problems, specifically in cases of alcohol abuse.

Natural beverages – herb/fruit teas, coffee substitutes, mineral waters, rosehip syrup. Over the last 10 to 15 years, fruit and herb teas have gained popularity as a pleasant alternative to tea and coffee. Many of them also seem to help with various health complaints. Some of the ones that are widely available are listed on page 453.

GEMS AND MINERALS

Colourless fluorite can be used to stimulate the crown chakra, and also cleanse and energize the **aura** (2). It brings rapport between the intellect and the spiritual and helps one recognize what is not useful in furthering the spiritual nature. It can be used to align the chakras as well as opening the route between the universal energy and the physical body. It can also be used to clear the eyes, which in turn stimulates sight.

Chrysoberyl The colour range of chrysoberyl includes various shades of green, honey, yellow and red. The following applies to the yellow and honey chrysoberyl. The mineral provides personal power and spirituality. It bonds the energies of the third and seventh chakras, helping one to use the intellect in all tasks. It helps to open and activate the crown chakra, promoting astuteness as to the progression of spirituality. Chrysoberyl makes us more generous and forgiving. It can bring peace of mind to the user and understanding in relationships. It can be used to treat incontinence, moderate cholesterol levels and disorders of the pancreas, kidneys and liver.

Clear calcite releases electrical impulses when placed under pressure and is an energy amplifier. It can help the mind and body to remember – the mind to recall information brought to our attention during **astral travel** and channelling (see **Medium**) experiences (2). During disease it helps the body to recall the state of perfection in order to return to normality and health. Calcite facilitates awareness and appreciation of the creative forces of nature and is a very good stone if studying science and art. Clear and golden calcite are very good energy sources for use at the crown chakra. Clear calcite can also be used with all chakras in order to amplify available energy.

Calcite can be used to help the kidneys, pancreas and spleen and is a balancing agent for the assimilation of calcium within the body.

Quartz crystal is both a transmitter and receiver of energy and power. When used specifically in relation to the crown chakra, it enables the individual to create a clear pathway to spirituality. It will often highlight blockages and difficulties on the lower chakras, particularly if those problems are in any way associated with the will. It can also provide a very subtle energy to enable one to dispel those blockages, although for some that action may be initially disruptive. Quartz allows clear communication with the **higher self** (2).

Spinel has been known as the stone of immortality, because it can bring a lightness to one's exertions, and make things seem fresh and new. It is the energy of beauty and, particularly in its colourless form, enables all the chakras to be aligned with the crown chakra in the movement towards full enlightenment.

GLANDS AND ORGANS

Brain From a physical point of view, the development of the seventh chakra brings about an improvement in the functioning of the brain. This is partly to do with the increased blood supply available through the practice of yoga and other disciplines, but is also aided by the discipline of thought. There is a famous saying which suggests that we only use one tenth of our brain power – development of this chakra gives us access to considerably more than just one tenth.

Discipline through meditation and the effective use of thought processes can considerably enhance daily life, enabling us to make better decisions faster than previously and to make better use of strategy and planning. Memory, both long and short term, is also considerably enhanced. Spiritually, when we are living our lives effectively, we have more 'room' for the concepts applicable to the seventh chakra. The level of consciousness achieved is freedom from the cycle of rebirth, and recognition of the potential for enlightenment. This suggests that if we reach enlightenment on the seventh chakra we may not have to keep coming back. Three aspects are needed for this: concentration, ethical conduct and penetrative insight.

Whole body The development of the seventh chakra brings about an awareness of the sanctity of the human body. It puts us in a position of being able to care for and nurture it on all levels of existence. Awareness of union with the divine means that we can look after ourselves physically, emotionally, mentally and spiritually.

Pineal gland Very small in size, the pineal gland is located at the base of the brain and attached to the mid-brain. Some alternative practitioners and occultists believe it to be the seat of the 'Third Eye' (Sixth Chakra).

Although the pineal gland is not directly connected with sight, it is nevertheless still linked with light. It is responsible for producing the hormone melatonin – a process dependent on daylight – which in turn regulates our sleep patterns. Sleep is an altered state of **consciousness (2)** and, of course, mediumistic activities rely on various degrees of altered states. It is worth noting that the pineal gland has been found to be bigger than normal in **mediums (2)** and channellers. The pineal gland is thought to atrophy around puberty as the individual becomes more involved in physical life. It is possible that the pineal gland of mediums and channellers either does not do so, or can be reactivated through spiritual development.

Other spiritual practitioners and teachers associate the pineal gland with our highest spiritual capacity, the seventh chakra, and believe that it connects us with whatever we perceive the ultimate to be.

NEGATIVE QUALITIES

The most important problem that can be experienced through the development of the seventh chakra is alienation. It can sometimes appear that one loses all sense of belonging to the physical world and does not wish to take part in normal, mundane, everyday activities. This is all right if one is allowed to lead the contemplative life of a monk or nun, but it can lead to misunderstandings and difficulties if one has to function in the so-called real world. Another problem that can arise is the feeling that in such a vast arena what one does (any action one takes) is meaningless. This is the opposite effect of taking responsibility for one's actions and could be dubbed 'Stop the world, I want to get off'. A further problem can occur when, recognizing one's union with the ultimate, one feels overcome by having to live in two worlds. Through experiencing the duality of the inner and outer worlds – the physical and the spiritual – confusion can arise as to which is 'real' and which is not. It is akin to the confusion that a young child experiences in trying to be good (see **Splenic Chakra**).

POSITIVE QUALITIES AND LESSONS

The main quality gained in working towards enlightenment is the experience of true silence. Described by the seemingly paradoxical Eastern phrase as 'the sound of one hand clapping', it is the knowledge of the ineffable peace and tranquillity that is experienced through union with divine energy. It is recognition of a reality which does not contain the 'busy-ness' of the material world and gives the individual the opportunity to become discerning and free from attachments. The physical body becomes healthier, and although initially there may be some unusually receptive mental conditions, the individual can gain control over his feelings and is able to experience emotions at a deeper level. Psychic skills increase and the ability to make correct decisions for oneself is enhanced.

Through learning to meditate, concentration on normal everyday matters is improved, and it would appear that at the same time memory expands. One also tends to be able to assimilate more detail in activities such as study. Many spiritual teachers feel that it is not possible to give practical, general techniques for developing the seventh chakra, because such development is extremely personal and individual and can only be gained through personal teaching. It is often at this point, however, that help becomes available to the individual apparently through coincidence, but actually through **synchronicity** (2). If the need is there the help will come.

As the qualities of the seventh chakra develop the individual recognizes the validity of his place in the evolving scheme of things and is often able to help others to undertake spiritual development. This should be done in a spirit of humility, because no one can know everything.

The actual experience of the opening of the seventh chakra may be described as the top of the head 'opening' to receive and emit a golden light. The sensations of the physical body are lost, and it can sometimes feel as though one is light – or pure energy – itself. It is a truly ecstactic state which can hold within it some sadness at having to return to the physical world.

With the awareness that comes with the opening of the seventh chakra, we are able to take responsibility for creating the present – as with the sixth chakra – and also for creating a world which has a sustainable future and is fit for others to live in. We recognize that what little we can do in the immediate has a profound effect on the overall picture. Just as a stone dropped into a pond can be perceived to cause ripples in the airwaves beyond the pond's rim, so the effects of our actions can be far-reaching.

EXERCISE FOR GROWTH
It has already been suggested that techniques and tips cannot be

taught at this level of awareness, but it is perhaps worth putting forward some subjects for consideration or meditation which may widen your perception.

● Consider what you perceive enlightenment to be.

● Contemplate the idea of each and every thing containing a 'divine spark'. Is this different in each thing?

● What does the phrase 'Is, was and ever shall be' really mean?

● How do you wish to be remembered?

● Finally, recognize that in having undertaken this journey of exploration, you have worked hard and carefully. Does the life you have matter to you?

USING THE CHAKRAS:
GUIDED MEDITATION

When we have studied the chakras individually and discovered how to apply the knowledge we have learnt in a practical way in our lives, it is helpful to put all that knowledge together and reach within ourselves for our highest potential. One way of doing this is to use a guided meditation which enables us to tap into each spiritual centre in turn.

Find a place where you will not be disturbed for at least an hour. Take the telephone off the hook and ignore the doorbell. If you have only a short time to meditate, you could extract the stage dealing with the chakra you are most interested in and simply use that. However, in order to make the best use of the knowledge you have, it is better to be able to complete the whole exercise in one go.

Having chosen your quiet spot, breathe easily and deeply until you have established a gentle rhythm. Close your eyes and allow the rhythm of your breath to quieten your mind. Visualize a path in front of you. In the distance there is a mountain which you wish to explore. You can see the greenery at the bottom of the mountain which gradually changes colour through blue and various shades of purple until you reach the snow-capped peaks at the top.

Approach the mountain with reverence and admire its perfection. Feel the warmth of the sun on your back as you walk forward, and at the same time become aware of the breeze as it blows gently in your face. Feel the earth under your feet, and – somewhere in the background – you can hear the splashing of water as it tumbles down the mountainside. All this makes you feel relaxed and happy and ready to enjoy your experiences.

As you walk to the foot of the mountain you become aware of a different quality in the air. It is softer, but also more vibrant than before and you know as you climb your own mountain that you will become much more aware of this quality the further you progress. The earth under your feet is a deep rich red, almost black, and you are conscious of how rich and fertile it is. You want to remember this moment, so you pick a flower, perhaps a rose or a geranium (one which is bright red), and tuck it into your buttonhole.

The quality of the earth changes, and there are rocks scattered around. Now you can locate the water you heard earlier. It is a small stream and you lean forward and drink with your hands from the stream. The water is icy cold, and as you drink you can feel it cleansing and refreshing you. In the stream is a gem, a carnelian, which you pick up and put into your pocket. You find yourself thinking about your relationships, and are aware that when you come back from your journey you will have something to share with the people you love. Sit for a while and remember them, and think about what will please them.

When you are ready to move on, look up ahead where you will see a cave in the rock, in front of which is a stretch of yellow sand. It is a little cold now, so you move into the cave in which is a warm fire. You stop to warm yourself, for you know that you will soon be moving on, and you wish to be prepared. Someone has left food for you and you eat it greedily, but know that you will not be able to finish it all. You put some of the ripe fruit into your pocket so it will not be squashed, and move confidently out into the open.

Now the grass is very green under your feet, and you become aware of the quality of the air again. It is soft and gentle and your lungs feel as though they will expand tremendously. Your heart beats a little faster, but that is all right, because you will be able to make more effort. You have a feeling that there is something around which you must find, but you do not know what it is. Behind a stone you find a wooden box, which you do not wish to open yet, but you carry it carefully with you.

Once again you move forward, and now the way becomes a little more difficult. There is a wonderful blue sky above and the rocks are taking on a bluish tinge. You perceive that some of these rocks are real gems, but you decide to leave them there. Instead you find an old parchment tucked in the rocks which you pick up and put in the box you already have. Instinctively you know it contains information you will need, and you move upwards even more confidently.

Now the terrain is becoming a little more difficult. The rocks and earth underneath take on an almost amethyst hue. You are able to turn your attention away from the mountain and to look out over the way that you have come and to perceive how well you have done since you started. Your eyes seem clearer now and there is a small pulse beating in the middle of your forehead. You can almost hear the movement of the rocks, and it sounds something like a heartbeat. You feel the urge to sit down and to look out into the distance. That too seems to have a purple tinge, and yet within it are signs and symbols that you know you will eventually be able to interpret. You have a new sense of purpose and know that you will climb your mountain right to the top. Picking up your goods, you set your sights on the top of the mountain.

It is again a little cold, but you know that doesn't matter because you are warm from within. You move onwards and upwards and the air becomes finer, but at the same time seems to be easier to breathe. It is beginning to get darker but this still holds no fear because you are at one with your mountain and also with the elements around you. You reach the summit knowing that life will never be the same again because you have conquered your own fears and doubts and have achieved something that no one else could do. Look out away from the mountain and lose the consciousness of the mountain beneath you. It seems as though you might fly, and you know that is possible. You may choose to do this if you wish, or you may come back down your mountain to your path at the bottom. Be aware that you may climb this mountain whenever you wish, and each time your experiences will be different.

WORKBOOK:
PLANS FOR
CHANGE

PLAN FOR CHANGE: ROOT OR BASE CHAKRA

The changes I need to make are:

1. Colour – I need to use more . . . . in my life

2. Element – I need to use more . . . . in my life

3. Diets/Foods/Herbs – I need to include more

4. I could use gems and minerals by

5. The Questionnaires/Exercises show I need to use/be

6. I will take . . . . weeks to make these changes

7. I will know I have succeeded when

8. I will continue to monitor my progress after every day/week/month

Root/Base	Splenic	Solar plexus	Heart	Throat	Brow	Crown

Awareness						Problems
Spirituality (creativity)						Ambiguity and illusion of life
Spirituality (objectivity)						Loss of spiritual direction
Wisdom						Futility 'Why me?'
Self-knowledge						Self-control World pain Intolerance
Emotion						Inability to close down
Relationship with others						Extreme sensitivity
Self-image						Sexual identity

9 months	2 years	4-6 years	8 years	10-11 years	14 years	16-17 years

465

PLAN FOR CHANGE: SPLENIC CHAKRA

The changes I need to make are:

1. Colour – I need to use more . . . . in my life

2. Element – I need to use more . . . . in my life

3. Diets/Foods/Herbs – I need to include more

4. I could use gems and minerals by

5. The Questionnaires/Exercises show I need to use/be

6. I will take . . . . weeks to make these changes

7. I will know I have succeeded when

8. I will continue to monitor my progress after every day/week/month

Base of spine sexual	Splenic	Solar plexus	Heart	Throat	Brow	Crown

Awareness		Problems
Spirituality (creativity)		Ambiguity and illusion of life
Spirituality (objectivity)		Loss of spiritual direction
Wisdom		Futility 'Why me?'
Self-knowledge		Self-control World pain Intolerance
Emotion		Inability to close down
Relationship with others		Extreme sensitivity
Self-image		Sexual identity

9 months	2 years	4-6 years	8 years	10-11 years	14 years	16-17 years

PLAN FOR CHANGE: SOLAR PLEXUS CHAKRA

The changes I need to make are:

1. Colour – I need to use more . . . . in my life

2. Element – I need to use more . . . . in my life

3. Diets/Foods/Herbs – I need to include more

4. I could use gems and minerals by

5. The Questionnaires/Exercises show I need to use/be

6. I will take . . . . weeks to make these changes

7. I will know I have succeeded when

8. I will continue to monitor my progress after every day/week/month

Base of spine sexual	Splenic	Solar plexus	Heart	Throat	Brow	Crown

Awareness		Problems
Spirituality (creativity)		Ambiguity and illusion of life
Spirituality (objectivity)		Loss of spiritual direction
Wisdom		Futility 'Why me?'
Self-knowledge		Self-control World pain Intolerance
Emotion		Inability to close down
Relationship with others		Extreme sensitivity
Self-image		Sexual identity

9 months	2 years	4-6 years	8 years	10-11 years	14 years	16-17 years

PLAN FOR CHANGE: HEART CHAKRA

The changes I need to make are:

1. Colour – I need to use more .... in my life

2. Element – I need to use more .... in my life

3. Diets/Foods/Herbs – I need to include more

4. I could use gems and minerals by

5. The Questionnaires/Exercises show I need to use/be

6. I will take .... weeks to make these changes

7. I will know I have succeeded when

8. I will continue to monitor my progress after every day/week/month

Base of spine sexual	Splenic	Solar plexus	Heart	Throat	Brow	Crown

Awareness		Problems
Spirituality (creativity)		Ambiguity and illusion of life
Spirituality (objectivity)		Loss of spiritual direction
Wisdom		Futility 'Why me?'
Self-knowledge		Self-control World pain Intolerance
Emotion		Inability to close down
Relationship with others		Extreme sensitivity
Self-image		Sexual identity

9 months	2 years	4-6 years	8 years	10-11 years	14 years	16-17 years

JOURNEY OF A LIFETIME: WORKBOOK

PLAN FOR CHANGE: THROAT CHAKRA

The changes I need to make are:

1. Colour – I need to use more . . . . in my life

2. Element – I need to use more . . . . in my life

3. Diets/Foods/Herbs – I need to include more

4. I could use gems and minerals by

5. The Questionnaires/Exercises show I need to use/be

6. I will take . . . . weeks to make these changes

7. I will know I have succeeded when

8. I will continue to monitor my progress after every day/week/month

| Base of spine sexual | Splenic | Solar plexus | Heart | Throat | Brow | Crown |

Awareness

Spirituality (creativity)

Spirituality (objectivity)

Wisdom

Self-knowledge

Emotion

Relationship with others

Self-image

Problems

Ambiguity and illusion of life

Loss of spiritual direction

Futility 'Why me?'

Self-control World pain Intolerance

Inability to close down

Extreme sensitivity

Sexual identity

| 9 months | 2 years | 4-6 years | 8 years | 10-11 years | 14 years | 16-17 years |

PLAN FOR CHANGE: BROW CHAKRA

The changes I need to make are:

1. Colour – I need to use more . . . . in my life

2. Element – I need to use more . . . . in my life

3. Diets/Foods/Herbs – I need to include more

4. I could use gems and minerals by

5. The Questionnaires/Exercises show I need to use/be

6. I will take . . . . weeks to make these changes

7. I will know I have succeeded when

8. I will continue to monitor my progress after every day/week/month

Base of spine sexual	Splenic	Solar plexus	Heart	Throat	Brow	Crown

Awareness		Problems
Spirituality (creativity)		Ambiguity and illusion of life
Spirituality (objectivity)		Loss of spiritual direction
Wisdom		Futility 'Why me?'
Self-knowledge		Self-control World pain Intolerance
Emotion		Inability to close down
Relationship with others		Extreme sensitivity
Self-image		Sexual identity

9 months	2 years	4-6 years	8 years	10-11 years	14 years	16-17 years

PLAN FOR CHANGE: CROWN CHAKRA

The changes I need to make are:

1. Colour – I need to use more . . . . in my life

2. Element – I need to use more . . . . in my life

3. Diets/Foods/Herbs – I need to include more

4. I could use gems and minerals by

5. The Questionnaires/Exercises show I need to use/be

6. I will take . . . . weeks to make these changes

7. I will know I have succeeded when

8. I will continue to monitor my progress after every day/week/month

Base of spine sexual	Splenic	Solar plexus	Heart	Throat	Brow	Crown

Awareness		Problems
Spirituality (creativity)		Ambiguity and illusion of life
Spirituality (objectivity)		Loss of spiritual direction
Wisdom		Futility 'Why me?'
Self-knowledge		Self-control World pain Intolerance
Emotion		Inability to close down
Relationship with others		Extreme sensitivity
Self-image		Sexual identity

9 months	2 years	4-6 years	8 years	10-11 years	14 years	16-17 years

ACKNOWLEDGEMENTS

Whenever one writes a book such as this, there are inevitably people whose contributions need to be acknowledged for the value they have added to the publication. In more senses than one this has been a team effort. I could not have done it alone and I am indebted to the many disparate, forgotten sources that have added to my knowledge during the thirty years I have spent in the business of personal development.

The help that is needed in pulling together such information and presenting it in a coherent form involves painstaking research and attention to detail. Often arising from a half thought, James Eden took my incoherent ramblings and went off and found out where they had come from (and often where they were going to). His help has been absolutely invaluable, because coming to it with a fresh mind he has had the ability to query certain points, which though obvious to me, would not be obvious to the beginner. His patience and good humour have been, as ever, a rock of stability.

When my language has been too 'way out' and esoteric, my daughter Fiona, as she has done since she was very young, has brought me back down to earth with 'You can't say that – it doesn't make sense.' (Incidentally, she accuses me of not having learnt how to punctuate a sentence.) My comment that 'commas hold you up', means that her job as scribe – together with the early mornings and late nights – has never been easy. To her, also, my gratitude.

My thanks must also go to Tessa Rose who bravely went 'where angels fear to tread' and edited the chaos of words and hidden meanings which this book originally was. Her support has been of inestimable help.

Finally, I must acknowledge all of our sources and helpers, too numerous to mention and too widespread to be recollected. If words and phrases sound similar to those of other writers and authors, I can only plead that we all have access to the same truths, and I believe that nowhere have I deliberately plagiarized someone else's work. In some ways this book cannot be totally original because it is based on Universal Truth.

My thanks again to all my sources.